PLACES OF TENDERNESS AND HEAT

PLACES OF TENDERNESS AND HEAT

THE QUEER MILIEU OF FIN-DE-SIÈCLE ST. PETERSBURG

OLGA PETRI

CORNELL UNIVERSITY PRESS
Ithaca and London

First published 2022 by Cornell University Press

Library of Congress Cataloging-in-Publication Data

Names: Petri, Olga, 1985– author.
Title: Places of tenderness and heat: the queer milieu of fin-de-siècle St. Petersburg / Olga Petri.
Description: Ithaca [New York]: Cornell University Press, 2022. | Includes bibliographical references and index. |
Identifiers: LCCN 2021054745 (print) | LCCN 2021054746 (ebook) | ISBN 9781501763779 (hardcover) | ISBN 9781501763786 (pdf) | ISBN 9781501763793 (epub)
Subjects: LCSH: Gay men—Russia (Federation)—Saint Petersburg—History—19th century. | Space—Social aspects—Russia (Federation)—Saint Petersburg—History—19th century. | Space—Political aspects—Russia (Federation)—Saint Petersburg—History—19th century. | Gay men—Legal status, laws, etc.—Russia (Federation)—Saint Petersburg—History—19th century.
Classification: LCC DK568 .P485 2022 (print) | LCC DK568 (ebook) | DDC 947/.21086642—dc23/eng/20220107
LC record available at https://lccn.loc.gov/2021054745
LC ebook record available at https://lccn.loc.gov/2021054746

For my mom

Contents

Figures and Maps

Acknowledgments

I envisaged this project twenty years ago when I first devised to write a book about "my" city, the city where virtually all my known ancestors lived and died and where I was born, raised, and educated. Being fifteen and given to dreamy perambulation, I wanted to write about hidden love and romantic hideouts in my city. The poetry of the early twentieth-century writer Mikhail Kuzmin hit the spot: it is mysterious, yet bright and full of a passion both artistic and romantic. The idea has been long in gestation, but the topic emerged only relatively recently when I took up my studies in the UK. My fascination with the methods of cultural and historical geography could be pursued effectively in my new intellectual home and opened up different ways of looking at St. Petersburg as a city "where the sky poured some kind of love," according to Kuzmin.

Before I left St. Petersburg, I was fortunate to encounter many people who supported my project and me personally. The Faculty of Geography and Geoecology (now the Institute of Earth Science) at St. Petersburg State University is my alma mater. I note my especially deep gratitude to Nikolai Vladimirovich Kaledin, who encouraged me to pursue endeavors in human geography that lay outside the typical scope of projects pursued there.

My move to the UK geography opened up new horizons and challenges, and the people I met there have supported and inspired my interdisciplinary leanings. Back in 2012, discussions with Richard Dennis, Matthew Gandy, Pushpa Arabindoo, and Andrew Harris during my time in the geography department at University College London (UCL) helped me make my project concrete and transition it out of its long gestation into an archival research program and broad plan of study.

The Department of Geography at Cambridge University provided a supportive and inspiring atmosphere for intellectual exchange. First and foremost, I wish to thank Philip Howell. This book would have been much poorer and less fun to write without him. His profound erudition, empathy, and brilliant conversation helped me crystallize my thoughts. He is a constant source of inspiration. I also owe an enormous debt of gratitude to my colleagues: David Nally, David

Beckingham, Alex Jeffrey, Francesca Moore, Liz Watson, Tim Bayliss-Smith, and Maan Barua. Their comments and advice helped me recognize and refine my project's scope and direction early enough to avoid serious trouble. I was fortunate to be reunited with Matthew Gandy upon his move to Cambridge, where he provided me with insightful feedback on the drafts of this monograph. Philip Stickler from the Cartography Unit helped produce the figures and maps with unstinting professionalism. I was fortunate to meet many exceptional students while writing this book. Special thanks to Ellie, Elo, Romane, Harvey, and Léo.

Beyond Cambridge and UCL, I am also immensely happy to have met Miles Osborn, Stephen Legg, and Dan Healey, who helped me recognize that revision is also a creative and inspiring process. Daniel Beer provided timely feedback when it was most needed. I owe a great debt of gratitude to Ethan Pollock. Our collaborative meetings, as well as his scathing reviews, have been among the highlights of my academic life so far. Perhaps a few of those mentioned above will recognize the parts of the book that draw on their inputs, thoughts, and reflections. Although I take full responsibility for all remaining oversights or flaws, their contributions reinforced any strengths the book may yet have to recommend it.

I am especially grateful for the institutional support of Emmanuel College, the Department of Geography, Cambridge, and the Leverhulme Trust for supporting this project and my broader research agenda. Wolfson College kindly provided a publication grant for which I am very grateful.

The librarians and archivists at the St. Petersburg Historical State Archive, the Russian State Historical Archive (St. Petersburg), the State Archive of the Russian Federation (Moscow), the National Library of Russia (St. Petersburg), the Russian State Library (Moscow), the St. Petersburg State Archive of Photo and Cinematic Documents, and the Slavonic Library of the University of Helsinki eased the process and helped dispel my fears about entering the archival labyrinth and never coming back.

At Cornell University Press, I wish to thank especially Roger Haydon, who took an early interest in the project; Emily Andrew and Susan Specter, who helped nudge it over the finish line; and Allegra Martschenko for their enthusiasm and support. Special thanks also to my anonymous reviewers, who took the time to read my monograph and provide empathetic and clear feedback that helped me find the remaining sand in the cogs.

I should note that some of my earlier efforts to investigate and conceptualize late imperial St. Petersburg's queer milieu were published as journal articles. Chapter 2 is an expanded version of "Discipline and Discretionary Power in Policing Homosexuality in Late Imperial St. Petersburg," *Journal of Homosexuality* 66, no. 7: 937–969. Chapter 4 is a substantially rewritten version of

"At the Bathhouse: Municipal Reform and the Bathing Commons in Late Imperial St. Petersburg," *Journal of Historical Geography* 51: 40–51. I would like to thank Elsevier and Taylor and Francis for granting me permission to reproduce parts of these articles.

Finally, I could not have written his book without my family and friends. Nic was the friendliest reader, and discussions with him taught me a great deal not only about my work but also about myself. I thank him for his patience, encouragement, and love. My children Zina and Georg were and remain a constant source of inspiration. Perhaps they will return to this book and remember their mom during its writing.

Friends and relatives have been hugely supportive throughout the project. My dad continues to inspire me when in my recollection or imagination I join him on his walks in St. Petersburg. My older siblings, Polina and Sergei, showed me that being little offers a privileged perspective and that I am allowed to look up in awe and wonder. My Aunt Ira taught me about the importance of persevering, not just in sport. Katharina, Eberhard, Lena, and Peter welcomed me into their family and showed me what it means to be part of a big family. My friends Polina, Dima, Jura, Nariman, and Simon met up with me after my long sessions in the libraries and archives and in our conversations we often continued exploring the city that so often brought us together. I was incredibly lucky during a stint in Serbia to meet Dragana, who taught me how to speak, write, and be friends in English—something I could not have imagined before meeting her. My warm, warm thanks go to Anja, my best friend anywhere, who has also been my constant supporter and ally in St. Petersburg for the past twenty years. She always gives me a reason to smile and continue plodding along, even when I think everything looks unpromising. In Cambridge, I was fortunate to meet many amazing people who supported me in my endeavors: Lesley, Tess, Soile, Oksana, Dave, Mak, Sophie, Edward-John, Mags, Seniz, Rebecca and Daniel, Sylvie and Chris, and Helene and Mark.

Finally, I dedicate this book to my mom, who infected me with her passion for St. Petersburg. She collected so many books in our apartment that I had to either read and love them or resign myself to feeling lost among the shelves and piles. She also helped me with my archival hunts: from playing with Georg and Zina while I was away and helping me figure out where to look next, to deciphering the most recalcitrant nineteenth-century shorthand. Her moral courage and intellectual curiosity continue to inspire me to care about what goes on and what happened in my city and in the world. I hope that this book will also prove slightly encouraging to people navigating its queer geographies today, which may be no less challenging than it was four or five generations ago.

A Note on Transliteration, Translations, and Dates

In transliterating Russian titles, quotations, and names, I have used the Library of Congress system (2012 edition)—except in the case of well-known names of persons or urban locations, such as, for example, Dostoevsky, Nevsky Prospect, and St. Petersburg (not Sankt-Peterburg). In the notes and bibliography, I adhere strictly to the Library of Congress system. I capitalize place names, such as, for example "Liteinyi Prospect" or "Tavricheskii Garden," even though, in the original Russian texts, these would not have been capitalized.

All translations, unless otherwise noted, are my own. I provide my own translation of quotes from Mikhail Kuzmin's diary, even in cases, where translations were available from other sources.

Dating follows the Julian ("Old Style") calendar.

A Note on Terminology

The terminological and methodological challenges are central to this book. In navigating the nuances of contemporary and historical terminology, Rudi Bleys describes terminological as a "trope of narration," where "the historical meaning of words and concepts is co-defined by their applications in wider contexts."[1] While Bleys focuses on changes of meaning over time, words with the same etymological roots may also have different meanings in various linguistic contexts. In the present discussion this involves the translation of terms from Russian into English. Even some terms with the same roots are used slightly different in the Russian and English contexts. (This may apply to the term "homosexuality" itself, which will be discussed later in this section.) Even where there are standard translations for certain Russian words, at times, these fail to capture important nuances intended by the original term, requiring additional explanation, which I have provided in the text of the book, the notes, and below.

The word "queer" in this book comes closest among the alternatives to capturing the amorphous nature of non-heterosexual sexualities. In its present-day usage it helpfully extends to practices other than sex, but nevertheless is associated with sexuality. Although I apply this term cautiously, citing the original terms and their transliterations where applicable, the retroactive application of "queer" has important benefits for the study of spatial patterns associated with non-heterosexual sex in the historical city. First, it is sufficiently, but not excessively, broad in scope. Second, it comes closest among the alternatives to being non-stigmatizing. Third, it is to the point. It emphasizes sexuality over sex and espouses the ambiguity and fluidity of attitudes, behaviors, expressions, appearances, and perceptions associated with non-heterosexual desire and eros instead of seeking to bundle problematic classifications of individuals based on the sex acts in which they engage. Finally, the term fills a gap in the verbiage used at the time. Take, for example, a constable who is determining his actions vis-à-vis a male subject he suspects of seeking sex with another member of his own biological sex. Without having anything but the most indirect and speculative indication that these subjects engaged in, or are even eager to engage in, homosexual sex, the constable describing them might have chosen any number of terms in use at the time—all of them derogatory and presumptuous. Protocols and directives from the period covered in this book contain a range of terms from the intelligently euphemistic "given to the Greek vice" to the humorously condescending "auntie" or the outright criminalizing "pederast"—all in translation or transliteration. I wish to subsume them all under a maximally neutral term that captures the varying states of knowledge underlying these documents, which often did not include recorded evidence of sexual acts, but rather relied on speculation or self-identification of their objects as interested in illicit homosexual sex. In this vein and in the specific case of the constable interviewing Johan, whose story is explored in the introduction of this book, I would argue that "queer comments" might in fact be a substantively more correct translation of the Russian phrase strictly translated as "suspicious comments." This example illustrates my practice in this book of staying close to original terminology and their accepted translations while transparently deploying the term "queer" as an overarching category linked to them retroactively by my own interpretative discretion. The fit of this category is, I believe, well-illustrated by the archival stories and excerpts offered in "strict" translation. For example, regardless of how certain the constable interviewing Johan was that the latter had engaged in criminal sex, his protocol offers no plausible alternative as to what made Johan's comments "suspicious." Lest this term, however, be understood as subsuming only the verbiage of ostensibly hostile observers, I should clarify that in using the term "queer" I also intended to encompass insiders' perspectives. "Queer" echoes the term "literate" (*gramotnyi*) and several others used by participants in the queer milieu that denoted any man willing to participate in flirtation, caresses, and sexualized physical contact with someone of his own sex. Describing a person in these terms would not have confirmed a settled sexual preference, or even have testified to a preparedness to engage in anal sex as the only explicitly criminalized form of sexual contact between men. Notably, much like "queer," the term "literate" was expansive and could include individuals regarded by the authorities as men, but who challenged a definitive gender assignment in their dress or behavior. "Queer" is thus a similarly broad term, which, although not applied by contemporaries, bridges the informal language used by participants and the dry euphemism or criminalized categories of spectatorial and surveillance reports. I should note here that the term "queer" itself also has the added attraction of etymologically capturing a spatial metaphor, potentially deriving from the German "quer," meaning "across," "aslant," and "askance." As the queer feminist scholar Sara Ahmed points out, "queer" is a "spatial term, which then gets translated into a sexual term, a term for a twisted sexuality that does not follow a 'straight line,' a sexuality that is bent and crooked."[2] Occasionally I use the term "homosexual," but not to describe a person. I use it in the way it was used in early Russian medico-forensic reports, where it is necessarily linked to an act and is close to the contemporary English category (preferred for its avoidance of questions of identity or identification) of "men who have sex with men." Dan Healey rightly observes an evolution of this term along similar lines to that taking place in Western literature around the fin de siècle, whereby to an ever greater degree "homosexual" and related terms came to be used in reference to something akin to a psychological condition.[3] But this is not the usage I employ here, as the term used to describe people is necessarily exclusive and definitive, which risks anachronistically exposing "the very incoherence at the core of the modern notion of homosexuality."[4] Given the often close link between these two terms, it is important here to make a distinction in my usage between "homosexuality" as a characteristic of a sex act between two males and "queer," which I use to characterize, for example, the full range of socio-spatial patterns performed in public and semi-public urban spaces by or with the participation of individuals classified by the law at the time as men and who were at least under certain conditions prepared to reveal an interest in sexual contact with individuals thus classified. Here, I do not wish to imply in my usage of "queer" that participation in spatial patterns that created opportunities for sex between men (or male persons in the legal sense appropriate to the place and time) necessarily determined an identity. In many, if not most, cases it did not. Thus, I accept the criticism that I am cherry-picking among the possible nuances intended and kindly request the reader's forbearance in espousing the inclusive, sexualized, but not necessarily sexual aspects of the term "queer" and suspending during their reading of this book any *binding* association of the term with individual fixed identities.

In this book I further propose to use the term "queer milieu" when talking about a group of men, who were prepared to make themselves known to one another and who had overlapping but varied sexual predilections. While I discuss the term further in chapter 1, a note is in order here. The queer milieu may have been anchored in the movements and encounters of queer men, but it was not composed of "homosexuals" in the modern sense. The unquestionably diverse category termed "queer men" in this book is used with the cautious aim of referring to men who regularly or occasionally had sex with other men, desired to do so, and communicated this desire to others to any extent. Again, as Kuzmin's diary and his novel *Wings* reminds us, many of these men would not have identified themselves as having a characteristic that marked them as permanently homosexual or, in this context, fundamentally different from others whose sexual desires were unproblematically directed only at members of the opposite sex. Many simply had occasional "lapses" or "adventures" or periodically "indulged themselves." Others had sexual "destinies" that sat comfortably with otherwise unremarkable social roles, and still others lived and expressed their personality in terms of male-to-male eros or the adoption of nonnormative gender roles to varying degrees. The use of the term "queer milieu" as a general term is, of course, simplifying, but does not stand in the way of detailed attention to individual expression. It merely reflects the aim of deploying a non-forensic term to capture a commonality that was recognized on all sides of the barricades, both by participants in the queer milieu who used very broad terms like "literate" and "experienced" to capture a similarly defined category as well as derogatory terms of similar scope used by those writing about queer men as from an observer's perspective. Moreover, the usage employed in this book corresponds to the broadly supported conclusion reached by Healey on the basis of medico-forensic discussions taking place in late imperial Russia: the capital's queer milieu did not consist of homosexuals in a modern sense. Instead, queer men, as I have called those whose participation in the queer milieu was at least occasionally linked to the objective of meeting or finding a male sexual partner, for all their diversity had as a common denominator their desire for homosexual sex as well as their occasional or frequent willingness to make this desire known to others. Some of them, like Kuzmin, were thoroughly embedded in this milieu, but some—including many of the bathhouse attendants, cabbies, and government officials mentioned in this book—only occasionally dipped in and out of this world. In part for this reason, it would be mistaken to assume that the queer milieu had a stable composition. Instead, it constantly assembled, disbanded, and reassembled, making it all the harder to pin down for the contemporary and historian alike.

PLACES OF TENDERNESS AND HEAT

Introduction

Imperial St. Petersburg, like a lost civilization, lies beneath the soot and rubble of the cataclysmic twentieth century. The city and its inhabitants suffered, lived, and loved through repeated ruptures. Much of the evidence of life before the events that caused these ruptures has been destroyed: social lives, private lives, love lives. This makes it especially difficult to reconstruct aspects of prerevolutionary lives that were intentionally hidden or kept opaque—illicit loves above all. As a result, the story of late imperial St. Petersburg's queer milieu has remained largely obscure, although significant scholarly attention has been paid to past and present efforts to explicitly regulate homosexuality in Russia. The pursuit of telling a story more focused on the queer milieu itself, how it evolved and functioned despite or because of regulatory efforts, is a natural and important extension of previous work. The present investigation, challenging as it may be, allows us to reconstruct neglected aspects of the experience of living in late imperial St. Petersburg and to juxtapose patterns of everyday life in this city at this time with the aspirations to urban order that were enshrined in its manifold laws and regulations.

This book looks at the spatial history of queer men's experience of St. Petersburg and the attempts of municipal authorities to manage what I call the queer milieu. Although it is intended as a contribution to the social and sexual history of St. Petersburg, it also tests and explores exegetical methodologies and conceptual approaches that will prove useful in the historical geographies and histories of sexuality more generally. By recovering the spatial stories constituting late imperial St. Petersburg's queer milieu, this book speaks to readers interested in the historical spatial expression of urban sexuality and gender relations. *Places of Tenderness and Heat: The Queer Milieu of Fin-de-Siècle St. Petersburg* is the first dedicated study of the male homosexual or queer milieu of fin-de-siècle St. Petersburg, specifically during the period 1879–1914. It focuses on the negotiation between queer men and municipal authorities of spatial patterns of movement and encounter in the historical city.

The period covered begins in 1879, two years before the assassination of Tsar Alexander II, whose reforms ushered in an era of unprecedented population growth and modernization, but whose death supported the preservation of substantial leeway in state surveillance and arbitrary administrative repression. It opens with the introduction of bathhouse reforms in 1879–1881, which targeted one of the city's premier spaces for homosexual sex and socialization (among many other perceived social ills). It ends in 1914, when the city became thoroughly militarized before entering its tumultuous revolutionary phase, during which it ceased to be the nation's capital and lost its dominant economic and cultural role, along with much of its population. The prerevolutionary queer milieu did not disappear but the conditions of its emergence changed decisively: as war segued into revolution, St. Petersburg turned into a garrison town from whence Soviet authorities orchestrated the dismantling of the imperial bureaucracy, the reallocation of privilege, and the collapse of Russia's markets and industry before moving camp to the Kremlin. This phase marks a disruption of a uniquely devastating character that, by way of contrast, sets apart the preceding period of gradual, if not unperturbed, modernization. With this violent end to its halcyon days, St. Petersburg ceased to be the "natural place for thinking about Russia and the modern experience."[1] The goalposts of the negotiation over queer spatial patterns also shifted with the abrogation of sodomy laws and the reevaluation of methods and priorities in municipal governance and policing. It was the end of an era for queer men in the city as well as the end of an era for the city as a whole.[2]

Archival stories are at the heart of this book's contribution, even when they are marked by gaps and omissions, circumlocutions and codes, moral condemnation and condescension. Many of these stories needed first to be discovered and pieced together for this study, while others were already known and acquired a richer patina by virtue of being revisited and inserted into a better-populated context that covers the full range from discreet tenderness to illicit sex or, metaphorically, heat, as the title suggests. The sources to which I refer capture and reflect a set of carefully negotiated spatial patterns that queer men used to navigate these extremes. They are, I argue, constitutive of a setting and situation that I term the "queer milieu" (see "A Note on Terminology" as well as the discussion below). Some of its archival traces are, of course, explicitly and obviously those of queer men and those who surveilled them. Most are more ambiguous. Each is specific and unique to perhaps a few individuals. But taken together, they encapsulate queer St. Petersburg at the end of the nineteenth and the turn of the twentieth century.

Here is one poignant example: the story of Johan and Dmitrii.

On June 12, 1910, twenty-one-year-old Johan Vol'mon came to the Kazanskaia Borough police station to report the disappearance of his friend and roommate, seventeen-year-old Dmitrii Gusev. The latter had not returned home after he and Johan had taken a stroll together two days earlier.[3] On an initial reading, the report composed on the occasion of Dmitrii's disappearance appears to be a haphazard collection of unconnected information. The shorthand notes of the constable questioning Johan inform us that the latter originated from Estlandiia, a province of the Russian Empire near the Baltic Sea, now Estonia. Dmitrii, in turn, was a peasant from Yaroslavskaia province, a region in the heart of European Russia near the upper Volga and far from the Baltic Sea. Here the report begins to deviate from the kind of detail necessary for a mere search for a missing person. The constable who composed it draws attention to the circumstance that the two young men not only came from entirely different regions but also worked in different factories and had learned very different trades. And yet, despite this, they lived together. These preliminary facts would have allowed contemporary readers to eliminate village connections or shared employment among the factors typically motivating young migrants to board together.[4] These two men lived together because they had chosen to do so. They had found each other in the metropolis and formed a friendship strong enough for them to share a room.

The remainder of the report contains a nuanced investigation of Johan and Dmitrii's relationship, eschewing altogether the topics required for a missing persons investigation. A physical description of Dmitrii, for example, is conspicuous by its absence. Instead, the report accumulates detail after detail to indicate that Johan and Dmitrii's relationship was queer, but without ever quite making this suspicion explicit. Informed by an awareness of the city's queer topography, it is a clear instance of "flagging": this record would have been transparently legible to police colleagues. The report precisely describes the route along Konnogvardeiskii Boulevard where the two young men had walked when they were together for the last time. This tree-lined street with a pedestrian island in the middle, similar to the parallel Galernaia Street, would have been well-known to the interviewer and his peers as preeminent cruising sites frequented by queer men and male prostitutes. Along these streets, men who were interested in sex with other men strolled, tarried, or observed from the numerous cafés and restaurants, and agreed on rendezvous in more intimate venues. These streets were also located near the barracks of a major infantry regiment, whose members were variously reported to engage in homosexual sex, sometimes for money.[5] The constable interviewing Johan did not, however, stop at spatial clues. He inquired into the details of the interaction that took place between Johan and Dmitrii when they were last on Konnogvardeiskii Boulevard. As he notes, not without a touch of pathos, Dmitrii had given Johan a *porte-cigares* (cigarette case) "as a farewell present." To make the situation abundantly clear, Dmitrii had declared that he wished to move out of their joint lodgings the same evening and part ways for good.[6]

Johan's decision to disclose this information is no less significant than the constable's decision to record it. In a single-minded pursuit of his intention to trigger a search for Dmitrii, Johan should have known better than to relay the interlude with the *porte-cigares*. The predictable price he paid for this indiscretion is that he failed to mobilize police resources for a major search effort. However, the comfort he took in telling his story to an attentive listener in this vast and dangerous city may well have compelled him to let down his guard for a moment.

The protocol is an exquisite example of bureaucratic communication. Indeed, the very possibilities that reward a close contextualized reading today would have been transparent to the constable's colleagues. The issue at hand is presented not as a truly worrying disappearance, but rather as the end of the two young men's intimate relationship—a breakup, not a suicide. In his masterful summary, the police constable and recordkeeper laid the basis for refraining from any immediate action and further work, while keeping himself above reproach by leaving the case formally open, "due to questionable statements of the applicant."[7]

Taken in the context of other cases explicitly linked to queer policing, the accumulated detail and the final decision in the protocol relegate the story of Johan and Dmitrii to the largely tolerated sphere of consensual queer relationships and offer a glimpse into the wider history of queer St. Petersburg, of queer lives as well as queer policing. Based on their choice of venue for a "farewell date," their decision to live together, Dmitrii's resolve to part ways, and Johan's insistence on finding him, if the proposed reading has any merit, these two young men moved through the city as friends and lovers, not just as sexual partners. They might very well have belonged to the loose-knit community of "familiar strangers," many of whom knew one another at least by sight, but shared crucial common ground even if they did not. Their perambulations and encounters, their contacts with the wider urban world, including the constable to whom we owe their fragmentary story, all contributed to the larger project of carving a queer milieu out of the bedrock of a reluctantly hospitable city.[8] In this milieu, "queer" and "normal," regulation and chaos, temptation and anxiety blurred in deceptive but partially decipherable ways, as this book undertakes to show. Ambiguous and cryptic as it may be, Johan and Dmitrii's story opens a small window onto an otherwise opaque aspect of the city's history that can only be reconstructed by assembling a sufficient number of adjoining pieces of this intriguing mosaic.

St. Petersburg, City of Contrasts

If we turn from the micro to the macro, from the fate of two young men to the population of the city as a whole, we see that Johan and Dmitrii inhabited the very center of the world known to them. Late imperial St. Petersburg was the cultural, political, and social center of one of the largest empires in world history. In the period under review, the city grew impressively, adding about 1.5 million inhabitants between 1880 and 1914, reaching a population of around 2.2 million in 1914.[9] During this period, the imperial capital transformed from a court and administrative center into an industrial-commercial metropolis of global significance. This transformation was easily visible on an international scale. From 1850 to 1900, St. Petersburg held its place as one of the most populous cities in Europe, trailing only three or four of the other great European capitals of the nineteenth century.[10] The city's demographic cauldron held elites eager to adopt the commercial, cultural, and technological achievements of the West in an unstable suspension with illiterate migrants, domestic and menial workers, and fortune-seekers of all brands, who, having recently abandoned rural lifestyles that were older than the empire itself, inevitably attracted the paternalistic attentions of authorities eager to curtail indiscriminate mixing and resultant threats to political and social order.

St. Petersburg was a city of contrasts—perhaps even more so than other cities its size. To some scholars, such as Marshall Berman, these contrasts seemed incapable of resolution. The city's barely hidden cankers fatally undermined its pretense to modernity. In his famous discussion of St. Petersburg's "modernism of underdevelopment," Berman remarks that St. Petersburg's shining modernity disguised the ugly consequences of its ramshackle rise: "Use of space behind the building façades was completely unregulated, so that, especially as the city grew, imposing exteriors could conceal festering slums."[11] To others, these contrasts were incongruous in appearance only, masking a complementarity of opposites, incendious but symbiotic, which is an established theme in the writing of Russian history.[12] In this sense, St. Petersburg's shocking mismatch between urbane pretense and primordial squalor merely reflected the intimate economic and demographic connections between misery and plenty in the empire's particular mode of development.[13] Peasant men and women drawn from its vast contiguous landmass, who were often racially indistinguishable from their masters, had built and sustained the palaces of its capital city. During the last two decades of imperial rule, their occupants continued to amass wealth by dipping into an increasingly mobile labor pool at world-beating rates, fueling a boom in Russian industrial production, but also reinforcing the concentration of income inequality in the empire's largest cities.[14]

Here, as elsewhere, the complementarity of contrasts shaped not only the physical but also the moral topography of the city, spatial and behavioral discontinuities that presented themselves as opportunities for transgression. An imaginary landscape to which Miles Ogborn refers in his discussion of pleasure, license, and commerce in London's eighteenth-century Vauxhall Gardens is an illustrative example and speaks back to Berman. A satirical, moralizing piece in the *Weekly Register* from 1732 describes "Virtue" leading "Curiosity" to four pleasure palaces in the garden: love, wine, ambition, and money. Behind each of the facades lurk ungainly courts, undercrofts, garderobes, and kitchens, with all the sordid, but necessary, consequences of the temptations displayed with such appealing luster in the front-facing staterooms.[15]

The title of this book, *Places of Tenderness and Heat*, refers to a similar set of contrasts and complements, but their juxtaposition and context emphasize the locally specific connections between queer socialization and sex rather than any inherent contradictions between them. The aim of this book is neither to pass judgment on the city's abortive transformation into a modern metropolis nor to diagnose the germination of identities connected to illicit sex.[16] Instead, the book stays close to the ground to explore the relationship between the management of space and behaviors ranging from informal communion to outright sexual transgression. It emphasizes a dynamic negotiation over the use of urban space and the patterns of movement and encounter that instantiated the city's queer milieu.

On the most literal, geographical level, this book's title refers to a spatial pattern that played an important role in late imperial St. Petersburg's queer milieu. This pattern straddled and connected one of the city's parks and several nearby bathhouses. In the park, the Tavricheskii Garden, men interested in sex with men met, talked, and socialized. "Tenderness" refers to the latent possibility of sex, friendship, and even love that drew men to this garden. "Heat," by contrast, refers to sexual passion that could not conveniently be consummated then and there, but might be pursued in the semipublic spaces of the nearby Znamenskaia or Basseinaia Baths. The title reflects this book's ambition to capture a range of activities far broader than the single-minded pursuit of sex, but nevertheless tethered to the possibility of it. Recognizable if often discrete patterns of movement and encounter played a crucial role in facilitating sex as well as nonsexual communion among men with broadly diverse but consistently illicit sexual desires directed at persons of their own physiological sex.[17] In places of tenderness such as the Tavricheskii Garden, the latency of sex, meaning the opportunity for men to meet other men with whom they might have sex, was an essential feature, but it often slipped into the background as looks, encounters, conversations, and perambulation dominated the playbook of activities. The possibility to transition from tenderness to heat, nevertheless, exerted an almost magnetic effect in arranging even seemingly casual queer spatial patterns near spaces where "heat" could be contained and accommodated. The transition between tenderness and heat, usually involving a spatial journey, posed one of the fundamental challenges underlying the spatial negotiation addressed in this book.

The terms are not my own. The title is gleaned from the 1906 diary of Mikhail Kuzmin, a poet, composer, and writer of the so-called Russian Silver Age.[18] He and his onetime lover, the painter Konstantin Somov, conceived of a map and a poem as a fanciful reflection of their own spatial patterns (more on this in chapter 5). As an idiomatic reference or mnemonic encapsulating the overarching topics of this investigation, the title reflects the complementarity of observable socialization among queer men in the city's public spaces with the more intimate interactions that took place in the city's private or semipublic spaces, such as bathhouses.[19] Importantly, it emphasizes subterfuge and calibration of behaviors to settings, insofar as part of the map's purpose was to help its users navigate the city and avoid getting caught. The title, thus, corresponds to my engagement with and, I hope, my contribution to scholarship on queer urban sexualities. In this book, I explicitly foreground the negotiation around the use of space as an important feature of urban modernity and I prioritize this over what has been called its "experiential dimensions."[20] The latter subject has warranted much attention in the context of a search for the origins of modern queer identities and subjectivities, but it has also proven doggedly elusive, especially in places where very few firsthand accounts survive. I build on the scholarship concerning queer sexualities, but this book's main contribution is in investigating and conceptualizing the relationship between the bureaucratic management of space and queer spatial patterns. It is both locally specific and, I hope, internationally relevant.

The choice to focus on movements and encounters instead of subjective experience and identities may seem inconsequential at first, but in fact it has important implications. First, a focus on the city comes at a price: readers in search of the historical origins or precursors of familiar gay or queer identities will find this subject addressed only very indirectly via a discussion about the use of urban space.[21] Second, this approach breaks an alternative path to reconstructing the lives of queer men, given the challenges of penetrating into the psychology of desires and relationships whose expression was carefully constrained by their subjects and often suppressed by their contemporaries. The associated subjective experience and identities are undeniably salient to a by no means merely prurient interest in the historical city, but an indirect approach to them is an opportunity born out of necessity. In some locales, an effort to understand *what* a great number of queer men actually did is both possible and, surprisingly, still outstanding, whereas the surviving smattering of statements from a few of them about *how* they experienced it has received ample, perhaps even excessive attention, but has proved difficult to contextualize. Moreover, by looking at movements and encounters quite broadly and in the context of efforts by municipal authorities to implement spatial controls, one stands to learn not only about the queer milieu but also about the historical city as a whole and the formal and informal regimes of governance in use within it.

This approach, which I describe as a geographical one, opens up new possibilities for the study of historical cities, particularly in their queer dimension. First, it adds to the tools available for expanding the pale of reasonable analytical ambition beyond the great Western cities—first and foremost London, Paris, Berlin, New York, and San Francisco—whose queer cultures, at least by the fin-de-siècle era, are unusually well-illuminated by surviving biographical evidence and have since become ever more visible and assertive. Second, it addresses one of the trends underlying urban modernity that has received either too little attention or only a certain kind of attention. Whereas alienation and commodification are front and center in most discussions of urban modernity, administrative management of space is something of a lonely stepchild, often studied through the prism of legislation and court cases alone, rather than through evidence of more routine street-level operations.[22] In fact, Foucault's project, which was groundbreakingly ambitious in its attempts to trace the insidiously subtle qualities and effects of spatial ordering, was built into his overarching critique of bourgeois capitalist society. The perceived urgency of this critique has receded since the collapse of communism as a preeminently visible contrasting system, but this does not detract from its chief merit of drawing attention to the ways in which the state aligned itself with various economic interests to propagate spatial measures that circumscribed and defined the grid of opportunities for transgression, sex, commerce, and communion. Picking up here, but treating the phenomena he describes as characteristic of state bureaucracies per se, rather than particular to any specific ideology or tradition of government, this book seeks to reconstruct an important but little-discussed feature of queer men's lives that influenced their behavior precisely at the times when they ventured out to pursue or cautiously disclose their desires: the on-the-ground negotiation over the appropriate use of the city's public and semipublic spaces.

In retracing this negotiation, the unique historical discontinuities in the development of St. Petersburg during the twentieth century are an advantage. Unlike other queer urban cultures that have attracted a disproportionate share of historical scholarship, St. Petersburg's queer milieu did not continue to evolve in communication with an internationally permeable cosmopolitan tradition of sexual and gender dissent.[23] Kuzmin and Somov's trips between places of tenderness and places of heat epitomize a milieu that, although permeable at the time, was soon to be cut off. Its idiosyncratic trajectory and inability to permanently resurface at least for another century imposes unique discipline on the retroactive hunt for queer modes of engagement with the city, insofar as a trajectory toward instantiating more familiar sexual and gender identities cannot be taken for granted. No backward inferences are possible. This singular historical configuration demands the nonforensic, emplaced, and dynamic analysis of a milieu that once was—independently of whether it contained the seeds of more assertive cultural communities associated with later gay rights movements or even the nonbinary identities (re)emerging more or less concurrently in major Western cities.

Peering over the Edge in St. Petersburg

Late imperial St. Petersburg, however, is booby-trapped in its own way for anyone with a propensity to read historical periods in the light of what followed. If in the West it is difficult to look back at the cultural expression of homosexual desires without thinking of gay liberation and emerging queer identities, in Russia it is difficult to look at the fin-de-siècle period without immediately thinking of the Revolution of 1917. The temptation to focus on its possible causes has often lent to this violent upheaval the sheen of inevitability. In fact, however, the last decades of imperial rule were not only a time of rapid economic growth and social tension but also an era during which a variously frustrated modernization drive by St. Petersburg's sophisticated, educated, liberal elites, looked less like a last-ditch effort than a promising return to Peter the Great's project of better integrating his empire and, in particular, its capital with Western Europe.

City authorities during this period tried to control and harmonize reformist influences, calibrating doses of liberal reforms to the demands of continued authoritarian surveillance of dangerous spaces as well as deviant individuals.[24] Like the well-maintained facades, the city's public and semipublic spaces enjoyed the benefit—or, depending on one's perspective, bore the brunt—of attempts to govern and control. Initially following the city's founding, this regime of spatial control had a straightforwardly military rationale, namely, to enable the swift movement of troops from one side of the fortified city to the other. During the period addressed in this book, however, the cultivation of an orderly choreography in the streets was paramount.[25] Conversely, what happened in the teeming, crime-infested spaces of courtyards, apartments, and boardinghouses or the interiors of elegant city flats and palaces remained largely unrecorded, barely visible to municipal and imperial authorities. Those authorities worried about such undergoverned spaces and made sporadic efforts to penetrate their obscurities, but in the end consistently fell back on promoting order in the streets and associated public spaces of St. Petersburg.[26]

The authorities were aided in this by the city's pleasingly legible architectural configuration, which enabled and encouraged mutual visibility across vast spaces and enhanced disciplinary ambitions, not least in the regulation of sexuality. The straightforward sightlines of late imperial St. Petersburg's most prominent and central public spaces facilitated the policing of crime and conduct, as they had facilitated the quick movement of troops across the city in decades past. At the same time, this legibility—aesthetically reminiscent of another planned city, Washington, DC—contributed to the production of a flourishing queer milieu.

Queer men, here as elsewhere, exploited the tension between the legibility of urban spaces and the private nature of their business in the public realm. As the story of Johan and Dmitrii illustrates, the late imperial capital married sexual opportunity and governmental surveillance in an uneasy, but arguably effective negotiation over the use of urban space. Queer men who observed certain constraints on their behavior could exploit the city's unique combination of panoptical public spaces and nearby bolt-holes of every brand and color. Men who desired sex respun the urban fabric by beating paths between the city's streets, gardens, and squares and the less visible, largely unpoliced realm of private or semipublic enclosures.

The traditional historiographical narrative concerning late imperial St. Petersburg underexploits this complementarity of once-illicit activities and an uneven urban landscape, emphasizing instead the fissures and cankers as seeds of revolution. This is not the only perspective available and it risks being undermined by recent scholarship.[27] Several influential works go so far as to call out the supposedly incendiary tension between authoritarian social discipline and oppressed groups in the city as something of a Soviet-era stereotype, influenced in hindsight by the onset or orchestration of fratricidal conflict.[28] A strong case can be made that the authorities had long lost the battle to implement an effectively oppressive disciplinary society even in the capital. Turn-of-the-twentieth-century St. Petersburg and Russian society as a whole were in many respects notoriously chaotic and if anything loosely governed. Disorder, breaches of law, and deviant behavior of all sorts were ubiquitous and had been so for decades. This disorder was the source of much anxiety about public life, including sexual activity, and perhaps erupted in what has been referred to as a full-blown moral panic in the years immediately preceding the Revolution.[29] But the underlying ubiquity of deviance was older and not strictly incompatible with economic, cultural, and even political progress. It extended to all social classes, including those involved in the work of government, and represented an unmissable opportunity to engage in behaviors in the liminal zone between tolerance and oppression.[30] Perhaps anticipating this perspective, Louise McReynolds in her analysis of this untidy autocracy and the opportunities for individual expression calls for a fundamental reevaluation of the supposed antagonism between the state and the individual, or elites and the masses in late imperial Russia and its capital city. She suggests that "the first task of the Petersburg writers is to resolve this antagonism, to accept that the city helps to shape the individual."[31] How this shaping took place can be observed more readily on the municipal scale when resisting, at least for a moment, the temptation to pit against each other privilege and resistance, oppression and freedom, the authoritarian state and the inhabitants of the "underground."

In expanding on a narrative of contrast *and* complementarity, one of the decisive contentions in this book is that what appears to be chaos and disorder was, in fact, a relatively stable and decipherable spatial entente between urban actors, particularly various municipal governing bodies, the police, and queer men. As illustrated by the case of Johan and Dmitrii, consistent patterns of covert and partially visible deviation from the normative public aesthetic targeted by legislation and regulation were enabled by and sustained this entente, whereas efforts at containment periodically shifted its boundaries, sometimes in unexpected ways. Deciphering these patterns and constraints was at least as important to a would-be participant in the day as it is to an archival investigator looking back. In their minutiae as well as in their aggregation, these patterns suggest that state and municipal autocracy were not monolithically coercive, nor was the broader population consistently and systematically recalcitrant, but rather that both were bound to one another by conventions of discretion and compromise over the appropriate use of urban space and the risks of defying a much-contested authoritative vision of order and propriety. A review of the surviving evidence allows us to reconstruct in some detail how this complementarity worked in practice. The interactions of queer men with the urban environment illustrate how this particular group of men was, on the one hand, subject to the vision of public order communicated downward by municipal authorities, but on the other hand, able to modify its imperatives to accommodate wholly incongruent desires.

In Search of the Queer City

In terms of size, wealth, and cultural and political importance, late imperial St. Petersburg ranked among the great cities of continental Europe. Visitors reported abundant sexual opportunities.[32] Despite this and with the notable exception of Simon Karlinsky's and Dan Healey's work, it has remained outside the main current of scholarship on queer urban life for several reasons. The first and most important of these is that "*the* dominant paradigm in historical analysis of male sexualities has been the correlation of the emergence of visible queer cultures with the experiential dimensions of urban modernity."[33] Relying on relatively abundant firsthand accounts of some cities, notably including London, Paris, Berlin, and New York, this paradigm traces the "'making of the modern homosexual'" with "singular linearity" to a set of more or less uniform aspects of urban modernity.[34] Neither pole of this classical dyad is neatly available for late imperial St. Petersburg. Very few firsthand accounts by queer men survive, and following Berman's influential characterization of the city's development, the unproblematic application of the term "modernity" to its state in the fin-de-siècle era would have required substantial justification.

In a subtle but important shift, Mark Steinberg and, to a degree, Joan Neuberger have softened the latter constraint by painstakingly disentangling fin-de-siècle journalistic, legislative, and forensic discourses from the supposed realities they describe. Looking at these discourses as cultural realities specific to late imperial St. Petersburg rather than as reliably accurate characterizations of a uniquely defective urban society and model of municipal governance, they argue that a radically anxious self-reflection penetrated many levels of society and that this anxiety or discontent had less to do with a lack of progress in reducing actual inequalities of living standards than with an ever sharper divergence of responses to social, economic, and technological change. Importantly, dissatisfaction among the urban poor found vocal reflection in the radical social criticism of elites shut out from governance and deeply divided about their diagnosis and prescription for the city's ills. "Here on the margins of Europe," as Steinberg notes, "Russians were exceptionally well-positioned to see and understand most acutely the dark sides of modern life. They could and did experience, and rapidly, the harshness of modernization and capitalism."[35] This localization of popular anxiety and radical social criticism marks a subtle departure from the Marxist paradigm of a singularly oppressive and inevitably doomed model of municipal and imperial governance.

The shift in perspectives contributes to new opportunities to conceptually distinguish between historical discourses about homosexuality in late imperial St. Petersburg and the activities and encounters of queer men whose lives are reflected in them only to a highly uncertain degree. Whereas important previous work has looked at journalistic, medical-forensic, and legislative representations of homosexuality in Russia, the historical production of St. Petersburg's queer spaces and their on-the-ground governance appeared to be singularly challenging and, in any case, largely subsumed in the professional and public portrayals. The recognition that the story has at least two sides, that systematic discrepancies might exist between the often stark discursive realities of journalists, medical luminaries, judges and lawmakers, and other no less discursive, but frequently more ambiguous realities of queer men, constables, sanitation inspectors, bathhouse operators, and other passersby adds a compelling motivation to at least partially reconstruct the latter. This project must be undertaken without the essentializing objective of unearthing the seeds of rupture and conflict, nor indeed that of detecting the origins of necessarily congealing boundaries between "deviant" and "normal" male sexualities.

There is, of course, fertile ground to build on. Although far less voluminous than the studies of queer historical London, Paris, Berlin, New York, or San Francisco, the literature on male homosexuality in St. Petersburg has passed some of the same milestones.[36] Following some early publications in the 1970s and 1980s by the Russian American historian Simon Karlinsky, historical scholarship in this area mainly played catch-up during and after the era of glasnost, focusing squarely on a *coming out* or *becoming visible* of the imperial capital's queer milieu.[37] The liberal atmosphere engendered by the reforms of the 1860s, it has also been claimed, created the necessary conditions for homosexuality to emerge and assume recognizable forms in "both Russian life and literature."[38] The reforms of 1905, though subsequently aborted, further underscored the overlap between sexual and other modes of dissent. During the period covered in this book, urbanization, industrialization, and political reforms congealed in a social transformation that, within the Russian Empire, affected St. Petersburg first and foremost. Shifts in the traditional social fabric were particularly noticeable in the capital. Symptomatically, for example, consistent application of the traditional system of social castes defied even the most dyed-in-the-wool government bureaucrats (discussed in chapter 1), and nontraditional sexual practices came to be thoroughly established as a topic for public discussion via medical accounts, journalistic publications, and legal debates.[39]

These discussions, combined with a few surviving surveillance records, lend themselves to the narrative of visibility—and, by extension, liberation. They are the subject of works by Karlinsky in particular, as is the book *The Other St. Petersburg* by the Russian historian Iurii Piriutko.[40] Although very different from one another, both writers combine fragmentary biographical information about the city's prominent queer residents with broader evidence of the city's "queer topography." Their work rests on descriptions of what we might today call "cruising sites," or locations providing opportunities for sexual encounters such as the city's bathhouses, as well as the goings-on in certain theaters and restaurants in which queer men met and socialized. Whether these sites had only recently started to provide such opportunities or had been doing so for a substantial time without attracting much attention is not considered, and this is almost impossible to ascertain in retrospect. Karlinsky and Piriutko instead make the plausible assumption that their appearance in the historical record coincided with their becoming increasingly popular and visible to the wider public.

Archival evidence discovered by Piriutko in particular in the mid-1990s quickly prompted further commentary from Russian historians.[41] In their paper "The Police and Gays: An Episode from the Era of Aleksandr III," Vladimir Bersen'ev and A. Markov examine the role of the physical city, of police and governmental regulation, and of public perceptions on homosexual socialization and sex in the late nineteenth century. They conclude that "there was no major gulf between Russian and European realities" as far as regulation and surveillance of queer activities were concerned. According to them, St. Petersburg essentially followed the path of its European peers in the emergence of a distinctive homosexual milieu.[42] They return St. Petersburg's European context, drawing valuable parallels with the experience of homosexual men elsewhere, though inevitably at the expense of locally specific particulars.

A different cohort of scholars, including, most importantly, two Western historians, Laura Engelstein and Dan Healey, have rightly questioned this view, putting increased emphasis on local, or rather Russian, "peculiarities." Engaging systematically with the discursive formation of sexuality and gender via medicalization, legislative debates, and public discourse in late imperial Russia, they look at the country as a whole.[43] Both correctly suggest that public debates, scientific literature, court records, and official policy engaging explicitly with issues of homosexuality, sexual deviance, prostitution, and gender constitute important points of departure for reconstructing often conflicting public perceptions around these topics. Both see the professional discourses on homosexuality, in particular, as increasingly integrated with Western medical and liberal legislative thought and, therefore, ever more at odds with imperial legislation. Healey does not focus on this disconnect, but concludes that by the last decades of imperial rule, the courts had essentially thrown in the towel in trying to prosecute sodomy cases. Almost none were brought to trial, insofar as the surviving evidence can be relied upon. Engelstein's analysis places far greater emphasis on the disconnect between public debates and policy. She describes it as essential to the radicalization of the left and the confused moral conservatism of reformers, both of which followed a locally specific trajectory and crystallized around issues of sexuality.

Importantly, Engelstein prominently acknowledges the constraints inherent in writing about sex without having broad evidence of actual sexual practices, as these were recorded only in rare and unusual instances.[44] Healey, working around the same constraints, focuses not so much on queer lives as on their regulation—a qualification he makes clear by adding the subtitle *The Regulation of Sexual and Gender Dissent* to the title of his book *Homosexual Desire in Revolutionary Russia*. It is legitimate to assume that public discourse and regulation affected queer men, but the breadth, mechanism, and manner of their effects are notoriously difficult to ascertain. Engelstein's decision, therefore, to focus on the discourses themselves and on elites by implication is as consistent as her contribution to the cultural history of this time and place is vast. Healey's conclusions regarding "gender formation among Russian men," based on his review of how "disciplinary mechanisms were adapted to authoritarian power" via legislative acts, court cases, medical investigations, and other explicitly documented events, are, of necessity, more tenuous.[45]

Neither approach, however, tests the limits of reconstructing queer men's movements, meetings, and encounters at the micro level at a particular time and in a particular city. In this regard, their work is quite different from, for example, Georg Chauncey's discussion in *Gay New York*, in which the particular goings-on in various prominently queer settings receive detailed attention. In the context of Healey's project in particular, the specific manners in which queer men calibrated their behavior to *authoritarian power* might have been a salient extension, but it would have distracted from his central project of revising flawed characterizations of state views on homosexuality in the early Soviet period. To complement the empirical basis for a discussion of fin-de-siècle St. Petersburg's queer milieu, therefore, some essential work of historical recovery remains outstanding. Given the dearth of autobiographical and court records, this requires integrating a different set of sources, some of which do not explicitly name or label homosexual identities and activities. Here, it is precisely the lack of homosexual "visibility," or the remaining opacity, that is both challenging and intriguing. Shining an archival searchlight into these recalcitrantly opaque regions enables a discussion that not only productively complicates the familiar narrative of a gradual and inevitable "coming out" of queer sexual practice (in Petersburg as elsewhere) but also adds to our understanding of how queer men balanced the risks and rewards of pursuing their desires in the city's public spaces at a time when public debate about sexuality and deviance was heating up.

The methodological challenges of opening up this window into the day-to-day lives of queer men are immense, but they also present an opportunity. By researching the activities of queer men when no "momentary failure to negotiate the tensions inherent in queer urban life" exposed them to explicit forensic scrutiny as sexual "deviants," this book seeks to reconstruct the dynamics of a negotiation that was at once routine and dynamic.[46] It shifts the focus from queer subjectivity to queer spatial patterns—not in the sense that this is where queer men necessarily became "visible" and especially exposed to persecution, but in the sense that these patterns were central to their pursuit of sex and communion and brought them into contact with the larger urban environment. By their participation in these patterns, they carved out a queer milieu, a queer geography both obscure and overt, familiar and strange.

Men Who Got Caught

This book situates the queer milieu at the nexus of flesh and cobblestone, understood dynamically in the most literal sense and intermediated by the soles of many feet, not just those of queer men. It complements the soul-searching quest to reveal queer subjects and subjectivities as it provides an alternative to the—often useful—visions of a "Gay New York," "Gay Berlin," "Queer London," or "Queer Russia" awaiting discovery in the rubble of old photographs, diaries, and police and medical records, much as Helen's Troy awaited Schliemann's spade. Responding to the challenges and achievements of queer urban histories of Western cities and existing analyses of forensic homosexuality in Russia (or larger cultural histories of the period, such as Laura Engelstein's), this book emphasizes queer spatial patterns as characteristic modes of community formation and nonconfrontational dissent in late imperial St. Petersburg. Here, the queer city, if it might be said to exist at all, was inherently contaminated during its preservation and excavation, and this contamination needs to be taken seriously. In the lives of individual men, sexual and romantic desire competed with other aspects of the project of working out viable social roles. In the life of this city as a whole, queer spaces were only rarely exclusively or even predominantly queer. Instead, overlap, discretion, and compromise dominated the dynamic between queer spatial patterns and other patterns that enjoyed the full sanction of governmental authority. Their mutual contamination, bordering at times on indistinguishability, is—far from being a snare or complication for the scholars looking for the queer city—an intrinsic, even essential feature of the queer milieu.

Attention to this feature is, furthermore, epistemologically compelling. Only a small and not necessarily representative fraction of queer life in the city was ever explicitly documented, as for instance in the lead-up to prosecution for breaches of draconian sodomy laws. Most queer histories have, nevertheless, placed significant reliance on evidence of major raids and instances of prosecution for transgressions of laws regulating sexual practices (see chapter 2). Even Matt Houlbrook, who writes about "Queer London" and explicitly acknowledges the risk of relying on the number of court cases brought under sodomy laws as a measure of police oppression, advocates a counterintuitive reading of such court records as evidence that "men *were* able to create a place for themselves in the city." More important than their being occasioned by their subjects' "failure to evade the law," he reads these records as "paradigmatic sources" reflecting how "pain and pleasure intersect."[47]

Clearly sensitive to the moral and epistemological issues of amplifying the voices of those who oppressed and censured queer men, Houlbrook proposes no convenient alternative to relying primarily on prosecution incidents as the corollary to memoirist recollections. In a city, where at least by the fin-de-siècle period a number of relatively diverse nonforensic firsthand accounts help to round out the picture, and where even court records routinely contained statements or documents written by the defendants, this approach is not altogether imbalanced and possesses the charm of removing much of the ambiguity as to whether the communities and behaviors described in such sources bear a direct connection to criminalized sex. Still, it is important to recall that even for London this empirical basis is thin. In 1917, in a city of over seven million inhabitants, only sixty-seven incidents led to proceedings for breaches against laws specifically targeting homosexuality, of which more than half took place on two streets.[48] Perhaps surprisingly for anyone whose idea of queer life at the fin de siècle is shaped by the highly publicized trial of Oscar Wilde, very few queer relationships or sexual encounters ever resulted in court proceedings, even in London. The surviving court record of sodomy cases is thinner by far for many other cities, including St. Petersburg. Thus, these other cities offer a compelling and underused opportunity for the historical study of queer urban encounters and communities. Not only do they force us to look for less obvious hooks on which to hang our historical imagination of queer urban life, but they also require us to engage head-on with the very ambiguity of sexual valences.

In looking for something at once potentially more broadly representative than prosecutions explicitly linked to laws targeting sex between men and more locally specific than internationally osmotic public discourses about queer men, including legislative debates and medical paradigms, the negotiation over queer spatial patterns is, I would argue, a highly promising target.[49] Its study casts the net far wider than documented instances of sex (or sexual solicitation) and dredging up a broad set of activities and encumbrances that shaped queer men's everyday lives. If the promise of this approach can be demonstrated anywhere, then it creates a plausible prospect of capturing a more representative and complete picture of queer urban life in the cities, about which much has already been written, and of tackling other cities, whose surviving historical record contains very few court cases. St. Petersburg, as one of many cities for which ample autobiographical evidence from this period is also in very short supply (in fact, London, Paris, and New York are the exception rather than the rule), offers an ideal testing ground for a set of analyses proposed not so much for their ability to illuminate the psychology of individual queer men as for their power to reconstruct the world many of them inhabited, an urban modernity *at work* in the negotiation over queer spaces.

Building on familiar projects of mapping queer encounters, the work involved in this approach is at times counterintuitive. It reverses a traditional preference for the clear-cut case study by actively targeting ambiguity as an intrinsic feature of queer lives. Especially against the background of the subsequent disruptions caused by the Russian Revolution, this ambiguity or opaqueness of queer spatial patterns stands as though suspended in time, ready to tilt or unravel in any number of directions. Paying specific attention to the opaque negotiation around queer spatial patterns, therefore, helps to resolve the tension between coexisting, but at times contradictory associations of modern urban life with licentious sex and oppressed but recalcitrant preliberation sexualities. This is much the same contradiction Houlbrook flags in proposing to read court cases as evidence, simultaneously, of successful competition by queer men for sexual spaces and of their occasional failures to negotiate the risks of prosecution under sodomy laws. I am reluctant to accept that these were two sides of the same coin, that arrest was, in fact, nothing more than a momentary failure. Rather, I have come to see these failures as the tip of the iceberg in a system of controls on behaviors and responsive adaptations. As is typical with icebergs, the part sticking out is small and does not tell us much about the shape underneath the waterline. The dive below the waterline targets the quotidian movements of queer men and the many nondisastrous inconveniences they encountered, ranging from the possibility of arbitrary arrest to an unpleasant encounter with hooligans. It may be a slightly fuzzy picture at times, and it remains surface-bound in its own way, but it plays a critical role in revealing the contours of the often secretive queer lives of men who engaged in homosexual sex.

In implementing this approach, I too rely to a large extent on documents made and kept by actors employed by the state, the very organs often charged with keeping queer spatial patterns in check. Nevertheless, the kinds of documents targeted make a big difference. The work underlying this book certainly seeks to be responsive to documents explicitly related to sex or erotic desire between men and to previous scholarship referring to these documents, but it considerably expands the empirical basis for analysis by dredging the documentary trail of routine operation of the state in, for example, street-level policing, infrastructural development, and urban planning, insofar as it relates to spaces demonstrably used by queer men to meet sexual partners or to socialize. This more broadly understood spatial governance shaped the contours of the risk map or, put more plainly, the movements, encounters, habits, behaviors, and attires that could be most conveniently enacted, adopted, and repeated with negligible risk of prosecution, at least under statutes specifically targeting male homosexual sex. "While cities are sites of sexual freedom," as Phil Hubbard observes astutely, "they are also sites of power. Importantly, this power is principally that associated with the state."[50] True elsewhere, this was certainly the case in imperial Russia.

A protracted and very much locally specific negotiation of queer spatial patterns and their visibility in public spaces emerges. This negotiation antecedes or underlies the battle cries for resistance to state oppression of homosexuals, and, in the case of St. Petersburg, that resistance, if and when articulated at all, took the familiar form of a widespread gay liberation movement, only with considerable delay and never succeeding in the way it has in many Western cities. I would argue that this makes St. Petersburg particularly useful in studying partially visible and often ambiguous queer spatial patterns. A narrow conceptualization of behaviors associated with deviant sexuality or illicit sex as an "an effective political strategy for destabilizing existing and taken-for-granted assumptions about sexuality" and for contesting public space may speak powerfully in the context of histories of gay liberation, but could mean misreading the historical role of spatial patterns recognizably associated with male–male sex.[51] It might even be said that retroactive application of paradigms of resistance risks, by implication or extension, denigrating partially visible queer cultures that predate any explicit struggle for recognition of sexual civic liberties to a kind of inferior moral status as "effectively submissive." Against this background of interpretive pitfalls, the spatial patterns implicated in late imperial St. Petersburg's queer milieu illustrate that visibility serves an important role for any sexual minority and that this role was, perhaps, even more essential to the constitution of a queer milieu than any nascent or yet-to-be-conceived political agenda: After all, visibility, even when partial and ambiguous, facilitates sex and communion. This basic sexual and social purpose required regular, frequent repetition of discrete patterns, many of which involved movement through or congregation in the city's public and semipublic spaces. Queer visibilities, therefore, regardless of whether they were complete or overtly political, had to be sexual and, I would add, social.[52] This basic functionality required careful calibration and negotiation with other stakeholders of the city's public spaces, primarily but not only the state.

The emergence of a queer milieu, therefore, was premised on at least partial success in this negotiation. In it, the rewards of compromise, complicity, even collusion, were at times much greater than those of defiance or overt resistance. This dynamic played a crucial role in queer men's lives and in the emplacement of the very communities that, under different circumstances, might eventually have sought to redraw the lines of broadly acceptable sexuality. It stood in particularly sharp relief in St. Petersburg, where the discrepancy between the state's autocratic ambition and its effective governance was stark by all accounts and the transition of queer life into a more assertive phase did not follow. The case of St. Petersburg, therefore, illustrates not just that but also how the pursuit of opportunities for sexual deviance functioned as a coherent principle for spatial ordering and competed, at times effectively, with normative conceptions of the proper use of space. Thus, much as queer spatial patterns may have challenged "normality" in late imperial St. Petersburg, they also confounded, undermined, and co-opted it, producing a remarkably stable and locally specific network of queer spaces and patterns of movement that, for some men, constituted an accessible and navigable refuge or harbor in the city. This book is as much about the interaction of the body and its desires with its urban environment and those charged with imposing normative order on it as it is about a negotiated entente, discernible to both the contemporary and the historical observer, that might supplant, to a degree, a lose-lose war of attrition in our historical imagination of queer life in the imperial city.

Queering the Archive

By affixing a decidedly "spatial lens" and simultaneously widening the aperture to also capture documents not related to prosecution under sodomy laws, nor even necessarily bearing any explicit association with homosexual sex, but testifying to the management of movements and encounters between queer men, we can broaden both our investigative tool set as well as our understanding of St. Petersburg's queer milieu. This book draws extensively on a number of lesser known sources, including municipal administrative archives. Although these records reflect the operations of the city government on the street and building level, in some important cases they also provide new information regarding city-wide policies or initiatives. For instance, in reviewing police files and lower-level administrative correspondence, I came across documents involving the implementation of major legislative acts or administrative directives, some of which were, in fact, explicitly directed at curbing queer socialization, while others directly affected the availability and use of spaces with strong relevance for the queer milieu (such as bathhouses). These acts failed to leave prominent traces in the larger national archives or to provoke extensive contemporary journalistic discussion. As a result, they have not entered the historical record at all. Fortunately, copies had been appended to lower-level administrative correspondence and can now be considered in their historical context. No less importantly, archival evidence of day-to-day patterns of interaction and movement—although far from comprehensive—allows us to revisit in unique detail the nature of the queer milieu in imperial St. Petersburg and, in particular, the specific spaces in which queer relationships unfolded.

Based on the juxtaposition and close textual analysis of archival sources, the results of this investigation demonstrate that the dry facts of police logs, administrative correspondence, and case files are neither dry nor, as it turns out, straightforward to interpret. For example, the potentially far-reaching implications of arrests for petty crimes become apparent only once a sufficient number of adjoining tesserae from the mosaic of queer policing are reassembled: in the absence of a practically useful regulatory framework for policing homosexual deviance, at least in some instances petty crimes arrests were made by constables to manage the visibility of deviant sexuality. The archival records pertaining to such arrests and a plethora of other mundane matters, such as shopping mall reconstructions, building regulations, sanitary inspections, and so on, inform the rich texture of an ongoing negotiation over the city's queer spaces. In reassembling this mosaic, I juxtapose what we can cull from hitherto neglected records with what we know from existing historical work and primary documents explicitly concerned with criminal sexuality. I contextualize the resulting history and geography of late imperial St. Petersburg's queer milieu via known autobiographical sources and the secondary literature about legislative trends, economic history, grassroots movements, and technological innovation in the imperial city. This unapologetically eclectic approach provides us with the resources to significantly broaden our understanding of late imperial queer life.

In this renewed and systematic dredging of primary archival documents and their integration into the historical record, omissions can themselves offer important clues. For example, as alluded to earlier, explicit mention of suspected homosexual acts in a police interrogation protocol would have mandated the immediate launch of a targeted investigation, on which the author of such a protocol may not have wished to embark. The protocol about Johan and Dmitrii offers several strong indications that the constable composing it employed subtle ways to make his suspicions transparent without, however, ever making them explicit in the sense of naming the crime of which he suspected them. The code he used—or seems to have used, as we can never be quite sure—can be deciphered today in approximately the same manner as it could be by his peers and superiors. In the same vein, important inference can also be made from the sorting of documents. For example, in one case constables making an arrest shortly after an anonymous denunciation recorded no evidence that the man arrested was the very man denounced. However, they filed the denunciation together with the arrest record, *implying* by inclusion of the two documents in the same case file that this man was arrested for an activity similar to that described in the denunciation or was, in fact, the very man (see chapter 2). Analogous to the nature of homosexual cruising and socialization, much is implied by context, but little is immediately made explicit. Thus, our understanding of queer spatial patterns in the historical city, as well as the intentions behind some of the city government's attempts to contain and manage them, is supported by nonexplicit, potentially salient, and surprisingly consistent evidence in peripheral aspects of archival organization, including grouping of documents, substantive omissions, response, and lack of response.

It is important to recall that I focus my analysis of the queer milieu on movements and encounters that became manifest in public or semipublic spaces. In part this is a consequence of the decision to prioritize the negotiation around queer spatial practices. As some of the evidence suggests, these were rarely contested when both private and effectively hidden from casual observation. In part, however, this is also a convenience. The already scarce evidence of queer lives dries up almost completely when we try to enter men's homes and residences. Even with the focus on public and semipublic spaces, the constraints inherent in the available archival sources are considerable. Therefore, several caveats are in order. The most significant of these is the circumstance that the vast majority of archival administrative records of a city obsessed with recordkeeping were destroyed during the Revolutions of 1917 (both in February and October 1917).[53]

Even this surviving sample of administrative archives poses considerable impediments to scholarly review, and perhaps for this reason it has not been extensively drawn on. The small preserved fraction of records is contained in poorly cataloged files wrapped in packages with enticing titles such as "Third Police Precinct, June–December 1908." The fragmentary documents they contain are mostly in stenographic shorthand and, in many cases, have not been touched since the day they were filed. Because of their partial nature and lack of cross-indexing across institutions, it is highly unlikely that the complete documentary record of a single case can ever be reconstructed from arrest to sentencing. It is not unusual for case records to be fragmented, but the St. Petersburg records are particularly troublesome. One must, therefore, treat these fragments with the knowledge that any conclusions drawn from them may be demonstrably plausible, perhaps even likely, but cannot be definitively established, insofar as the cases relied on may have taken unexpected turns not reflected in the remaining portion of the archival record. This constraint is I think acceptable, as the fundamental imperative of this effort is not to debunk an established view of forensic sexuality and set up a definitive new one in its stead, but rather to draw the mundane into the historical record, to reconstruct the terms of engagement of queer men with urban spaces, and to recognize the ambiguity facing both them and those who sought to constrain the expression of their illicit desires.

Chapter Overview

Five chapters follow. Within each, the chronological order of events is respected, but each chapter covers the entire period of investigation. The sequencing follows a geographical framework rather than an overarching chronology. It traces the negotiation over the city's public and semipublic spaces by first looking at its fundamental citywide mechanisms and then zooming in on several of the spaces that particularly defined the queer milieu. Chapter 1 starts with a—characteristically problematic—bird's-eye view of the city's queer milieu from a perspective associated with the country's central governing authority, which was, of course, also located in St. Petersburg and preoccupied with goings-on in the capital. The chapter straddles the tension between place and discourse by revisiting both a central spot in late imperial St. Petersburg's queer spatial patterns, Anichkov Bridge, and a secret dossier discovered in the personal archives of a former minister. Together, they open up valuable perspectives on the key themes of ambiguous visibility, social class, and punitive responsibility that inform the remaining chapters. Chapter 2 is about policing. In this chapter I look beyond laws and court cases at the role of street-level constables in regulating the circulation of illicit desire in the city's public spaces. In particular, the broad discretion of constables is important here in iterating the informal principles of spatial management that largely displaced the enforcement of impractical criminal sodomy laws. Chapter 3 is about street life in the city center with a particular emphasis on the Liteinaia Borough, which stretched from Nevsky Prospect to the Neva River in one direction and from the Summer Palace to the Tavricheskii Garden in the other. Aside from being one of the most central city boroughs, it was recently constructed, commercially well-developed, and readily accessible with its even grid of large thoroughfares, proximity to the city's main train station, and connecting bridge to one of the city's populous industrial regions. Its state and development serve as the context for a discussion of the unique blend of risks and opportunities facing queer men as they ventured into the city center in search of sex and communion. Chapter 4 marks the transition to semipublic spaces: it addresses the failure of bathhouse reforms to resolve the tension between queer spatial patterns associated with bathing and the visions of order pursued by the city's governing authorities. Here, I look at the idiosyncratic adaptations of commercial bathing to an evolving urban context that made it so notably convenient for queer encounters. Finally, chapter 5 seeks to expand and anchor the emotional range of queer spatial patterns at one end by examining the experience of a particular group of men in the Tavricheskii Garden, where they gathered to socialize and make new acquaintances and from whence they fanned out to locations more hospitable to intimate exchange. Notwithstanding a gradual progression from a citywide perspective to a microgeographical one, the chapters themselves are not only conceptually connected but also sewn together by the movements of queer men between spaces and regimes of indifference, scrutiny, and obstructive control.

In retracing the steps from places of tenderness to places of heat, and back again, this book sets out how the forays of queer men into the city's public and semipublic spaces entangled them with the materiality of the city in all its dynamism, and with a broad range of governmental attempts to regulate the use of urban space, not just those specifically targeting queer activity. As already mentioned, these attempts largely spared queer men's bedrooms, boardinghouses, and private apartments. While sex and communion in private spaces was, of course, an important part of queer men's lives, it was not contingent on an ongoing negotiation over the use of space to the same degree as the goings-on in public and semipublic spaces. Very little ever came of the few known attempts to challenge a regime of de facto noninterference in sexual affairs between consenting adults at home and behind closed doors (see chapter 2). More importantly, however, the queer milieu as both spectacle and refuge was constituted in public and was accessible, at least in principle, to all.

Its accessibility and partial visibility was at once its chief advantage to participants and a source of anxiety to those charged with containing it.

A critical question, which may be posed early on, is why I propose this particular selection of geographic themes. One consideration is completeness along a number of important dimensions. Chapter 1 covers the queer milieu taken as a single amalgamation, but does so with little prospect of correcting the errors of vision that clouded the eye of bureaucratic authority. Chapters 2 and 3 about policing and streetlife capture aspects of the queer milieu that have broad implications. Chapters 4 and 5 are deep dives into two related and, by all accounts, prominent queer spatial patterns: bathing and cruising. Taken together and in their progression they address a significant portion of what can be discovered about queer spatial patterns in the historical city. Further extending the scope of discussion, while always desirable, might in fact skew the picture more than it supplements it. For example, adding detailed discussions about queer encounters in cabarets, restaurants, and musical theaters would invariably skew the resulting image toward the experience of well-to-do and highly literate queer men—a tendency that is hard enough to counteract as it is. A further consideration is the relevance of each of the chosen themes in shaping the dynamics of the initial encounter—not sex, but rather the moment of mutual recognition that might lead to sex or simply friendship, companionship, and communion within a larger network of queer men. Finally, I have sought not only to contribute to our knowledge about the semi-opaque lives of queer men in a particular city and during a particular time but also to expand the methodological arsenal available for historical studies of the urban queer. The case studies chosen, therefore, also illustrate elements of the conceptual toolbox, including the ideas of a contested urban common and a refuge that I believe may be especially well-suited for the analysis of spatial patterns in other cities as well.

Chapter 1

St. Petersburg and Its Familiar Strangers

By the late nineteenth century, St. Petersburg's queer milieu had developed a clear and recognizable footprint. One of its central locations was Anichkov Bridge, part of the city's largest traffic artery, Nevsky Prospect. Completed in 1841 to replace a smaller wooden structure, Anichkov Bridge crosses the second-largest of the city's rivers, the Fontanka.[1] To allow the passage of boats underneath, the pavement of the bridge was raised about six feet above the ground level of most of St. Petersburg. Its elevation is an architectural anomaly in the flat landscape of a city reclaimed from the Neva estuary. Looking out from the bridge, one's eyes follow the natural curve of the river and its embankments as well as the impressive vistas east and west along the grand boulevard that is Nevsky Prospect. It is the only location in St. Petersburg from which one can oversee the entire two-mile expanse of Nevsky Prospect from the Admiralty Building to the city's largest railway station on Znamenskaia Square.[2] The very lines of sight that make this a panoptic and popular space facilitate both cruising and surveillance. Someone standing on the bridge has an unparalleled opportunity to observe a densely peopled section of the urban landscape, the advancing and retreating passersby, the strolling boulevardiers and flaneurs. But it also exposes people, whether they want to be observed or not, to the suspicious or desiring eyes of others.

The authorities were perfectly aware of the advantages of the site. Throughout the nineteenth and early twentieth centuries, a constabulary post was permanently positioned at the center of the bridge, flanked by the statues of four virile bronze horses and their tamers who held fast the straining bridles—a classically respectable parade of ideal masculinity but also transparently homoerotic. In a lewd colloquialism that made no distinction between animal and human virility, the bridge was termed "the bridge of the eighteen testicles," a collection that was completed by the attributes of a constable, whose perennial presence on the bridge, whether by night or by day, was as reliable as that of the immovable figures.

Anichkov Bridge, naturally, had much to recommend itself as a location not only for watching the waxing and waning of the anonymous crowd but also for meeting up with a lover or encountering a stranger who might become one. Its central location, panoptical elevation, and homoerotic allure were only some of the properties that made it a linchpin in the city's queer choreography. Part of a stretch of Nevsky Prospect that was illuminated with gaslights even before 1850, the bridge was convenient for nighttime cruising as well as casual promenades, all the more so when these practices intertwined. Anichkov Bridge also served as a nexus of pedestrian traffic opening onto both sides of the Fontanka Embankment and Nevsky Prospect. Police surveillance enhanced the personal safety of passersby—an important factor in this city afflicted with violent crime. Although this may have made cruising more risky at quieter times, it did little to encumber meetings and observation between queer men at the busiest times and it provided a visible warning to anyone contemplating violent assault.[3] A public convenience installed in the late 1880s on the embankment immediately to the northeast of the bridge became a prominent location for more intimate sexual reconnaissance. The bridge was also conveniently located between several nearby sites offering a little or a lot of privacy, all famed and frequently mentioned in archival documents relating to the historical city's queer milieu. These included some of the city's largest commercial bathhouses, various cafés, the elegant restaurant Palkin, the Malyi and Mikhailovsky Theatres, the city's main circus—the Ciniselli Circus, the sites of seasonal fairs like the Manezh on Mikhailovskaia Square with paid-entry amusements and a nearby roofed shopping arcade called the Passazh at 48 Nevsky Prospect. Finally, it offered diverse opportunities for an extended stroll in nearby public spaces, including a small park behind the circus, the Fontanka Embankment itself, Mikhailovskiaia Square, and the Ekaterininskii Garden next to the nearby public library. These semipublic and public spaces were obviously rife with opportunity for queer encounters, and Anichkov Bridge was ideally situated among them to serve as a place in which to loiter in the hope of a chance encounter or as a starting point for a rendezvous with a lover or a group of acquaintances (see map 1).[4]

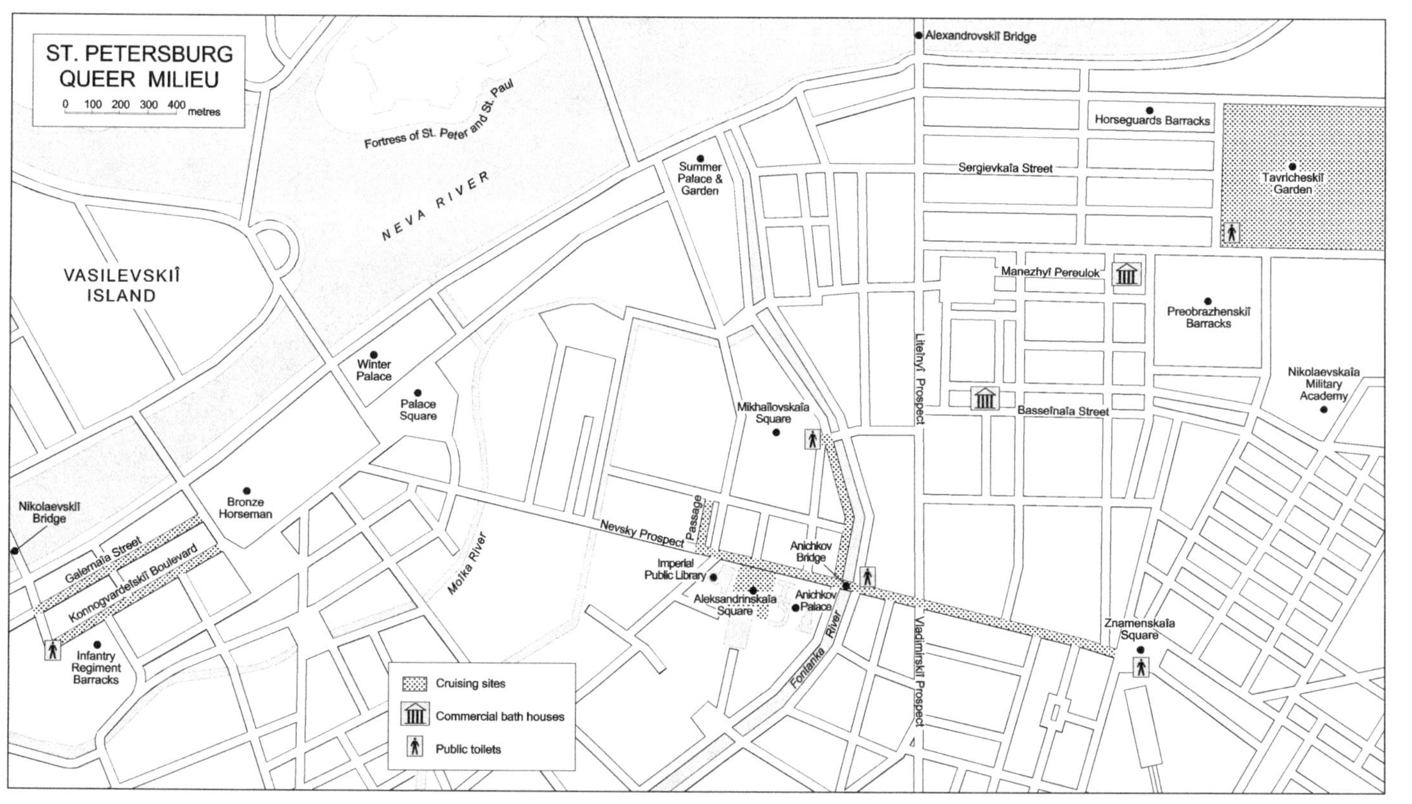

Map 1. St. Petersburg's queer milieu.

The centrality and popularity of Anichkov Bridge rendered these queer meetings relatively discreet but also sometimes remarkably open to view and in numbers that indicated a community of like-minded strangers rather than merely individual *deviants*. The visibility of a milieu of queer men lingering on and near the bridge and fanning out to various nearby locations was first documented, as far as we are aware, half a century after the reconstruction of the bridge. The earliest known snapshot of a cohesive network of men pursuing opportunities for sex with other men in late imperial St. Petersburg is in a report by an anonymous government official, which was preserved in the personal archives of Mikhail Ostrovskii, who was an imperial minster from 1881 to 1893 before becoming chairman of the Imperial Governing Council's Legislative Department, a position he held until 1899. This report acknowledges that the phenomena described were already "deeply rooted." It singles out Anichkov Bridge and its environs. These sites were thereafter fixtures in the various mappings of the city's queer milieu. The anonymous official's report, or dossier, as I will call it, was rediscovered in 1997 by Iurii Piriutko. It was subsequently dated by the Russian historians Vladimir Bersen'ev and A. Markov to the early 1890s, based on the persuasive hypothesis that the ages of individuals named in the dossier are the same as those given in the police files once maintained for each of them, assuming no corrections had been made for the time since their respective filing.[5]

The first half of the dossier contains a timetable of activities we would describe today as cruising, along with commentary regarding common sexual and gender roles and their relationship to social class. Its anonymous author draws urgent attention to the threats posed by homosexuality, which he (we must assume the author is a man, as the ministries only employed male officials) positions as a growing urban affliction to the state and the military alike. The second half of the dossier consists of a list of named individuals with brief but impressively informed comments on their sexual predilections and mutual connections. Three aspects of the dossier are remarkable. The first is its emphasis on the visibility of the queer milieu and the preparedness of some of its participants to "act openly," even or especially if this meant encounters with men who might be unwittingly caught up in their cruising, potentially as objects of propositions. The second is its underlying view of the composition of the queer milieu, notably its class-based structure and the notion that a relatively small number of wealthy individuals served as the glue binding a loosely affiliated network of men with overlapping interests or pursuits to one another. This suggestive analysis of the queer milieu's composition serves as the background for a third notable aspect of the dossier, which is the assignation of blame for the milieu's relatively recent emergence as a rapidly growing community to a small interconnected cluster of well-to-do "aunties" (*tetki*): middle-aged queer men who took various roles in the queer male cohort. "Patron," in its double meaning of mentor and consumer, perhaps comes closest to reflecting the social and economic interface between "aunties" and their male partners.

Before discussing each of these in some detail, however, it is important also to acknowledge the obvious: the explicit topic of the dossier is a "circle" or a "society" of men known to each other and with shared but varied sexual predilections. The recognition of such an *assemblage*, as we might call it today, or a *milieu*, as a contemporary might have termed it, is itself historically significant.[6]

According to the *Merriam-Webster Dictionary*, a milieu is "the physical or social setting in which something occurs or develops." Etymologically, the word derives from the French roots "mi" and "lieu," translated as "middle" and "place."[7] Literally, then, the term denotes the middle of a place, a physical location. In reading this etymology geographically, Anichkov Bridge could not have been far from the dossier's physical center. In its common usage, however, the term refers to events, actions, and people who share a connection to geography and each other. I employ it according to this usage. By calling the aggregate of men and shared patterns of movements and encounters a "milieu," I am on the one hand connecting and ordering disparate notions employed in archival documents, journalistic accounts, medical publications, and forensic reports from the period of study. On the other hand, though, I am explicitly disavowing the frequent imputations in such documents, including the dossier, of formalized and unambiguous bonds, such as a "society," an "association," or a "circle." Instead of these terms, my use of "milieu" reflects an acknowledgment of a fuzzy or fluid boundary between queer patterns of movement, encounter, and association and their broader urban context. Rather than assuming, as the authorities were wont to do, the existence of an unambiguously delineated community of queer men or pederasts who used the city and its sites to satisfy their "depraved" desires, I refer to a spatial phenomenon: the structured but often ambiguous interplay between desiring men and the sites, spaces, places, locales, incitements, and opportunities they variously encountered. The hybrid term "queer milieu" is then a descriptive convenience denoting the movements and encounters of men who sought opportunities for sex with other men and met regularly in the same locations where, in some form or other, they disclosed their disposition to one another. It points toward a recognition that the city's geography was itself an actor in these men's queer experiences.

Certainly this geography changed from time to time, and not all the locations implicated in it were public or even semipublic. Some of them were nothing more than private lodgings. Naturally, these changed frequently. The most public and visible patterns of encounter involved in the production of the queer milieu nevertheless displayed a remarkable degree of inertia during the period covered in this book. They might shift temporarily as a result of building measures or intensified surveillance, but, as will become clear from several examples, they quickly resumed their former places when the temporary inconveniences subsided.[8] Within and across these patterns, the demographics and infrastructure of the city directly affected the nature of encounters as well as their relative ease in different locations. In a word, the spatial patterns constituting the queer milieu were subject to the city's modernization and other historical forces at play, but they also inscribed a consistently legible, if necessarily partly opaque, alternative *script* onto the urban spaces most profoundly associated with this milieu. Meanwhile, the degree and implications of participation in these spatial patterns were quite diverse. In some cases, belonging to the queer milieu was a central characteristic of a certain individual who frequented the same location, always dressed in drag, and threw "unmistakable" glances at younger male passersby. In other cases, an individual might be linked to this milieu more tenuously, perhaps by no more than a furtive and inconsequential visit to a park with a questionable reputation.[9]

In this chapter, I look more closely at the ministerial dossier mentioned above as a starting point for exploring the visibility and composition of late imperial St. Petersburg's queer milieu. Building on this, I address the prism of social class, the dossier's emphasis on decadent and exploitative cross-class encounters, as this is the predominant trope of its anonymous author in his characterization of the city's queer milieu. Subsequently, I set out the preliminary position of the dossier vis-à-vis other key historical sources and, most important, the forensic-medical discussion of "homosexuality." Aside from diverging views on questions of guilt as a factor ultimately underlying opinions of how municipal authorities ought to suppress male-male sexual deviance, I summarize certain themes highlighted in the dossier that are repeated in other documents from around this time. In adding a level of complexity to the spatial or geographical structure of the book, this section sets out some of the conceptual themes that reappear in the subsequent chapters. These themes all prefigure prominently in the dossier and include the tension on the part of the city's governing authorities between suppression and toleration, the implications of streetlife for the queer milieu, its use of semipublic spaces, and finally, casual queer socialization (as opposed to explicitly sexualized cruising). These four themes are first integrated here based on their discussion in the dossier and they correspond to the geographical plot of each of the subsequent chapters. The themes themselves are not necessarily unique to the dossier or even initially raised there, but the dossier first collates all of them in a single document. We can argue, in fact, that the city's queer milieu first becomes visible to the eye of authority—and ultimately to the historian—in this late nineteenth-century report, which languished in the archives until its rediscovery a hundred years later. At the end of this chapter, the historical dimension of the queer milieu as a phenomenon that was first exposed to scrutiny during the period covered by this book is the context for a brief description of looking simultaneously at geographical *and* historical dynamics.

During the time period addressed in this book, a number of milestones that affected the queer milieu stand out. Some of these shaped the lives and spatial patterns of queer men quite specifically. These include predictable events such as the issuance of police directives, but also events more obscure in their agency such as the rollout of electric lighting or the sanitary regulation of bathhouses, to give but two examples. Moreover, broader developments on a national scale affected the city's queer milieu and the ordering of both space and sexuality. These include the state-driven policy of rapid industrialization and urbanization during the last two decades of the nineteenth century, the debate about a new legal code around the turn of the century, and the revolution of 1905 with all its consequences for urban policy. In addition to these influences on a municipal and national scale, we have archival documents and published records at our disposal that disclose changes in the spatial patterns as carried out, regulated, or perceived at specific locations within the city over the period under review. The implications of changes at these intersecting scales are discussed in each of the chapters in a direct commentary on the themes mentioned above. Nevertheless, it is important to point out that the historical and geographical lenses compete for primacy, and my emphasis is consistently on the geographical lens. From this perspective, which may not be immediately comfortable to the historian, the period of nearly forty years on which this book focuses should be considered a snapshot, a single image in which motion produces just a minor fuzziness of certain figures due to prolonged exposure, and even these can be discerned only by careful study of a few individual streaks. This should be acknowledged where relevant and even analyzed and discussed at times, but it should not be allowed to become a distraction from what is on the whole a remarkably stable set of spatial practices that constitutes late imperial St. Petersburg's queer milieu as first described in a known historical document in the ministerial dossier that is the topic of this chapter.

Official Reconnaissance of the Queer Milieu

Let us turn then to what the dossier's anonymous author has to say about the queer milieu, since he has perhaps the first claim on its discovery to the ever-watchful eye of authority. The dossier asserts at best a partly opaque visibility of this queer milieu to outsiders that is helpful and frustrating in equal measure. We must presume the author is an outsider, given his accusatory stance toward the subjects of his report, though his information about queer individuals and activities demonstrates a degree of acquaintance and interest that is itself suggestive. All the same, his assertions are murky and at times even contradictory with regard to the visibility of the queer milieu. He does not disclose his sources or explain whether his insights have been gained by direct observation, interviews, or by some kind of clandestine reconnaissance under the guise of potential participation. Most likely, it is a combination of all these approaches.

To be sure, the dossier contains some fundamental inconsistencies, which should be acknowledged at the outset. For example, the author claims that "this mischief has, visibly, taken deep roots in the capital."[10] Consistent with the assertion that its growth had become odiously apparent, he points out that the phenomena he describes were "well known to society in the capital."[11] In the same section of the dossier, however, he points out that this "mischief is hidden under the plausible cover of private family gatherings and revelry in hotels" and that the "members of the society . . . protect their craft by all possible means from the danger of persecution."[12] Their supposed secrecy and eagerness to avoid persecution clearly lose their sinister aspect insofar as this "mischief" was already supposedly "well known" to St. Petersburg society, including the dossier's author himself! The most plausible explanation for this apparent inconsistency is that the most egregious offenses, including criminalized sex, remained hidden, whereas other aspects were visible, if not brazenly displayed, and endowed with no more than a thin veneer of deniability. In a similarly revealing inconsistency, the dossier's author claims that "aunties, as they call themselves, recognize each other at first glance by some signs, elusive to outsiders."[13] He singles out such "aunties" as "well-to-do individuals for whom sexual intercourse with women has become repugnant as a result of sexual oversatiation."[14] A few lines later, despite the alleged elusiveness of their signs to outsiders, he claims that their victims, including soldiers and cavalrymen, "know the aunties by sight and a soldier passing one of them, looks at him pointedly, heads for the water closets and, looking back, checks whether the auntie is following him."[15] So the dossier's author assumes that these soldiers—who apparently do not as a rule share their clients' sexual proclivities but instead engage in sexual activities with them only for pay—have also learned to "recognize" them. Thus, the claim that aunties were recognizable only to one another sits uncomfortably with their evident recognizability to soldiers. Again, the visible script of dress, movement, timing, and glances seems to have been no more elusive than what would be compatible with successful sexual barter. These and other apparent inconsistencies are revealing not only insofar as they suggest a unique combination of clandestinity and visible promotion of the queer milieu by its participants. They also echo in their confused fearmongering the hysterical imputations of conspiracy that characterized bureaucratic surveillance of civilian groups following the assassination of Tsar Alexander II by anarchist terrorists in 1881. Their imprint on official perceptions of the queer milieu as a subversive threat to the military and the state and its institutions remained a constant in descriptions of the queer milieu for decades.[16]

The appendix of the dossier breaks down the issue of visibility to the level of the individual. Next to the names, titles, occupations, ages, and other identifying characteristics of each named man, the dossier contains their specific sexual preferences (this prurient list includes "mutual masturbation," "oral sex," "active role in anal sex," "likes soldiers," "likes to use good-looking school boys," "uses actors," "primarily Cossacks," etc.), connections between them ("considered Berg's lover"), and in most instances, an indication as to whether the individual in question "acts openly" or "hides" his "debauchery." In the examples given, "hiding" can mean either avoiding gatherings of queer men altogether or at least avoiding those that take place in public or semipublic spaces such as the Passazh or bathhouses, respectively. As though to indicate the quality of the author's information, the dossier contains minute details even about those individuals who are "very much in hiding," noting, for example, that a certain wealthy Bliambenberg "lives with a young man, Pavliusha, for whose upkeep he pays. His procurer is G. I. Depari."[17] Altogether, the dossier contains seventy-two such entries.

These notes on individuals fit with another comment included in the dossier as an aside, which lends further credence to the hypothesis that the author in fact aggregated information contained in police records. Among the disastrous consequences of homosexual sex and socialization he cites the suicides of young men: "Many cases of suicide of young men were discovered in some instances to be those of victims of pederasty, involuntary victims who did not have sufficient will power to free themselves from the debauched nets into which they fell."[18] Besides the bold extrapolation from "some instances" to "many cases," the emphasis here is on the occasional discovery of a link between suicide and homosexual behavior. A police protocol from ten years later provides an example of just such a connection. In 1903, the body of an urbanely dressed man was fished out of the Finnish Bay into which he was assumed to have floated from one of the city's main rivers. In the report on the incident, the presence on the body of a red handkerchief seemed to its authors to warrant particular emphasis. The red handkerchief, we know from other sources, was used as an element of apparel by which queer men sought to render themselves recognizable to one another.[19] The dossier's mention of suicides, which were always investigated by police, is revealing insofar as it concerns the deaths of less well-to-do victims, who were unlikely to be the subject of society gossip, to which the dossier's author also professed to have access. Against the background that various sources from around this time acknowledge the police practice of compiling files on individual queer men who were not necessarily arrested but instead kept under some degree of surveillance, the mention of suicides "discovered" to be those of queer men supports the suggestion that the dossier's anonymous author was either a high-ranking police official or worked with the police in compiling his report.[20] The slight inconsistencies in the ages of the individuals listed in the dossier are a further indication of the author's reliance on police files.[21]

It is important to note that by this time the queer milieu had a clearly identified spatial dimension. The dossier provides a detailed overview of seasonal gathering places and links some of the individuals mentioned to specific locations. These observations, consistent with other archival documents and with journalistic reports from later years, appear rather more reliable than some of the views expressed in the dossier, including the probably spurious claims regarding rigidly understood membership and formal vows of secrecy. As they gathered in groups, socialized, or pursued opportunities for sex, queer men could be observed by nonparticipants, including constables. The dossier contains some indications as to the signs and patterns by which the queer milieu became distinctly recognizable. First, dress and style are indicators: some of the men listed in the dossier are marked as "dames" or "ladies" (*dama*). These references correspond to the description in the dossier of a queer ball at which several guests and the host himself wore "ladies' dresses."[22] One "dame" mentioned in the dossier's list of individuals is said to regularly attend public balls and private gatherings in dresses. In the street, it is likely that such dress was toned down, but makeup was still worn and effeminate behavior remained in evidence. A forensic-medical report from the preceding decade, for example, mentions a young man wearing rouge and eyeliner in public view. In his diary from the decade following the one in which the dossier was composed, the poet Mikhail Kuzmin recollects wearing an extravagant yellow shirt and makeup during strolls and describes members of his "circle" wearing a yellow flower, a narcissus, on their lapel specifically to identify themselves as men sexually or romantically interested in other men.[23] Thus, elements of dress and style served as markers of belonging to the queer milieu. They were thus readily recognizable to outsiders as well as insiders and they could be used to establish connections between participants.

Second, the patterns of movement of queer men included observable sequences that distinguished them from others (map 1 shows most of the locations mentioned below). For example, the dossier mentions "soldiers and young men who wish their members to be touched for money and who swarm near the pissoirs by Anichkov Bridge, near the water closets on Znamenskaia Square, around the public library, and by Mikhailovskaia Square, where aunties also look in."[24] This particular type of sexual reconnaissance took place in the toilets themselves, as the dossier informs, and aided "aunties" in the selection of a sexual partner. On a given evening, an "auntie might repeat this type of touching several times."[25] This was clearly a pattern that could be observed by attentive outsiders—sometimes with disastrous consequences.[26] Repeated and unusual patterns of movement allowed participants to recognize one another and enabled observers to extrapolate from one or two visibly queer individuals to others with whom they came into contact, jointly entering a public toilet or departing to a space permitting greater and more extended privacy, such as a bathhouse.

Based on these visible signs of attire, movements, and encounters, our anonymous official goes on to list seasonal patterns of cruising in the city, the key fixtures of which remained consistent at least until World War I. As places where "aunties" "go for strolls" during the summer months, the dossier lists the zoo, Anichkov Bridge, Nevsky Prospect (particularly the stretch between Znamenskaia Square and Anichkov Bridge), the Fontanka Embankment from the Sheremetev Palace to the Summer Garden, the Ekaterininskii Garden near the public library, and Konnogvardeiskii Boulevard, where Johan and Dmitrii met. Its anonymous author further describes a daily and weekly routine, with afternoon strolls along Konnogvardeiskii Boulevard, for example, preceding visits to the zoo during the late evenings on workdays. Notably, the dossier points out that such strolls might be interrupted by visits to commercial establishments, such as a pastry shop, from whence observation could be continued or an encounter might be discreetly pursued. Gatherings were particularly populous on "Saturdays and Sundays, when [soldiers] come from their camps and when young noblemen, army choristers, cadets, gymnasium pupils, and apprentices are free from their occupations."[27]

In the winter these patterns obviously had to shift, given that the days shrank to as few as six hours and temperatures remained well below freezing. As a result, Saturday gatherings took place at or near the Mikhailovsky and Malyi Theatres and weekday gatherings started in cafés or at the ballet and then spilled into restaurants during the later evenings. On Sundays during the winter "aunties stroll along the upper gallery of the Passazh, where cadets and pupils come during the mornings and soldiers and apprentices arrive at around six in the evening."[28] During the colder months, ice-skating rinks were also popular gathering spots where "aunties observed the figures of young male skaters, inviting them subsequently to pastry shops or home."[29] During holidays or at Shrovetide, "aunties stroll between the stalls and rides during the day and in the horse-riding hall in the evening."[30] Finally, the anonymous official describes parties in hotels and private apartments, some of which he calls "jours fixes," or repeating, regular events, which were obviously less seasonally constrained.

It is worth noting, of course, that the author's myopic prejudice, itself inconsistent with some of his notes on individuals as it is, grinds the very lens through which he recognizes and describes these peculiar patterns. He assumes that the "aunties," who were usually wealthy, were the instigators of such gatherings, whereas less well-to-do participants were merely hangers-on who made themselves available for sex in exchange for payment. It is against this background that the author emphasizes locations such as theaters, pastry shops, restaurants, bathhouses, or private apartments, access to which clearly presupposed a willingness and ability to pay. If the reader recalls the story of Johan and Dmitrii from the introduction to this book, however, such gatherings could just as easily involve partners who paid neither for access to semipublic locations nor for sex. An archival file regarding Lieutenant Raikovskii and college assessor Sarkisov similarly complicates the paradigm established in the dossier. Neither Raikovskii nor Sarkisov was wealthy, but both were at least financially secure. The space they used for their meeting was provided by the state. According to the affidavit of Sarkisov's wife, she caught the two men in flagrante delicto in Raikovskii's room in one of the city's military garrisons.[31] So, the official's viewpoint and his idées fixes are likely to have rendered him blind to other aspects of the queer milieu that simply did not fit his preoccupations.

And yet, regardless of whether the dossier's generalizations hold true in all cases, its author establishes a plausible and even probable connection between the queer milieu and a plethora of decidedly noncriminal phenomena visible to outsiders. In compiling a description of key spatial patterns carried out by men seeking sex with other men and attempting to provide a comprehensive list and timetable of their activities in the imperial capital, the dossier testifies to the visibility of these patterns. It is sufficient evidence to suggest that an observer armed with the dossier could recognize patterns that might otherwise have escaped his or her attention. The descriptions of individuals in the second part or appendix of the dossier, the name list, reinforce its author's claim that these patterns were carried out by an interconnected "society" of men, and the public scandals mentioned—in particular the court cases of a certain school headmaster Bychkov and the engineer Iolshin, who were accused of seducing young men or boys—anchor these descriptions in proven sexual crimes, as if to say "where there is smoke, there is fire."[32] Taken jointly, these observations revealed, beyond bureaucratic deniability, an interconnected community of men living in the capital, who pursued an interest in sex with other men under the watchful but impotent gaze of the machinery of state. Although unremarkable from a present-day perspective, these revelations are important in their context because they constitute the earliest known aspirationally comprehensive description of St. Petersburg's queer milieu by and for the state's administrative apparatus.

To be sure, some deeper research by the dossier's author, including a consultation with medico-forensic works on the new phenomenon of homosexuality, might have dispelled some of these notions or at least made their assertion more challenging. And yet nothing indicates that he was insincere in his conviction that his dossier was groundbreaking. The author clearly believed that the extent and coherence of the queer milieu, its spatial patterns in particular, as well as the dangers emanating from its expansion were news to his superiors. He relied on the unproven assumption that the phenomenon he was describing was specific to the capital and also relatively recent.[33] According to him, the circle of homosexuals "has developed in the capital": "it has existed for several years, but never reached such a scale," it had now "taken deep roots in the capital," and "the development of this mischief has not only not stopped, but intensified."[34]

The Queer Milieu and Social Class

In describing the queer milieu's composition, the dossier, like several subsequent reports and some of the preceding forensic-medical literature, places heavy emphasis on class distinctions. However, in segmenting the queer milieu according to class, the dossier's author is again idiosyncratic, which makes his argument more complex than it first appears. He does not, for instance, rely primarily on the imperial system of social estates in use at the time, which would have been immediately familiar to his colleagues and contemporaries. In a document that constituted official bureaucratic correspondence, this is both remarkable and understandably practical. Under the imperial system of estates, which had been introduced by Peter the Great and was still in force in the 1890s, membership in a social estate determined one's civil rights and obligations. Adult men belonged to the aristocracy or the clergy or else they were to be countered as "honored citizens," merchants, tradesmen, townspeople, peasants, foreigners, or—in something of a classificatory shrug of the shoulders—"persons of miscellaneous rank." An adult man's membership in an estate often constrained his fate and that of his family, limiting his field of action and ambitions to a narrow range of probable socioeconomic outcomes. The assignation determined, for instance, whether or not he was free to relocate and whether he was subject to taxes, military service, and corporal punishment.[35]

Someone's estate was usually marked in his or her traveling papers and any official documents concerning one's person. In police reports from this time, the system was still strictly in use and arrest record or interrogation protocols tended unambiguously to assign the individuals mentioned to one of the various estates or another, perhaps as a result of bureaucratic inertia and a desire to follow correct procedure, as opposed to blind faith in the accuracy of its assignments. Not so in the dossier on the queer milieu, however. Although the dossier does mention the estate of a few of the named individuals listed in the appendix, it draws the primary dividing line, simply and somewhat brutally, between rich and poor.

This simplified, wealth-based class paradigm is separate from the inherited political categories, though of course with overlap. It is, however, consistent with developments in the city and society around this time. Starting with the emancipation of the serfs in 1861 and the administrative reforms of Alexander II, the system of social estates and the table of ranks introduced by Peter the Great had begun to recede in importance, especially in the city. They were no longer quite applicable to any recognizable reality in the capital. The country's rapid industrialization, which gathered steam in the last two decades of the nineteenth century thanks to the efforts of Count Witte in breaking down tariffs and attracting investment, meant that with regard to members of at least one very numerous urban class, factory workers, the assignation of peasant no longer hit the mark. At the other end of the property spectrum, a critical mass of individuals from all classes, including some peasants, managed to defy the constraints of their estate and accumulate wealth, sometimes considerable wealth, with the opportunities that city life offered. Describing a well-do-do entrepreneur as simply a *peasant* or *tradesman* no longer reflected the reality of this urban propertied class.[36]

This was not lost on contemporaries and, in fact, imperial policy adjusted to the new property paradigm relatively quickly despite the state's reputation for stubborn and stolid conservatism. As a result of Alexander II's so-called Urban Reforms, after 1870 the municipal representative bodies all over the Russian Empire, including its capital, no longer had membership quotas based on estates. Instead, electors and representatives had only to meet personal property qualifications.[37] The new policies were not necessarily more inclusive, but they more appropriately reflected the empire's urban class differentiation based primarily on wealth. They recognized the new realities of urban modernity, but they certainly were not democratizing or power sharing in any Western sense. For example, the property qualification for St. Petersburg's highest elected legislative body assembly (the City Duma) was adjusted in 1892 to reduce the number of voters in St. Petersburg to around seven thousand, still a tiny minority of the urban population, at this time over a million strong. Still, by the late nineteenth century, wealth was clearly crowding out membership in the estates as a determinant of social class and political influence in the city.

Characteristic of the attitude of the *enlightened bureaucracy*, the dossier's author chose wealth as the main principle driving the demographic segmentation of the queer milieu. He describes the core of the queer milieu as "primarily composed of rich people," and adds that its subsequent expansion drew in impecunious, literally "property-less" young men who joined reluctantly "in pursuit of advantages and the means for merry and easy existence."[38] This picture of concentric circles is as significant as the sweeping division of queer men into a rich minority and a mass of proletarians, made deviant not so much by nature as by the opportunity provided by the former.

According to the class paradigm deployed in the dossier, a populous swarm of poor opportunistic sexual partners circled around a small core of wealthy "aunties," attracted by the gravitational pull of money. This imagery of circles is as suggestive as the hierarchy of wealth. The spatial image employed in the description permits an analogy to the empire itself, composed of a contiguous landmass governed from a single point, its capital city. Even this city itself was spatially and conceptually composed of such concentric rings, with the integrally planned center couched in a chaotically expanding periphery, and the imperial bureaucracy gently tugging the strings of the remote and often inefficient machinery of state. The central analogy employed in describing class is not therefore that of the social pyramid, but rather the city or the empire itself, whose sphere was ever expanding. Even the dossier's reference to the queer milieu's "highest protector," quite possibly a member of the royal family, as is heavily hinted, is analogous to the radial structure of the state, the city, and the empire, with the palace and person of the tsar at its center.[39]

Class-based segmentation and its circular motif are essential to the dossier's central message about the corruption of the poor, the young, and the morally weak by lascivious men of wealth. The latter are at least initially grouped together as "aunties," and we need to return to this concept with more care. Presumably, this description had initially entered the language as a translation of the French *tantes*, also used to refer to queer men.[40] Here the dossier's author provides no definition, except to specify that the men in question used it to refer to themselves and each other. He also links the appellation to both wealth and sexual debauchery. It would be a mistake, however, to take the term too literally and attribute effeminacy to the rich men who, allegedly, formed the core of St. Petersburg's queer milieu. In fact, the dossier specifically indicates *which* "aunties" were also "dames" (*dama*) and goes on to point out that only some of these "dames" wore female clothing or had female features. So the term "dame" designates a subgroup of "aunties"—specifically, men whose bearing was effeminate. Yet even these "dames" did not necessarily wear female clothing. Conversely, therefore, the "aunties" who were *not* "dames" did not distinguish themselves, according to the dossier, by effeminacy either in bearing or appearance. A much later journalistic report uses the term "auntie" to refer to a group of middle-aged men who sat on benches in the Tavricheskii and Summer Gardens, "not forgetting, by the way, to cast quite unambiguous glances at passing youths."[41] The term's usage in the dossier is consistent with this and other later reports insofar as "aunties" are simply wealthy queer men who were no longer young but were not necessarily effeminate in appearance, dress, or manner. This reading is also consistent with the dossier's notes on individual men. Further supporting such a circumscription of the central term used in the dossier, the composer Pyotr Ilich Tchaikovsky describes himself as an "auntie" in his posthumously published diaries.[42] By no means effeminate, the married Tchaikovsky perfectly illustrates the model of the older, wealthy homosexual man caricatured as a kind of apex predator in the anonymous dossier, but one who might see himself rather as patron and protector, lover and friend, rather than an exploiter of the young and vulnerable.

The key function of these aunties in the homosexual "circle," as the author of the dossier calls it (which I prefer to term a milieu), was to provide private or semipublic spaces for the most lascivious gatherings, to pay young men in exchange for engaging in sexual acts with them, and to provide administrative cover or protection to the milieu and its participants as required. The dossier also alleges that procurers usually created the links between "aunties" and their "victims." Several examples of such individuals designated in the dossier as procurers indicate that these are not rich men themselves—one is supposedly a craftsman, the other a waiter, and the third a twenty-year-old man of unknown profession. As ever, we have to treat such allegations critically. According to the notes in the dossier itself, organized, professional matchmaking or, as the dossier calls it, "prospecting" or "recruitment," was not a factor in all or even the majority of liaisons between aunties and their young and less well-to-do *victims*. Still, the author paints a stark picture of a queer urban world marked by constellations of class and age, resulting in mutual exploitation as well as privilege-based victimization.

Notable here is also the imputed role of aunties as "protectors" and guardians of the queer milieu. The dossier mentions, for instance, the toasts raised to "preeminent protectors" of their "society." Moreover, two men who are not themselves listed in the appendix or name section of the dossier are specified in comments next to the names of other men as having facilitated their careers. Aunties are thus portrayed as constituting a kind of freemasonry of sexual deviance. These prominent people held the positions of "director of the Imperial Theatres" and "head of the Central Committee of Prisons." But this point requires further explication. By doing painstaking archival research, the Russian historians Barsen'ev and Markov have unearthed ties that were either not known to the author of the dossier or were purposely omitted. These include links between a number of the men named in the dossier to a certain government inspector, Tertiia Filippov. Filippov was close to the director of the Imperial Theatres, Vsevolozhskii, and he corresponded with and frequently received in his home the chairman of the Imperial Governing Council's Legislative Department, Ostrovskii, in whose personal archives the only known copy of the dossier was discovered. Filippov later hired Gusev, a man named in the dossier who had previously served under Ostrovskii, and promoted him to the rank of privy councillor. Finally, Filippov was a friend of Count Mesherskii, who figures prominently in the dossier as an "auntie" who offered young men favor and protection in exchange for sex. Count Mesherskii later tried to interfere with high-level army appointments in order to facilitate his liaison with an army trumpeter. The fact that he was subject to scandal and frustrated in this attempted meddling did not prevent him from rising to particular prominence several years later under Tsar Nicholas II.[43]

Neither these revelations about so-called high-ranking patrons and "protectors" of the queer milieu, nor historical evidence testifying to further connections between them, nor even the impressive careers of certain individuals identified in the dossier indicate that the anonymous author was justified in suspecting the existence of a sinister secret society. The mixing of sex and ambition is by no means unique to queer men, and networks of patronage, even corrupt ones, could be constructed for virtually any group of friends and acquaintances. What it does demonstrate, however, is that inclusion in the secret dossier did not necessarily adversely affect the careers of prominent individuals. In fact, the author of the dossier points the accusing finger toward the "inaction of the authorities, who have not taken any measures whatsoever to uproot this malicious debauchery."[44] Court case compendiums and instances of police harassment of queer men, as well as evidence of more systematic measures of the state bureaucracy vis-à-vis queer spatial patterns, complicate the dossier's naive and categorical claim concerning universal inaction by city or national authorities. The claim itself is remarkable, nevertheless, given that the basis for the dossier was in all likelihood lists and case files compiled by the police. In other words, in the instances noted here, the records reviewed by the anonymous compiler of the dossier did not include any records of prosecution, which would have made such a claim immediately refutable and, therefore, unwise. It can be said with some confidence that the existence of such lists was not directly linked to prosecution or even to the passing over for promotion of suspected "sodomists" in the government bureaucracy. What, then, was the purpose of such a list and why did Ostrovskii preserve it in his personal archives, among all the papers that must have crossed his desk?

Several theories have been proposed. One is that Ostrovskii hoped to refer to it in arguing for changes to the sodomy statutes of the new legal code, known as the Code of 1903, on which debates began in the mid-1890s. As chairman of the Imperial Governing Council's Legislative Department, Ostrovskii would have been a prominent participant in these debates. Although we have no known record of his personal influence on the redrafting of sodomy statutes in article 995, we know that a significant broadening of the scope of prosecutable crimes related to homosexuality eventually made it into the final draft. Similarly, the dossier may have been laying the groundwork for a complex bureaucratic charade in which the amalgamation of queer men into a society akin to the illegal freemasons might support their classification as "unreliable persons" dangerous to the state and enable their persecution under the Emergency Legislation. Until 1893, Ostrovskii as a member of the Council of Ministers would have been charged with overseeing the use of the emergency legislation, and he may have retained a professional stake in the issue even after his subsequent appointment.

One the other hand, the emergency legislation and debates around the criminal code may merely have provided official cover for requesting the dossier. Ostrovskii's motive might have been more subtle, even Machiavellian. It has been suggested that he hoped to use the dossier in bureaucratic and court intrigues. Equally plausible, however, is the intriguing possibility that Ostrovskii or his immediate associates were themselves implicated, such that they wished to discover how much was known to the police. The close social links via Filippov between Ostrovskii and two of the prominent queer men named in the dossier suggest as much. This impression is supported by the highly odd inclusion of Ostrovskii's own former appointee, the discreet and careful "dame" Gusev, as a kind of afterthought in the list. His entry is appended on a separate page at the end of the list and is the only exception to the otherwise strictly observed alphabetical order. One might speculate that this name figured only in Ostrovskii's personal copy and was discreetly omitted in other copies. Given Ostrovskii's well-known ambitions to head the Ministry of the Interior, which included the police, this might have been a prudent precaution on the author's part vis-à-vis a potential future superior.[45] The same precautionary bureaucratic courtesy might help explain why a copy of the dossier ended up in Ostrovskii's hands in the first place. We will likely never be sure, but the ambiguity of Ostrovskii's involvement itself embodies the entanglement of surveillance and classification with the complex representation and realities of queer experience in the metropolis. Our anonymous author indicts the "aunties" who preside over the queer milieu, only for his dossier to circle through the government bureaucracy onto the desk of one of its potential patrons. The dossier provides vital information on queer life in St. Petersburg at the end of the nineteenth century, but its fate might itself be implicated in the alleged conspiracy it describes.

It is important to note that the class paradigm constructed in the descriptive section of the dossier alleges that the wealthy men who formed the queer milieu's core were not only socially interconnected but also nefariously complicit in maintaining and organizing the spatial patterns that sustained the milieu's operation and drew in its young victims. They form for the author a single group, irrespective of bureaucratic rank or aristocratic lineage. What binds them together as a kind of deviant estate are their shared sexual tastes and the desire to advance their corporate interests.

Unlike the men at the queer milieu's core, those at the periphery, according to the dossier, are a much less monolithic circle and are highly differentiated both in terms of professions and modes of engagement. Farther from the center of the queer world—from its conspiratorial core—revolves a diverse constellation of male bodies, sometimes in near orbits, regularly encountered and closely aligned, or sometimes meteorically as occasional and infrequent visitors. In reducing this alleged periphery to its essentials, the dossier's author concentrates not on the men themselves and their natures as much as on where and when they are to be found. The dossier links the supposed victims of prowling "aunties" to different spatial patterns based on their professional activity. These are army choristers, cadets, gymnasium pupils, apprentices, soldiers, cavalrymen, and guardsmen. Comments in the appendix extend the list to include doormen, waiters, carriage drivers, servants, and bathhouse attendants. Their only shared characteristics are that they are young and impecunious and that they appear in specific places at predictable times according to a schedule described in the dossier. For example, on the weekends, junior officers, army choristers, and cadets visit the zoo. On Sundays, as mentioned above, cadets and gymnasium or officers' school pupils arrive in the mornings, and soldiers and apprentice boys come after six in the evening. Thus, social distinctions, not in the hierarchical sense but in terms of profession and participation in various spatial patterns, play a role at the periphery of the queer milieu, which is populated by reluctant joiners in pursuit of coin rather than—or rather than just—pleasure.

This paradigm is, of course, a gross simplification in every way. Above all, we must suspect the dossier's generalization of exploitation as the queer milieu's fundamental organizing principle. For example, I have mentioned the archival testimonies of a sexual relationship between two men of roughly equal rank and age, Raikovskii and Sarkisov, which unfolded directly in the military accommodations of the former without the detour of a visit to one of the cruising sites mentioned in the dossier.[46] This kind of relationship simply does not fit in the world that the dossier writer describes. Moreover, the author is not even internally consistent in reflecting the bipartite demographics of wealthy "auntie" and young indigent victim in its inventory of stock characters populating the queer milieu. For example, the thirty-five-year-old Berklund fits neither category. As a cutter employed in a tailor shop, he was not rich, nor was he young by the standards of the dossier and according to the perceptions of the time, when average life expectancy in imperial Russia was around thirty.[47] The same could be said of the thirty-eight-year-old Danaurov, a censor. Conversely, several men included in the list were not only wealthy but also young. Some are explicitly described as "handsome" and had no obvious need to resort to the victimizing behavior described in the main body of the dossier, such as paying for sex and maintaining would-be lovers in a constant wine-induced stupor. One such man is the twenty-year-old son of a senator, described as a "high-class courtesan." Another is twenty-three-year-old Ekimov, member of a prestigious regiment. He is identified as the former lover of thirty-year-old Rauch, a decommissioned officer from another prestigious regiment. In fact, three out of four of Rauch's former lovers identified in the list have a settled situation or a steady income, again failing to fit the description of destitute young men.

These inconsistencies are important not because they debunk the detective work that the dossier represents, but precisely because they draw attention to the obvious: the reality of queer life—even the sliver of it that the dossier's author acknowledges in his notes on individuals—was clearly more complex than the dossier's convenient extrapolation from a single plausible scenario of class and sexual relations to a highly centralized and exploitative milieu. Conversely, this is not to say that the exploitation of vulnerable young men by men of privilege did not take place, in some cases perhaps even in line with the playbook described in the dossier. It is hard to imagine that the sexual economy failed to respond to a number of encouraging circumstances in St. Petersburg. And yet the subtle internal inconsistencies of the dossier and the contravening evidence of other fragmentary archival sources from around the same time are a reminder that the dossier reflects a prurient and partial view of the queer milieu—and one conveyed with a distinct political or bureaucratic agenda.

The myopic character of the dossier's view of the queer milieu is itself revealing in the specific aspects of urban reality it alleges or describes as well as in its implications for the potential administrative suppression of queer sexual expression. Both issues are related to the assignation of culpability for purported illicit sex and especially the overlap between prostitution and the queer milieu because exploitation of the poor by the rich (and sometimes the other way around) is a constant theme in the discourse of sex between men.

The general theme of sex as a mode of class-based exploitation is, of course, by no means unique to imperial St. Petersburg, to this dossier, or even to sex between men. Historical discussions of paid sex tend to recognize a broadly consistent set of circumstances as highly conducive to the prostitution economy.[48] These include uneven wealth distribution, rampant urban poverty, and a high rate of migration to the city by young, uprooted, vulnerable people. In this sense, late imperial St. Petersburg experienced a perfect storm. The accounts of foreign travelers of this time consistently draw attention to the striking prevalence on St. Petersburg's streets of "muzhiks": poor, disheveled-looking peasants who looked thoroughly out of place in the city. We know from census data reviewed and compiled by James Bater in the 1970s that by 1900, 88 percent of the capital's population lived in rented accommodations, with the average number of people officially registered to an apartment reaching 7.4—probably still a gross underestimation.[49] Conversely, 12 percent of the population owned virtually all the real estate in the city. Many renters lived in shared rooms where they occupied only a corner of a room (*ugol*). Over half of all renters or lodgers (52 percent) were unattached young people.[50] Many of these young people lived in what Bater calls the "festering slums" that dotted the less visible parts of the city center, nestling in the extended systems of courtyards between the well-maintained and sumptuous street-facing vistas of St. Petersburg's main thoroughfares.[51]

The unevenness of the city's wealth distribution and rampant urban poverty were underpinned by decades of migration to the city from the countryside. After the emancipation of the serfs in 1861, the reforms of Alexander II and the industrial boom under his successor attracted young would-be wage earners to the city. Most of them left their families behind in their villages or had no families. The 1881 census of the Russian population reveals that in St. Petersburg a mere 19 percent of married wage earners lived with their families.[52] Urban migration was also driven by outright poverty and famine in the villages. The famine of 1891–1892 led to half a million deaths at a time when the economy was growing by a massive 8 percent per year.[53] Many migrants arriving in the city impoverished and alone retained attachments to their distant villages, returning there to help out with the harvests. This high degree of transience was an important feature of the capital, where the population remained predominantly single, male, and relatively young.[54]

Thus, consistent with the dossier, St. Petersburg had attracted a large mass of impoverished young people, whose precarious economic situation has been linked by contemporaries and historians to increases in female prostitution.[55]

The same forces encouraged male prostitution, several instances of which came to the attention of the legal and medical authorities in the decades preceding the issuance of the dossier. One of these was the 1866 court case of a young bathhouse attendant, Vasilii, reviewed by the venereologist Vladislav Merzheevskii in his influential 1878 handbook on forensic gynecology. In his initial testimony, Vasilii implicated himself and several of his colleagues as having received tips for engaging in sexual intercourse with bathhouse patrons. Two of these fellow attendants were recent migrants to the city from the same village as Vasilii. The latter blamed them for initiating him into this practice during his first day on the job. He concluded his initial testimony with the sweeping assertion that "attendants in all of St. Petersburg's bathhouses engage in the described (crimes)" (parentheses added by Merzheevskii). Vasilii soon withdrew most of his initial testimony, notably his admission of having engaged in anal sex and all his statements implicating his colleagues. In the end, however, he alone was found guilty and condemned to six months' confinement.[56] Demographically speaking, a large proportion of the urban population consisted of poorly paid young men like Vasilii. When they came into contact with wealthy patrons interested in homosexual sex, some or many responded to the incentives of agreed payment or tips, and from this grew the male prostitution economy, which by all accounts was a feature of late imperial St. Petersburg. The dossier mentions that the "procurer" Zaitsev, a waiter in the elegant restaurant Palkin, "supplies boys and soldiers to reveling groups of aunties, for which [service] he accepts payment."[57] The incentives would have been significant. Merzheevskii noted as an aside that the going rate for sex with a "kined"—a term used to describe a male prostitute—was roughly the same as that of female prostitutes. The dossier itself contradicts this view, however, indicating that male clients paid male prostitutes "3–5 rubles," twice the typical price of a visit to a female prostitute in a mid-tier registered brothel and almost half of the average wage for an uneducated laborer in the city.[58] This rate would have left plenty of room for "procurers" or other complicit individuals to skim off the top.

Prostitution, however, was of course not the only avenue for sexual exploitation between men. Veniamin Tarnovskii, in his 1885 forensic-medical treatise on the origins of perversion of sexual sentiment, mentions testimony from another sodomy trial of a young apprentice, who was also a recent migrant to the city. He had engaged in sexual acts with his master or instructor. Here no payments were made, but the master's crime of sodomy was found to have been aggravated by virtue of his having abused the dependent position of his underage apprentice. The master was prosecuted in 1874, but the apprentice's acts of criminalized sodomy were overlooked because his participation was found to have been involuntary and his position vulnerable to such an extent as to excuse the crime.[59] At times, however, the situation was less clear. The dossier describes several instances of so-called sponsorship, which included paying for room and board and providing the means for "revelry." For example, in the dossier, twenty-three-year-old Linevskii is alleged to have been successively sponsored by three named individuals, and another twenty-year-old is said to have been "sponsored by many."[60] More generally, the author of the dossier claims that young men lived at the expense of their "auntie-sponsors."[61]

The significance of the monetary sexual economy for the queer milieu lies in part in the fact that commerce, whether in goods, sex, or other services, benefits from at least a degree of visibility that enables would-be consumers to attach an unspecific desire to a specific object or person and to find and retrieve offerings of a similar kind in known locations. The same factors that created incentives for young men and women to return regularly to the same locations and venues offering sex for tips, pay, or sponsorship, therefore, also helped to unmask the queer milieu vis-à-vis a broader urban population. Sometimes, however, the sexual economy may have been no more than a convenient artificial lens through which to view the queer milieu. Andrew Ross, who writes about homosexuality and female prostitution in nineteenth-century Paris, notes not only that the scripts of public sex of all kinds were readily readable but also that regulators found it more palatable to draw an analogy between homosexual solicitation and female prostitution than to acknowledge the uncomfortable reality of mutually voluntary interclass mixing accompanying sex between men.[62] The dossier's author clung fast to his notion that poor young men engaged in sex with older wealthy men against their own inclinations and for material gain, the author's own cited evidence to the contrary notwithstanding.

Placing "the Blame"?

The dossier's class paradigm of wealthy predator and poor victim is remarkable not for its empirical merit or its problematic generalization but for its exclusive assignation of criminal culpability or blame to wealthy "aunties." The author's emphatic exculpation of their sexual partners relies on alleging elaborate efforts by wealthy "aunties" to seduce their indigent young victims, whose only fault lay in "insufficient willpower," even this tempered by broadly assumed extenuating circumstances, including perpetual involuntary inebriation.[63]

This portrayal of the poor as victims echoes a prominent strain of social thought in the literature and cultural commentary of the time. From the racially biased philosopher and literary critic Vasilii Rozanov to political commentators such as Nikolai Chernyshevsky and even the novelist Lev Tolstoy, the notion had gained currency that the urban monied elite was failing as a class to establish a new social order following the eradication of the old one via the emancipation of the serfs. The state, the bureaucratic machinery, and the landed aristocrats who often remained away from their villages, preferring the aloofness of fashionable city residences, were faulted, among other failings, for not having provided newly freed serfs with access to sufficient land to secure their livelihood. Slavophiles, liberal reformers, and reactionary conservatives alike bemoaned the deplorable conditions and socially vulnerable position of former serfs and other poor members of the provincial population who had fled the countryside in the hope of finding a better existence in the city.[64]

Given his audience and the robust conservative credentials of his clandestine muckraking, the dossier's author had little to lose and something to gain by adding his own voice to this chorus of critical voices. Ostrovskii's deceased brother Alexander, a playwright, had been one of the most prominent critics of the aristocratic establishment, and sexual corruption visited by the rich upon the poor was one of his central topics. In one of his last plays, the central plot is the attempted seduction of a young actress by a middle-aged count.[65] The anonymous official's exposé on the queer milieu strips away much of the nuance of the literary perspective and squarely places the blame for the corruption of weak and exposed young men on the shoulders of their well-to-do corrupters. In this sense, the dossier is taking the boldest of stances. In the case of the bathhouse attendant Vasilii, not even the jury that had proposed leniency toward an uneducated minor would have gone quite so far as to exculpate him entirely. The author of the dossier, however, demanded nothing less than the complete pardon of the corrupted victims, alleging that their tempters had caught them in "corrupting nets, not sparing, as is well known, any means for their subsequent seduction."[66]

This particularly tendentious view of the queer milieu and its hierarchies of privilege and blame stands in sharp contrast to some of the most prominent examples of the Russian forensic-medical literature of the preceding decades. The prominent physicians Merzheevskii and Tarnovskii, writing seven years apart in 1878 and 1885, give a number of examples of court cases involving blackmail or extortion. According to Tarnovskii, "one of St. Petersburg's highest-ranking administrative officials" became the victim of one of the earliest such cases at the beginning of the 1870s. Following his "exposure for pederasty, he was dismissed from his position forthwith and, without trial or any sort of announcement, sent into foreign exile." His accuser was apparently a "pederast-for-hire, a carriage-driver's son, without means and education, a dimwitted and sassy youth," whereas "his victim had been married, had children, was considered a good family man, had an outstanding mind and education and a brilliant career, who lost everything thanks to an accusation of some unknown tramp." This case, according to Tarnovskii, had been "widely talked about." It and others like it encouraged victims of blackmail to pay up.[67] Here, of course, the nature of the exploitation is the other way around, with the poor in the role of predator and the rich in that of victim. The moral repugnancy of these cases is heightened, perhaps, by the circumstance that money and, therefore, greed was the occasion for such blackmail, with the sexual nature of the case doubtful and in a secondary position, even occasioning a degree of sympathy where the victim is not represented as a wholly innocent party.

In each of the cases of blackmail described by Merzheevskii and Tarnovskii, well-to-do men, no longer young enough to be called "young men" or for their age to be listed as a defining characteristic, were accused of having engaged in sodomy with youths, whose age is always given (between seventeen and twenty-five years old). Most of these youths are explicitly described as poor or as being waiters, lackeys, unemployed, or engaged in menial professions. In all the reported cases, the wealthy clients initially paid the blackmailers in order to avoid exposure and a fate similar to that of the above-mentioned high-ranking official brought down by scandal. Courts, however, seemed to take a sanguine view of allegations of sodomy in cases where it was demonstrated that extortion had taken place. Sometimes, although not often enough, as Tarnovskii laments, the blackmailers were themselves brought to trial. He relates, for example, the case of the seventeen-year-old son of a low-ranking retired military officer, who was sentenced to six months in prison for extortion and theft, but it appears that neither of the well-to-do men whom he had accused of having seduced him were prosecuted.[68] Merzheevskii points to and condones this judicial practice. He mentions that in another case involving extortion, "the merchant M., whose guilt was obvious, was found not guilty by the jury."[69] Here again, the ingredient of blackmail seems to have played the crucial role in rendering the testimony of the alleged blackmailer biased and all but overwriting the crime of illicit sex with that of extortion. By contrast, in comparable cases involving well-to-do men with impecunious youths, but not involving blackmail, Merzheevskii expressed no particular sympathy for either party, both of whom were convicted.[70] Of primary importance here, however, is not the court practice, which in Russia we are provided with only sporadic examples, given the paucity of sodomy cases actually brought to trial, but rather the attitude taken by the leading Russian medico-forensic experts. They emphasize blackmail and avarice, which, far from exculpating, exacerbated the guilt of young men who engaged in criminalized sex with other men for gain, whether in the form of sponsorship, tips, outright payment for sex, or extortion.

Based on this stance, Tarnovskii explicitly describes his paradigm of juridical punishment. For him, the dividing line between victimhood, deserving of compassion and condescension, and vice, requiring punishment, runs not along class lines. The medical professionals already held a slightly more nuanced view of homosexuality, according to which a predisposition toward homosexual sex could, at least in many cases, develop among men of all classes through no fault of their own. It should therefore be regarded as a medical or psychological condition rather than a crime, unless, of course, it compelled them to engage in sex with aggravating circumstances, such as physical coercion or child abuse. In cases where an inclination toward homosexual desire is an involuntary perversion, Tarnovskii explains, this condition ought to be treated as a medical and psychological abnormality and treated accordingly by medical professionals with a view to curing or at least subduing it. On the other hand, it is precisely the poor young men engaging in sex with other men for pecuniary motives, despite their otherwise "healthy" sexual instincts, who deserve punishment given that their free volition makes them culpable, analogously to cases of theft. Adopting a tack common among the members of his profession, Tarnovskii insists that "however it may be, in cases of acquired pederasty punishment is justified," even if the punishment may have to be adjusted depending on whether the perpetrators are world-wise cynics or "stupid village boys."[71] Similarly, the legal scholar Ernst Bukhner, writing in Russia as early as 1870, recommended treatment rather than punishment for men caught having sex with other men, insofar as their acts were motivated by a perverted sexual inclination, not committed with a minor, and not involving violent coercion.[72] Here perverse pleasures might be met with therapeutic care, but venal motives deserved the full measure of criminal prosecution.

In contrast to these views, of course, the dossier assigns blame strictly along class lines, exculpating the poor young men as participants in the queer milieu merely for gain. It is as if the increasingly medicalized understanding of homosexuality did not exist. Even though the attached list of names and its commentary would seem to partially undermine the dossier's simplifications, the clearly stated objective of the proposed "measures by the administration" is the salvation of the poor young men at the periphery of the queer milieu from the clutches of the queer "aunties" at its core, who should be prosecuted by means more "paralyzing" than brief prison sentences.[73] This divergence of views on criminal responsibility between the dossier and the leading forensic-medical texts could not be more stark and has wide-ranging ramifications. For one, the assignation of criminal responsibility to rich "aunties" alone makes the threat allegedly posed by the queer milieu to the military, educational institutions, and the bureaucracy of the state appear more compact and manageable. It is consistent with the views expounded in the first paragraph of the dossier that the origins of the queer milieu are relatively recent, specifically urban, and limited to the decadence of a small group of sexually oversatiated wealthy men who seek to overcome their ennui by corrupting impoverished and vulnerable youths. Having a villain makes the problem manageable, and only if it is manageable does the dossier serve any purpose besides perhaps satisfying the prurient interests of some of its readers. The "auntie" fits the bill as the picture-book villain driving young men to suicide and isolation and causing their moral downfall with no motive but his own distraction. This focused villainization is critical to the dossier's naive assessment of the authorities' ability to "stamp out this malicious debauchery," since it traces the phenomenon back to a small circle of mutually connected wealthy individuals.

Whether or not these individuals were to blame had implications for, among other things, the ongoing debate about the criminal code, which continued until 1903, when a new draft was proposed to the State Council (Gosudarstvennyi sovet).[74] The fault lines in this debate were the same as those between the dossier and contemporary Russian forensic-medical literature, except that around the draft criminal code a direct engagement took place, but no evidence indicates that the author of the dossier had so much as read the work of his medical colleagues. Had he done so, he might have come across Tarnovskii's varied examples of male homosexual practices from a wide range of cultures, geographies, and historical periods. In his work addressed to doctors and legal professionals and published in St. Petersburg a few years before the anonymous dossier, Tarnovskii had argued clearly against the opinion that "pederasty is like some kind of infectious disease," an opinion explicitly professed in the dossier.[75] Widely citing the work of Western European colleagues, Tarnovskii concludes that "as an illness pederasty could be observed always and everywhere."[76] The dossier, on the other hand, describes a highly local phenomenon of the past "couple of years," owing its existence to the wanton decadence of a few known villainous "aunties."[77] As long as the responsible individuals could be identified and their activities suppressed, the phenomenon could still be uprooted.

The draft criminal code of 1903 contained an attempt to do just that. Ostrovskii, as the chairman of the Imperial Governing Council's Legislative Department, would undoubtedly have had an influence on its formation and, as mentioned above, the dossier may have been prepared to guide or support him in legislative discussions. The proposed change to antisodomy statutes, which was hotly debated but never enacted, was to replace the term used for anal sex (*muzhelozhstvo*) with the more malleable "indecent acts of passion" (*liu-*

bostrastnye deistviia).[78] This latter term meant that proof of anal sex would no longer be a prerequisite for prosecution. Instead, queer men could be prosecuted for a broad range of actions, but only insofar as the motive of illicit passion could be established.

Compared to the status quo, this change would have eased prosecution, even while narrowing the scope of individuals to which it applied in principle. The requirement to prove—often with the help of forensic-medical expertise—that an act of anal sex had taken place had long acted as a constraint on more extensive prosecution under the sodomy laws.[79] The removal of this requirement would ease the prosecution of allegedly queer men. Strictly speaking, it would not even be necessary to produce evidence of any sexual act whatsoever because solicitation alone could arguably qualify as an "indecent act of passion" and serve to incriminate would-be participants in an encounter. This catchall nature of the proposed definition of crimes related to sex between men, however, applied broadly only to men for whom no material motive could be established: that is, wealthy men of exactly the type described in the dossier. With regard to poor men, the shift in legal terminology implied that participation in the same act for money or under coercion was a priori excused or at worst relegated to the status of an administrative offense.[80]

The proposal, although consistent with the dossier's assignation of blame to wealthy corruptors and perhaps its call for "measures by the administration," immediately attracted sharp criticism from the more scientifically minded camp. Vladimir Nabokov, a leading Russian criminologist and lawyer who was actively involved in drafting the new criminal code, astutely recognized that this rewording would assign criminal responsibility precisely and exclusively to those who, like his own brother, struggled with a sexual desire beyond their volitional control. He also pointed out that the proposed term "fails to clarify any of the unique characteristics of the acts to which it applies or their criminal relevance."[81] This ambiguity, he argued, accorded unacceptable leeway to the police, as it shifted the burden of defining the crime from the legislator to the enforcer. The proposed change, however, reveals two things. First, it suggests that legislators were very much prepared to accord the police broad discretion in operationalizing antisodomy laws. Second, it shows that a considerable contingent of the leading men within the imperial administration were unprepared to relax the legislative suppression of homosexuality, seeking instead to upgrade their arsenal of statutes with laws that would enable the prosecution of precisely the kinds of men described as "aunties" in the anonymous dossiers from Ostrovskii's personal archives.

Aside from any connection the dossier might have had to legislative debates, the dossier's assignation of all blame to wealthy queer men had the potential to reposition even those statutes that were already in effect at the time of its writing and remained in place until the Russian Revolution, given that the relevant parts of the draft criminal code of 1903 were never enacted. The call for clemency for young, penniless participants in sex between male partners opened up procedural avenues for the focused judicial persecution of well-to-do queer men under existing antisodomy statutes. After all, *if* these young men participated "only as victims," as "pitiable young victims," then their acts of sodomy could be understood as entirely passive in the judicial sense, if not in the sexual sense as well.[82] The dossier's paradigm of seduction, therefore, and its appeal to extend one-size-fits-all extenuating circumstances to some participants in criminalized sex, such as their involuntary inebriation and the elaborate efforts of the "aunties" directed at their corruption, go far to justify a blanket amnesty for penniless would-be informers. Even under the existing statutes, any "victim" could hardly also be the offender with regard to one and the same sexual act. Given that hard-up youths were actually the most likely witnesses and informers in the known court cases under existing sodomy statutes, the acceptance of such a paradigm, unlike those proposed by Merzheevskii and Tarnovskii, would have had the obvious appeal of operational convenience in mustering a cohort of prosecution witnesses willing to confess their reluctant participation in criminalized sex. If only courts could be instructed to recognize young, poor participants in male homosexual sex as victims of the crime they were reporting, then prosecution under sodomy laws might become much more straightforward, since witnesses could avoid incriminating themselves. Thus, unsurprisingly, the dossier's assignation of blame to rich "aunties" had potential practical implications for the containment of the city's queer milieu.

A First of Sorts

Aside from any practical implications, internal inconsistencies, dubious motives, and homophobic biases, however, the anonymous dossier from Ostrovskii's personal archives establishes many of the themes that characterize both the queer milieu and the archival documents that contain its surviving testimony. Notwithstanding that this and other such archival documents were written by those looking in at the queer milieu with the ostensible objective of constraining its participants and their activities, a number of the themes raised by the dossier were of defining importance for the queer milieu. These themes form a red thread running through subsequent testimonies until 1914, including those composed in a nonforensic context by its immediate participants.

Each of these themes aligns to a significant degree with one of the remaining chapters of this book, even though the latters' scope is defined geographically.

The first such theme to emerge from the dossier is the tension on the part of municipal and imperial authorities between toleration and suppression vis-à-vis the queer milieu, and this can be seen most clearly in citywide policing. The dossier decries the government's failure "to take any measures whatsoever."[83] In apparent contrast to this assertion, the dossier's notes on individuals are evidently based on information gathered by the police. Moreover, the alleged pedophile and gymnasium headmaster Bychkov, whose case is mentioned in the dossier, was sent to Siberia according to published court rulings, and spent five years there before being permitted back and kept under house arrest with curtailed rights.[84] The dossier's anonymous author seems to dismiss surveillance and isolated instances of prosecution as entirely negligible measures. "Court judgments," he notes, "are powerless in this respect because, regardless of the strict sentencing of the above-mentioned individuals, the development of this mischief has not only not stopped, but has intensified."[85]

Something more is needed, but the dossier's author does not specify what he has in mind. He leaves no doubt, however, as to the presence of broad support in the government bureaucracy for more aggressive action. Several government departments, including the powerful Ministries of Defense and Education, he further alleges, already intend to demand a "stringent inquiry." Against this background, the dossier's author considers the time ripe for "strict measures." He only specifies these measures to the extent that he calls them "measures of the administration," distinguishing them from court-imposed sentences.[86] Although no government measures can be directly traced to the dossier, its author seems to have been far from alone in advocating this approach. Chapter 2 of this book discusses policing and provides a number of examples of such "measures of the administration," ranging from the prosecution of alleged homosexuals for petty crimes, circumventing the courts, to a more general—although ultimately abortive—effort to compile complete lists of well-to-do men who held parties in their apartments, where they corrupted young men. "Administrative measures" was in fact bureaucratic code for use of the emergency legislation to stamp out unwanted behaviors using extended royal prerogatives as opposed to legal due process under the criminal code. The tension on the part of municipal and imperial authorities between toleration and suppression of the queer milieu resulted in a relatively fluid regime of police discretion, which I reconstruct and describe in chapter 2.

The second theme clearly articulated in the dossier is queer streetlife: the spatial patterns, geographical footprint, and interconnectedness of the queer milieu. With regard to historical St. Petersburg, the dossier is, at least for now, the first known document to describe many of the recurring spatial patterns of encounter and engagement taking place in observable public spaces. Many of the most important venues, which are also mentioned in diaries and other archival files, are first combined by the dossier into a single inventory of queer spatial patterns in this city.

Moreover, the dossier's author first hypothesizes that these patterns were not just thematically connected to sex between men but in fact carried out by men loosely or intimately familiar with one another in a single citywide network. The soldiers and other impecunious young men who had sex with "aunties" "know all of them by sight." The terms "society" or "circle" used to refer to the queer milieu are always used in the singular: "All members of the society are connected to one another by a special kind of oath, [as] once practiced in Masonic lodges."[87] A number of opinions and specific customs, including nicknames for certain members of their circle, are shared "among aunties," implying an ongoing exclusive but universal exchange. Furthermore, several individuals in the dossier's list, including the wealthy heir and actor Vorobets-Spasskii, are "acquainted with all aunties of St. Petersburg."[88]

The author probably underestimates the number of men fitting his description of an "auntie" in the city, almost certainly overestimates their degree of organization, and unduly generalizes their mutual social intimacy, but he is undoubtedly onto something in alleging the interconnectedness of queer streetlife. Other sources from the early twentieth century emphasize the connection between spatial practices and social ties. For instance, Kuzmin describes himself as firmly rooted in a network of social relationships by means of joint participation in overlapping spatial patterns. Kuzmin describes "his" queer milieu not as a matter of oaths and secret societies but as a loose network of "familiar strangers." In carrying out their habitual strolls, he and his "gang" met other groups of men, among whom he frequently spotted familiar faces. Some of the social and sexual connections implicated in these patterns breached customary class boundaries, suggesting that the queer milieu indeed functioned as an independent and partially subversive community. Vladimir Ruadze, writing in 1908, and Pavel Kovalevskii, writing in 1909, return to these themes, alleging that homosexuality was a specifically urban phenomenon lodged primarily in the streets of the capital and involving men who "are all acquainted with one another."[89]

This view of the social and geographical interconnectedness of the queer milieu was something new. It is obviously a far cry from Merzheevskii's considered view that "Petersburg . . . evidently does not have a well-organized community of pederasts similar to that of Paris."[90] It marks an almost equal degree of evolution from Tarnovskii's observation that "pederasts . . . live to a certain extent in communities," as if they formed a heterogeneous array of small clusters.[91] In the dossier, the queer community is presented as existing in the singular, extending to the very bounds of the city and prominently interpenetrating demographic and geographical space within these bounds. Despite its author's positioning of male homosexual desire as the exclusive characteristic of well-to-do "aunties," however, he calls a manservant an "auntie" and notes at the end of a detailed description of male-only balls and private dinners that "servants at such parties are usually . . . chosen from among their crowd."[92] Thus, prey and predator, victim and corruptor join the concentric motion of the queer milieu around a common demographic and geographic center where rich and poor, young and old, "dame" and soldier meet. If we accept the astronomical metaphor, queer streetlife is better represented by way of an orrery, something that is both dynamic and structured. Just so, Anichkov Bridge exercised a unique gravitational pull across the city and formed one of the main entry points to the Liteinyi Borough, where the quickening of commerce, leisure, and surveillance turned out to be so uniquely conducive to queer streetlife. The streetlife of this borough and its implication for the city's queer milieu are the subject of chapter 3.

The third theme described in the dossier is the interplay between public and private spaces in the urban landscape. Near Anichkov Bridge or at the zoo, would-be-partners slip out of sight by entering public conveniences. A number of the cruising grounds here identified, including Ekaterininskii Garden, Znamenskaia Square, and Mikhailovskii Square, enable a similar pattern of encounter and engagement. According to the dossier's anonymous author, a queer couple's final destination might be a private apartment or a bathhouse, where privacy of sorts could be carved out of the public world. Similarly, the progression toward these same destinations for a sexual encounter might begin on an ice rink and occasion a detour via another semipublic space such as a café in a confectionery shop. From one of the theaters or *cafés-chantants* (the nineteenth-century equivalent of a jazz café), the pattern might lead into the private rooms of one of the restaurants specifically catering to queer clients. Near the Passazh, the pattern might segue directly into the adjacent hotel with rooms let by the hour or, again, into one of several nearby bathhouses with private rooms.[93] An entire set of potential "administrative measures" was premised on such observations. These measures could, in principle, be tailored to each step in the progression. On the street, policing might take on a cosmetic form insofar as men obviously recognizable as male prostitutes might be removed under any convenient pretext and surveillance intensified to force queer men to adopt no less effective and extensive but more discreet spatial patterns.[94] In relation to progressively more secluded spaces, authorities tried out more intrusive "administrative measures," ranging from the modifications of physical space, as in the case of the design of public urinals and the renovation of the Passazh, to the attempted reform of bathhouse operations. The last of these is particularly revealing and is the subject of chapter 4 of this book.

Finally, the dossier's disclosure clearly implies the existence of social groups of queer men for whom sexual opportunity was not the only or even the primary reason for gathering. The dossier includes a description of a "ball," one of many "held by rich aunties for greater communion." At this ball, the "rich aunties" arrived in the company of their lovers and "departed in couples . . . some to their homes, others to hotels and bathhouses."[95] The intermittent interlude would have been expendable had the objective been merely the identification of a partner for sex. A more direct route for rich men and their lovers to private spaces convenient for sex was available. The purpose of the ball, described as "greater communion," was thus objectively to foster a community. The dossier's description of the event itself supports this interpretation. The attendees "pronounced toasts, befitting of the present gathering, notably including a toast to the highly placed patrons of the society who were not in attendance."[96] Similar to Mikhail Kuzmin's description of his strolls in the Tavricheskii Garden, in which he communed with his group of queer friends and acquaintances in a significantly tamer but by no means discreet manner, "cruising" was not tantamount to the pursuit of sex, nor was the queer milieu barren of social charm and comfort, at least for those lucky enough to escape police interference, if not scrutiny. The experience of the queer milieu as a social environment, albeit from the very particular vantage point of a poor aristocrat and poet, is the topic of the fifth and final chapter of this book.

Between Evolution and Revolution: A Word on Historicity

The dossier may be a first of sorts, but neither the prejudices revealed in it nor the phenomena described are likely to have been entirely new at the time of its submission to Ostrovskii—the author's conviction to the contrary notwithstanding! Given that sex between men was a crime and, then as now, would-be-perpetrators generally knew better than to "put their crimes in writing," historians of queer urban life must rely largely on historical documents about the queer milieu composed by those charged with suppressing queer expression, whether in terms of spatial patterns, sexual acts, or even outwardly visible identities. The almost insurmountable challenge lies in being able to distinguish between historical perceptions of queer men and government action toward them, on the one hand, and the reality on the streets, in the bathhouses, and in private apartments, on the other. One compelling option for avoiding the pitfalls involved in this challenge is thus to describe only one side, tracing the historical arc of the queer milieu, for example, in terms of its reflection in evolving perceptions of queer men in the medical community and in the courts, or the history of government action directed at queer sexual expression. But some limitations in this body of work call for a reevaluation of homosexuality in the late imperial era and for a return to evidence such as the anonymous dossier, which complicates the established account.

The late nineteenth century witnessed the evolution of legislation and medical views of homosexuality where the medical discussions in the late imperial era gradually shifts away from an almost exclusive focus on sexual acts and ways to prove them toward the psychology of sexual perversion. Beginning with the first extensive works on the topic, such as Merzheevskii's 1878 textbook-style *Forensic Gynecology: Instructions for Doctors and Legal Professionals*, Russian forensic-medical professionals had been drawing on the work of Western European colleagues. The evolution of views in Russia, therefore, reflects that in the Western literature. Merzheevskii, referring to the work of Auguste Tardieu in France, devotes much of his writing on the subject of homosexuality to observations on the presumed physiological indications of past anal intercourse. Tarnovskii, writing only seven years later, is already more focused on the etymology of guilt in sexual crime and its relationship to the psychology of personality formation and sexual perversion. Another decade later, Vladimir Bekhterev and other contributors to his journal, *Views on Clinical Psychiatry, Neurology, and Experimental Psychology* (*Arkhiv psikhiatrii, nevorologii i sudebnoi psikhopatologii*), are focused almost exclusively on diagnosis and treatment of sexual deviance and not on questions of forensic medicine. This gradual transformation of the scientific literature took place during the period this book covers and, doubtlessly, informed the views of legal reformers, including Vladimir Nabokov, whose efforts to decriminalize consensual sex between adult men came to naught.

However, the combination of stagnant sodomy legislation and a scarcity of known cases brought to trial did not result from official policy or changes in the intentions of the dominant factions of lawmakers.[97] Rather, a watering down in the transmission system from law to enforcement took place in this sphere as in many others and was symptomatic of a generally inefficient autocratic state and erratic law enforcement.[98] The opinions of leading legislators did not become more tolerant of homosexuality toward the end of the imperial era, despite the emergence of some prominent voices for the defense of sexual freedoms in the debate around possible revisions of the legal code around 1903.[99] Given the absence of any indication that the evolution of medical views of homosexuality, which traced the arc of the Western professional discourse, had any direct and significant influence on late imperial St. Petersburg's queer milieu, its impact might have been achieved via the medical community's support of revisions to the criminal code. From what little is known about these drafting processes, however, it is more likely that medical views of homosexuality were simply ignored by those involved in revising the wording of homosexuality statutes in the draft 1903 criminal code or in subsequent revisions.[100] If one's interest is primarily in the city and its queer milieu, therefore, clear limits exist regarding what can be achieved by studying medical views or even legislation that remained unchanged during the late imperial era and was by all accounts virtually a "dead letter."[101]

The view from outside in, such as that expressed in the dossier, is particularly helpful in revealing the signs by which interactions between queer men began to project the appearance of an interconnected community or milieu. This book will explore each of the themes first assembled in the dossier as so many windows through which to look into the queer milieu, but it does not take these representations for granted or see them merely as a kind of discourse. I link these themes to specific geographies, but in discussing them, I draw—for corroboration or critique—on a number of independent sources, including police logs and correspondence, diaries, and information about events that affected the queer milieu and connected it to broader, national events or developments. The evolution of the queer milieu as a historical phenomenon, however, must remain largely elusive because, even across the thirty-five-year period of investigation, the available evidence is not sufficiently dense and comprehensive to provide for year-by-year or even decade-by-decade comparisons of spatial patterns and cultural factors. Instead, the period is precisely chosen for its relative stability, which allows us to open the aperture wide and long enough to capture the limited light available for historical geographic research into one of the city's most elusive phenomena. A shorter period would have left the phenomenon in the dark, whereas a longer period would have made it unrecognizably smeared and streaky. To tackle the objective of re-creating a single but representative snapshot of the patterns of policing, streetlife, ablution, and socialization that defined the queer milieu of late imperial St. Petersburg, the period from 1879 to 1914 is just about right because a significant degree of consistency in the spatial patterns of the queer milieu can be demonstrated, and at least some key pressures on these patterns can be historically investigated.

The duration of this snapshot exposure is deliberate but so is its timing, as explained in the introduction to this book. Aside from the major events that mark the beginning and end of the period covered in this book, important publications concerning male homosexual sex and the queer milieu fall on either side of it. They underscore both the evolution and the relative stability of the broader environment over this period. In 1879, a year after Merzheevskii published his seminal textbook on forensic gynecology with a review of sodomy cases in the capital, city authorities began their most ambitious and protracted attempt at sanitary reforms of communal bathing practices. Toward the end of the period, in 1908, the journalist Vladimir Ruadze published a pamphlet on the homosexual milieu, *On Trial! Homosexual St. Petersburg* (*K sudu! Gomoseksual'nyi Peterburg*). Although most of the phenomena described in it had been revealed to the authorities years earlier, its significance lies in the fact of its publication as the first or one of the first accounts directed at a large public audience. The resulting degree of exposure marked yet another milestone in the gradual becoming visible of the queer milieu.

Besides the fact of its publication, however, Ruadze's account of the queer milieu is a testament to the continuity in external perceptions. All the key aspects that defined the dossier's characterization of the queer milieu reappeared with similar substance and emphasis. As before, queer streetlife warranted extensive description and followed similar patterns in familiar geographies, except perhaps the addition of a newly built concert and exhibition center, the Narodnyi Dom, and the Tavricheskii Garden. A class-based view of relations within the queer milieu and of its origins remained more or less unchanged, again following a wealth-based principle rather than the empire's official social estates and feeding into a unilateral assignation of blame to the well-to-do corrupters of poor folk "from the streets." The only minor deviations in the picture are the anomaly of "Count K-gelm [who], just like a homosexual prostitute, sells himself, capably attaches himself to rich men and plays the role of procurer," and the observation that alongside mature "aunties," "young men, the sons of wealthy parents, who chose debauchery as their calling due to an inborn tendency toward that vice" are equally worthy of blame.[102] Here at least, the utterly untenable age distinction superimposed on the rich–poor binary has been abandoned. These are at best, however, minor corrections of an otherwise more or less unchanged picture.

As with the dossier, the class paradigm expounded in Ruadze's publication primarily serves the assignation of criminal responsibility for the presumed growth of the queer milieu to wealthy corrupters of young men. As in the dossier, the cast of rich instigators of debauchery contrasts markedly with "pitiable youngsters, who deserve all compassion, who fell into poverty and are cut off from their families."[103] Ruadze describes the poor participants in queer spatial patterns in revealingly geographical terms, grouping them together as "people from the street," whom he describes as "victims, yes, only victims." He writes that "[although] I launch myself with such hatred against these socialite and bourgeois criminals, I speak of these [people from the street] without anger."[104] Just as the anonymous author of the ministerial dossier has done, Ruadze decries police inaction. Even the format of his exposé is the same, with general prosaic observations on spatial patterns, private parties, class relations within the queer milieu, and the need for state action followed by a list of names with comments. Thus, in tracking down the historical phantom of late imperial St. Petersburg's queer milieu, these two documents offer the only known attempts at its comprehensive description by contemporaries. This skewed and ostensibly external view, this imprint accessible by observation, indicates that change was minor, and evolutionary rather than revolutionary over this period—an impression largely confirmed by firsthand sources. In the following chapters, however, the snapshot will show some blurs and streaks where things did change during the thirty-six-year exposure time employed in this book, thus upsetting the sense of immobility and revealing some of the ways in which the entente between a generally unsupportive state, a largely indifferent public, and queer men emerged and changed in different spaces and contexts within the late imperial city.

The tension between enabling better containment of queer spatial patterns and inadvertently helping the very men who seek to navigate them is a characteristic feature of many documents about the queer milieu, even the most secret ones. Careful perusal of Ruadze's accusatory pamphlet, for instance, conveniently betrays where and when men in pursuit of sex with other men met, and may have prompted some of the furtive reveries or determined expeditions of queer men strolling along the Fontanka Embankment and across Anichkov Bridge. The dossier had its own ambiguous valences. It may have been written with the intention of unmasking and damaging the career of a government bureaucrat like Asterii Gusev, who is described as a "dame" and a client of male prostitutes in the city's bathhouses, but in fact the inclusion of an entry about him in the copy provided to Ostrovskii gave his superiors the opportunity to protect and promote him, as they did. Whether Ostrovskii and other influential men provided this protection *because of* or *despite* Gusev's inclusion in the dossier's list of prominent "aunties," we will never know. Undeniable, however, is the potential for misuse of any document concerning ineradicable but illegal or illicit activities. Such "devious" potential was far greater still in the instance of Ruadze's publication *K sudu!* than that of the dossier. Under the public's very eye, here was a clear and specific guide to queer "cruising," available to anyone who cared to pick it up and read it. Its cover page included the titillating and enticing subheading, "Orgies and Parties (Fontanka, Tavricheskii Garden, and Narodnyi Dom)."

The inscriptive power of the historical documents used in this book to reconstruct the spatial patterns that characterized late imperial St. Petersburg's queer milieu can hardly be overstated. This is the case for police logs or secret dossiers, the very existence of which could severely affect the lives of the individuals mentioned in them, as well as for published documents. Ruadze's *K sudu!* could be used by both administrative officials and the police in targeting the queer milieu, albeit with caution. In any case, insofar as it achieved its aim of drawing attention to the very existence of the queer milieu, it could not but promote a kind of arms race between queer men and those eager to suppress their expression. These arms were, on the one hand, regular and recognizable spatial patterns that enabled queer men to meet while preserving a sheen of deniability. On the other hand, they included "administrative measures" ranging from targeted policing efforts to changes of the urban landscape itself proposed by planners and sanitary commissions to either combat or simply contain the very patterns that constituted the queer milieu. It may be tempting to read archival documents as merely descriptive, just as it is tempting to regard laws and court records as merely reflective of the reality on the streets, but this would leave the constitutive power of the documents in question unattended to. As will become even more evident in chapter 2 about policing, the eye of authority is never just an oculus but part of a larger structure. Like the observer effect in physics, whereby the mere fact of observation itself affects the phenomenon being observed, these documents testifying to St. Petersburg's queer milieu can best be understood when the likely influence of their composition on its readers and subjects is borne in mind. The same is true for this retrospective. The documents available to us such as the dossier are not simply descriptions of queer activity but also products of and interventions in the queer milieu.

Chapter 2

Policing Sex and Desire

On September 25, 1900, at two o'clock in the morning, a middle-aged unemployed peasant from the Vitebskaia region, one Ludwig Adamovich Zimmel', was arrested on Nevsky Prospect in the heart of late imperial St. Petersburg.[1] The arrest was prompted by an anonymous denunciation and was hardly unusual. This part of Nevsky Prospect was frequently mentioned in the police logs of the neighboring boroughs in connection with a range of recorded offenses of vague description such as "loitering for the purpose of debauchery." Men and women were arrested there almost every night for purported offenses against civil statutes or a broadly defined public order. Their crimes included those of a sexual nature, notably prostitution, though most arrestees were released without being charged.[2] The story of Zimmel', however, is unusual in two ways. First, his punishment was exceptionally harsh: Zimmel' was barred from residing in the city for two years. Second, the anonymous denunciation included in his file links his arrest to the phenomena of queer cruising and male prostitution.[3] In marked contrast, a series of diary entries recorded by Kuzmin a few years later in 1906 contains descriptions of relaxed meetings between recognizably queer men in a park just a few blocks away from the place where Zimmel' was arrested. These men, this time, did not seem to fear arrest. According to Kuzmin, his friends were obviously identifiable to constables as queer from their behavior and appearance, but felt sufficiently impervious to persecution to risk teasing nearby constables and passersby.[4]

The starkly contrasting responses of the constables in these two instances have everything to do with the aspects of policing that are the focus of this chapter.[5] I argue that the differentiation of police responses to everyday events on the streets of St. Petersburg are symptomatic of a developing compromise between the vision of spatial order pursued by the city's governing hierarchy, on the one hand, and the inevitable incursion of behaviors wholly incompatible with this vision, on the other. This compromise was operationalized by the police, whose actions or inaction produced such seemingly contrasting outcomes.[6] It would be misleading, however, to assume that the trade-offs involved in this compromise were weighed by high-level bureaucrats and communicated explicitly and precisely to the city's precincts and the constables on the street. This compromise was sought or achieved not on the basis of the archetypical model of centralized decision-making one might well expect to discover in a famously autocratic state and society. To understand the locus and method of decision-making which in many instances took place at the street- or precinct level, it is important to understand the actions and rationale of constables themselves in staking out the terms of the trade-offs between spatial order and transgression. In this context, the development of models of policing that are reflective of the agency of members of the lower-level police hierarchy in application to late imperial St. Petersburg is long overdue. To set up and describe such models, I build on Michel Foucault's description of street-level constables as arbiters of illegalities vis-à-vis the queer milieu.[7] The term "arbiters" rather than "law enforcers" emphasizes the possibilities of rule-based and yet highly discretionary street-level sexual policing.

This is the model of the policing of sexuality I explore in this chapter. On the basis of my analysis of newly discovered evidence contained in the surviving precinct-level police archives, I argue that day-to-day policing in St. Petersburg frequently involved the use of nuisance laws and administrative prerogatives but was also instanced in thinly veiled refusals to carry out direct orders to manage the spaces and environments in which queer men acted out their desires. This regime involved the exercise of broad police discretion and can be plausibly reconstructed based on the surviving evidence of police activity—or inactivity—in relation to queer spatial practices in the city. I refer to this as a regime of *queer sexual policing*, by which I mean the decisions and actions of constables and officers in conducting surveillance of men presumed to be amenable to having sex with other men, curtailing opportunities for sex between men, or targeting behavior understood as a precursor to sex between men. More generally, queer sexual policing encompasses a revealing range of modalities of informal policing. It addresses the liminal space between law and lawlessness in the city, taking into account the obvious difficulty of detecting, let alone preventing, actual breaches of sodomy laws.[8] Understanding and providing plausible interpretive models of queer policing helps reveal how a vision of spatial order held by the city's administrative elites was made operational on the streets.

Much of this queer policing was accordingly focused on space rather than on sexual acts or identities. Precinct-level archives provide important evidence of the decisions made by constables with regard to queer men and the spatial patterns in which they participated. This evidence consists of patrol and arrest logs, interrogation protocols, and administrative correspondence. Although they are often incomplete and ambiguous, these files are worth the effort it takes to decipher and contextualize them. They offer perhaps the only opportunity to examine day-to-day policing routines, which in all likelihood represent the majority of contacts between representatives of state authority and the queer urban milieu.

The role of police constables emerges in sharp relief here. Constables were on the one hand subjected to the visions of public order communicated by their superiors and expressed in legislation and direct orders, but on the other hand they were the less-than-all-powerful agents charged with establishing and maintaining this order.[9] The tension inherent in this dual role is important in understanding the projection of state authority onto urban space. Constables made up the broadest class of the police hierarchy and were the final members in a chain of delegation that linked the city's public and semipublic spaces to the offices of legislators and high-level bureaucrats. These constables were far more than a gearbox or transmission system charged with imprinting—however imperfectly—the letter of the law or even the decrees of the state onto the recalcitrant reality of the streets. Here it is particular challenging, but for that reason no less important, to look for patterns in the apparent laxity or inconsistency of law enforcement and to recognize instances of decentralized decision-making as distinct from either a general regime of "tolerance" or, alternatively, administrative inefficiency analogous to grit in the gears.

Rapid urban migration, an outdated criminal code, and inefficient state bureaucracy, including that of the courts, have been variously faulted with contributing to the Russian Revolution.[10] Whether or not that is true, these realities certainly placed unique constraints on the choices of individual constables and precincts in the imperial city. Their choices are significant because they directly reflect the trade-offs that the police, here as elsewhere, routinely had to make regarding the geographical extent and nature of the order they aspired to maintain. Looking at the surviving evidence of day-to-day police responses to the challenges posed by queer sexual policing helps refine models of policing in the historical city. Policing has been seen either as chaotically inadequate and brutally overbearing or both at the same time, depending on the situation. Limited as it is, the evidence of actual policing in the concrete urban spaces of fin-de-siècle St. Petersburg suggests at least some method to the apparent madness. Constables, in evident recognition of their limited influence on transactions between individuals in the public domain, found ways to negotiate a broadly consistent mandate of queer policing that satisfied their superiors but at the same time treated their target population with discretion.

To present this argument, the first section of this chapter describes the ambiguous relationship of constables and street-level policing to antisodomy legislation. Understanding this relationship is key to broadening the range of recognized public response to the spatial patterns in which queer men engaged. The second section focuses on models of policing other than straightforward law enforcement. As alluded to in the introduction, these models address the limitations on using criminal law to promote order on the streets. They also allow the possibility that inactivity of the police in the face of illegal activity might in fact be entirely consistent with the kind of order actually targeted. Here I ground my analysis in a small number of archival stories that are nevertheless highly revealing of instances in which constables employed discretion to manage the city's public spaces.[11] The third section of this chapter explores the relationship between constables, subjects of policing, and the police hierarchy by looking at attempts to regulate homosexuality in the city. The fate of a secret directive of 1910 illustrates how constables consistently and successfully resisted the imperative to expand the spatial remit of queer sexual policing. The final section of the chapter positions constables' actions in a broader discussion about a sexual "economy of illegalities."[12] Here I hope to resolve an apparent contrast between abstracted versions of Foucauldian coercive discipline and a view of tsarist policing in late imperial St. Petersburg as inefficiently "tolerant." These seemingly contrasting conceptions are reconciled within the model of queer sexual policing proposed here, where constables exercised a degree of coercive power precisely by making compromises tailored to particular situations and by negotiating their mandate with both their subjects and their superiors.

The City, the Law, and the Police

The City and Antisodomy Laws

The Criminal Code (*Ulozhenie o nakazaniiakh ugolovnykh i ispravitel'nykh*, hereafter the Code) of the Russian Empire specified the nature and punishment of all crimes, including sodomy. Issued by imperial decree in 1845 and modified several times thereafter, it remained in effect until 1917. Among sexual acts, the Code specified as criminal offenses adultery, bestiality, and "sodomy, a vice contrary to nature," in the sense of anal sex but not specifically male prostitution. Article 995 of the Code stipulated a prison term of four to five years for anyone convicted of sodomy.[13] The next article of the Code, Article 996, raised the penalty to imprisonment with hard labor for nine to twelve years if anal intercourse was aggravated by the use of violence or performed with an underage or a mentally defective partner. Lesbianism, in contrast, was not mentioned and was thus not criminalized under tsarist law.

The Russian Article 995, like Article 175 in Germany or Section 11 of the 1885 Criminal Law Amendment Act in Britain, formally criminalized only the specific sexual act. Significantly, however, no supplementary legislation was explicitly directed at cruising or male prostitution, in contrast to the British Vagrancy Law Amendment Act of 1898, which referred to "men who in any public place persistently solicit or importune for immoral purposes" and was instrumental in criminalizing "a putative homosexual identity."[14] In St. Petersburg, therefore, the time-honored criminalization of sodomy was not matched by a legislative machinery that specifically targeted the ways in which homosexual men met each other and socialized in the city's streets and public spaces.

Given the well-recognized challenges of detecting consensual sex between men, this left St. Petersburg police with a grossly inadequate legal arsenal for addressing activities such as cruising and male prostitution in the city's public and semipublic spaces. This challenge was not unique to St. Petersburg, nor was the fact that the city's police were forced to improvise. In Berlin, for example, police "found creative methods for enforcing the German anti-sodomy statute, Paragraph 175." One instance where such methods were used was a raid in 1885 on Steeger's restaurant, a well-known queer site. The men in the restaurant on the night of the raid were arrested, prosecuted, and sentenced to between three and four months in prison for "disturbing the peace" rather than for offenses against any laws or regulations specifically targeting homosexual sex, cruising, or socialization. Nevertheless, this raid is understood to have been a singular and unique event that inaugurated an era of general police tolerance toward public cruising. Regarding Berlin, historical evidence even shows that this tolerance was policy, or was at least passively condoned by the highest administrative authorities.[15]

No equivalent regime was in evidence in the Russian capital. In fact, legislative support for antisodomy legislation remained strong right to the end of the imperial era.[16] Similarly, the city's highest administrative authorities, the offices of the police chief and the mayor, initiated an effort to set up a central register of suspected homosexuals and even attempted to expand queer sexual policing into the spaces of private apartments, where consensual homosexual sex was presumed to take place farthest from imperial oversight. These and other initiatives not mentioned in previous work on late imperial St. Petersburg's queer milieu demonstrate that at least on some occasions, constables were expected to and did respond to behaviors indicating a propensity to engage in homosexual sex rather than merely the unmistakable breaches of antisodomy laws. This imperative required constables to use the law and their administrative prerogatives "creatively" because the bulk of detectable queer behaviors clearly did not fall within the narrow remit of the laws according to which men had to be witnessed in the act of sodomy.

Finding Queer Sexual Policing

As mentioned in the introduction, specifically in the section "Men Who Got Caught," to date the focus with regard to queer life in imperial Russia has been on the laws against male sodomy, court cases, medical reports, scattered biographical information about queer men, and, overall, the deficiencies of the tsarist state in policing homosexual offenses. A closer look at the day-to-day business of maintaining a vision of order in the streets contributes a different dimension to the discussion of queer sexual policing in late imperial St. Petersburg. Little has been known about the surveillance routines in place or attempted in St. Petersburg, thus making the conclusion that "police devoted little energy to this crime" appear almost inevitable.[17] Compounding this appearance, the "low incidence of sodomy prosecution" in the city and in Russia as a whole assumed the guise of further evidence of the low priority attached by authorities to managing sex between men.[18] While I do not dispute the paucity of cases brought to trial and I rely on the definitive work conducted on these cases, in particular by Dan Healey, the cases do not exhaust the resources available to the archaeologist of queer sexuality and the response of the authorities. The attitude of the state administration and the police toward queer men and their behavior, habits, and environments can be identified, even where these men were never subjects of criminal prosecution, using limited, in some instances explicit evidence of police interference with the spatial patterns of queer life, even if—especially if—this did not involve sexual transactions. What is more, certain aspects of day-to-day police routines can be plausibly linked by circumstantial evidence to queer policing. This evidence provides a useful context for considering the representativeness of instances in which a suspected propensity to engage in male homosexual sex was explicitly noted. Each of these new sources adds information as well as important nuance to the widely shared perceptions of Russian sodomy laws as a "dead letter" and of constables as relatively incompetent, scarce, and corrupt executors of official orders and enforcers of written laws and regulations.[19]

Taking these next investigative steps to uncover more of the presumably vast realm of "gray-zone policing" of sexuality is necessary but challenging in ways hardly unique to imperial St. Petersburg. Historians of queer sociability and sexual policing have sought to expand our understanding of queer life in other cities by trawling for evidence of day-to-day policing of a range of crimes and offenses, all the while acknowledging the considerable difficulties involved. In Britain, for example, court documents and newspaper reports offer voluminous evidence of police activities, in part because under the Vagrancy Law Amendment Act homosexual socialization itself was criminalized, unlike in Russia.[20] Nevertheless, it is unclear whether the police continued to use the likes of the nuisance laws to contain queer spatial patterns in cases where the application of the Vagrancy Law Amendment Act was too cumbersome.[21] Looking at the implementation rather than the letter of the law thus requires a concerted attempt to uncover the "underbelly" of historical cases involving either no court prosecution at all or prosecution under statutes other than those specifically targeting male-to-male sexual solicitation or sex. Even when such cases can be recovered, some of them left no court record of an alleged breach of law, and others are not explicitly linked to queer identities or activities at all. The point is that the small number of explicit prosecutions leaves unaddressed the possibility that queer men were subject to street-level policing not authorized by sexual legislation, which resulted either in their blending into the woodwork of lists concerning other offenses or—in instances where they successfully calibrated their behavior to the predictably circumscribed forbearance of constables and police authorities—their complete absence from the case record. The ellipses, therefore, are also important and can be addressed by looking specifically at the evidence of police discretion to see how it was deployed.

Against this background, sexual policing in eighteenth-century Paris also offers a surprising, if slightly incomparable, set of parallels to late imperial St. Petersburg. In France, the legal situation for sodomy was fundamentally different from that in Britain or Russia: sodomy had been decriminalized since the French Revolution. In a city like Paris, for instance, consensual sex between adult male partners in private spaces remained outside the pale of the law throughout the nineteenth century, much as it did in St. Petersburg in practice, if not de jure. Nevertheless, state resources were deployed in Paris specifically to manage the cosmetic effect of queer spatial patterns on public spaces.[22] Constables developed a range of approaches to address the challenges of firming up evidence to the standard required for successful criminal prosecution. On occasion they got lucky. Sometimes they engaged in elaborate setups to bring a case into the narrow scope of their official prerogatives. In yet other cases, vagrancy statutes were used to harass and inconvenience queer men, sometimes banishing them from the city—a practice also in use in imperial St. Petersburg.[23] Again as in St. Petersburg, lists of men suspected of having sex with other men were compiled, presumably either to focus surveillance or to exercise pressure on queer subjects in the gray area between the law and the amorphous requirements of propriety.

Building on these rarified asides in discussions of other European capitals, specific attention to the scope of police activity directed at the queer milieu but not necessarily at criminal prosecution offers a clear prospect for expanding our understanding of queer spatial patterns in late imperial St. Petersburg in particular.[24] This is especially necessary given the lack of any specific legislation targeting queer cruising, socialization, or solicitation. A focus on police "work-arounds" that facilitated spatial ordering without recourse to the criminal law requires consideration of a wider range of sources telling stories about the realities confronting constables on the beat.[25] Fragmentary as they are, the spatial stories found in these sources expand our understanding of the ways in which government—governmentality, to use Foucault's terminology—was involved in the negotiation over the late imperial city's queer spaces.

We see this in the arrest and banishment of Ludwig Zimmel', to return to a familiar example. Cases like his offer unique insight into the notoriously elusive histories of homosexuality by indicating how the law could be used "creatively" to manage queer forms of expression in the city's public spaces. Just as important, we must consider cases where the criminal and administrative arsenal was not used at all; it was held in reserve but was considered unnecessary or inappropriate. In this sense, the case of Lieutenant Raikovskii, mentioned in chapter 1, is a telling example. Raikovskii stood accused by a former lover of having engaged in sodomy. Street-level constables declined to investigate further, ostensibly because his putative crime was contained and did not threaten to "spill out" into public space. They arrived at this conclusion after interviewing, at the suspect's apartment building, a yard keeper who noted that the accused man "does not have visitors and rarely goes out." This statement apparently constituted sufficient justification for closing the case.[26] Nonprosecution cannot be interpreted as evidence that Lieutenant Raikovskii had been cleared of breaching antisodomy laws. It simply indicates that the constables who had been asked to investigate concluded that neither criminal prosecution nor other measures were advisable in the circumstances. Perhaps the evidence was not good enough for prosecution in the courts or the degree or risk of public disturbance did not suggest that other measures were necessary. Here and elsewhere—including the familiar case of Johan and Dmitrii—the key questions in the operationalization of regulation were whether or not the police should become active at all in the face of a suspected breach and if so, which tools to use. Patterns in the decisions where the police refrained from action are as revealing as the modalities of active responses, and they suggest the same calculation, in which constables confronted the trade-offs between the risks and costs of unsuccessful prosecution and those of being perceived by their superiors as insufficiently alert to alleged moral crimes.

The use of the *positive* and *negative* evidence of police discretion thus usefully complicates descriptions of policing in late imperial St. Petersburg directed at sodomy as "sporadic or indifferent" insofar as these characterizations place excessive weight on the scarcity of convictions under laws banning sex between men.[27] In the archival documents at our disposal, the constables' choices are not binary—that is, between *never* or *always* bearing down on spatial expressions of the queer milieu. Instead, these constables emerge as active arbiters seeking a balance between the vision of public order they were enjoined to promote and the often recalcitrant realities confronting them on their beat. Fragmentary documents about the nature of this policing allow us to start filling in this aspect of the picture of late imperial St. Petersburg's queer milieu. At the same time, they help reposition police practices in this city in relation to Western examples. The obvious but sometimes neglected lesson is that the way order was maintained or established on the streets of the city did not correspond directly to the ways that laws were devised in government bureaus.

Sexuality in a State of Emergency?

Although the police in late imperial Russia have typically been described as a mixture of the overbearing and the incompetent, an emphasis on the modalities of precinct-level police activity prompts a question about the cumulative effects of its responses. Was queer sexual policing broadly consistent in the application of its discretion, and if so, was it potentially more effective than has previously been assumed in managing public spaces with limited police resources?[28] Is another choice therefore possible—neither bluntly autocratic nor hopelessly ineffective, but pragmatic, discretionary, and perhaps efficient?

To even begin to answer these questions, it is not enough to look just at the decisions of constables in their interactions with the likes of Zimmel', Raikovskii, Johan, Dmitrii, and Kuzmin. We have to place these decisions within a larger context of street-level queer policing. Although sodomy laws were not invoked and applied in cases like these or in police responses to broader efforts by the city's governing authorities to target spatial patterns associated with the queer milieu, the police nevertheless did find ways to apply pressure that was aimed primarily at reducing the visibility of these patterns. The conclusion that laws against consensual sex between men was "virtually a dead letter in the largest Russian cities by the end of the imperial era" is important and serves as a starting point of this investigation.[29]

For the St. Petersburg police, in addition to the familiar difficulty of obtaining reliable witness testimony as evidence of illicit sex between consenting partners behind closed doors, other, locally specific factors contributed to the reluctance or inability of the police and courts to apply Article 995.

First, Russian members of the medical professions were more willing than their Western counterparts to acknowledge the limited relevance of their expertise when support for aggressive prosecution under the sodomy laws was requested. This comparatively lower aspiration of and reliance on medico-forensic expertise can plausibly be linked to the circumstances under which doctors were compelled to provide evidence in courtroom proceedings. In Russia, doctors were required by courts to examine suspects and write affidavits free of charge, in contrast to most places in the West where such services were compensated.[30] They had little incentive to boost their expertise and the work was unpleasant and tedious as well as unpaid. This particularity of the Russian legal system was a systematic impediment to the court prosecution of sodomy, but it did not apply to other forms of police coercion of queer men, where the tenuous tenets of sexual psychology and physiology were not at stake.[31]

A second factor was the existence of a parallel legal universe that persisted alongside the realm of criminal law and relied on the exercise and delegation of so-called administrative prerogatives. These allowed for the procedurally far less cumbersome inconveniencing or persecuting of men suspected of engaging in sex with other men. The state simply had other ways to address the indiscreet pursuit of consensual sex between men, which to a greater extent than in many Western cities lay outside the scope of criminal prosecution. The exercise of these administrative prerogatives was sufficiently pervasive that it stymied the progress of liberal reforms favoring legally enforceable rights and obligations.[32] The tsar's appointed government appropriated the institutional appurtenances of the rule of law (legal codes, an independent judiciary, trial by jury) but continued to exercise absolute sovereignty through the mechanisms of the administrative state, albeit an often inefficient one.[33]

St. Petersburg's governor commented explicitly on this state of affairs in 1906. He blamed the need to bypass the criminal justice system on the incompetence of "judicial and administrative authorities, Russia's unsophisticated criminal law and the weakness of the procedural system," noting that "not one of the inhabitants is shielded from the *proizvol* (arbitrary power) of gendarmes."[34] Writing about the emergency legislation in late imperial Russia, Jonathan Daly points out that "administrative Russia coexisted uneasily with an independent judiciary and a powerful procuracy, especially when juries acquitted defendants clearly guilty."[35] These conclusions likely applied to defendants accused of sexual as well as political crimes, in particular to sodomy. Healey, citing a 1910 statistical analysis of criminal cases, concludes that "the justice system prosecuted these cases much less successfully than the average crime, with only about 41 percent of sodomy indictments leading to conviction (compared with a conviction rate of 66 percent for all other crimes)"—this despite a dwindling number of cases being brought for prosecution in the first place.[36]

The emergency legislation passed by imperial decrees starting in 1866 was instrumental in maintaining a system parallel to that of the criminal courts. This system was commonly described by both contemporaries and historians as consisting of "administrative measures." Here, we recall the "administrative measures" cited as an alternative to court sanction by the author of the dossier discussed in chapter 1. As if to draw its readers' attention to this other side of the law, the aforementioned 1910 case compendium notes that "the autocratic state itself was inclined to apply administrative punishments that would obviate any courtroom session." Unfortunately, it does not provide any examples or detail of such cases, which is understandable given the compendium's own reliance on courtroom evidence.[37] Action taken via the recourse of "administrative measures" remains obscure as a result. But Laura Engelstein persuasively concludes that "while few men were ever prosecuted in tsarist courts for the crime of consenting (homosexual) sodomy, it is not the case that imperial legislation, or even the dominant opinion among progressive legal scholars and lawmakers, exempted sodomy from repression. The tsarist regime was notorious both for ignoring the law (acting through imperial fiat or passing 'emergency legislation' that superseded formal procedures and guarantees) and for laxity in implementing the laws it did endorse."[38] Such "emergency legislation" protected vestiges of the administrative system of extrajudicial punishment but it was by no means a dead letter. Often misread as a rolling back of the civil liberties enshrined in the laws of the judicial reforms of 1864, this legislation in fact carved out an already much-reduced share of formerly vast administrative prerogatives.[39] But this turf was still significant and jealously defended by government bureaucrats, initially with the support of the great reformer himself, Tsar Alexander II.

The specific modalities of sanction associated with administrative prerogatives included arbitrary detention, banishment from a region, forced exile to a specified location, state-mandated professional discharge, prevention of public gatherings, and closure of businesses—all without recourse to the courts. These prerogatives and forms of sanction remained largely consistent from 1866 until World War I and the Revolution. They were constantly tweaked and renegotiated, resulting in an uncomfortable entente between "partisans of the rule of law and the supporters of unencumbered administrative discretion."[40] The focal node for this negotiation was the council of ministers, who could declare and renew a "state of extraordinary security" for a geographical area, fine-tune the scope of administrative prerogatives, and define the procedures required for various methods of sanction, notably including banishment for "depraved behavior" (*porochnoe povedenie*) or "political unreliability" (*politicheskaia neblagonadezhnost'*).[41] Thus, an opportunity or a threat existed depending on one's perspective: sexual crimes or perhaps simply the expression of illicit sexuality could be addressed with the powers conferred on the city authorities by the authoritarian state. This did not mean, in itself, that queerness and homosexuality were aggressively policed, but the legacy of autocracy gave municipal authorities greater leeway in policing the queer milieu in ways that did not involve prosecution under sodomy laws.

Governors certainly made extensive use of their so-called administrative prerogatives, routinely resorting to banishment, professional discharge, and detention. From St. Petersburg alone, nearly forty-four thousand people were exiled between 1884 and 1895 for nonpolitical reasons and an unknown number for political ones.[42] The sanctions of professional discharge and detention without warrant were also widely used, often explicitly on the basis of the emergency legislation. These measures were known to be used in response to suspicions of sex between men.[43] In defense of these prerogatives, the governor of St. Petersburg annually renewed a state of "reinforced security" from 1881 until 1905, and further enhanced his autonomous powers by raising the declared threat to public order to a state of "extraordinary security" in 1905. From 1905 until 1910, this state of "extraordinary security" was annually renewed with the support of both the Council of Ministers and the tsar himself.[44] These rolling states of emergency set the scene for police work in the late imperial era, in particular in the empire's capital. The prosecution of "unreliable" or "depraved" persons entered the standard police repertoire in dealing with perceived threats to public order, and these threats were interpreted broadly.[45]

Third, and finally, one needs to emphasize the institutional weakness of the police force itself. According to both historians and contemporary commentators, the Russian police were chronically understaffed, underqualified, and poorly supervised, including in the imperial capital.[46] As stated by the historian Neil Weissman, in this predicament, the police force adopted an "arbitrary and coercive operational style" as an expedient.[47] Weissman does not see much merit in this approach. As with Foucault in his discussion of patchy law enforcement regarding weavers in fifteenth-century France, Weissman unhesitatingly links this arbitrary and coercive style not only to structural constraints but also to police corruption. In the context of queer sexual policing, however, condemnation of corruption is not sufficient. A special power may be at work in arbitrary policing beyond its unfairness. After all, the terms "arbitrary" and "arbiter" are closely related. The more arbitrary the exercise of authority in the context of all three of the locally specific factors described above, the more important the role of the arbiter. It is therefore imperative to ask: Was the use of arbitrary police authority really as catastrophically inconsistent and thus inefficient as has been assumed? Might there have been at least some method to the madness? Scholars of queer sexual policing have mainly relied on the documentary traces of prosecution or treatment for criminalized sex. This is perfectly understandable, but it leads to the neglect of discretion in the policing of queer sexuality and its expression. In order to evade the very constraints that arbitrary power seeks to overcome, the exercise of police discretion is inevitably poorly documented, but scattered evidence extends our understanding of queer life in late imperial St. Petersburg. Queer spatial patterns may indeed offer the ideal litmus test for an investigation of arbitrary policing, not only because the failure to enforce sodomy laws was nearly complete but also, more important, because constables nevertheless made real efforts to control perceived deviance. Their arsenal of methods as street-level arbiters in queer policing as well as the record of their decisions help to fill in the picture of how governance actually operated on a day-to-day level in the streets of the capital.

Queer Policing in Action

The arrest of Ludwig Zimmel' and his notably severe punishment open up a view into the world of police discretion that had little to do with the formal procedures of the criminal justice system. His story mirrors that of many other men and women who were arrested on Nevsky Prospect and in neighboring areas for various misdemeanors. Their arrests suggest that at least during the first decade and a half of the twentieth century, constables on the beat undertook to manage certain kinds of "deviant" behaviors in the city's public spaces and curtail spatial patterns associated with homosexual sex, all without recourse to the criminal courts. This is a world of "discretion" that is largely invisible in the records of prosecutions but is no less pertinent for the policing of the queer milieu.

Some further details of the Zimmel' case should be added here. On September 23, 1900, the mayor of St. Petersburg, Count Kleigel's, received an anonymous letter claiming that "last year a new class of debauchers joined those already populating Nevsky Prospect—pederasts. One of them is a Polish man who wears a brown coat and hat and frankly offers his sexual favors."[48] The author goes on to proclaim that "there has never been such debauchery in St. Petersburg. The public cannot fight by itself."[49] In response to this letter, as the archival file containing it further informs us, on September 25 at two o'clock in the morning, a peasant from Vitebskaia region, Ludwig Adamovich Zimmel', a middle-aged (thirty-seven-year-old) unemployed man with a recognizably German name was arrested on Nevsky Prospect. The file makes no further mention of the color of his coat or anything particularly "Polish" about him. Even the part of Nevsky Prospect on which he was arrested, Spasskaia Borough, is not the one specified in the letter. It is entirely possible that Ludwig Zimmel' is not the man described in the letter at all, but simply a queer man previously known to the constables making the arrest as a habitué of Nevsky Prospect or one coincidentally observed by them that night and arbitrarily linked to the anonymous letter. In the absence of any description of the activities of Zimmel' at the time of his arrest, it appears that the anonymous letter along with the unstated and unsubstantiated link between Zimmel' and this letter sufficed not just for his arrest and detention but also for the subsequent ruling by a magistrate court.

Here police action does lead to prosecution and to severe punishment that is seemingly disproportionate to the dry account in the archives. The case of Ludwig Zimmel' demonstrates a crude efficiency in speedily responding to a citizen's tip-off. Little more than a day passed between receipt of the letter and the arrest of Zimmel'. As the file "regarding the pederast Ludwig Adamovich Zimmel'" reveals, he was promptly removed from the city and barred from returning for two years, all for the petty crime of "soliciting members of the public" (*pristavanie k publike*).[50] This is probably explicable because Zimmel' had previously served three months in jail for "peddling stolen goods," making him a repeat offender under petty crimes statutes, which were not subject to the demanding procedural constraints on district courts for prosecution of more serious crimes, including sodomy.[51] But other things can be learned from his exemplary punishment. The story of Zimmel' shows that the constables and magistrates handling his case had no qualms about their determination that Zimmel' was not only *a* pederast, but *the* pederast mentioned in the unspecific anonymous complaint, and they had no misgivings about banishing him for a crime for which no evidence at all had been put on record. The anonymous tip-off served as the only evidence in his file. So even when prosecution was the result and the harshest available stricture was employed, arbitrariness—or discretion, as I prefer to call it—is the dominant theme. It is, of course, impossible to make statistical use of this case, but it is remarkable that such a degree of discretion was applied seemingly as a matter of course even in a single instance without the encumbrance of procedural safeguards for the civil liberties of Zimmel'.

The case is unique archivally in the sense that it has been preserved in its entirety and contains a documented link between allegations of homosexual cruising or prostitution and prosecution under petty crimes statutes. It may not be unique in other ways, however. Similar procedures or the threat of them following arrest were applied in other cases as well, including when no anonymous correspondence was involved, no allegations were taken as truth, and their vagueness, again, was no barrier to the swiftest and most decisive action. Some of these other cases are linked to queer spatial patterns in ways that underline the role of circumstance in police decision-making. The etymology of the word "circumstance" is standing "around," encircling, or encompassing. For example, police logs of arrests in the Kazanskaia Borough adjacent to the boulevard on which Zimmel' was arrested provide some helpful context. These case logs contain an abundance of notes regarding arrests for loitering and soliciting in the area. Several of them indicate that the intention of the police was to bear down on "debauchery," meaning moral and sexual offenses in general and not queerness specifically.[52] A few cases stand out as those involving individuals engaged in prostitution, another important facet of sexual policing. Elena Sazonova, for example, was arrested in 1910 on Voznesenskii Prospect for "loitering for the purpose of debauchery."[53] Not only was Voznesenskii Prospect famous for prostitution, but the note taken together with the circumstance that Sazonova was arrested at one o'clock in the morning and sent to the Medico-Forensic Committee, an institution ambiguously tasked with both preventing prostitution and improving hygiene, strongly indicates that she was a prostitute or sex worker and renders probable the connection of her arrest to sexual policing.[54] In many other cases, women who had been arrested were released in the morning after several hours' detention. The same procedure was applied with men who were arrested for various vaguely defined minor disturbances of the public peace. Most of them were eventually released without the matter ever being referred up to the magistrates' courts. The standard of documentation required for such arrests was particularly low, thanks to the emergency legislation and the declared state of "extraordinary security."[55]

The existence of an anonymous letter in the case of Zimmel' uniquely links to queer sexual policing what would otherwise simply have looked like another of these routine arrests and inconspicuous magistrate court proceedings for "soliciting members of the public." This case, along with an abundance of territorially consistent nighttime arrests for similar misdemeanors, makes it plausible that all-purpose petty crimes statutes were deployed by constables against queer spatial patterns, fulfilling their mandate—in the highly general terms of a contemporary police handbook—to conduct "surveillance of common order in public places, markets, restaurants, pubs, and similar places, everywhere that anyone has free access."[56] Against this background, the presence of the letter in the Zimmel' case file is an indication of the expectations of the city's highest police authorities. By forwarding it from the office of the city's mayor and chief of police to the precinct level, superior authorities sent a signal that indiscreet queer behavior in central public spaces was to be addressed by aggressive police management of these spaces. The citizen's tip-off or complaint would have increased the urgency of this issue, but Zimmel' might have been arrested that night even had no such letter ever been written. Perhaps the existence of the letter, although fortuitous for us in trying to understand the ins and outs of queer sexual policing, merely contributed to the misfortune of Zimmel' in possibly prompting his referral to a magistrate court, while many otherwise similar arrests remain nontransparent to the historian.

The practice of using petty crimes statutes to respond to observable sexual solicitation in the city's busiest commercial areas would be broadly consistent with the observation that few consensual sodomy cases were brought to trial. It helps reconcile the observation that sodomy laws were in effect a dead letter with the remark of Engelstein stating that support for the curtailment of homosexual activity remained strong in administrative and legal circles. Both views are surely correct. The practice in evidence in the case of Zimmel' and quite plausibly in a wider range of cases may in fact be the missing link between the dearth of criminal cases related to consensual sex between men and the persistent intention, at least among some members of the administrative elite, to subject such sex to repressive action. This conception of police activity goes well beyond the discovery of grit in the gears of the administrative regime. It suggests instead that the motion desired by the driver—the city's elites in this analogy—was supported by mechanisms other than antisodomy legislation. We have to turn from that legislation, and even from the lower police courts, to the world of the streets where the precinct constables played the preeminent role, even if they were not—especially if they were not—all-powerful agents of authority.

Teasing the Police

The picture on the streets was multifaceted, to be sure. It is complicated by the circumstance that the police response to recognizable and visible queer behavior was not always so swift and robust as in the case of Ludwig Zimmel'. Kuzmin, to whose diary and novels I return throughout this book, recorded a very different instance in May 1906, when his male friends "teased constables" in the Tavricheskii Garden.[57] This public garden is a brief walk away from Nevsky Prospect and was also a famous cruising site.[58] It is clear from Kuzmin's diary entries that his group's behavior could be described as anything but discreet. According to Kuzmin's reports, he and his friends dressed extravagantly and considered it quite acceptable to hold hands with a lover during strolls in the Tavricheskii Garden in unmistakable reference to a sexual relationship.[59] It is clear that he and his friends did not fear police interference in their activities, despite the fact that the constables had a range of options available to them. Arrest, even administrative sanction, would have been at least as straightforward in 1906 as it had been in 1900, if not more so, given the escalation of the city's declared state of emergency by a further notch. Why then did Kuzmin and his friends act so seemingly rashly?

Several complementary explanations all point toward a nuanced but broadly consistent approach in the application of discretion in queer sexual policing and the management of spatial order. One such explanation is that the behaviors of Zimmel' and Kuzmin may have fallen on different sides of unrecorded and historically difficult to establish boundaries of accepted public sexuality. In the case of Zimmel', who was arrested alone at nighttime and whose arrest was linked to a letter making reference to "frankly [offering] sexual favors," a commercial element or prostitution may have been particularly pronounced, whereas in the case of Kuzmin and his friends, their interactions and flirtations in the Tavricheskii Garden seem to have been of a primarily social and noncommercial nature.[60] It is possible, even probable, that the behavior Kuzmin could get away with was very different from that attributed to Zimmel', although queerness was a common denominator.

A second possible explanation, equally probable, is that social class played a role. Kuzmin was an aristocrat, albeit by no means rich. What is known about him clearly indicates that his manner of dress and speech would have made him recognizable as such. Regardless of his appearance, however, if his behavior were ever to have prompted police action, his status as an aristocrat would have been clarified among the first orders of business by the police. Constables scrupulously recorded the social estate of any arrestee, including that of Zimmel', for example, who, according to recorded statements he made at the time of his arrest, tried unsuccessfully to pass himself off as a "burgher" (*meshchanin*), one notch above the peasant status he actually held. With Kuzmin, the police might have been more reluctant to test the boundaries of their arbitrary powers. Not only did the law treat him differently (for example, he was not subject to corporal punishment), but merely by virtue of his social status he was more likely to have connections in the city's administrative apparatus. The sensitivity of constables to the implications of such possible connections should not be underestimated. In the course of the prosecution for sodomy of an aristocrat mentioned in the ministerial dossier discussed in chapter 1, letters were mobilized from many influential people on behalf of the accused, including ones to the tsar himself.[61] This would have exposed police to considerable scrutiny, especially in a less clear-cut case. Better, perhaps, to err on the side of caution with a man like Kuzmin.

It would not be unique to St. Petersburg that petty crimes statutes were routinely applied to contain queer socialization and solicitation by lower-class men, whereas lists, surveillance, and the threat of exposure might be deployed against upper-class men suspected of similar activities.[62] This explanation, however, can only be taken so far. His social class alone was not a sufficient explanation for Kuzmin's immunity from police interference on his strolls in the Tavricheskii Garden. Kuzmin describes his "friendly gang" as consisting of a mix of men from *all* classes, numbering aristocrats and lower-class men alike. On the occasion mentioned above he was joined by two shop clerks. Their sense of relative impunity appears to have applied to them as a group rather than just to Kuzmin or other individuals within it. Moreover, a different and decidedly lower-class group of men, so-called hooligans, enjoyed a similar degree of noninterference from police in the Tavricheskii Garden, according to Kuzmin's diary and independent archival sources (for more, see chapter 5).[63] Perhaps most notably, Kuzmin *was* later fined for pornography when his definitively unpornographic novel *Wings* was published.[64] It seems that he was not personally immune to harassment, if one uses an expansive interpretation of the law. It is rather more likely that his group's immunity was situational, which returns us to the discretion shown in regard to the spatial policing of sexuality.

The differences in approaches between the Zimmel' case and Kuzmin's recollections might indeed have been mostly related to the development of an understanding between constables and the regulars of the Tavricheskii Garden. This understanding, or entente as I have called it, had far-reaching consequences such as the acquiescence of constables to abandoning the monopoly on violent coercion by sharing its prerogatives with men like the hooligans. In accepting this state of affairs, constables may have been motivated by fear of trouble, a lack of resources, or even corruption. It is likely that for some in the community of so-called hooligans, a commercial element played a role in this power-sharing arrangement. Such commercial connections may have penetrated the queer milieu as well. Both Kuzmin and his friends at times had sex with these hooligans. Kuzmin records interactions that demonstrate a degree of social familiarity if not overlap between the groups of queer men and hooligans: the latter could thus be companions, lovers for pay or pleasure or both, as well as adversaries to be feared more than the police (for more about the complex relationship between queer men and hooligans, see chapter 5).[65] It seems from Kuzmin's recollections that unlike the male prostitutes on Nevsky Prospect where Zimmel' was arrested, these hooligans did not publicly solicit for sex, but rather socialized with their potential partners, patrons, or clients.[66] The circumstantial evidence suggests regular sexual and monetary exchange between hooligans and queer men of Kuzmin's circle, which may have been underpinned not only by desire and opportunism but also by the threat of violence or exposure. The queer milieu was negotiated between queer men and the police and with the other groups who shared this public space.

Constables on patrol in the Tavricheskii Garden had every reason to recognize the garden as a functioning social ecosystem that was to be interfered with only when certain boundaries were crossed.[67] The nature of the queer subsection of this ecosystem is the subject of chapter 5, but here suffice it to say that both queer men and hooligans were to some extent perpetrators against good order, and the mantra of noninterference also removed the need to protect either group from the other—the one against violence and extortion, the other against sexual corruption. Finally, it should not be ruled out that hooligans shared the proceeds of their activities with constables, although the historical record contains no positive evidence of such a connection. Regardless of whether constables were motivated by a well-considered sense of their priorities or personal greed, it is evident that Kuzmin's and his friends' cruising as well as the various activities of hooligans in the Tavricheskii Garden benefited from constables' predictable and consistent restraint in applying their mandate of curtailing "impudent and seductive behavior in public places" to the activities of both groups in this particular space.[68]

The Secret Directive of 1910

If the stories of Zimmel' and Kuzmin illustrate wide variations in police responses based on observable behavior, class, and location, then understanding the robustness of accepted constraints on arbitrary police authority becomes a priority both for participants in the queer milieu and for anyone looking back in time. Recently discovered archival materials testifying to what is an extreme case of inaction on the part of constables in the face of direct orders from their highest-ranking superior to surveil patterns of queer socialization and sex are fortuitously illuminating. The materials in question include a secret mayoral directive from 1910 that has been preserved together with precinct-level responses to it. Together these documents shed further light on the manner in which the scope of police activities vis-à-vis queer spatial practices was defined and operationalized. The directive itself indicates that at least on this occasion police hierarchies targeted the spatially ambitious enforcement of "public decency and peace" by repressing sex between men even in private residences. The far-from-enthusiastic responses from constables in various city boroughs, however, illustrate the important role that precinct-level police played in negotiating the geographies of homosexual sex and cruising.

Regarding the secret directive, then, on October 21, 1910, Count Vendorf, deputizing for the city's mayor and head of police, sent a dispatch to all police stations requiring them to identify and collect information about men suspected of hosting gatherings at which these men and their guests engaged in homosexual sex in private apartments:

> According to information to which I have become privy, certain individuals, who have sufficient material means and live by themselves, receive regular visits from students of institutions of higher learning as well as other young men. These young men then engage in unnatural relations of homosexual intercourse with the hosts and with one another.
>
> Given the need for determined action to protect our youth against the scourging influence of debauchery, I request that you provide—within two weeks—detailed information about such individuals, who according to their behavior give reason to suspect such inclinations.
>
> The chief of the Secret Police is to render all necessary assistance to the boroughs in the execution of this order.[69]

On the face of it, the directive delivered an unambiguous message to constables to monitor a demographically circumscribed group of individuals who were potentially willing to engage in homosexual intercourse. As a matter of course, the directive underscores the stereotype familiar from the ministerial dossier of the early 1890s of the debauched well-to-do male preying on vulnerable young men. Aside from reinforcing such stereotypes and in fact explicitly marking men fitting this demographic description for surveillance and further "determined action," as opposed to, for example, exempting them based on their social status, the directive also represented formal grounds for intrusions by constables into private apartments. Had the hunting season for well-to-do queer men who discreetly constrained their illicit activities to their apartments finally opened? It seems not. Despite its aggressive aspirations, the directive seems to have engendered little more than a flurry of internal police correspondence. The archival evidence indeed suggests that whatever initiative Vendorf had in mind got bogged down at the first step. As far as one can tell, constables conducted no interviews, made no new arrests, and did not even produce any of the requested lists in response to the directive. The city's secret directive appears to be even more of a dead letter than the state's antisodomy laws.

What turned the directive into a dead letter is precisely the matter at hand. An analysis of the responses from boroughs, precincts, and "watch areas," fortuitously filed in the municipal archives along with a copy of the directive, suggests that constables decisively resisted this mandate.[70] Constables from seven of the eight precincts within the Spasskaia Borough flatly denied the existence of any suspicious individuals of this sort in their precincts.[71] One went even further, writing that "there are neither apartments nor individuals who engage in homosexual sex."[72] The author of the Narvskaia Borough's consolidated response flatly denied the presence in his borough of any individuals "who might give rise to the suspicion of engaging in the unnatural Greek vice." He added, in apparent reinforcement of the directive's class paradigm, that in this relatively poor district, "apartments are rented by families and groups of individuals and their occupants and lifestyles are well known to us."[73] The response from Narvskaia Borough is also remarkable for its author's confidence—sincere or merely professed—that in the eyes of his superiors his generalized assertion of knowledge regarding the residents of his borough provided robust grounds for refraining from further action. Perhaps the most creative and suggestive reply comes from the Liteinaia Borough. In the precinct's response, a previously known suspect was identified as a target for action under the directive. The man in question, one Otto Tard'e, fit the bill perfectly. He was an aristocrat and titular councillor. The author of the precinct's response underlined Tard'e's high social status in his response.[74] In the reply he received from Vendorf's office, he was tersely informed that no further action was required in this case. He was reminded of what he should already have known: Tard'e had recently been arrested in 1908 and 1909, on the latter occasion "for indecent behavior and solicitation with an inappropriate proposal to Gerasim Adamov."[75] The surviving responses do not indicate that a single previously unknown suspect was identified in response to the directive.

A modern-day reader of police documents may be tempted to see the reason for the directive's apparent failure to achieve its objective in its lack of instructive detail. Were constables free to ask questions and disclose their objective of searching for men suspected of having homosexual sex? What was the intended next step? Would men suspected of having homosexual sex be monitored until adequate proof could be obtained and then arrested? Were constables free to improvise other measures to prevent the gatherings described in the directive from taking place? While the lack of detail regarding these questions may be jarring to a contemporary reader, the directive is no exception in the proliferation of these apparent ellipses. Contemporary police instructions are characterized by textual ambiguity and vague orders, especially on issues of sexual policing, which suggests that the higher reaches of the police hierarchy conveyed the desired spatial order in quite general terms, thus leaving plenty of leeway to constables in interpreting and operationalizing the orders they were given. For example, in July 1908, following unsavory incidents at the hotels Dunai and Olimpiia, the police conducted raids and discovered "two men and two women simultaneously staying in a single hotel room for the purpose of debauchery." As a result, Daniil Drachevskii, for whom Count Vendorf had been deputizing when he issued his directive targeting queer men, ordered the police to "take measures to avoid allowing the likes of this in the future, in recognition of the circumstance that the concurrent occupation of one hotel room by several men and women does not accord with the requirements of public order and decency."[76] In a vein similar to Vendorf's 1910 directive, Drachevskii remained notably silent as to the nature of the actions constables were to take in the absence of applicable legislation to prevent any recurrence.[77]

The omission of instructive details in the directives of this time is consistent with the degree to which their authors felt they could rely on constables to make their own prudent judgments regarding matters such as the sexual inclinations of the inhabitants of their boroughs and to come up with measures to achieve the desired but loosely defined objectives. It is likely, therefore, that the reasons constables avoided providing the requested lists and "detailed information" under the 1910 directive targeting queer men lay beyond the text of the directive itself. One plausible explanation, which I propose here, is that the constables who responded to the secret directive were reluctant to expand their mandate of "defending security and tranquility" beyond prominently visible public and semipublic spaces into private apartments. The problem with the directive, it seems, is that it would commit the police to move beyond the policing of indiscreet and highly visible queer spatial patterns to action against queer sex and, more important, socialization regardless of where it took place.

The historical record provides several indications, including the directive itself, that the vision of spatial order pursued by the city authorities was incongruent with readily recognizable male homosexual socialization, but resources for the suppression of this phenomenon were deployed selectively. For example, between 1880 and 1900, a small contingent of constables was routinely deployed to a closed shopping arcade near Nevsky Prospect with the express goal of monitoring and curtailing what we would today call queer cruising (see more about the Passazh and its refurbishment in chapter 3).[78] Police were also regularly deployed to raid the private rooms of the city's large commercial bathhouses (see chapter 4). Despite patchy enforcement, these and other efforts suggest an aspiration on the part of members of the city's administrative hierarchy to hamper homosexual socialization and male prostitution as well as illicit heterosexual encounters by subjecting spaces presumably used for these encounters to surveillance and policing. The regularity and consistency of these efforts, however, is unique to spaces that were at least in principle accessible to the public. The police focused their efforts against spaces of "debauchery" rather than against queer men as a cohort. This does not mean "tolerance" of homosexuality, but rather the operation of a regime of discretionary policing, even when this meant resisting the sporadic enthusiasm of the higher authorities for more aggressive moral campaigns.

The fate of the secret directive of 1910 against the backdrop of arrests on Nevsky Prospect and the stories recounted in Mikhail Kuzmin's indispensable diary suggest that the city government's aspirations were only selectively operationalized by precinct constables.[79] Implementation was limited to certain areas and situations in which a practical impact was realistically attainable and that for some reason—whether an anonymous complaint, the proximity of prominent ministries or embassies, or interference with commercial interest—attracted the eye of the municipal government or threatened to do so.[80] In the resulting entente between queer men, constables, and the broad class of governing agents, a remarkably stable topography of both homosexual prostitution and cruising emerged. This entente consisted of a concentration of police resources—at least those devoted to sexual policing—in several known public or semipublic spaces where the most egregious offenses were observed by the general public or administrative authorities. Queer men of all social classes, by adapting their behavior to what was permissible in each location, could significantly reduce the risk of harassment by members of the police and frequently did so, as suggested by the experience of Kuzmin, the subjects of the secret directive, or even men like Johan and Dmitrii. These instances of policing are entirely consistent with contemporary newspaper clippings in demonstrating that the spatial extent and behavioral scope of this entente was known not only to queer men and constables but also to many members of the public.[81]

As the correspondence engendered by the secret directive of 1910 makes clear, constables played a critical role in negotiating which efforts were to be made to curtail opportunities for sex between men and homosexual cruising. The surviving evidence makes it plausible, indeed likely, that the ambitious vision of spatial order indicated by the directive of 1910 flew in the face of a relatively stable entente about queer policing. Its aims were systematically frustrated by the unwillingness of street constables to expand the scope of their operational mandate and draw resources away from other tasks felt to be more important, including those related to sexual policing in general. This mandate was shaped not only by characteristics of the crime (consensual, noncommercial sex vs. prostitution, rape, or child abuse) and the social class of the offenders (constables incurred greater risks of attracting scrutiny by interfering with the activities of men of a higher social status), as has been previously recognized, but also by the negotiated and selective designation of spaces in which enforcement was feasible with reasonable effort.[82]

Against the background of this geographically selective "moral hygiene," the directive acquires three important dimensions worthy of final emphasis. First, as an expression of the expectations of the highest levels of the police hierarchy, it demonstrates an ambition to expand forms of police surveillance and, possibly, enforcement to private apartments to undercut consensual male homosexual sex and socialization, including—perhaps especially—among men of high social standing. Second, it reinforces a view of day-to-day policing in the late imperial city according to which urban authorities relied heavily on the discretion of constables in determining which actions to take in achieving objectives of spatial order. Third, and most important, the surviving correspondence indicates both the reluctance of constables to accept the implied expansion of their mandate and their superiors' lack of insistence. All three aspects evidence a degree of consensus (or, indeed, an entente) within the police hierarchy about the scope of activities to be carried out by constables in selectively enforcing the vision of spatial order implied in the directive and targeted by other administrative efforts.

Projecting Order onto Urban Space

The exercise of police discretion suggests that a kind of negotiated, even complicit mode of policing announced a disciplinary regime in which authoritarian ambition coexisted with constraints on police action. The resulting picture appears less chaotic than Weissman's portrayal of the tsarist police's "arbitrary and coercive operational style," a picture influenced by hindsight given its subsequent disintegration.[83] The discretionary but broadly predictable style of policing in evidence in late imperial St. Petersburg calls for an acknowledgment of a degree of method, but it also occasions adjustments to the model of disciplinary power proposed by Foucault for the analysis of policing and surveillance in the workings of Western governmentality. The simplified model of the disciplinary society, which pitches popular resistance against monolithic state oppression, is complicated by a more nuanced view in which police discretion is indicative of a systematic compromise between state ambition, police agency, and the motives of "deviant" and delinquent subjects.

The seeds of such a view can be identified in the work of Foucault, according to whom the deployment of specialized police forces contributed to the emergence of a disciplinary society. The earliest, more tentative versions of this thesis (somewhat obscured in the published form of *Discipline and Punish*) linked these developments straightforwardly to the interests of the dominant class in conditions Foucault referred to as a kind of "civil war," such that activities constituting a threat to these interests were efficiently identified and punished as both moral retribution and pragmatic deterrence.[84] The organization of reproduction, its confinement to the family and to private space, as well as the designation of public space for commerce were key interests in this context. Approached in this manner, the directive of 1910 looks like a classic instance of the Foucauldian disciplinary surveillance of sexual impropriety serving to advance this project by combating sex between men. To keep things neat, this view would imply brushing aside the monolithically consistent resistance of constables in boroughs and precincts as merely symptomatic of the poor state of the imperial police. Tempting as that interpretation may be, I have proposed what I believe is a more compelling and contextually consistent alternative that has the advantage of being responsive to the available evidence. Insofar as consistency exists in the action and inaction of lower-level police constables, the dichotomy between state and individual and the narrative of oppressive reordering and resistance needs to be adjusted. These dichotomies ignore the imperfect link between law and subjects, and between the agency of the constables and other administrators charged with operationalizing laws and the visions of order held by their superiors. Patterns of police discretion, aside from constituting that imperfect and often poorly documented link between law and subject, also remind us that constables are themselves subjects of the state. As the known instances of street-level sexual policing targeting queer men in late imperial St. Petersburg indicate, discretion was not necessarily haphazard and could be accompanied by efficient execution and bureaucratic finesse when required. If the measure of its effectiveness was indictment for sodomy or the prevention of any breaches of sodomy laws, the exercise of police discretion was a glaring failure. If, instead, the measure to be applied is an aesthetic one expressed in terms of a spatially and behaviorally differentiated regime of suppression of visible queer socialization, then there are some indications that police measures must be understood as a nuanced and surprisingly autonomous negotiation of the aesthetic principles reflecting the avowed interests of the state with a varied topography of deviance.

Police discretion, as a complication of cruder models of sexual oppression or assumed general toleration, has in fact attracted some degree of attention in discussions of Western cities, but more often as an aside than as a central topic in discussions of urban queer life. Historians including Harry Cocks, Matt Houlbrook, George Chauncey, and Andrew Ross point us toward patterns of police discretion that fail to sit neatly on a spectrum between oppression and toleration. Instead, these patterns consist of apparently lenient oversights in law enforcement in the face of egregious breaches coupled with inexplicably heavy-handed responses in seemingly benign situations.[85] Ross is perhaps boldest in articulating that the explanation for these patterns may lie in the circumstance that police activity was not in fact directed primarily at preventing or punishing the crime of sodomy but rather at managing the most blatant affronts of queer sexual transactions against an aspirational aesthetic of urban space.[86] Instead of representing minor inconsistencies in the process of law enforcement, the discretion of constables thus emerges in sharp relief as soon as one accepts their less formal role in the disciplinary construction of urban space. In St. Petersburg, as in some other locations, constables were not the impersonal agents of an abstract state enshrined in an immutable set of criminal laws, they were creative agents negotiating a locally specific entente between ineradicable deviance and authoritative visions of spatial order.

Outside queer histories, the discussion of police agency has focused mainly on the contemporary Western city and a range of phenomena from benefits and service provisioning to biases in the use of coercive violence against marginalized populations. Michael Lipsky, who has been championing the topic since the 1980s, notes that street-level bureaucracies are often ill-equipped to implement policy as articulated at the highest levels of the state, and therefore they improvise and adopt informal practices that deviate from documented policy. In his 2010 preface to a new edition of his book, he points toward a subtle repositioning of the theory that could be particularly relevant in the context of queer spatial patterns. "The gap between policy as written and policy as performed" is, he writes, at times so significant that "devices [street-level bureaucrats] invent to cope . . . actually *become* the public policies."[87] As a result, "policy is not fixed . . . but negotiated in the course of its implementation."[88] The promise of bottom-up readings of policy from practice, however, sits uncomfortably with the essentializing prioritization of commonalities between state employees in vastly different fields of work and organizations, which treats citizens as they come into contact with street-level bureaucrats as client-sponsors of the state. Related work on so-called pedestrianism in the revanchist city informs this approach to some extent, insofar as it looks more narrowly at the reasons for spatial unevenness in policing, which is understood as involving the work of not only the police but also planners, engineers, courts, and even private entrepreneurs or investors.[89] These discussions have focused on homelessness, begging, immigration, race, prostitution, and political dissent but understandably less on queer spatial patterns. This activity, at least in the contemporary Western cities that have attracted the bulk of scholarship, is either subsumed under prostitution, or is, in the form of cruising, neither illegal nor in fact generally treated as a breach against public order.

The look at historical geographies of policing and police discretion vis-à-vis the queer milieu of late imperial St. Petersburg thus not only complements queer urban histories but also speaks to these broader approaches to the state and policing by highlighting a situation and setting in which police constables could not but recognize the punishment or prevention of criminalized sodomy as quixotic. It was therefore not a question of tailoring impartial policies to the individual but one of the wholesale substitution of informal spatial management for impractical criminal law. Practice here displaced legislation to a degree more extreme than a mere deviation from official policy. The question thus becomes not whether the bounds of discretion were employed in line with the policy objectives but whether the discretion employed was itself consistent and successful in not only pursuing but also articulating an alternative policy and set of objectives to those enshrined in legislation. This is what I mean by "bottom-up readings of policy from practice" that are notably absent in Lipsky's project and that have been the subject of this chapter. Interestingly in this context, in their blurring of the lines between what has been termed "strong" and "weak" discretion in the queer policing of late imperial St. Petersburg, constables could be seen to be "playing the system" to such an extent as to destabilize the very primacy of the association of the police with the bureaucracy, or the state, rather than the street.[90] Their ability to constrain queer spatial patterns was in fact so limited that, in effect, street-level constables had to treat the upper echelons of the police hierarchy as their clients rather than as the queer men with whom they interacted, which would be consistent with most discussions of street-level bureaucracy. Thus, to the extent that enforcing sodomy laws was impossible, the challenge became one to which sex was all but peripheral: How to create a spatially differentiated order that suppressed or at least concentrated in a few acceptable places those behaviors associated with queer socialization that were the most troubling to high-level bureaucrats, informed as they were by anonymous denunciations and internal reports.

Nowhere is this clearer than in the discipline of queer policing in late imperial St. Petersburg, where the police were particularly resource constrained, unaided by supplementary legislation explicitly directed at cruising or male prostitution, and unlikely to make a dent in the actual number of breaches of sodomy laws that took place behind closed doors, even while the management of order in the city's public spaces was of utmost importance to the prestige of both the municipal and national governing autocracy. Police discretion was therefore at the heart of a historically underemphasized and internationally relevant local dialogue between constables, suspected offenders, and the administrative hierarchy. This dialogue deserves broader scholarly attention beyond the present context in order to complement more traditional analyses in queer histories focused on the enforcement of criminal laws, including sodomy laws, and conceptualizations of the state via more or less acceptable deviations from democratically legitimized policy objectives.

As the cases of Zimmel' and Kuzmin and the fate of the secret directive of 1910 suggest, police constables could act quickly and decisively to arrest a putatively queer man on a central street, using expansive administrative expedients to approximate a vision of spatial order communicated by their superiors. But only a few years later they turned a blind eye to homosexual cruising in a nearby park and passively resisted orders from the city's chief of police to expand their mandate regarding queer sexual policing. No evidence suggests that the discretion employed by constables in these instances was merely collusive, simply oppressive, or in fact arbitrary, in the sense that this was so random as to be impossible to reckon with. Instead, the order police enforced in these instances is broadly consistent with the scattered cases and accounts available to us. Raikovskii, the lieutenant, was not arrested because his crimes took place behind closed doors and he did not apparently go out in search of trysts. A number of the men listed in the ministerial dossier discussed in chapter 1 avoided certain places, acting discreetly, but others frequented places of moral surveillance, thus making themselves and their intentions visible to potential partners but knowing how to behave in such places to avoid the risk of arrest. Johan did not hide the dramatic nature of his parting with Dmitrii, but he did not, of course, admit to being in a romantic relationship. This was not a regime of tolerance, and queer men had much to fear not necessarily or not only from the police.[91] Rather, the sensitivity of police responses to behavior, person, and place reflects a regime of spatial governance in which the situational decisions of constables and lower-level administrators were critical instruments, perhaps *the* critical instrument, in managing the queer urban environment and projecting state authority into the city's spaces.

It is in this sense that I seek to nuance Foucault's model of the disciplinary society that has been so convincingly challenged by Laura Engelstein in its application to late imperial St. Petersburg, but to do so by merging it with Foucault's own parallel construction of the police as an "arbiter of illegalities."[92] From the vantage point of such an arbiter, the goal of discretionary policing did not necessarily have to be the extraction of illicit benefits such as sex or bribes, or in fact the detection and punishment of blatant breaches of law and morality. Instead, the probable objective appears to have been much humbler but at the same time unspectacularly pragmatic and more realistic: to constrain certain kinds of activity and people in certain places and at certain times—that is, to manage the urban environment, including its sexual economy and queer spaces. In the resulting "economy of illegalities," to use Foucault's terms, it was perfectly reasonable to expect the display of blatant insinuations of sexual relationships between men to remain unpunished in one area and situation, but in another a man merely suspected of being a "pederast" should be banished from the city for the ostensible crime of soliciting. The reflexive relationship between constables, the subjects of policing, and the police hierarchy outlined in this chapter as a factor shaping the projection of state authority into city spaces contrasts with both the highly abstracted Foucauldian models of collusive or coercive policing and a historical view of the tsarist police in late imperial St. Petersburg as primarily inefficient and secondarily "tolerant" of consensual homosexual sex.

The proposed modified historical hypothesis and theoretical model rereads evidence of police actions and adds new cases of police discretion. I emphasize the critical role played by street-level constables in the spatial projection of administrative power, recognizing their constraints as well as their powers of discretion. This role is realized in the dialogue between what Foucault calls "the impersonal machinery of the state" and its subjects—except that this "impersonal machinery" was not in fact quite so impersonal.[93] Foucault rightly acknowledges that the police, in occasionally colluding with citizens, granted "a little extra life—and, by doing so, suppl[ied] the state with a little extra strength." Nevertheless, in his description of the disciplinary society, discretion can appear as merely another ruse of power and one of many tools in the service of the disciplinary state.[94] In looking at the urban queer milieu and addressing this apparent reductionism in Foucault's view of the disciplinary society, I suggest replacing the idea of collusion with the concepts of *discretion*, compromise, and constant multilateral negotiation, as entertained by Foucault himself in his 1973 lecture on police complicity with rampant law avoidance by the weavers' guild in eighteenth-century France. In the lecture, he described the police as "arbiter in an economy of illegalities."[95] The resulting model fits remarkably well with queer sexual policing in imperial St. Petersburg.

Foucault famously argues that power is not a possession but a relationship. In the case of queer sexual policing, this relationship between queer men, constables, members of the police hierarchy, and the general public required constables to preserve and exercise a degree of power precisely by making compromises. These compromises were tailored to particular situations and negotiated in a discernible fashion with their subjects and their superiors. By replacing collusion with a multilateral compromise involving, among other aspects, the spatial scope of the police's mandate vis-à-vis queer spatial patterns, we not only create a framework that can help make sense of the instances of policing described above, where it is far from evident that constables extracted illicit gain or favors, we also constructively broaden the scope for application of Foucault's concept of an "economy of illegalities."

Taken together, the events described in this and other chapters of this book compose a fragmentary but still cohesive image of queer policing in late imperial St. Petersburg. These events are reflected in the police records of the city, particularly the ones I have chosen to highlight in this chapter—the arrest of Zimmel' for solicitation, Kuzmin's and his friends' recognizably queer but remarkably unencumbered "cruising" behavior, and the ill-fated 1910 secret directive requiring the police to enumerate men in their precincts who had a propensity to engage in homosexual sex. These and other archival materials as well as previous historical work allow us to adjust our view of the queer milieu by juxtaposing and partly reconciling different examples of the ways constables engaged with queer subjects with some of the modalities by which queer policing was made to work in the city.

I hope that the stories told in this chapter are illuminating with regard to certain otherwise obscure aspects of the policing of homosexuality. These aspects include the divergent reactions of street-level constables to orders to penetrate the homosexual milieu by identifying suspected homosexuals and their apartments as well as using ambiguous petty crimes statutes and administrative measures to deal with individuals denounced as queer. As it so happens, these cases are only superficially incongruous and their close contextual reading illustrates the complementary aspects of compromise and discretion that are so central to an understanding of queer policing beyond an instrumental model of law enforcement in the disciplinary society. This is a practice that lies beyond the traditional focus on sexual crimes and law enforcement in the modern-day sense and contributes important nuance to now-classic narratives of gay oppression, resistance, and visibility.

In the context of this practice of queer policing, constables played the crucial role of "arbiters of illegalities," to again draw on Foucault's terminology. Where Foucault describes the police as an arbiter in certain historical circumstances but characterizes the relationship between criminals or deviants and constables as collusive, we can recognize the full implications of discretionary power. The practices of constables in their relationships with queer men include elements that did not constitute mere collusion in the sense of bribery or the extraction of sexual favors. Instead, these elements had much to recommend them to constables by virtue of being discreetly effective in supporting a characteristically urban entente that appeased municipal authorities and morality campaigners insistent on a degree of apparent order, decorum, and public decency in the city's public spaces without requiring impossible and inhumanely exhaustive policing of queer sexuality.

What these cases reveal is not so much the disciplinary power and ambition of the state when it comes to the policing of illicit sexuality, but the role of compromise and discretion in shaping the encounters between queer men and the men on the beat. Even in this famously authoritarian society, the limits to the "eye of power" are obvious in the context of queer policing. It is inevitably tempting to see this merely in the thematics of tolerance or resistance, though both simplify and essentialize the dyad of police and queer victim, thus contributing little to our understanding of the state's responses at the level of streets, precincts, and magistrates courts. Nor should we be led to see apparent tolerance as just another ruse of power, the regulation of an "economy of illegalities" that in the end only serves the interests of the state or a tiny elite. Instead of focusing on the incendiary and familiar fault lines of discipline, resistance, and tolerance, this chapter has made a case for a discretionary model of spatial management that has some of the trappings of disciplinary policing in this imperial city, but can, or perhaps should, also be read as reflecting a nuanced and effective negotiation of behavior at the street level.

The possibility of a systematic link between police discretion and the spatial projection of state authority onto urban space may be particularly relevant for histories of queer sexual policing, though it has received scant attention from queer urban historians. Focusing overwhelmingly on Western experiences, some scholars note discretion and contingency in policing homosexual practices, but the reflexive relationships between constables, the administrative hierarchy, and queer men have been left on the table as topics for further investigation.[96] Given the recognition that depersonalizing the laws and regulations of "the state" constrains the historical discussion of queer sexual policing, a focus on the decisions of constables and police administrators helps us understand how laws and regulations were operationalized or even displaced by other considerations by low-ranking constables who came most directly into contact with the spatial patterns constructed by queer men. In the instances where known practice obviously failed to coincide with legal requirements, anachronistic concepts of tolerance or haphazard inefficiency or even tweaks to explicit policy objectives can be constructively spun into a recognition that constables and queer men negotiated the use of urban space with each other, as they did with other groups in the city. Even a patchy view of the process and results of this negotiation substantively extends our understanding of the historical queer milieu and helps us move well beyond the more generalized question of degrees of oppression. It also provides a telling example of the manner in which the state sought to project visions of moral order onto the city and its queer milieu and, within some of its organs, ranked this objective higher than straightforward law enforcement.

On this basis, it is possible to raise a general caution that decrees and laws, unless informed by an understanding of the practices of the individuals on the front line of their operationalization, are insufficient and potentially misleading bases for a discussion of the historical trajectory of urban sexual policing and the projection of state authority into the city's spaces. To extend and correct such a discussion, it is necessary to lift the lid on what appears to be the transmission box between state and civil society, between law and order, between the higher levels of the administrative hierarchy and queer men, and to reveal not immutable cogs and unwanted grit inside but agents making broadly consistent, far from trivial decisions that in the end accumulate to construct more or less consistent, or at least legible and predictable, informal policies toward queer spatial practices in the city.

Chapter 3

Queer Streetlife

Queer men, like all city dwellers, found challenges and opportunities in the rapid spatial, demographic, and technological transformations so characteristic of urban modernity.[1] Although modernity promised "adventure, power, joy, growth, transformation of ourselves and the world," it also placed "all into a maelstrom of perpetual disintegration and renewal, of struggle and contradiction, of ambiguity and anguish."[2] In late imperial St. Petersburg in particular, rapid urbanization and industrialization during the last decades of the nineteenth century profoundly disturbed and shaped urban life. Coming less than a generation after the emancipation of the serfs, disastrous crop failures in the 1890s uprooted millions of peasants who left their villages in search of temporary or permanent employment in urban areas.[3] In the imperial capital, the decades around the turn of the twentieth century were marked by unprecedented population growth. From 1880 to 1914, the urban population grew by 170 percent, adding on average forty thousand inhabitants per year.[4] Not surprisingly, such substantial migration-driven growth transformed the urban fabric and gave rise to a huge housing shortage, a peak in crime rates, and mass poverty.[5] It created opportunities for large-scale deployment of workers in industrial enterprises as well as for consumption, shopping, and leisure. As Mark Steinberg notes, the streets played a significant role in reshaping newcomers as consumers, pleasure-seekers, workers, pickpockets, prostitutes, cabbies, and others, gradually grinding them urbane.[6] The streets were also, of course, a site of purposeful or accidental encounter in an increasingly crowded and anonymous city. In this chapter, I explore how a particular group of St. Petersburg residents, queer men, structured their social and sexual worlds in response to the stimuli engendered by the city's transformation. Queer men in late imperial St. Petersburg negotiated the crowded streets, trading off the risks and rewards of cruising and socialization in this rapidly modernizing authoritarian city.

In this chapter, I explore the ordering, the experience, and the performance of the queer city in the streets by connecting key phenomena symptomatic of urbanization and modernization to reports of queer life. In the first section of the chapter, I look at cruising by drawing on parallels between flaneurs and queer men, both of whom exploit the unique characteristics of modern urban streetlife for opportunities of observation and exhibition. Then the focus of the chapter narrows to one particular location, the Liteinaia Borough, which was home to Anichkov Bridge and a critical mass of other sites that played an important role in queer spatial patterns. The discussion of this borough helps visualize a panopticon analogous to Bentham's but fundamentally frustrated in its function by seemingly insignificant deviations from the abstract model. From here, the focus once again broadens as we track certain infrastructural themes that penetrated the Liteinaia Borough but also expanded beyond it: public transport, streetlights, and public toilets. All these were, of course, intimately connected to commerce and entertainment as well as to the queer milieu. I conclude the chapter with the story of a particular public commercial space located a few steps from the Liteinaia Borough: the roofed shopping arcade called the Passazh. Its refurbishment uniquely reveals how municipal authorities and the Passazh's owners attempted to enforce a vision of spatial order that was irreconcilable with what we would today describe as cruising.

The Flaneur and the Queer City

Particular attention to modern streetlife in any book about queer history should hardly be surprising.[7] Fleeting opportunities for contact and encounter on and near the streets implied new ways of moving, seeing, and sexually experiencing the city. Queer streetlife put the physical and functional spaces up for grabs and made them host to sexual opportunity and socialization. The spatial and technological innovations characteristic of modernity in many Western cities interacted with the historical fabric of this particular city—its current social, demographic, political, and economic conditions—to frame its queer streetlife.

The resulting transformation of St. Petersburg's busy streets allowed for alternative and divergent types of encounter.[8] If modernity as a category of inquiry is to remain analytically useful, then "it must capture a singular condition or process that all societies experience, albeit in their own ways."[9] This singular condition, I would say, can be provisionally summed up as the creation of "a society of strangers," a condition characteristic of the late modern period but uniquely experienced by each particular city.

The male flaneur, or downtown pedestrian who makes walking and observing his pastime, is the ancestor of the modern tourist. Ostensibly, he watches without any clear objective. His temporary activity defines him, and this activity does not imply a permanent identity. When he is finished being a flaneur, he can go back to being, for example, a government official, a bank employee, or a man of leisure. The category of the male flaneur in the historical city is less restrictive than many other categories.[10] To qualify temporarily, one had to be strolling without going anywhere, observing without becoming a spectator. The flaneur's dress also needed to be of sufficient quality to avoid any confusion of his activity with one that was altogether less respectable and, in fact, illegal: "loitering." If he qualified, however, the flaneur ceased for a while to be the government official, bank employee, or man of leisure (to stick with these by no means exclusive examples) and became someone defined by his patterns of movement in the city, his flânerie. His anonymity was essential to his presumed enjoyment, for his activity was voluntary. As he engaged in it, he was exploiting a paradox between the multiplicity of directed motion and its amalgamation into a directionless business. The flaneur might rightly have claimed that other people's business is his leisure, their visibility his hiding place.

The parallels between the flaneur and men participating in queer spatial patterns are obvious, insofar as the two are, of course, overlapping categories. Both congregate in the city center. Both keep their cards close to their chests, avoiding any exposure of their objectives or even denying that they have any. The movements of both will appear directionless to outsiders. Nevertheless, both are at least potentially recognizable to the attentive observer by these very movements that mark their participation in uniquely urban categories of contingent identity. Like the flaneur, the man participating in queer spatial patterns, who might in fact stop being a flaneur on any given occasion, exploited the anonymity of the city and the business of its streets. The queer flaneur, however, might at least in principle be prepared to signal that he welcomed company, lest he continue his stroll alone indefinitely and remain merely a flaneur. Queer spatial patterns, after all, were like flânerie only insofar as they might appear directionless to observers. To fit that definition, queer spatial patterns had to have at least some participants who carried them out in order to encounter men who shared their desire for illicit sex.

Like the strolls of the flaneur, queer spatial patterns were situationally performative and responsive to what people do most in the street. To address and recognize this, analogously to our attention to day-to-day policing in chapter 2, it is important to revisit the experienced reality of the city's streets, the "production of new kinds of spaces" in the daily lives of many. To this end, as Peter Andersson warns us, it is imperative to avoid getting too "caught up in things like riots or city planning or representations of the street that only a select few have the ability to convey."[11] Beyond the singular events prominently recorded in history books or even the readily retrievable master plans of urban development, the experiences of flaneurs and queer men were shaped by what they encountered when they entered the street. They entered a specific urban topography of man-made and natural spaces, they walked past or even into public toilets, passed under electric streetlamps, and enjoyed the use of a growing transport infrastructure and opportunities for shopping and commercial hospitality or entertainment. All these encounters shaped both their experience and the city's "practiced places" in which queer men met.[12]

In looking at the movements of queer men, the proximity of semipublic or private spaces to the busiest public spaces in the city center is, of course, a key consideration and one that necessarily widens the aperture beyond mere flanerie. My starting point in this respect is the contrast between the panoptic view of a place like Anichkov Bridge, which provides anonymity and a legible spatial order, and the sheltered nature of nearby semipublic spaces that provided opportunities for more explicit spatial improvisation or intimate encounters.[13] Queer men took advantage of both, weaving them together in a single tapestry of spatial patterns as they moved and met in the crowded and illuminated streets, shopping arcades, cafés, theaters, and bathhouses; used new public conveniences and transportation; or met in a park. Characteristic of their streetlife were the opportunities created by the proximity of panoptical and more occult spaces that linked ostensibly innocent flanerie in the former with the possibility of illicit intimacy in the latter.[14]

The material conditions of the street and its dual nature as both exposed and anonymous contributed to the production of the flaneur, whether he be queer, heterosexual, or asexual in his motivations, who walked among strangers and wished to see and be seen. In such a *society of strangers*, the flaneur encounters people and spaces in something akin to narrative continuity, the route of the stroll being intimately connected with the kinds of encounter potentially on offer.[15] Mikhail Kuzmin's "familiar stranger" overlaps with the category of the flaneur. In fact, to most, they are indistinguishable, and that is the point. His movements and objectives are also a play on (or perversion of) the theme of urban indifference.[16] And yet he could be relied upon. He appeared from behind a bend in the park, emerged from a public toilet or confectionery shop, or strolled up and down the balcony in a certain roofed shopping arcade—all according to discernible patterns, which queer men read, followed, and reenacted. Like the flaneur, the "familiar stranger" as a participant in the city's queer milieu could be observed, made himself available to view, and ostensibly displayed an attitude of leisure, but most often failed to be noticed by those using the street merely as a means of getting from the proverbial point A to point B. The queer flaneur, however, was there to meet a "familiar stranger" with whom he had something in common—a desire for illicit sex. Although perhaps keen to appear indifferent and content to be alone, he was not merely an aloof observer. He was implicitly or explicitly a participant in a queer milieu that purposefully penetrated urban space in predictable and retrievable ways. Late imperial St. Petersburg met all the necessary conditions as a setting for the activities of the flaneur and the "familiar stranger," both of whom exploited an atmosphere of indifference, a blasé attitude of city residents to one another. Queer men, whether as ostensible flaneurs or in less discreet appurtenances of the queer milieu, participated in urban streetlife and created a "deviant normal" of flaneurism that was visible and invisible at once.[17]

Queer urban streetlife was thus an important and revealing by-product of the city's modernization. As Richard Dennis observes, "within modern cities, rationalism—the search for spatial and economic order and efficiency, as embodied in planning, zoning and regulation—made space for pluralism—an increasing diversity for social, ethnic and gendered identities."[18] The characteristically modern combination of rationalism and pluralism implied a "production of space" where representations conceived by planners and city authorities were reappropriated and absorbed into the evolving spatial patterns of opportunistic deviance.[19] Geometric lines drawn by urban planners became meaningful, at times "disorderly," elements in people's lives, in both lived space and the spaces of representation, as they were incorporated into "spatial stories," narratives through which individuals relate their urban encounters to places and each other.[20] Queer men's "spatial stories" were, of course, subject to all the factors that shape urban spaces: pedestrian traffic, residential and commercial development, planning and reconstruction in the city center, development of transport and hygienic infrastructure, climatic and natural light conditions, technological innovations such as streetlights, and a fast-evolving culture of consumption and leisure. All these set the text and texture of queer men's relationships with each other and constituted the context for the "shrill, uncouth, and inchoate" Russian, or more specifically, St. Petersburg "modernism of underdevelopment," as Marshall Berman famously termed it.[21]

The Compromised Panopticon of Liteinaia Borough

Nowhere were these "spatial stories" as tightly interwoven as in the city center. The Liteinaia Borough, situated at the heart of modern St. Petersburg and separated from its royal palaces and gardens only by the Fontanka River, features in this chapter as an area that emblematically combined the anonymity of crowds with opportunities for unobserved encounters. In this context, I refer to Jeremy Bentham's panopticon. The metaphor is both a useful and a problematic one in thinking about ways that queer men in late imperial St. Petersburg participated in the life of the streets. As we shall see, the spatial arrangement of the newly developed Liteinaia Borough in the late nineteenth century bears analogy to Bentham's panopticon, but its function was notably perverted. As a technology of discipline, Bentham's panopticon is originally conceived as a circular space with wholly visible prison cells arranged in a circle around an unseen guard. The guard can observe the cells and their inmates whenever he wishes. Since the inmates do not know when they are being watched, they are (in theory) forced to choose either controlling their behavior at all times or risking punishment. This machine is more than just a convenience for the guard. It also does away with any vestige of privacy because the inmates can see each other and begin to exert a disciplinary function vis-à-vis one another.[22]

Recent conceptualizations of the panopticon, however, focus not just on the authoritatively condoned disciplinary effects of observation but on the many secondary effects of urban pedestrian culture. The city and its intensively policed and well-illuminated central boulevards, parks, and squares, in particular, attracted crowds in search of spectacle. The very concentration of bodies in transit or at play ensured that "the audience was very much part of this spectacle." Miles Ogborn traces the panopticon as an urban spectacle—"a machine of vision that created ways of looking"—to the mid-eighteenth century as exemplified by London's Vauxhall Gardens.[23] These "ways of looking" were not necessarily the ones intended by planners and administrators, although in certain places they were, of course, met with benevolent condescension or even encouraged with commercial acumen. Ogborn cites a contemporary observer who understood as early as 1752 that sex was essential to the mix. "'Here the Splendour is so great,'" the observer writes, "'that the juvenile Part of both Sexes may enjoy their darling Passion:—the seeing others, and being seen by them.'"[24] But spectacle was not the only side effect of this unprecedented expansion of busy, wide-open panoptical spaces subject to police surveillance. As Simone Browne notes, the urban panopticon bred methods for prioritizing the attention of those charged with surveillance as well as a gamut of behavioral responses from those most exposed to unwanted attention. The art and habit of "rendering one's self out of sight," is therefore also a characteristic effect of modern surveillance and the panopticon.[25] All these secondary effects as well as the architectural hallmarks of straight vistas across vast and populous urban spaces are in evidence in the Liteinaia Borough of late imperial St. Petersburg. Here, in a grid of broad streets lined with commercial establishments, constables stood in sight of one another and kept watch as pedestrians, shopkeepers, cabbies, and street peddlers exchanged glances, observed, and beckoned to each other. The visual configuration of the Liteinaia Borough shaped queer *streetlife*, which emerged as a permanent interplay between various movements and glances: the vigilant gaze of a constable, a flaneur's idle observation of the crowd, a stroller's look in a shop window, a passerby's fleeting glimpse, or the reciprocated look of recognition between two queer men. A contemporary postcard depicting Liteinyi Prospect shows the seemingly infinite sightlines, pedestrian traffic, horse cabs and electric streetcars, storefronts, and streetlights that all contributed to spectacle, opportunity, and risk in this contested urban panopticon (see figure 1).

FIGURE 1. The contested panopticon of Liteinaia Borough. The image bank "Lori," Izobrazhenie 3072203, Liteinyi prospekt v Sankt-Peterburge: staraia pochtovaia otkrytka, 1909. Courtesy of the image bank "Lori."

The long straight boulevard shown in figure 1 is Liteinyi Prospect, an urban artery of people and vehicular traffic that facilitated the movement of people and goods through the borough and between boroughs; provided access, light, and air to the buildings lining the street; and created opportunities for pedestrians to stop and linger before shops, cafés, and restaurants or wait at tram stops. These functions were not coincidental. The notion that the habits and character of citizens could be welded and improved by shaping urban spaces is what informed policies regarding the physical and functional reconstruction of entire boroughs, including Liteinaia Borough (see map 2).[26]

The destruction of most legacy buildings in Liteinaia Borough and the imposition of a new layout with broad straight boulevards was part of the city's third wave of expansion and reconstruction carried out after 1830 to meet the commercial, residential, and administrative needs of a growing urban population.[27] The reconstruction of the borough provided for wider and straighter streets and thus a better flow of people, animals, vehicles, and air through the city. It even saw the conversion of the two rivers intersecting the borough from picturesque landmarks into useful transport routes, as their waters were deepened and dredged and their embankments enhanced by a multitude of small stairs and jetties. This modern district took into account the physical dynamism of modern urban life. In a telling detail, the pavement was specifically chosen to support vehicular traffic. The borough's even streets were paved with "uniquely durable twin layers of stones."[28] No less effective was the reconstruction of most of its buildings, which enabled an unprecedented rise in population density, and its neoclassical style conjured up the image of modern European or American metropolises.[29]

Nowhere were these modern and European aspirations of the reconstructed borough more palpable than on its central artery, Liteinyi Prospect, which crosses Nevsky Prospect and connects the Liteinaia Borough to the workers' district across the metal and steel Alexandrovskii (Liteinyi) Bridge. Liteinyi Prospect was lined with shops, restaurants, hotels, and cafés, but also had factories and military barracks. It was itself a space for intensely varied encounters. Illustrating the experience of a typical early twentieth-century flaneur, figure 1 shows a man turning the corner near a shop window in the right-hand corner of the photograph. Another man lurches into the street from the left-hand corner to join the almost palpable hustle and bustle on Liteinyi Prospect. The experience of mixing and mingling would have been reinforced by the borough's diverse social composition in terms of the occupations and social status of visitors and residents, which included factory workers, domestic servants, aristocrats, and urban professionals (doctors, administrators, and lawyers). As a contemporary description of the borough informs us,

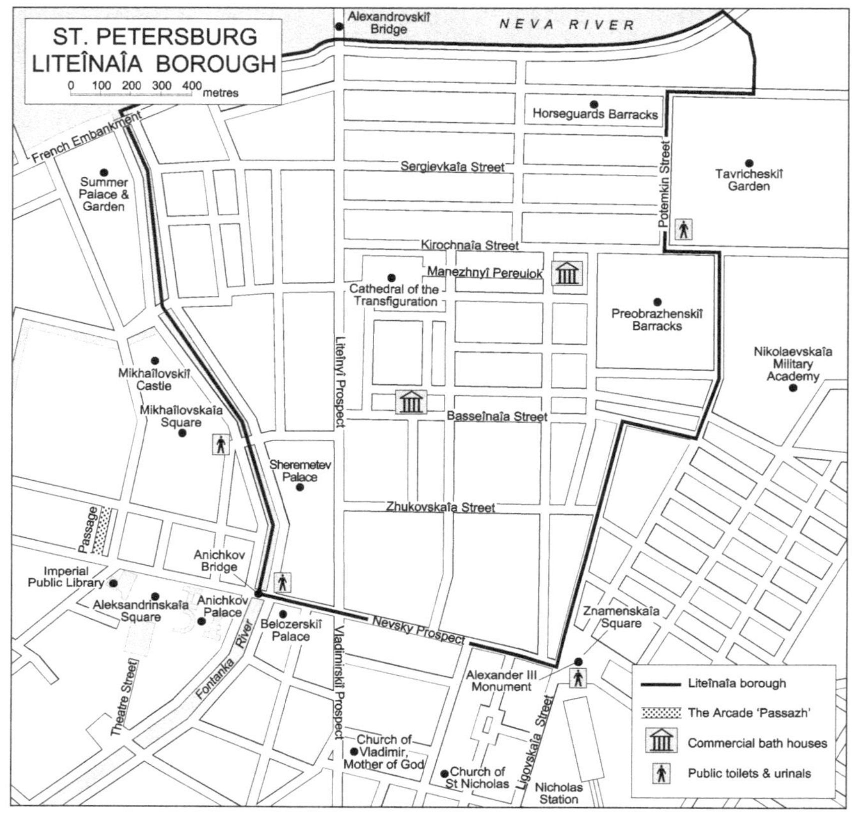

Map 2. Liteinaia Borough and its queer geography.

> The population of the borough differs from the population in other central city boroughs. The streets, including Sergeevskaia, Furshtatskaia, a part of Kirochnaia, and Mokhovaia as well as Gagarinskaia Embankment are populated by the rich and members of the hereditary aristocracy and also by foreigners. The proximity of the Army Medical Academy . . . compels students and professors and other academy staff to choose the Liteinaia Borough. The wide boulevards of the Liteinaia Borough, including the right side of Nevsky Prospect from Znamenskaia Square to Anichkov Bridge [and] both sides of Liteinyi Prospect are occupied by shops. In the fourth ward of the borough, one finds the cartridge factory of the Saint Petersburg Munitions Works with 1,200 workers and the armor factory of the Artillery Division [of the army] with 290 workers. The population of the borough also includes military elements living in the army barracks of the cavalry guards and the Preobrazhenskii Division, the sniper guards, the artillery division, and the Personal Imperial Guards.[30]

The exceptional diversity of local residents that resulted was further enhanced by numerous visitors to the borough, who came to work, shop, or stroll.[31] It created a tapestry of opportunities for the disinterested flaneur and cruising queer man alike.

It is no coincidence that the picture in figure 1 also shows a constable standing in the middle of the street. He looks straight at us and must have caught the photographer's attention as the man most visible, but also as the one with the most privileged vantage point for observation. The constable's position in this spot would have been strictly specified under the city's "reactive system of policing," according to which constables remained at fixed posts and maintained constant lines of sight to at least one, if not several other constables at nearby posts.[32] This approach allowed for the rapid summoning of reinforcements if required and seemed to close any gaps in surveillance. The intensity of police surveillance exercised in the Liteinaia Borough was exceptional compared to other city boroughs. Part of the rationale behind this was the need to protect various prominent institutions and residences located in the borough, including most foreign embassies, several ministries, and a series of palaces, one of which belonged to members of the royal family and another one occupied by the minister of internal affairs to whom the police were subordinated.[33] Analogous to Haussmann's reconstruction of Paris, the layout of the Liteinaia Borough never served just aesthetic objectives. Instead, the borough was laid out and designed in such a way as to facilitate observation and spatial control. Its grid of long wide boulevards created unobstructed lines of sight.

These intersected and facilitated efficient surveillance of all points by constables positioned within shouting distance of one another.[34] The surveillance grid on the streets was supplemented by yard keepers who were obliged by city regulation to keep courtyards closed at all times and who routinely provided information to constables about the goings on in their courtyards and the activities of residents in their buildings.[35]

Analogous to information overload on the internet today, however, the sheer number of people populating the street at any one time made surveillance more problematic than had perhaps been expected. Anything but an open brawl or traffic accident could only be spotted with the minutest and most uninterrupted attention. As the photograph in figure 1 illustrates, the constable standing in the middle of the street could hardly hope to follow the movements of individuals on both sides of the street. If the street offered protection in numbers, any ambition to enforce spatial discipline would have been further frustrated by the many available avenues of escape from the observable realm. A number of archways and alleys, shops, and cafés lined the street. The photograph thus depicts not an ideal "machine of vision" but rather a compromised panopticon in which the lone authoritative observer is rather less effective—except perhaps in a symbolic sense—than the Benthamite model so worrying to Foucault. The legible and open public realm was too crowded and the ample opportunities for escape too proximate to fully yield to the watchful eyes of constables, plainclothes police, and even vigilante yard keepers and citizens.

The police discretion described in chapter 2 may be in part a response to the need to prioritize one's attention as a guardian of the street. It forced police officers to choose their targets, "thereby disregarding trivial factors that guided people's everyday lives."[36] Marking the cutoff for such trivial factors involved a great deal of discretion, as discussed in chapter 2, but it was clear that the wide boulevards of the Liteinaia Borough offered a strategic opportunity to queer men to mold their behavior and patterns of movement in such a way as to exploit the staggering concentration of people, carts, wagons, trams, and animals populating the streets at the busiest hours of the day and night. Here, the metaphor of the panopticon illustrates first and foremost the aspirations of planners but also highlights the impossibility of the ideal model's stringent implementation in a crowded city borough bustling with traffic and commercial activity. As surveillance yielded ground to spectacle, the circumspect flaneur could disappear in the crowd at the drop of a hat, if he ever stood out at all, as could queer men of every stripe and color. In fact, insofar as these two groups were even distinct rather than merely overlapping, constables could hardly hope to reliably track the less disinterested among the flaneurs, thus enabling the urbane strollers to successfully challenge the boundaries between the licit and illicit.

Urban Innovations and Queer Streetlife

Queer streetlife successfully adapted to a number of changes brought about by the modernization of the urban environment, including the improvement of means of public transport, the introduction of electric streetlights, public toilets, and the advent of new forms of consumption and recreation. All these factors affected queer urban encounters and influenced the spatial patterns of cruising. The streets of the Liteinaia Borough were shaped by competing groups and uses. Here in this central borough's public spaces, a wide range of biographies, predilections, attitudes, and behaviors were elaborated. Its largest boulevards, Nevsky Prospect, Liteinyi Prospect, and Nadezhdinskaia Street, wore many guises. They married transient traffic with permanent commercial activity, were at once a destination and a thoroughfare, provided a stage for anyone from advertisers and newspapermen to street magicians and soapbox evangelists, and, of course, they facilitated the characteristic anonymity of the crowd and the convenient confluence of friends and strangers alike.[37] As city planners agreed on the layout and improvement of the streets, investors and entrepreneurs opened shops, restaurants, cafés, music halls, theaters, and shopping centers. Construction workers built them and employees came to serve in them. A wide range of clients, from workers to members of the bourgeoisie and even the aristocracy, came to spend their money in them or simply enjoy the spectacle. Urban intellectuals grappled with the future implications of increasing population density and an accelerating pace of movement, and public moralists lamented the past and criticized the effects of streetlife on morality.[38] Contemporary journalistic and biographical accounts single out streetcars and cabbies, electric lights and window shopping, constables, street musicians, hooligans, and queer men as hallmarks of urban modernity. They are all part of the mosaic of streetlife that created evolving risks and opportunities for queer men. Centrally planned measures such as the appearance of streetcars, the rollout of electric lighting, and the erection of public toilets all contributed to the gradual becoming visible of queer men in certain areas of the city and were all hotly debated by contemporaries in books and the press. These debates together with archival sources and existing histories of the period reveal much about the ways in which the city's residents performed the physical and mental actions required to thrive within the bustling public and semipublic spaces of St. Petersburg's city center.[39]

Public Transport

A visitor to the Liteinaia Borough around the turn of twentieth century would have witnessed a range of modes of public transport, but might not have immediately noticed the opportunities they provided for men to explore transport as a means to participate in queer spatial patterns. A photo of Nevsky Prospect from around this time illustrates some of the various modes of transport available on the streets (see figure 2). Above all, the abundance of horse cabs and streetcars is evident. By the end of the nineteenth century the number of cabbies had grown to over thirty thousand, more than doubling in the seventeen preceding years and roughly matching the rate of population growth. This led, of course, to an ever-more-impressive concentration of vehicles in the city center.[40] Even as early as 1874, as the visitor Theophile Gautier remarked, "what struck me especially was the immense throng of carriages—and a Parisian is not apt to be astonished in this respect!—which were in motion in the broad street; and above all, the extreme speed of the horses!"[41]

The cabbies were a second-rate solution for the city's logistical challenges. Regardless of rapid population growth and the imperial government's initiatives to build out long-distance railway lines connecting the capital to other major cities inside and outside Russia, the municipal government "was far from enthu-

FIGURE 2. Traffic on Nevsky Prospect next to Liteinyi Prospect. TsGAKFD SPb, G6867, Uglovoi fasad doma # 49/2 po Nevskomu prospektu (gostinitsa "Moskva"), unknown author, okolo 1900-kh. Courtesy of TsGAKFD SPb.

siastic about technological innovation in public transport."[42] These attitudes reflected national priorities. The country was more focused on "opening up the east" and was allocating huge investments to the infrastructure development projects that would bring its resources closer to export markets. Nevertheless, shortsighted decision-making by the City Council may have delayed developments in lower-priced alternatives to horse-drawn cabs for individual transport. According to James Bater, the City Council was focused on the taxes and duties paid by the owners of horse cabs, which were expected to decline if multiclient vehicles were introduced. They seem to have missed the bigger picture and the role that convenient mass transport could play in the city's development. Lobbying by the center's landlords may also have had an effect insofar as it required workers, domestic and service-sector employees to live near their places of work.[43] As a result, cabbies enjoyed a certain primacy as means of public transport all the way up to the dawn of World War I and the Russian Revolution.

A cab was, however, not altogether inconvenient for the queer visitor to the streets of the city center, provided he was also a man of sufficient means to afford one. It provided him a view from above the crowd, extended his reach, and was itself a semipublic space in the middle of the hustle and bustle of the crowded streets. Queer men used cabs to travel to popular cruising sites, survey the crowd, and engage in intimate conversation away from the eyes of constables, plainclothes police officers, and even hooligans, all of whom observed the Liteinaia Borough in their different panoptical capacities. Kuzmin, who himself lived in the Liteinaia Borough, recorded in his diary several instances on which he rode along Nevsky Prospect in a horse-drawn cab. In his entry regarding June 4, 1906, for example, he described a drive near Liteinaia Borough, along Suvorovskii and Nevsky Prospects. He wrote in his diary: "Having driven along Suvorovskii, we saw a group of people, three of them were playing accordions and dancing. I told the cabbie to slow down, and then he himself suggested turning back, since, as he said, he also enjoys this type of entertainment. We returned and stopped. The musicians were still playing, but there was no more dancing. The cab driver sang. One of the accordionists came to me and said: 'Shall we ride together?' 'Where?'—'Just along Nevsky, if you like.'"[44]

This passage illustrates several important functions of horse cabs for queer streetlife. First, Kuzmin's ride in a horse cab was part of his cruising practice. The cab provided an elevated vantage point for observation, and at an appropriate speed, individuals could be picked out. Taking advantage of these conveniences, Kuzmin asked the driver to bring the cab up to where he could speak to the street musicians. Incidentally, this is not the only occasion when Kuzmin recollected cruising in a cab. He described several other occasions when he and his friends used a cab for similar purposes.[45]

Second, cabs provided spaces for a conversation or even a degree of intimacy. Kuzmin invited one of the musicians to take a ride with him at the musician's prompting. Once in the cab, they spoke intimately and kissed. With the roof drawn up, this could be done quite discreetly. With the roof tucked away, however, the risks were considerable, as Kuzmin learned on June 4, 1906, when his cab was stopped by a constable and its driver fined for speeding on Nevsky Prospect. (In the context of other cases of queer policing, one might wonder whether the driver of Kuzmin's cab had actually breached any speed limits.) To add insult to injury, hooligans, whose unwanted attention they had also attracted during their licentious ride, attacked them as they alighted from the cab. This did not deter Kuzmin for long. A few days later, he describes an evening on which he first met a man, Pavlik Maslov, who would become his long-term lover. Having met through mutual acquaintances at a restaurant, the two men took a horse cab to Kuzmin's apartment. Kuzmin writes, "Already in the cab he demonstrated his 'literacy' and intrepidness," by which he meant a familiarity with queer sexual possibilities and a preparedness to engage in unambiguous intimacy.[46]

Third, horse cabs facilitated cruising insofar as they made it possible for men from all over the city to gather in certain places in the city center. They quickly delivered men living on St. Petersburg's ever-expanding periphery to the center and dispatched them with equal ease, allowing for a higher concentration of like-minded individuals in established spatial patterns of reunion and encounter. Horse-drawn cabs helped connect Liteinaia Borough to the rest of the city and made its streets, theaters, and eateries attractive and convenient not only for much of the city's population but also residents of the borough. Moreover, cabs shortened the time required to move between cruising sites and apartments, hotels and bathhouses, creating a geographically extended cruising routine.

Fourth, and finally, as Dan Healey explains, cabdrivers in Moscow as well as St. Petersburg "supplemented their income (or simply took pleasure) in this fashion," referring to their willingness to engage in sexual encounters with male passengers, making them immediate and direct participants in the queer milieu.[47] Kuzmin also describes an occasion when the driver of a cab in which he and his shop-clerk friend, Stepan, were riding participated in their homosocial revelry. Stepan "tickled the cabdriver, who laughed and drove on with a gesture as though he were playing a trump. It was stupid, but fun."[48]

Thus, the ever-growing number of cabbies in late imperial St. Petersburg created new opportunities for cruising, which, based on indications from contemporary sources, were essential to the spatial patterns of queer cruising.

Horse-drawn trams, or *konki* in the Russian vernacular, also featured in the production of queer streetlife. Figures 3 and 4 illustrate the defining presence of two-story horse-drawn trams in the central boroughs, where they finally began to appear in greater numbers around the turn of the century. Nevertheless, their numbers were still not nearly sufficient. The two photographs reveal one of their most notorious features: permanent overcrowding.[49] Horse-drawn trams and buses were introduced around 1890, when the shortage of public transport, including cabs, had become a major factor constraining the city's commerce and growth.[50] Even the new trams and buses were soon quite full, but according to contemporary accounts, conductors allowed passengers on until they stood or sat closely pressed together in the overcrowded open-air sections. The resulting intimacy among strangers, the mixing and opportunities for spontaneous conversation, struck observers as emblematic of modern city life.[51] As one contemporary journalist observed, streetcars and trams were part of the adventure of the street, a place for watching and listening in on the variety of people and voices of the city.[52] For queer men, the crowds waiting at tram and bus stops also offered ample opportunity to mingle, exchange glances, and converse. The stops were a natural place to linger. In the Liteinaia Borough, Nevsky and Liteinyi Prospects had intersecting tramlines. Liteinaia was the only borough that had two lines. In 1908, it also became the first borough to be equipped with electric trams. These facilitated even quicker travel to and from the city center as well as

FIGURE 3. Crowds, cabs, and horse-drawn trams on Nevsky. TsGAKFD SPb, E16166, Perspektiva Nevskogo prospekta ot gorodskoi dumy k Znamenskoi ploshchadi, atelier of Carl Bulla, early 1900s. Courtesy of TsGAKFD SPb.

FIGURE 4. A horse-drawn tram and the view toward Anichkov Bridge with a constable standing in the street. TsGAKFD SPb, G18514, Konka na Nevskom prospekte, unknown author, 1906–1907. Courtesy of TsGAKFD SPb.

between various locations within the city center such as factories, barracks, parks, shops, restaurants, and residential areas. Like cabs, the less expensive trams, whether electric or horse-drawn, supported cruising both by allowing men from various boroughs to congregate in the city center and by giving rise to encounters on their decks and at their stops.

Lighting: Streets and Windows

Electric lighting did more than just extend the day on the street; it created an entirely different set of opportunities for shopping, movement, encounter, and entertainment. According to contemporaries, "in the evening the light was switched on and a special life started."[53] In their joint memoirs from the turn of the twentieth century, Dmitrii Zanosov and Vladimir Pyzin highlight the transformational role of electric streetlights. They describe a new nighttime atmosphere in the illuminated streets. For queer men, streetlights played an important role, though not an altogether unambiguous one.

The municipal administration pursued the rollout of electric streetlights with the explicit intention of facilitating nighttime policing of the city's busiest streets.[54] This connection between lighting and surveillance was not unique to St. Petersburg. In rolling out electric lighting in other cities, urban authorities effectively laid claim to the city's downtown spaces, thus emphasizing their intention to exercise redoubled administrative control over them. For example, in nineteenth-century Paris, a key motivating factor for the decision to implement state-operated public lighting was to allow more effective around-the-clock surveillance on high-traffic streets. In the process, electric lighting became "closely associated . . . with the repressive function of the police."[55]

As so often happened, however, these measures assumed a fixed and unresponsive set of behaviors and subjects. This proved to be a fateful miscalculation. Improved illumination opened up the nocturnal city to wider ranges of uses and users. As a result, the difficulty of policing the now-busier nighttime street scene grew in at least equal measure to any benefits of surveillance. The rollout of electric streetlights supported nighttime access to settings where one could patronize a range of new leisure-time establishments, including billiard halls, dance halls, cabarets, smoking lounges, and late-night restaurants or cafés. These activities drew huge crowds and added to the bustle on the newly or better illuminated streets, giving rise to urban nightlife as we understand it today: "a set of socialites played during the hours of darkness, enabled by, and symbolised through, artificial lighting," writes the urban geographer Phil Hubbard. Nighttime promenades, he continues, became "a leisurely amalgam of strolling, loitering, and importantly, gazing at the urban spectacle." Lighting supported the emergence of nighttime strolling and leisure as a characteristic urban ritual in the downtown areas of major Western cities such as Paris, London, New York, and Berlin.[56] St. Petersburg was not much different in this sense. According to an enthusiastic, if decidedly unscientific early twentieth-century account, Nevsky Prospect and other central boulevards and streets were electrically lit and provided a variety of new leisure spaces:

> Nevsky is lit by a sea of lights. Electric lights form a long chain; their glow mixing with that of shop windows, also brightly lit by many smaller lamps. . . . Crowds move along both sides of the street. . . . There are many cafés and overcrowded restaurants, in which the public occupies all tightly packed tables. Here and there the sounds of restaurant orchestras break forth. Horse-drawn vehicles continue their polonaise along and across Nevsky, delivering their passengers to their abodes, others to the many theaters, restaurants, and clubs of the capital.[57]

The difference between electric lights and old-fashioned gas and oil lamps cannot be overstated. Even the early electric arc lights were about ten times brighter than gas lamps, and gas lamps were to oil lamps what electric globes were to the gaslights they replaced.[58] As in London, electricity and spectacle were connected. Electric streetlights not only enhanced the show initially, "it *was* the show."[59] St. Petersburg was not late to the party. A mere five years after Pavel Yablochkov's spectacular presentation of the electric arc light at the Paris Exhibition of 1878, Nevsky Prospect was electrically illuminated from the Admiralty to the Fontanka River. Three years later, this network of lamps already stretched all the way to the Nikolaevskaia Station on Nevsky Prospect and covered a number of other key streets, including the Fontanka Embankment itself and Bol'shaia Morskaia Street.[60] On the eve of World War I, the city center was lit by over three thousand electric streetlamps, most of which were of the newer incandescent kind.[61] In 1912, emboldened by this success to write a history of street lighting in St. Petersburg, the city's onetime chief streetlight inspector, Georgii Semenovich, concluded that in the eyes of many of his contemporaries, a city could not consider itself modern unless it had an extensive network of electric lights.[62]

The bright lights installed at the behest of the City Duma by the Russian branch of Siemens & Halske reinforced the preeminent splendor of the city's central boulevards, which penetrated the Liteinaia Borough and constituted the main arteries of the capital's streetlife during the hours of darkness.[63] In St. Petersburg, darkness could last as long eighteen hours a day, from 4:00 PM to 10:00 AM in December. The newly lit streets and boulevards thus saw an ever-increasing concentration of nighttime activity.[64] Secular trends, such as continued migration into the city, the increase of disposable income and wealth among certain groups of inhabitants, and the improving accessibility of the center thanks to public transport all combined with electric lighting to attract shoppers, diners, partygoers, and flaneurs to the Liteinaia Borough and neighboring boroughs in ever greater numbers.

Bright as it was, this burgeoning nightlife was associated with illicit activity, some of which was queer in nature. Both the journalist Vladimir Ruadze and the author of the ministerial dossier discussed in chapter 1 refer to a number of the locations included in the early days of electric illumination as sites of queer spatial patterns.[65] Nevsky itself attracted queer men from all over the city.[66] Its accessibility, illumination, and crowdedness made it an ideal spot for queer encounters. Just as in central London, it was a site that provided "pleasure in being looked at as well as in looking."[67] The lights, the shop windows, the cafés, restaurants, dance halls, and theaters provided opportunities for queer streetlife, and bright lights connected them all! As one contemporary urban resident recalls, "throngs of people basked in this light, this heavenly light."[68] Far from undercutting illicit activity, lighting was thus critical to mutual visibility among strangers and a factor particularly conducive to queer streetlife. Queer urban historians, including Healey in reference to late imperial Russia, emphasize the importance of the "significant glance" between strangers in the phenomenology of cruising. Healey notes that "the single most important gesture of discreet self-proclamation by men seeking lovers on the street was the significant glance."[69] Streetlight made faces and figures visible, made glances discernible even at a distance, and increased the field of play by drawing bigger crowds of pleasure-seeking men out from work to the city center.

More than streetlights played a role in patterns of cruising. Some of the largest streets were lined with electrically illuminated display windows and brightly lit commercial venues, and in one case even bordered on the well-lit enclosed shopping arcade known as the Passazh (see figure 5). In fin-de-siècle St. Petersburg, "much attention was paid to such displays . . . with the use of lighting for effect, and various stars made of electrical lights."[70] For queer men, illuminated display windows or windows at various venues provided an excuse to linger and look at the displayed goods and interiors—to engage in "window-shopping" even at night, when most stores and some venues were

FIGURE 5. Passazh, electrically illuminated after its reconstruction. TsGAKFD SPb, E539, Vnutrennii vid Passazha na Nevskom, vpervye osveshchennogo elektrichestvom, atelier Carl Bulla, shortly after 1901. Courtesy of TsGAKFD SPb.

shut. Mark Turner connects practices of cruising and window-shopping. His analysis of autobiographical sources and court cases suggests that shop windows provided queer men with that ever-important sheen of deniability as they lingered with their backs to the street, able to discretely exchange glances or even engage in brief conversation.[71] Queer men in the well-lit shopping districts of the Liteinaia Borough could stop at the many illuminated windows to follow up on a fleeting glance from a like-minded stranger and strike up an initial acquaintance. Internal public or semipublic spaces situated along the streets and boulevards of the Liteinaia Borough were also more and more often electrically lit well into the night, creating further opportunities indoors. It is perhaps no coincidence that the formerly gloomy Passazh shopping arcade, which will be discussed in more detail toward the end of this chapter, regained its status as one of the most famous or infamous cruising sites after its reconstruction and the installation of electric lamps in 1901.[72]

Public Urinals

As a third technological innovation contributing to queer spatial patterns in the city center, public conveniences were no less important than public transport and lighting in creating opportunities for queer men to meet. By commissioning the installation of public urinals, the municipal government unwittingly created a network of public, freely accessible male-only spaces, where opportunities for sex or sexual reconnaissance were helpfully concentrated. Urinals were constructed in streets and stations shortly after the introduction of a municipal wastewater system in 1871.[73] They constituted a liminal social space in which the unique interplay between public and private sustained complex opportunities for an explicitly sexual approach or encounter.

The use of public toilets for spontaneous and anonymous sex is an archetypical urban phenomenon with a long cosmopolitan history. For example, in his history of queer London, Matt Cook describes the role of the public urinals near Piccadilly Circus.[74] Matt Houlbrook, who also writes about London, describes the practice of "cottaging" (engaging in homosexual acts in a public toilet) in the interwar years.[75] William A. Peniston describes public urinals as favored locations for queer sexual encounters in late nineteenth-century Paris.[76] Most recently, in his work on the queer geography of nineteenth-century Paris, Andrew Ross devotes an entire chapter to public urinals, which he describes as critical, albeit partially counterproductive, instruments in successive municipal administrations' efforts to discipline, contain, and enable the male body. In effect, public urinals in Western cities were important sites of queer sociability and actively "shaped the particular ways men met one another."[77]

According to historical sources testifying to life in late imperial St. Petersburg, public conveniences were fewer and farther between but nevertheless important to the city's queer milieu. As in Paris, their location and layout influenced the ways queer men used them to initiate sexual encounters. The dossier discussed in chapter 1 singles them out as key sites of encounter and sexual reconnaissance. The public toilets located in or along the periphery of the Liteinaia Borough were architecturally very different from one another, but, according to the dossier, even the smallest and most exposed served as hubs for queer spatial patterns. By the early 1890s, pedestrians in the Liteinaia Borough could steer themselves toward public urinals on the Fontanka Embankment near Anichkov Bridge, on Znamenskaia Square, in the Tavricheskii Garden, by the Mikhailovskii Manezh, or on Mikhailovskii Square.[78]

The appearance of these urinals in or near the Liteinaia Borough was a relatively recent phenomenon at the time. The city's first public toilet, or so-called *retiradnik* (from the French verb "retirer"—to withdraw) did not open near Mikhailovskii Manezh on Mikhailovskii Square until the summer of 1871. This public toilet was a characteristically urbane, fashionable, and expensive affair. Its design was ambitiously responsive to local constraints and the municipal government's somewhat self-conscious aspirations for cleanliness and propriety. Underscoring the importance of the project, the architect commissioned to design and supervise the construction of the first public toilets in the city was none other than the mastermind behind the build-out of the city's sewage and freshwater systems, Ivan Merts. Conveniently, Merts was also a prominent member of the City Council. As he explained, not without a certain stake in the matter, "the lack of public toilets in a city as large as St. Petersburg comes as a surprise to everyone and especially to those who have had the opportunity to visit the big cities of Western Europe and see these conveniences there almost ubiquitously. St. Petersburg's backwardness compared to the generally accepted norms of Western European cities, of course, results partly from the severity of our climate, our hard frosts, and finally, from the lack of proper underground canalization to evacuate sewage from the city in general and from each house separately."[79] Merts's observations about the Petersburg climate are pertinent and indicate one difference between the city's experiences and the more familiar Western European exemplars. The first public toilet was a well-insulated wooden structure in which the temperature could always be kept comfortably above the freezing point. It had two externally symmetric but internally differentiated halves with a separate entrance on each side—one for women, one for men. Each side had a guard who doubled as a stoker. Guards were employed by the city and served in shifts to permanently heat, monitor, and clean each site. They were posted to small guardrooms next to each entrance and entered the interior space through a door from their watch room.[80] Merts's public toilets were aesthetically conservative, replete with a decorative roof, two small courtyards, high ceilings, and brass fixtures, but technologically quite up to date, with heated running water and effective plumbing.[81] A mere five such *retiradniki* were built in the 1870s and only a few more followed in the 1880s and 1890s. A competing, drastically simpler design emerged that included only urinals for men and had no doors or heating. The first four such toilets were installed before the turn of the century. The overall pace and scale of this initiative was far from impressive, however. By the turn of the twentieth century, St. Petersburg had a grand total of thirteen public toilets, not counting ones installed in railway stations and other public buildings. All were located in the city's central boroughs. By contrast, Paris had around 3,500 public toilets or urinals as early as 1893.[82] St. Petersburg's citizens, including its queer citizens, were underserved by the municipality.

Despite their small number, however, public toilets in St. Petersburg still played an important role in the spatial patterns so characteristic of queer life in the city center. Most if not all of the newly built public toilets were in or next to major cruising sites. Some of these sites, such as the Zoological Garden and the Fontanka Embankment near Anichkov Bridge, may have risen to prominence as sites of queer spatial patterns in part owing to the installation of public toilets there. The available reports of their role in queer spatial patterns concur about one thing: St. Petersburg's public toilets served queer men primarily for what I have referred to as sexual reconnaissance. Echoing the anonymous dossier from the 1890s, Ruadze describes the activities of queer men near the Mikhailovskii Manezh around 1908: they "form entire processions . . . queues. They familiarize themselves with [each other's] intimate anatomy, and then agree where to go next."[83]

It is not improbable that the change in design of public toilets at some point during the late nineteenth century already reflected much earlier observations similar to Ruadze's, as well as a number of other constraints that pointed in the same direction toward far less elaborate public toilets offering less room for privacy or unseen illicit activity. In any case, the next generation of toilets, to which the ones near Anichkov Bridge belonged, were spartan indeed compared to those conceived and built by Merts. Instead of the large, decorative brick building with small courtyards to either side, the new design consisted only of a small, erect metal tube containing two separate urinals. The grand designs of the imperial city gave way to the embarrassing functionality of cost-effective hygiene infrastructure. The design, however, struck a very different balance between privacy and publicity. It reduced privacy to a degree that challenged the borders of propriety that were so assiduously observed in Merts's design. By the same token, the new design seemed destined to inconvenience the kind of homosexuality that was recognized as arising in closed, publicly accessible spaces not only in St. Petersburg but also in the cities of the West. In this, however, it was only half successful.

An early twentieth-century photo of Anichkov Bridge shows a public urinal in the foreground. It was one of four similarly shaped iron urinals set up in the city center. It handily illustrates both the constraints and opportunities afforded by this type of urinal for queer *streetlife* in the Liteinaia Borough (see figure 6). This tubular construction lacked doors and was permanently open to both the street and the sky. A circular exterior enclosure provided privacy by blocking the view from the outside. A T-shaped interior wall divided the internal cylinders into halves separated by a wall. Each half offered enough room for two men to stand in close proximity but hardly enough room to move, let alone risk engaging in criminal sex without closed doors and near a permanently manned police post.[84]

While not, perhaps, convenient for a sexual encounter, such urinals were used for the kind of sexual reconnaissance described above, according to several reports.[85] Ruadze's pamphlet and the ministerial dossier attest to the importance of even these simple public urinals in facilitating queer spatial patterns. Archival

FIGURE 6. The public urinal near Anichkov Bridge. TsGAKFD SPb, E17035, Anichkov most i panorama naberezhnoi reki Fontanki s vidom na Anichkov dvorets, atelier Carl Bulla, 1910s. Courtesy of TsGAKFD SPb.

sources corroborate such claims. These include the anonymous letter from 1900 that led to the arrest of Zimmel'. In it, the author decried the inaction of police and complained that "pederasts primarily gather around Anichkov Bridge next to the urinals, and in the evening next to the water closets at the Moscow Train Station."[86] The dossier similarly mentions these two toilets in the same breath, referring to the toilets near the train station by their address on Znamenskaia Square. Neither anonymous denunciator draws any attention to possible differences in the activities that went on in and around the small tubular urinal by Anichkov Bridge and the elaborate toilets on Znamenskaia Square. In terms of their role in the queer milieu, it seems that both held their obvious attractions. In the case of the larger toilets, the benefit of doors and heating was at least partially canceled out by the presence of a guard, whereas in the case of the small tubular urinals, the constraints on the space were mitigated by the difficulty of observing the minor misdemeanors that went on inside (see also figure 7, which illustrates the typical hustle and bustle on and around this bridge). In the end, much as in London or Paris, St. Petersburg's public toilets—designed, of course, to clean up and sanitize the city center—had the opposite effect in many cases and became hubs of queer interaction. Thus, the small number of public toilets and their concentration around the Liteinaia Borough had, if anything, the effect of increasing the importance of that borough and each such facility for the queer spatial patterns woven around them.

FIGURE 7. Crowds, cabs, and tram on Anichkov Bridge. TsGAKFD SPb, G6918, Konka na Anichkovom mostu, atelier Carl Bulla, 1906. Courtesy of TsGAKFD SPb.

Passazh: Shopping Center Turned Cruising Site

Very near the Liteinaia Borough and also off Nevsky Prospect was a shopping center called the Passazh. It doubled as a thoroughfare connecting Nevsky Prospect to the parallel Italianskaia Street, which intersected with another frequently mentioned nexus of queer spatial patterns, Mikhailovskii Square. The Passazh was completed in 1848 and consisted of a deep building enclosing a narrow street. The building had a glass roof, following the model of similar luxurious shopping arcades in the centers of Paris and London. On either side of this narrow street, or passage (hence the name), were initially located warehouses, shops, apartments, and a concert hall. By the late nineteenth century, it also housed a famous restaurant, a café, a billiard hall, a hotel, a bank, a miniature museum, and even a zoo described by Fyodor Dostoyevsky in his short story "The Crocodile: An Extraordinary Event; or, a Passage in the Passage." On the second floor, the shops were accessible on either side from a gallery-like balcony running the length of the building and from which it was possible to look down onto the neatly tiled floor of the central ground-floor passage (see figure 8). This balcony was perhaps the most recognizable cruising site in all of St. Petersburg, at least for those who were positioned outside the queer milieu. By the 1860s, it had gained a reputation as a preferred site for queer encounters.[87] Soon afterward, in

FIGURE 8. The Passazh at Nevsky Prospect 48 after its reconstruction. TsGAKFD SPb, E16717, Zdanie Passazha, atelier of Carl Bulla, early 1900s. Courtesy of TsGAKFD SPb.

what was a well-publicized police sting operation and subsequent public trial, members of the so-called Mikhailov Gang, a group of young blackmailers, were caught and prosecuted in 1875. They had been approaching queer men in the Passazh as well as at a nearby restaurant, Dominic's.[88] During the last decade of the nineteenth century, the upper gallery was variously described as a space in which young men chatted in low voices; middle-aged laymen picked up soldiers from the nearby military compounds, sometimes for pay; and cross-dressers and boys wearing the attire of apprentices watched and walked in small groups.[89] Queer activity was apparently hardly hidden and could be observed throughout the day. The Passazh was not physically shut at night: it remained well-lit then and during the long, dark winter days.[90]

The strolls and encounters of queer men in the balcony and ground-floor passage of the Passazh communicated seamlessly with the many queer spaces located nearby. These included hotel rooms directly accessible from the Passazh as well as the two largest commercial bathhouses in the city, the Znamenskie and Nekrasova Baths, which were only a short walk away. Similarly, it was not far from a number of restaurants offering private rooms. Immediately adjacent were also the busy and crowded sidewalks that stretched along Nevsky and the Fontanka Embankment from the Anichkov Bridge to Ciniselli Circus in one direction and to Znamenskaia Square in the other. Finally, St. Petersburg's smaller equivalent of Hyde Park, the Tavricheskii Garden, was less than two kilometers away from the Passazh. Even after extensive reconstruction from 1898 to 1901 following a fire, the Passazh remained an important queer hub. It did so irrespective of the fact that the reconstruction included several spatial modifications that constrained cruising activity.[91] When the Passazh reopened, its "moral" cleanup was quick to attract notice: "Not long ago I step into the Passazh and see the young lady students of one of the boarding schools walking in pairs in a long column and under the watchful eyes of their educators. This fact, itself not very significant, is of great importance for the Passazh. It categorically confirms the success that has been achieved in the attempt to remove from the galleries of the Passazh *the undesirable element*, which formerly so unfortunately affected sales, prior to major reconstruction."[92] Despite this observer's enthusiasm, the journalist Vladimir Ruadze insisted that the Passazh remained a meeting point for men on the lookout for sex with other men or had firmly reestablished itself as such a site even at the time of his writing in 1908.[93]

Queer men were not alone in according the Passazh a favorable rank among the places one might visit for stroll. In St. Petersburg, aside from a few luxurious bathhouses, which will be covered along with less luxurious ones in chapter 4, the Passazh was rivaled in style, scale, and elegance only by government buildings and a few private palaces, but it was freely accessible to the public, stood as a monument to consumption as a leisure activity, and symbolized the city's aspirational connection with other modernizing European capitals. Like the Parisian arcades, the Passazh illustrated even more clearly than the shop-lined streets and boulevards the elevation of shopping to the status of a respectable pastime. Here, as in Paris, visitors did not have to compete with carts, trams, carriages, and people moving to and from work.

The Passazh was uniquely valuable to residents and visitors of St. Petersburg, queer and not queer alike. In Paris, where one of the unique features of this type of space, protection from the elements, was far less critical, over fifty roofed passages or arcades were built between 1790 and 1850, and a similar trend developed in London. No such emulation of the concept took place in St. Petersburg. Despite its apparent success, the Passazh remained unrivaled during the late nineteenth and early twentieth centuries as a luxurious enclosed shopping facility in a city, where leisurely shopping in the outdoors for long stretches of the year required a great deal of hardiness.[94] In poor weather and for people wearing fancy dress, it was one of very few options for such an activity and certainly the most elegant one. The floors in these traffic-free spaces could be kept immaculately clean. Visitors marveled at the polished tiles. Here, this made all the difference. The mud and grime of horse-drawn transport passing through perennial sleet and snow would have been especially irreconcilable with a leisurely stroll. This gave the Passazh a certain seasonal pride of place during the long winter months as the geographical center of a certain kind of leisure culture but also of the city's queer milieu.

As a modern urban phenomenon, the arcades in Western Europe have attracted much scholarly attention. The German philosopher Walter Benjamin wrote about the Parisian arcades as the prototypical form. He suggests that Paris's arcades uniquely connected industrial capitalism with a broad section of the urban population during the nineteenth century.[95] In his history of this space, he describes them as part of the "phantasmagoria" of modernity, presented in distilled and attenuated form. The arcades promoted a commodity fetishism that displaced the previously all-important association of the value of a thing with its usefulness or the amount of labor required to produce it.[96] According to Benjamin, things were no longer valued for what they did or what they were worth but for how new and fashionable they were. In St. Petersburg's Passazh, homosexual sex, whether paid for or exchanged freely, was offered for consumption by men eager to cater to the fashions of the day. Even sexual fetishes fell into commoditized categories. Contemporaries write of times and areas in the Passazh where well-dressed "aunties" or *tetki* strolled up and down, where cross-dressers, soldiers, and apprentice boys offering sex for pay stood in habitual places and waited to be approached, and where students watched and mingled. In other parts of the Passazh or at other times, young workers smoked alone or in small groups, university and gymnasium students cruised and mingled with friends, and so on.[97] The reconstructed Passazh figures prominently as one of the city's main cruising sites.[98] After a brief hiatus during and immediately following the reconstruction, queer spatial practices adapted and perhaps became even more brazen. The Passazh's value for members of St. Petersburg's queer milieu was hard to beat. Strategically located in the vicinity of several queer sites, including two of the city's largest bathhouses, and surrounded by the part of the city center with the most active commerce and nightlife, it offered opportunities to linger and stroll in an enclosed space during the cold, dark months of the year. It is an example of the continual interplay between efforts to rationalize the layout of urban spaces by investors, architects, and city administrators and the behaviors of their residents, who apprehended and exploited these transformations in intuitive and opportunistic ways.

Urban innovations in the final decades of the imperial period shaped queer streetlife in St. Petersburg. The effects of these innovations were often far from obvious and not necessarily those expected by their proponents. In this context, Peter Andersson stresses the "multiplicity and simultaneity of the city beyond the procrustean language of modernity" as a partial explanation for the unpredictability of the effects of spatial modifications.[99] The queer streetlife of late imperial St. Petersburg emerges as both performative and responsive, situationally opportunistic in a modernizing public realm, and fundamentally characteristic of the metropolis. The growth of shopping and commercial hospitality, public transport, electric lights, and public toilets all played important roles in queer socialization and shaped the way queer men entered and used urban streets. Public transport provided a privileged vista and connected queer cruising sites to the expanding urban periphery and various semipublic locations in the city center. The introduction of electric streetlights coincided with and aided the advent of a range of new leisure activities, including new forms of commercialized urban spectacle. Public urinals were focal points of queer streetlife and served as public spaces out of the public eye. The role of specific cruising sites and the frustration of attempts to counteract the attachment of queer valences to these sites suggest the hardiness of queer spatial patterns, as illustrated by the reconstruction of the Passazh. This strange and often surprising fate of efforts to rationalize the layout of urban spaces and thus to reduce "illicit activity" in them carries us into chapter 4, in which I tackle the interaction between attempts to "clean up" the city's commercial bathhouses and the persistence of queer spatial patterns carried out in them.

Chapter 4

Bathing in the Queer City

Ten of St. Petersburg's sixty commercial bathhouses were completely or partially sealed by the authorities in the summer of 1887. Where the closures were partial, the so-called *nomernaia bania*, or family sections, which offered private bathing spaces by the hour, were shut and sealed. The closures took place on the authority of the previously discussed emergency legislation—specifically, the Security Law of 1881. The relevant injunctions note breaches of sanitary norms but as grounds for closure prioritize the allegation that operators had acquiesced to activities that had turned their baths into "dens of debauchery."[1] One of the bathhouse operators, a man named Adrian Gustov, submitted a telling affidavit in which he pleaded for permission to reopen and blamed any possible instances of prostitution in the *nomernaia bania* on attendants whom he had long since dismissed. As he did not hesitate to point out, this section alone ensured the economic sustainability of his operation.[2] When his and several other bathhouses were allowed to reopen, quite plausibly to avert the threat of bankruptcy, the hours of operation of the *nomernaia bania* were restricted to exclude nighttime.[3] The seemingly desperate petitions of Gustov and his colleagues or competitors are only the proverbial tip of the iceberg testifying to the failed reform of the city's commercial bathing facilities. This chapter seeks to reassemble the story to include what lies below the waterline. It is the story of a botched effort to raise bathing practices to a higher sanitary and moral standard. From 1879 to 1914, this effort claimed the attention of a generation of municipal legislators, medical professionals, and sanitary inspectors. It also threatened to erode the bottom line of operators and investors in a sector vital to the health and leisure of a large cross-section of the city's population. When all was said and done, however, it had little practical effect other than to produce a few adjustments to the way commercial bathhouses were set up and run and, as an inadvertent consequence, to reinforce the commercialization of homosexual sex as a feature of urban bathing spaces in late imperial St. Petersburg.

Even before the onset of reforms, these spaces were home to an internationally unique culture of communal bathing that accommodated and facilitated sex between men. And yet this culture was not frozen in time. Noting its evolution during the last decades of the imperial era, Dan Healey sees this "most singular institution of St. Petersburg's pre-revolutionary homosexual subculture" as a transition between two distinct phases of male prostitution.[4] He briefly explains that the more or less egalitarian work teams of attendants who pooled their earnings from sex with male patrons were replaced by tightly run commercial organizations of young male sex workers managed by an attendant, who was usually older. Healey notes that the "temporal threshold" between these two phases "remains indistinct from existing sources," thus placing it somewhere in the last two decades of the nineteenth century.[5] I believe that the Bathhouse Ordinance of 1879, which was yet to be retrieved at the time of Healey's writing, and the renegotiation of unofficial rights over the city's bathing spaces it necessitated are the most likely drivers of the increasing commercialization of male prostitution in bathhouses observed by Healey. This shift as well as the underlying role of bathhouses in the city's homosexual milieu further illustrate how the negotiation over space took place.

In this chapter, I look at the urban adaptations and peculiarities that made communal bathing in St. Petersburg so notably convenient as a context for queer encounters. From here, I go on to examine how the goalposts in the negotiation over this space shifted in response to government action in the form of the Bathhouse Ordinance of 1879. I describe how and why this unprecedented and ambitious legislation failed to achieve the intended reforms and instead reinforced queer spatial patterns and the commercial role of sex in the city's bathhouses. The failed reforms provide an important example of an evolving entente and negotiation regarding the city's queer spaces among urban administrative authorities, people who had a pecuniary interest in bathing, queer men, and the general public.[6]

Urban bathhouses were the site of a decidedly mainstream activity, but not an unproblematic one. As Ethan Pollock, the preeminent historian of Russian communal bathing, writes, they held a "privileged place as a marker of Russian identity." And yet the "late imperial Russian banya was both about 'hereditary love' of Russia *and* about sexual and moral transgression."[7] It is hence unsurprising that municipal and national authorities struggled to reconcile the disorderly actual practices of urban bathing with various competing ideals of social communion and hygienic ablution. Even contemporary Russian commentaries from the second half of the nineteenth century were pointedly divided as to whether Russian baths aspired to be trailblazing machines of rationalistic public hygiene to be held out as beacons to the West or, rather, ready-made bastions of traditionally Russian communion worthy, in all their sleaze, fun, and grime, of protection from Westernizing influences.[8] In fact, they were both. The tension between actual practice and conflicting ideals of bathing very much defined the struggle of St. Petersburg's municipal administration to manage this particular urban space and the persistence of sexual deviance within it. Toward the end of the imperial era, however, spatial regulation not only failed to bring under control what went on in the semipublic spaces of St. Petersburg's commercial bathhouses in the intended manner, they in fact underpinned the status of commercial bathhouses as the city's preeminent semipublic queer spaces.

How it happened is important. Over almost three decades of negotiated noncompliance, amendments to legislation, unsuccessful petitions, and subtle adaptations by owners and attendants, commercial bathhouses not only retained but even reinforced their place in the queer city. In St. Petersburg, the drive to extend governmentality robustly into the city's commercial bathhouses backfired. The defense and redoubled designation of bathhouses as hardly governable spaces available for illicit activity, including sex between men and male prostitution, was not achieved as a result of any resistance on the part of queer men. Instead, a proxy war pitched the exigencies of individual economy and powerful commercial interests against the concerted efforts of spatial governance by municipal authorities. Queer men gained in the mix. As this interplay reveals, the illicit practices associated with bathing remained largely beyond the reach of city authority precisely because they were nestled within the commercial sector. The social, affective, and sexual "commons" of St. Petersburg's commercial bathhouses, invitingly accessible for a relatively small fee, simply did not conform to the injunction that bathing be relegated either to the "private realm of the modern bathroom or the controlled space of public baths," which would have precluded the inappropriate mixing of people and pleasures.[9]

Thus, the city government's attempts to draw commercial bathhouses into an emerging public health movement ran out of steam due in large part to the fact that the city's bathing spaces were primarily subservient to commercial interests, unlike the spaces predominant in the West. As a result of inexperience in tailoring legislation to commercial incentives and the degree of discretion involved in spatial governance, these reforms inadvertently reinforced the role of queer spatial patterns as a mainstay of communal bathing.[10] The chapter tells the story of the commercial bathhouses' successful cultural and economic adaptation to the new era's legislation and constraints. The ordinance marked the transition from a bathing tradition in which prostitution was peripheral to one in which it was central to the commercial viability of this singular urban space.

Village Bathing Comes to the City

Water has long been an unruly force in St. Petersburg. The city's historical geography, its very mythology, is inseparable from the waters that surround, underlie, and interpenetrate it. Control of water has been essential to the Russian "imperial projection of power" in the capital since the time of Peter the Great.[11] Built on a swamp, furrowed by many rivers flowing into the Gulf of Finland, St. Petersburg, through all the decrees of tsars and presidents, has continually been confronted with the uncontrollability of water, most notably in the threat and reality of regular floods.[12]

Despite this abundance of water, St. Petersburg's rivers have typically been inaccessible for bathing and washing from October to May, when they are frozen over or covered with moving ice. In imperial St. Petersburg, with fuel also at a premium, Russians turned to another property of water to keep themselves clean. Instead of washing primarily with directly heated water, they found that steam offered the most economical solution, for one can sweat alongside others in a small space and then wash briefly with water at a temperature barely above the freezing point.[13] This technology obviated the need to thaw and transport vast quantities of water or bathe in holes in the ice, then reemerge into air temperatures dozens of degrees below zero.

Steam bathing, however, relies on cooperation and economies of scale. These could be harnessed most effectively in the form of communal bathhouses, which were a prominent feature of St. Petersburg long before the modern era of communal bathing in the West. Soon after the founding of the city in 1703, numerous bathhouses cropped up on the banks of the Neva. Construction workers and soldiers, forcibly recruited from the villages, built bathhouses in the manner they had observed and employed in the countryside. These bathhouses were physically familiar and the bathing practices in them had not yet substantially deviated from their rural precedents. Indeed, as described by the eighteenth-century historian Andrei Bogdanov, the earliest bathhouses in

St. Petersburg were small wooden huts in which men and women bathed together and which were collectively maintained and used.[14] In this way, Petersburg's citizens reproduced the norms and traditions of village bathing cultures in the city, and in so doing implicitly asserted their right to such amenities.

The new urban strand of the Russian bathhouse tradition began, however, to develop along its own trajectory quite soon. As early as 1704, St. Petersburg's bathhouses came under the influence of government regulation when Peter the Great noticed the small wooden bathhouses appearing along the riverbanks and decided to regulate and tax them.[15] The construction of bathhouses was henceforth restricted to certain parts of the riverbank, and they had to be built of stone and brick rather than wood. In addition, Peter the Great instituted a *bannyi nalog*, or bathhouse tax.[16] The burden of taxation necessarily favored large commercial bathhouses because it reinforced economies of scale. By 1751, the city had nine frequently visited commercial bathhouses, all of them cavernous and imposing.[17] A generation later, in 1783, mixed-sex communal bathing was outlawed in the city's commercial bathhouses in the interest of sexual propriety and spatial order, thus severing yet another link to village bathing traditions.[18] Finally, in 1843, price regulation was implemented, which had a defining effect on the subsequent evolution of commercial bathhouses, as it split the urban bathing public along economic lines.[19] Importantly, all these regulations were creative rather than transformational. They shaped an institution that was only just coming into being instead of trying to transform an already well-established one.

By the middle of the nineteenth century, however, the city's commercial bathhouses had gained institutional momentum and established themselves as distinctive spaces for ablution and certain manners of communion. In 1847, forty commercial bathhouses served an urban population of almost half a million residents.[20] The largest bathhouses offered all classes or levels of service under one roof with separate male and female sections corresponding to each level (see figure 9).[21] The scale and segmentation of these bathhouses made it possible to satisfy the needs of customers according to their means and preferences, to create more homogeneous—in some cases homosocial—environments in each section. They also maximized income for bathhouse owners. To borrow Peter Bailey's useful neologism, the commercial bathhouses were "segregarious"—that is, they provided communality tempered by disciplinary separation, albeit along gender and class lines rather than the more traditional separation into social estates.[22]

In the third-class section, the *prostaia bania* (or simple bathhouse), for instance, the washing facilities usually doubled as a self-service laundry. The steam room was often heated *po-chernomu*, that is, without a chimney, as in the villages, and

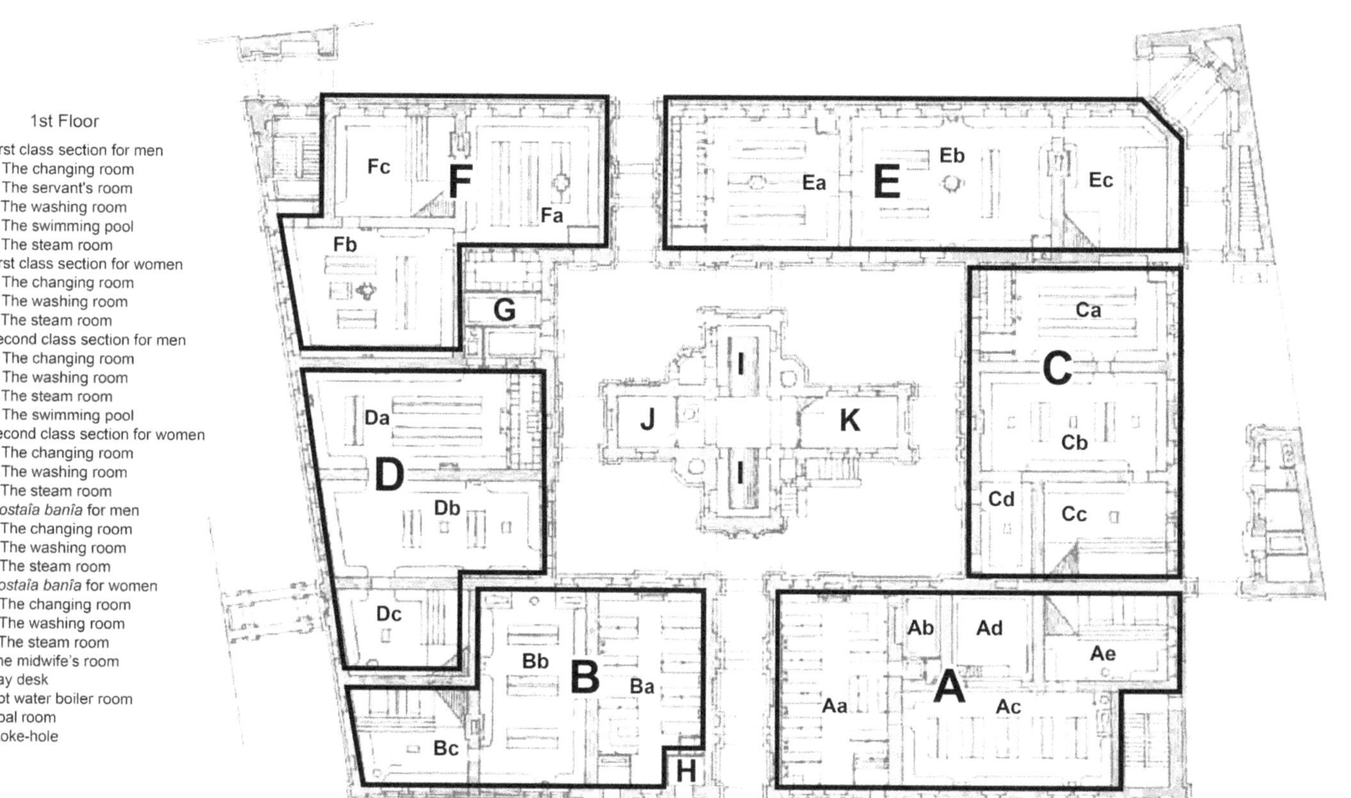

FIGURE 9. Layout of Voronin Bathhouse—first floor with large communal sections. Siuzor, "Torgovie (narodnie) bani Voronina," 5.

with predictable results: a contemporary physician described one such section as a place covered by "a thick layer of soot."[23] With a relatively low entrance fee fixed by city regulations, initially at 3 kopecks and later 5 kopecks, or 0.03 rubles and 0.05 rubles, respectively, the poorest urban residents, including coachmen and unskilled workers, could patronize these facilities.[24]

The second-class section was tidier, less crowded, and more comfortable and had an entrance fee at least twice that of the third-class section. In many cases it offered options such as a spatially separate full-service laundry, a restaurant-style kitchen, a masseur, and a barber who was often also trained in the application of leeches, hot cups, and bloodletting. These auxiliary services were available for additional fees, of course.[25] Although originally targeting merchants, officers, members of the urban professional classes, and even clergymen in the complex system of regulated social hierarchies or estates in Russia, this section naturally attracted the wealthier tradesmen and peasants and the poorer members of the bourgeoisie or the aristocracy.

Finally, the first-class section offered a decidedly luxurious experience, with semipublic stalls in the changing and rest area, often a large swimming pool, "soft rugs," "good copper washbasins," hot showers, and a price regulated to at least three times that of the third-class section. The same general services as those in the second-class section tended to be offered by attendants, but the ratio of attendants to patrons would have been higher, the facilities more extensive, and the furniture decidedly opulent.[26] This section would have targeted aristocrats and high-level state employees, a strongly overlapping demographic. In an urban reality defined by money rather than regulated estates, however, it soon became infiltrated by prosperous merchants and well-earning professionals such as doctors and lawyers.

The urban evolution of these bathing spaces thus went hand in hand with price regulation, the ban on mixed-sex bathing, tax incentives to capture economies of scale, and the increasingly ambiguous system of class divisions in the imperial capital. The mandated segmentation of the urban communal bathing experience should be taken with a grain of salt because, as discussed in chapter 1, the purely price-based segregation of the bathhouses imperfectly reflected the social estates. Even segregation based on sex left room for notable exceptions.[27] According to Pollock, "like late imperial Russia more generally, the banya was a place in flux, a place of mingling. . . . The banya was an 'egalitarian' and anonymous place, even as it became increasingly segregated in its services."[28]

The gradual transposition of rural bathing to the city thus produced a significant divergence from the various forms of village bathing commons, but not their wholesale displacement. One might be forgiven for thinking that whatever communal bathing traditions workers and soldiers brought with them from Russia's villages should have been wholly eradicated by the advent of large commercial establishments and their subjugation to municipal authority. And yet village traditions were clearly recognizable in the breadth of communal experiences and auxiliary conveniences that accompanied urban bathing. These had their precedents in the village bathhouse, which had a similarly important, albeit different communal function from, say, that of the pub in England. The village bathhouse was a location for communal feasts and socialization as well as a space associated in the peasants' mind with sex, though not of a particularly anonymous kind.[29]

As stalwarts of the urban incarnation of Russian bathing, St. Petersburg's commercial bathhouses also played a role in the life of city residents that went far beyond hygienic convenience. They were, in effect, the purveyors of "a set of livelihood qualities . . . over which rights are negotiated."[30] These qualities ranged from ablution and laundering to sex and socialization. The negotiation over these qualities was no less complex than the one discussed in chapter 2 involving the municipal administration, the police, queer men, and passersby in the use of public and open spaces for queer encounters. Urban communal bathing again involved the city government as the owner of the water used for bathing (revealingly, the main basis for taxation was the number of buckets of water consumed), but it also involved bathhouse owners, bathhouse operators, attendants, queer men, and members of the bathing public.[31]

Room for Sex in Urban Baths

The informal, licentious, and slightly chaotic communion of acquaintances and strangers in St. Petersburg's nineteenth-century commercial bathhouses was by no means a blotch in an otherwise perfect painting. Rather, it was quintessential to its appeal, both popular and intellectual. In Pollock's words, the urban commercial bathhouse was "like a club, but without exclusivity."[32] The bathhouse tantalizingly "obscured identities and required people to strip down with strangers . . . granted access to the Russian past . . . exposed people to disease, debauchery, and anonymity associated with modernity . . . inviting in turn both vulnerability and the possibility of the exploration of sexuality and sin."[33] In the late nineteenth and early twentieth centuries, the combination of license and communion as the essential accoutrements of urban bathing were hotly debated by Russian scholars and commentators, some of whom have celebrated these elements, even the problematic ones, as venerable features of the modern Russian city.[34]

In both the public discussion and the underlying negotiation over the use of commercial bathing spaces for sex and transgression, two specific ingredients of urban bathing are particularly worthy of attention. These are the role of the *banshchik*, or bathhouse attendant, and that of the *nomernaia bania*, or numbered baths, also known as the "family section." Taken together, these two uniquely urban adaptations had a defining influence on the city's culture of commercial bathing as it entered the last decades of the nineteenth century. In their combined effect, they were nothing short of a warping of village bathing traditions and thus highlight the many contradictions inherent in simply going for a bath in late imperial St. Petersburg.

Attendants, or *banshchiki* (in plural), took over many of the chores previously fulfilled by the village or family community in the rural archetype of urban bathing. In a world of increasingly anonymous and commercial urban interactions, they also held the keys to both the sanitary and salacious aspects of bathing. They serviced the urban bathing commons, washing, feeding, entertaining, and guarding the bathhouses' clients.[35]

Historically, the life of attendants would have been so completely intertwined with their place of employment that they not only worked all their waking hours in the baths but also limited their employment options by taking on large initial debts to bathhouse operators who brought them from the villages and housed them "in the banya's wash or changing rooms or sometimes in the basement."[36] *Banshchiki* offered services such as washing, soaping, scrubbing, rinsing, massaging, and assistance in the steam room. These were rendered on the basis of a conversation between visitor and attendant, and remuneration was a fee- and tip-based arrangement between visitors, operators, and attendants constrained by price lists and convention. Unlike menus and bathing accessories, their services did not always fit the standardized constraints of price lists. Instead, they were subject to informal negotiation. Attendants relied to a great extent on tips paid simply by goodwill, although these tips were often shared not just among attendants but also with managers and even the commercial operator.[37] Based on these informal and fluid arrangements, the *banshchik*'s services could be highly tailored to each visitor, especially in the first- or second-class bathhouse sections.[38] For example, Nikolai Leikin, a late nineteenth-century writer and journalist, reported that "one [visitor] likes to be scalded with boiling water, another would prefer cooler water."[39] (See figure 10, which, although it is a staged and stylized photograph, illustrates the role of attendants in bathing. It also shows the physical proximity of bathhouse attendants and clients.)

The attendants' role was critical to the functioning of the city's commercial bathhouses, but their own economic situations were always precarious.

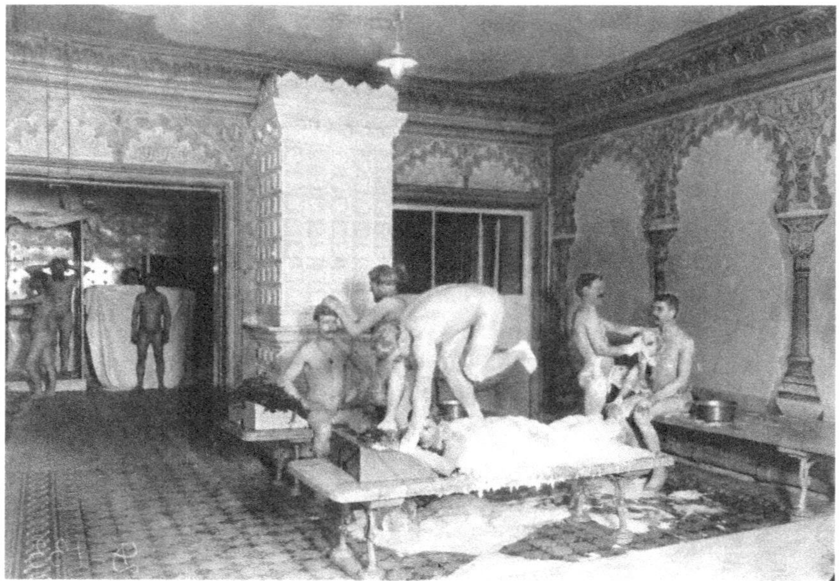

FIGURE 10. A staged photograph with the original caption "Bathhouse attendants washing patrons in the soap room, bathhouse of the brothers Egorovory." TsGAKFD SPb, D133, Banshchiki moiut posetitelei v myl'ne bani brat'ev Egorovykh, atelier of Carl Bulla, 1914. Courtesy of TsGAKFD SPb.

For the most part, attendants were recruited from estates and villages in the Russian countryside. Until the emancipation of the serfs, they were often doubly saddled with debts to both their employers and their fiefs. As a result of the feudal system and the general patterns of urban migration and recruitment, village relationships were transplanted and reproduced in the city, including those of conspiracy and cooperation. This cooperation was supported by village connections, attendants' parallel experiences of coming to the city, and the requirements of mutual assistance in the face of material adversity.[40] All these factors shaped a sideline for bathhouse attendants—male prostitution—into which young new arrivals were often initiated by earlier migrants from their own villages. As several sources indicate, including the much-publicized trial of a twenty-year-old attendant in the 1860s, many young bathhouse attendants participated in sex with patrons to earn comparatively large tips, which they sometimes shared among attendants alongside the proceeds from other services.[41]

Prostitution, however, did not necessarily take center stage. It was nestled among the many functions performed by *banshchiki* and carried out in the spirit of cartel-like cooperation. Many of their tasks required complex coordination and cooperation. As the range of services of urban bathhouses expanded, the role of *banshchiki* remained critical. Besides maintaining the bathhouse and assisting patrons in washing, *banshchiki* did laundry for clients; prepared and served food and drink; provided items such as birch twigs, hats, and towels; and in the higher-level sections helped clients undress and dress. They also maintained a modicum of order in the city's bathing spaces. They removed unruly clients and reminded patrons of house rules. Of course, discretion was in play here as well. *Banshchiki* were known to extract tips as a reward for looking the other way when clients breached house rules by washing their own fetid laundry or having sex with one another in the curtained stalls of the changing room, demeanor typical of the less expensive and more expensive sections, respectively.[42] So *banshchiki* not only maintained the city's commercial baths but were also instrumental in supporting the spirit of informality and licentiousness noted by observers of urban bathing around the middle of the nineteenth century.[43] Finally, whether as guardian of the spatial order or its nemesis, the *banshchik* was a central figure. His role also extended beyond the walls of the common sections: attendants also had an important role as gatekeepers of the *nomernaia bania*, to which I turn next.

The *nomernaia bania* was a second distinctively urban adaptation of Russian bathing customs that set St. Petersburg's commercial bathing culture apart and made it particularly amenable to illicit encounters and sex. Variously called "numbered" or "family" baths (*nomernaia bania* or *semeinaia bania*), they became de rigueur during the first half of the nineteenth century.[44] The *nomernaia bania* consisted of individual rooms, each equipped with a tub, arranged along a corridor as in a hotel or boardinghouse and offering a more intimate bathing experience than the communal bathing sections.[45] Because the ban against mixed-sex bathing did not apply here, entire families could bathe together. More than any other aspect of urban bathing, the *nomernaia bania* represents an "on-going dialogue between past and present," insofar as its family-sized rooms, the opportunity for legally condoned mixed-sex bathing, its freedom from price caps, and generally light degree of regulation all harked back to rural bathing practices, even while providing an altogether new urban format.[46]

This all seems perfectly respectable. However, in what is a distinctly urban twist, the *nomernaia bania* was used by visitors in search of privacy for sexual encounters of various kinds, whether with an attendant, another visitor of the same sex, a prostitute from outside, or a heterosexual lover. These uses were so widespread that the *nomernaia bania* became indelibly associated in the public mind with promiscuous sex, prostitution, and homosexuality.[47] In this way, the *nomernaia bania* significantly extended and complemented the large open areas described above. Highlighting its questionable role, an 1866 article points out, counterintuitively, that the *nomernaia bania* remained open even when the supply of water to the entire bathhouse was turned off. Clearly, clients had plenty of reasons to attend this section even when washing was not possible.[48] By the final decades of the nineteenth century the illicit uses of the *nomernaia bania* were not only the object of widespread debate but also the prerequisite for making bathhouse operations economically sustainable.

The *banshchik* and the *nomernaia bania* were at least as important as all the remaining characteristics of the urban banya combined in making the imperial capital's variant of the Russian bathing tradition both nationally and internationally distinctive. Their role was shaped by the banya's almost universal take-up by city residents, bathhouses' uneasy segmentation, their massive urban scale, the confluence of nudity and anonymity, and the overlay of traditions of leisure on hygienic ablution. In responding to these factors, *banshchiki* and the *nomernaia bania* transposed and preserved the heritage of village bathing. They helped ensure that the capital's commercial bathhouses retained a strong but commercially viable bent toward communion, disorder, and debauchery and continued to offer opportunities for intimacy, be it social, familial, or sexual. The commercial bathhouse enjoyed a definitive pride of place as heir to the pastime of bathing and not just the rational hygienic practice of doing so. As one contemporary described it, Russian fin-de-siècle urbanites shared a "hereditary love of steaming themselves with *veniki* (birch switches), relaxing in the changing rooms, and 'wagging their tongues' with their companions."[49] Moreover, as a contemporary medical practitioner explained, "baths turn out to be a type of club [for] washing, talking, leisurely snacks, etc., offering return of that series of pleasures da capo and da capo."[50] In the strange and contradictory intellectual climate of late imperial Russia, the routine mixing of ablution and communion, hygiene and sex gave rise to a confusing sense of pride in the tradition of communal bathing. "The banya—even in the cities—made Russians distinct and even superior to unwashed Westerners," but this superiority rested equally on their cleanliness and their capacity to engage in the regular, intimate, and uninhibited communion associated with bathing.[51]

Commercial Bathing's Pride of Place

Late modern bathing practices—in St. Petersburg as elsewhere—were situated at the intersection of two important trends during the second half of the nineteenth century, both of which emanated from municipal governments: first, advances in public hygiene, and second, the development of urban infrastructure, including the large-scale deployment of pipes and pumps for water provisioning.[52] Each of these advances reached St. Petersburg promptly. Water quality was identified as an important factor in the spread of diseases by the physician Ivan Eremeev, and the bacteria count became one of the most widely recognized indicators of water quality. Government authorities, including bathhouse inspection commissions in St. Petersburg, frequently referred to this indicator in their reports.[53] In parallel, significant progress in the use of pipes and pumps was made during the second half of the nineteenth century; steam engines were used as early as 1871.[54] Steam-driven pumps enabled water to be lifted into dispersed reservoirs and released under pressure to bathhouses, factories, and residential apartments.[55] Private water pipes and networks built by corporate utilities coexisted from 1862 until the creation of a municipal network in 1892 via the city government's acquisition of St. Petersburg's two largest water utilities.[56] Technologies for water filtration and cleaning were also developed and deployed; the first municipal water filtration and chlorination plants were launched in 1889 and 1911, respectively.[57] These developments meant that bathhouses could be built farther away from sources of water (mainly the city's many rivers). They could also be operated more efficiently and could offer more and fresher water for bathing.

Outside Russia, these two trends spurred governments to firmly establish public control over communal bathing through public investment and regulation. In Liverpool, London, and New York, to name the most prominent examples discussed in the historical literature on bathing, municipalities took the lead, creating municipal bathhouses at public expense.[58] In the West more generally, measures targeting improvements in communal bathing fit neatly enough into the context of rationalist reforms designed to endorse and enable the hygienic self-improvement of citizens. As Chris Otter explains, the late nineteenth century was alive with enthusiasm about the ability of science, technology, markets, private initiative, and rational government to act upon the citizen and make him (the discourse is undoubtedly masculinist) more reasonable, fit, and healthy to pursue both his own happiness and the public good.[59] Normative, progressive ideals of cleanliness, self-reliance, health, "character," manliness, racial superiority, and class emancipation all informed the discussion about bathhouse reforms in British cities, although the discussion sat uncomfortably with the opportunities for queer male cruising, which even the most sanitary single-sex communal bath offered "around the edges." Tom Crook has specifically considered Victorian public baths in Britain as "elaborate, if decidedly functional, institutions designed to produce clean, disciplined subjects."[60]

By no means was this rationalistic normative ambition confined to the Western world. The knock-on influence of colonial governmentality is also acknowledged, for example, in discussions of infrastructure and water usage in British Bombay, where the building and regulation of urban infrastructure can be seen as "attempts to conceive and influence agency and subjectivity, in this case through the enrolment of infrastructure in sanitary discourses."[61] Moreover, the interpenetration of sanitary bathing with commercial and public bathing traditions was decidedly bidirectional. For example, in the West, commercial bathhouses, including famous (sometimes notorious) Turkish and Russian baths, had numerous options for the well off and the not so well off, and for the sensually inclined as well as the sanitary-minded.[62] The point to make here, however, is that bathing in the great Western capitals, notably including London, was a mixed economy transitioning between scientifically administered public baths and the private baths gradually being rolled out in houses and apartments, even though it was undoubtedly the former that provided more people with bathing facilities than any other alternative well into the twentieth century. By contrast, what was so noticeable in urban Russia—as in places like Hungary, which also had a distinctive urban communal bathing tradition harking back to Roman and Turkish origins—was the predominance and cultural significance of the commercial bathhouses. Commercial prominence and preeminence were coupled with the complete absence of a municipal sector and minimal progress in the construction of domestic bathing facilities.[63]

Noting this unique and prominent urban tradition supported by commercial establishments, Russian doctors, policymakers, and public intellectuals during the latter half of the nineteenth century rallied to the cause of urban communal bathing. They described the country's commercial bathhouses as signifiers of collective identity and a source national pride. Russian bathing advocates saw the urban bathhouse as the "rightful heir to a long and venerable tradition among the 'civilized' nations of the world, from the Greeks and Romans in antiquity through Byzantium in the Middle Ages."[64] The architecture of St. Petersburg's largest commercial bathhouses visibly underscored this fanciful lineage.[65] Concurrently, doctors and policymakers in the mid- and late nineteenth century hoped to position the Russian bathhouse as a model for Europe's emergent bathhouse movement. Beyond the pale of national policy, public intellectuals such as Vasilii Rozanov celebrated the distinctive Russianness of the banya, its association with sensuality, emotion, communion, debauchery, and controlled violence, and saw it as a bastion of national authenticity juxtaposed with modernizing and Westernizing influences.[66]

The contradictory nature of these impulses did little to detract from the solidarity with which many Russian doctors, policymakers, and intellectuals in the late nineteenth century extolled the virtues of their country's specific tradition of communal bathing. Whether the provenance of urban bathing traditions was to be found in Greek and Roman antiquity or Russian village customs affected their enthusiasm very little. Similarly, regardless of whether urban bathing was to be celebrated *for* or in *spite of* the often unhygienic and debauched practices routinely observed in commercial bathhouses, apologists agreed that the urban strand of Russia's bathing tradition was worth preserving and, if possible, further improving as a source of national strength and identity. The question was one of direction—which aspects to encourage, which to suppress, and which merely to tolerate. However, in the absence of a clear and unified direction, St. Petersburg's bathhouses enjoyed an ambiguous and precarious prominence in the city's cultural landscape: "The banya was healthy and dangerous, purifying and sinful, socially levelling and exploitative, the symbol of all that was right with imperial Russia and all that was wrong with it as well."[67] Settled within the contradictions of the city's attitudes toward bathing and, at least in part, protected by them, sex between men was no jarring abnormality at the periphery of an otherwise efficiently administered and authoritatively condoned bathing culture, but rather an organic extension of the atmosphere of communion and homosocial exchange so characteristic of St. Petersburg's commercial bathing tradition. Unsurprisingly, however, for the capital of an ambitiously modernizing state, by the 1870s legislators had the city's bathhouses in their sights.

Disciplinary Ambitions Meet the Reality of Urban Bathing

Before the launch of systematic bathhouse reforms by the City Duma in 1879, the mayor's office made various attempts to understand and improve the situation in the city's commercial bathhouses. Concurrently with increasing attention directed at bathing by members of the medical professions, the city's mayor who, as already mentioned, was also its chief of police, assembled a commission of doctors, police, firefighters, and architects in 1870 to inspect all of the city's forty-six commercial bathhouses and later to obtain design plans for a model bathhouse.[68] The main conclusions of the commission's initial report on the physical and sanitary state of St. Petersburg's commercial bathhouses as well as the goings on within them were published in the official government gazette later that year.[69] The members of the commission argued that the city's bathhouses suffered from several shortcomings, including unsafe and unsanitary conditions and "immoral" behaviors by attendants, guests, owners, and operators. Based on these findings, the city hired a prominent architect, Pavel Siuzor, "to design bathhouses that could meet sanitary and technical requirements."[70]

During the 1870s, at least ten such bathhouses designed by Siuzor were built using the money of private investors, but the situation in other bathhouses improved little as a result of the new competition. Sanitary shortcomings and debauchery in the majority of the city's bathhouses remained a thorn in the mayor's side. To make matters worse, inspection reports, citizens' tip-offs, and publications such as Vladimir Merzheevskii's 1878 handbook on forensic gynecology all indicated that the problems persisted, and some specifically highlighted the role of the city's commercial bathhouses as places of sexual encounters between men, reinforcing commercial bathhouses' status as an urban space in dire need of additional reform efforts.[71]

These were not long in coming. In 1879 a major legislative initiative was passed targeting the sanitary and moral improvement of St. Petersburg's commercial bathhouses. In fact, it specifically addressed many of the shortcomings identified in the report of the commission on bathhouses from 1871. The "Bathhouse Ordinance," or simply the "Ordinance," was adopted by the City Duma in 1879 and set out requirements pertaining to the construction, layout, physical maintenance, and day-to-day management of the city's bathhouses.[72] The goal of the Ordinance was to standardize and regulate the physical characteristics and services of commercial bathhouses, to improve their sanitary conditions, and to suppress illicit or unhygienic behaviors such as doing laundry or having sex. It was not just another ordinance—it was the municipal administration's first and only boldly systematic attempt to extend the government sphere deeply into St. Petersburg's commercial bathing spaces.

The first part of the Ordinance set out exacting standards for the construction and internal layout of bathhouses—avowedly to ensure proper insulation and ventilation, to prevent drafts, and to manage other health and safety risks.[73] The second part of the Ordinance, however, had much more to do with what actually went on in the baths. It regulated the use of internal spaces, opening hours, entrance fees, and the conduct of bathhouse operations in what was undoubtedly an attempt to sanitize, standardize, and commoditize the bathing experience. Regulation severely restricted the provision of auxiliary services and regulated the work of bathhouse attendants. Medical services (such as cupping, bloodletting, and application of leeches) now had to be licensed by the Interior Ministry Medical Police and supervised by a doctor. Other services became subject to onerous restrictions, too: for example, any kitchen operating in a bathhouse now had to pass the same stringent inspections to which restaurant kitchens were subject, a ruling that would significantly increase costs.

Most importantly, perhaps, the role of *banshchiki* or bathhouse attendants was addressed with particular emphasis and care in the second part of the Ordinance, suggesting that their function as participants in or arrangers of sexual encounters had been earmarked by authorities for urgent reform. Attendants were no longer permitted to sleep in the bathhouse when off duty, eliminating the possibility of retaining sleeping bays in the cavernous bathhouse basements. They became subject to capped working hours that were far shorter than the duration of the traditional shift. This required operators to increase the number of attendants. Moreover, new regulation required attendants to leave the bathhouse promptly on completion of their shift.[74] Finally, they also had to pass regular, free medical checks, most likely intended to stem the tide of syphilitic infections.[75] Little did the legislators consider, however, that the combination of shorter shifts with higher expenses for external lodging left attendants even more reliant than before on tips from patrons.[76] Nor could pricing be easily adjusted so as to pay attendants more because a large share of revenues came from entrance fees, which were regulated.[77]

The third and final section of the Ordinance specified deadlines for compliance and the consequences of failure to comply, which were nonissuance or revocation of the license required to operate. Two years were given to bathhouse owners to implement all necessary changes. In 1881, city officials were to reinspect all bathhouses, and those that did not comply would be unable to operate until they did.[78]

All of this sounds stringent enough, but the attempt to regulate St. Petersburg's commercial bathhouses was not even remotely successful in its scope of aims. By early 1883, following two rounds of inspections, officials concluded that of the city's sixty commercial bathhouses, only eleven were compliant in all material respects.[79] Five had not been subject to inspections, but the remaining forty-two demonstrated the most egregious breaches. Of these, two were shut permanently, as "their further existence was recognized to be impossible."[80] The many others that had achieved partial compliance had to be left alone—an immediate and marked deviation from the injunctions of the Ordinance. Clearly, the city administration could not dispense with the vast majority of institutions. Thus, forty-two bathhouse operators were only warned and received an extension of six months to comply.[81] Without any formal framework for such decisions, discretion had been employed in deciding which bathhouses to close, which to impose partial closures or restrictions on, and which to simply allow continuing operations but with deadlines for improved compliance. None of this was foreseen by the authors of the Ordinance, who had treated compliance as binary.[82]

The majority of commercial bathhouse owners and operators had made costly adjustments to at least partially comply with the Ordinance, but nevertheless they now had to operate under the constant threat of forced closure, which created a sort of stalemate or suspended entente between authorities and bathhouse operators. Clearly, in this situation, further investments became problematic. On the one hand, sanitary inspectors and the municipal Sanitary Commission, which had been created in 1879 as a permanent institution responsible for monitoring the "general sanitary conditions in the city" and reporting directly to the City Duma, refrained from closing the majority of the city's bathhouses.[83] After all, it was also in the vital interest of sanitation to preserve capacity in the city's existing bathhouses for an ever-growing population. On the other hand, leniency was also a signal, one that conflicted with the ambitious and strict requirements of the Ordinance. Bathhouse owners and operators read the combination of signals and did just enough to remain open while shying away from the most costly measures. As a result, a new entente emerged. The threat of closure remained imminent and the prospects of full compliance slim. Most owners or operators whitewashed walls, sealed floors, replaced furniture, canceled services, and introduced new shifts and timetables. And yet they were reluctant to tackle building measures and, it seems, struggled or did not wish to exercise proper oversight over the activities of *banshchiki*.[84] It was a situation of who blinks first.

Not surprisingly, inspectors were at a loss about what to do next. In some rare cases, they even went so far as to explicitly acknowledge the futility and counterproductive nature of certain measures and lobbied to defend the need to let bathhouse owners and operators, bathers and attendants just get on with their business. For example, commercial bathhouses for a large section of the population provided the only access to running water during winter months. Inspectors observing this practice asked their superiors where else bathhouse visitors were to wash their clothes.[85] Similarly, on at least one occasion in 1881, limited carve-outs were created for existing bathhouses, granting permanent, legislated reprieves regarding a few of the most unrealistic demands of the Ordinance, such as ensuring that steam rooms, changing facilities, and washrooms always be located on the same floor.[86] For the most part, however, bathhouse owners and operators had to improvise at their own peril, seeking and finding protection only in numbers and calibrating their actions to the discretion of inspectors and municipal commissions.

The city administration, seemingly impervious to the challenges of implementing the Ordinance and unwilling or unable to directly address the stalemate it had achieved, decided to press on rather than take a step back. In 1887, the City Duma passed an amendment to further extend the moral ordering described in the second part of the original Ordinance with an expanded list of restrictions. This amendment stipulated that bathhouses had to remain closed during the night and that the *nomernaia bania* had to shut down before the other sections.

A 1903 revision of the Ordinance that did little more than incorporate various amendments continued this trajectory of unrealistic overregulation.[87]

The tension between ambitious legislation and far-from-perfect implementation was nothing out of the ordinary in this city. As we have seen in the context of the operationalization of laws and directives relevant to queer spatial patterns in public and private spaces, the experience of frontline officials was rarely reflected in realistic tweaks to orders and legislation or better drafting the next time around. The operational challenges were taken into account, albeit abstractly and preemptively, via the significant discretion afforded to state officials tasked with enforcing its laws and directives. As in the case of the 1910 directive targeting queer men in their apartments (see chapter 2), the response to the challenges of operationalizing this spatial order was not to scale back official requirements but instead to tolerate patchy and "creative" implementation and the often counterintuitive ententes that resulted. As a result, the correspondence about threatened or actual closures between bathhouse owners, inspectors, the mayor's office, and the Sanitary Commission continued to grow.

Meanwhile, the city government's flexibility and imperviousness to its own failure could go only so far, especially on a matter so vitally important to its self-image as bathing. Therefore, in 1910, after having tried for thirty years to make a dent in the city's "debauched" bathing customs, the city administration finally made a complete about-face and shifted the emphasis to a scheme more consistent with trends in the West. Legislation "for the establishment of municipal bathhouses" (*ob ustroistve gorodskikh narodnykh ban'*) was adopted, including the commissioning of construction plans for model bathhouses to be built at public expense, much as in Liverpool or Manchester. Again, the architect Siuzor won the commission. But this time the city government was going to control every aspect of the new municipal baths directly. They were to be endowed with separate sections for doing laundry and most importantly, would have no *nomernaia bania* sections, dipping pools, curtained stalls, or, in fact, any areas affording even a degree of privacy. They were also to provide spatially separate housing for attendants.[88] These deviations from any of the existing commercial bathhouses in St. Petersburg at the time, including ones designed by the same architect, Siuzor, indicate that the city government was well aware of the far-from-perfect and perhaps even counterproductive results of previous reforms. The implementation of this municipal project, however, was stalled and eventually canceled, first by World War I and then by the Revolution. And yet, as a reflection of a remoralized, entirely functional bathing institution, the intended state-owned bathhouses could hardly have been bettered.[89]

The Cost of Compliance

Why, then, in the absence of municipal bathhouses, was St. Petersburg's culture of communal bathing so intractable to the kinds of regulation and reform that would have curtailed opportunities for illicit sex and prostitution within them and aligned the city to a more rationalistic vision of communal bathing focused on ablution? How did the urban tradition of communal bathing and the operations of commercial bathhouses adjust to attempted reforms? In responding—if one is to go beyond the simple explanation of institutional inertia—it is helpful to look at how the Ordinance affected the economics of bathhouse operations. The severity of this impact is perhaps most evident in the pattern of new bathhouse construction.[90] Having previously kept pace with population growth, bathhouse construction virtually ground to a halt in the two decades following the introduction of the Ordinance, despite unabated population growth (see figure 11).[91] This was no fluke. Evidence shows that the Ordinance increased costs beyond what could be recouped via regulated prices, thus squeezing returns for operators and investors. Simultaneously, its excessive provisions raised the constant specter of forced closure.

Evidence that the Ordinance had a detrimental effect on existing bathhouses comes from municipal archives in the form of letters and petitions by bathhouse owners and operators as well as indirectly from the previously mentioned climb down of the city administration on a few particularly stringent requirements. The requirements for new bathhouses were always more taxing than for existing ones—a differentiation further reinforced by adjustments to the legislation.[92] Hence, whatever negative effects the Ordinance had on the economics of existing bathhouses would have been amplified for new ones.

The requirements of the Ordinance for existing bathhouses were already quite onerous. Repeated petitions by bathhouse owners bemoan the effects of regulation on their economics. As the petitioners plausibly claim, complying with the Ordinance meant significantly increasing the cost base by carrying out renovations, burning more fuel, hiring more attendants, and paying them more. Moreover, regulation concerning working conditions for attendants, stipulations about opening hours, restrictions on hospitality, and the provisioning of auxiliary services such as laundry all would have constrained important sources of revenues. Thus, it is unsurprising that bathhouse owners and operators started bombarding municipal authorities with suggestions and petitions to adjust taxation or entrance fees in order to enable both full compliance with the Ordinance and economically sustainable bathhouse operations. In the vast majority of cases they did not dispute or seek to soften any of the principally feasible requirements of the Ordinance itself. The respon-

FIGURE 11. The city population and number of bathhouses. Data sources: On population: B. Kochakov, *Ocherki istorii Leningrada, period kapitalizma, vtoraia polovina XIX veka*; B. Kochakov, *Ocherki istorii Leningrada, period imperializma i Burzhuazno-demokraticheskikh Revoliutsii*); on the number of bathhouses, TsGIA SPb, f. 792, o. 1, d. 3337, Po zaiavleniiu glasnogo V. I. Likhacheva; TsGIA SPb, f. 479, o. 22, d. 1479 O materialakh za 1900 (Spiski vladel'tsev ban'); and Bogdanov, *Tri veka*, 63.

sible authorities, however, were not quick to respond. With one notable exception regarding the taxation of *nomernaia bania*, official response was unsupportive. Finally, in 1900 the City Council, to which many of these proposals and petitions had been addressed, grudgingly acknowledged these difficulties, noting in a resolution that required ratification of the City Duma that an increase in entrance fees was required to "reestablish an acceptable relationship between costs and revenues of bathhouses and, thereby, avoid the possibility of closure of many of them as a result of their insufficient profitability." The Duma, however, rejected the price increase.[93]

The halt in bathhouse construction supports the assertions of bathhouse owners and operators that full compliance was not only detrimental to their bottom line but, indeed, prohibitively expensive. Against this backdrop, one might have expected the city government to respond to the pleas of bathhouse owners and operators with greater urgency. By the late 1890s, the situation had become difficult to manage, given the gradual overcrowding of the city's bathhouses, which was noted in many inspection reports and addressed in follow-up legislation.[94] By this time, complete closure had long been obsolete as the method of choice to combat poor compliance. Rather, the tables had been turned almost completely and closure had become the most effective threat of bathhouse owners and operators in their letters to the Sanitary Commission and the City Council. In 1900, the commission confessed its fears openly, justifying its support of relief for bathhouse owners with the injunction that "the existing number of bathhouses should under no circumstances be reduced." It proposed instead reducing taxes by lowering charges for water used in bathhouses, whereas the City Council preferred a straight-out increase in regulated prices.[95] The Duma accepted neither. Even given the freezing of investments in the sector and the perceived threat of closure of some of the city's bathhouses, official policy failed to adapt in response to the shared concerns of bathhouse owners, operators, and would-be investors. The City Duma held fast to its conviction that reforms should be possible by prescriptive authority alone. Thus, none of the pragmatic solutions proposed by owners and operators and endorsed by various municipal bodies were implemented. Given the failure of their petitions to elicit favorable adjustments to regulation or taxation, bathhouse owners had to navigate their economic difficulties on their own.

Renegotiating the City's Bathing Spaces

At least initially, bathhouse owners sought and found safety in numbers. The failure of five out of six bathhouses to fully comply with the Ordinance made it almost impossible for the Sanitary Commission and the City Council to take broad action.[96] The Ordinance itself was to blame. Having neglected to anticipate a collective noncompliance, legislators had relied on a simplistic binary concept of compliance and stipulated closure as the only available governmental response, even for minor deviations from requirements. By early 1883, this was obviously unrealistic. It took a while for inspectors and regulators to find their footing. Gradually a new entente emerged after a push for compliance and moral discipline in 1887, when the Ordinance was amended to shorten the hours of nighttime operations, especially for the *nomernaia bania*, and a flurry of unannounced inspections or raids took place. Subsequent evidence suggests that noncompliance could be negotiated along broadly predictable lines in what is yet another characteristic example of the broad discretion accorded to the state's frontline representatives in managing the city's public and semipublic spaces. The above-mentioned letters to the mayor from bathhouse owners whose establishments had been shut following inspections demonstrate that in some bathhouses, partial or even complete reopening was accompanied by tailored restrictions on opening times or obligations to replace attendants, despite continued noncompliance in other aspects. Similarly, an agreement on measures to address the most consequential breaches of the Ordinance or other requirements sufficed to warrant at least partial reopening or to temporarily stay the threat of imposed closure. For example, in 1837, the mayor's office allowed Timofei Kriukov to continue to operate his bathhouse in the Moskovskaia Borough under the condition that the *nomernaia bania* closed at 10:00 PM.[97] That same year, a Mr. Sorokin had to close his *nomernaia bania* bathhouse until more reliable *banshchiki* could be found.[98] This modus vivendi remained in place. In 1910, the bathhouse on Shpalernaia Street, which was in breach of the Ordinance's wastewater handling requirements, continued to operate for five weeks while the breach was successfully remedied.[99]

Negotiated noncompliance increased the prominence of the *nomernaia bania* and, as it turns out, paved the way for a grassroots response to the Ordinance that could not have been further from its authors' intentions, including a redoubled emphasis on and commercialization of the bathhouse's role as a sexual space in the city. Notable in the correspondence about noncompliant bathhouses is the concern demonstrated on the part of owners and operators that the *nomernaia bania* be reopened as soon as possible. In their petitions and in responses to enforced closures, owners described the *nomernaia bania* as the only part of bathhouse operations that remained profitable.[100] The bathhouse operator Adrian Gustov, for example, went so far as to claim that failure to reopen his *nomernaia bania* would inevitably lead to his bankruptcy and closure of the entire bathhouse.[101] His rationale was easy enough for his addressees to interpret. This was the only section for which prices were not regulated. The *nomernaia bania* thus competed freely for customers. Successful competitors could pass costs on to customers—with a healthy margin on top. In two other characteristic letters from 1887, bathhouse operators wrote that the *nomernaia bania* alone was offsetting losses from all the other bathhouse sections, which were subject to price controls.[102] The city government responded opportunistically. On the one hand, it permitted a number of bathhouses to keep this section open (or reopen it), even while other parts of the bathhouse remained closed.[103] On the other hand, in what is perhaps a textbook example of so-called sin taxes, the City Council proposed raising taxes on the *nomernaia bania*, which had not been touched since 1838. Perhaps to sweeten this bitter pill, the burden of the tax was transferred from operators to owners, who now had to pay up to 2 percent of the assessed rental income on their *nomernaia bania*.[104]

The resulting special status of the *nomernaia bania* under the Ordinance seems to have expanded the common ground available for all sides to find a new modus operandi. Regulators and inspectors were allowing owners to use the *nomernaia bania* to subsidize other parts of the bathhouse and fund partial, albeit skin-deep, compliance with the Ordinance. The municipal coffers obtained a share of the profits. *Banshchiki* and patrons had access to a barely regulated and classically opaque space in which illicit activities attracted little attention save from the prurient. Such prurient interest was, of course, eventually awakened by the press but, even then, did little to dent the popularity and prominence of the *nomernaia bania*, which gradually came to be publicly recognized as the geographical epicenter of queer male sexual activity in the city.[105] In effect, commercial bathhouses retrenched and offered a cocktail of subtle adjustments in response to overambitious legislation. Paint was refreshed, furniture replaced, *banshchiki* sent home at night; some of them even had to look for new places of employment.[106] At the same time, structural changes to the bathhouses were few and far between and *banshchiki* frequently continued their "mischief." Following a period of adjustment, the *nomernaia bania* funded the new entente among municipal authorities, bathhouse owners, attendants, and patrons. Symptomatically for the resilience of the urban commons and the way in which spatial regulation worked (or did not work) in this city, the capacity of commercial bathhouses—by now a key target of municipal authorities—could be prevented from declining only by the spaces that were the least susceptible to reform.

The increasingly prominent role of the *nomernaia bania* in bathhouse operations corresponded to a less visible but equally important adaptation in the culture and economy of sexual encounters in the city's commercial bathhouses. As we have seen, prostitution was hardly new to St. Petersburg's bathhouses. And yet several indications reveal that something changed following the passing of the Ordinance. In his discussion of bathhouses, Healey draws explicit and repeated attention to this change: "The peasant pattern of working in a team (the *artel'*) for an equally apportioned share of earnings, was observed among bathhouse sex workers from the 1860s to the 1880s."[107] He emphasizes a transition "between the formation of this 'depraved work team' and the arrival of more commercial prostitution, with a brothel-keeper managing atomized male sex-trade workers."[108] By the first decade of the new century, according to Healey, "male sex work was becoming more commercialized" and "youths selling sex, and pimps who organized them, were commodifying the sideline in 'sodomy' described by bath attendants a half-century earlier."[109]

This change left its mark on public perceptions of the bathhouse. A wealth of testimonials from the final decades of the imperial era speaks to the ubiquity of sex between men (as well as between heterosexual couples) in the bathhouses. Those focusing on instances of sex between men include the diaries of Kuzmin and the last tsar's brother, Konstantin Romanov; books by the prominent public intellectual Vasilii Rozanov; forensic-medical publications; travel journals of foreign visitors to St. Petersburg; and pamphlets and newspaper articles from the early twentieth century.[110] Summarizing these perceptions, Pollock writes that during the last years of imperial rule, the bathhouse's "reputation as a place of same-sex relations, mixed-sex prostitution and violence became increasingly visible."[111] Similarly, he notes that "by 1906 the idea that bathhouse workers could be paid for sex was not a well-kept secret."[112]

The voices drawing attention to illicit sex, especially to male prostitution in bathhouses, cannot easily be chalked up to a relaxation of censorship laws and practices after 1905, as only some of them were published at the time, and not all of them are Russian.[113] For example, around the time of Kuzmin's publication of the novel *Wings* in 1906, which, incidentally, was censored for "pornography," "foreign apologists for homosexuality in the modern, Western sense sang the praises of the Russian bath as a place of particular opportunity."[114] Perhaps even more revealingly, as early as 1887, the office of the capital's mayor and chief of police opened a dedicated file on cases involving prostitution and sex at bathhouses.[115] Here again the *nomernaia bania* features prominently. The file titled "Debauchery at the bathhouse" (*razvrat v baniakh*), consists mainly of complaints by anonymous visitors. Characteristically, one such letter writer concludes that the city's commercial bathhouses have "turned into dens of debauchery, which has reached its utter limits and is expressed in an entire series of phenomena of the most immoral character."[116] In several cases, responses from bathhouse owners or operators have also survived. Many of them—unsurprisingly—point an accusing finger at the *banshchiki*.[117]

Indeed, prostitution evolved from a side hustle, the financial rewards from which were shared just like other tips among attendants belonging to the same "artel," into a business line for *banshchiki*, if not their main line. Often they were organized by an older attendant—allegedly with the complicity and pecuniary participation of bathhouse operators.[118] This adjustment in the entente among city authorities, bathhouse operators, attendants, and patrons is hardly surprising, given the impact of the Ordinance on the position of bathhouse attendants. The Ordinance had barred them from living in the bathhouses and shortened their shifts. This change was relatively easy to monitor and did not require large up-front investments by bathhouse owners. In the surviving inspection reports, infringements of these rules were not recorded. As a result, *banshchiki* became ever more dependent on tips. This change in their circumstances pushed them toward activities that reaped the largest tips. The single most lucrative of these was sex with male clients. The result was ever more entrenched, organized, and commoditized prostitution.[119]

As early as 1885, the venereologist Veniamin Tarnovskii estimated that "three quarters of male attendants were willing to engage in [homosexual sex] for cash."[120] By 1897, the exigencies of the profession had produced a remarkable demographic among *banshchiki*. Almost all of them were young. For instance, in a city borough adjacent to the one discussed in chapter 3, the Kazanskaia Borough, only 14 percent of male *banshchiki* were over forty, whereas 74 percent of female attendants were over forty.[121] "High rates among *banshchiki* of syphilis and other venereal diseases, especially among those working in the numbered or family sections" also suggest the prevalence of male prostitution in St. Petersburg's bathhouses.[122] The Medical Police made comprehensive efforts to respond to the medical profile that was asserting itself among *banshchiki*, mandating, for example, universal regular medical exams for male bathhouse workers. In 1887, the City Council and the police even went so far as to close a bathhouse in the Vasilievskaia Borough after a *banshchik* there, a decommissioned soldier, was found to have successfully concealed his syphilitic infection from medical inspectors for three months.[123] These demographic and medical sources corroborate anecdotal evidence from diaries, newspaper articles, and literary sources that suggest that by the late imperial era the roles of *banshchik* and male prostitute had all but merged in the bathhouses.

The increasing prominence of commercial bathhouses as the purveyors of semipublic spaces for "debauched purposes," the dubious renown of the *nomernaia bania* within them, and the ever more prominent role of *banshchiki* as prostitutes or arrangers of prostitution encountered some feeble resistance, to be sure. Although municipal authorities had in large part only themselves to blame for overburdening bathhouse owners and operators with their ambitious sanitary and moral reforms, these same authorities, when faced with their apparent failure, resorted to a familiar set of authoritarian tools. In 1887—the same year that the Ordinance was amended to restrict nighttime operations of bathhouses and ensure that the *nomernaia bania* closed before other sections—the city's regular police joined the efforts of the Medical Police to suppress illicit sex in bathhouses. Had legislators of the City Duma and administrators in the mayor's office been more responsive to the pleas of bathhouse owners and operators or appropriately scaled down their ambitions to their subjects' propensity to fund them, the municipal government might have turned owners and operators into allies and reduced the incentives for tacit complicity in prostitution. As the case stood, the efforts of legislators and sanitary inspectors in constraining opportunities for illicit sex in bathhouses were clearly not having the desired effect.

Thus, the mayor's office enlisted the support of the police in directly suppressing "debauchery." To that end and on the basis of the Emergency Laws of 1881, several bathhouses in which such activity was allegedly taking place (and this included most of the big ones) were raided, perpetrators (*banshchiki* and patrons) were caught red-handed, and *nomernaia bania* sections or even entire bathhouses were closed, some for months.[124] Unfortunately, this high-cost effort could not easily be repeated and the strain of keeping some of the city's bathing spaces closed made this a one-off measure tailored to intimidate rather than to effectively uproot a practice that had become more or less universal in the city's commercial bathhouses. Moreover, the operators of the closed or partially closed bathhouses immediately and plausibly evoked the economic necessity of keeping the problematic *nomernaia bania* open to avoid impending bankruptcy and permanent withdrawal of their bathhouses from the supply of bathing spaces. This constrained the ability of police to effectively apply pressure, since, as was eventually evidenced in the Sanitary Commission support of concessions to bathhouse operators, the city's governing authorities were eager to ensure that the number of commercial baths be prevented from declining.[125] In addition, a carefully sustained sheen of deniability insulated owners and operators from most egregious breaches linked to illicit sex and, thus, further frustrated the municipal government's efforts to extend disciplinary control into the semipublic spaces of the commercial bathhouses, especially the *nomernaia bania*. To sustain this sheen of deniability and present themselves as cooperative, bathhouse operators were always quick to respond to any complaint by reporting on recent staffing changes or promising to make them and otherwise pleading their ignorance of specific incidents, noting, for example, that these had taken place "only on account of the staff, which have all been exchanged for new ones."[126] All bathhouses but one were reopened, but the debauchery, including sex between men and male prostitution, continued unabated.

Understood in the context of an ongoing negotiation over the city's semipublic spaces generally and those available for queer encounters in particular, the Ordinance appears to have been intended as the definitive reform of urban bathing, Russia's answer to the bathhouse movement in the West. Its objective was to create a rationalistic and sanitary oasis of self-improvement that would marry the best of domestic tradition and Western science. Almost the opposite was the result. The Ordinance's mix of unrealistic ambition and lack of responsiveness to the constraints of bathhouse economics instated sex—male homosexual sex in particular—as a mainstay of urban bathing. Previous urban adaptations had only to evolve a little to accommodate the increased role and commercialization of homosexual sex in bathhouses. The *nomernaia bania* provided the ideal space for sex, and changing and washing rooms were theaters for encounter. Higher demand for the *nomernaia bania* allowed bathhouse owners to ward off the worst economic consequences of the Ordinance and stave off "complete bankruptcy."[127] In turn, attendants, who were now working shorter shifts and had to pay for external accommodation, increasingly focused on prostitution to such a degree that this activity defined the demographics of the profession.

The stakeholders of commercial bathing had responded flexibly to the Ordinance, not by complying with all its requirements but by complying with some, and shifting the emphasis to an activity that had always been present as an optional ingredient in urban bathing and now became a prerequisite for the economic and social functioning of the city's bathing spaces. To be sure, the bathhouse sections offering a degree of privacy, especially the *nomernaia bania*, were not a poor man's world. A typical visit might cost as much as half an average worker's monthly salary and the cost of sex with an attendant was additional.[128] Thus, the reality of highly commercialized and commoditized prostitution in the banya could not but reinforce the paradigm familiar from the dossier discussed in chapter 1 that described the wealthy male client and the impecunious youthful attendant who was motivated by money alone. But not all visitors to the *nomernaia bania* were rich, as we know from the diaries of Kuzmin, who was not poor but also could not afford to live on his own and who struggled to pay a fine for pornography. Nor, if he or his fellow writer Rozanov are to believed, were all *banshchiki* reluctant.[129] The adjustment of St. Petersburg's commercial bathhouses to the pressures of attempted reforms affected the reputation of these institutions as a whole and nudged even the bathhouse spaces that were less critical to the sexual and prostitution economy a few steps closer to being perceived as centers of homosociality, debauchery, and sexual reconnaissance. In no small part owing to the gravitational pull of these adjustments, St. Petersburg's bathhouses had failed to morph into "factories for bathing," as legislators had hoped, but instead redoubled their claim to the urban market for "space[s] of pleasure and encounter."[130]

This seemingly perverse outcome of governmental legislation, which was passed with the explicit intention of making bathhouses cleaner, safer, and morally uplifting, reveals an important feature of St. Petersburg's queer milieu and its peculiar urban modernity rooted in a rural, communal past. On its face, the Ordinance failed because it contained insufficient elements to gain the support of the very constituency that had to fund and implement measures to meet its edicts. The evolution of the role of bathhouse attendants and the *nomernaia bania* in the purveyance of illicit sex, however, demonstrates that the self-organizing nature of the activities surrounding ablution contributed to the survival of commercial bathhouses that were under pressure from economically crippling legislation. Their resilience owes as much to their cultural heritage as modern adaptations of rural communal bathing practices, which ensured a high degree of general acceptance for the actual disorderly goings on in the city's bathing spaces, as it does to their intrinsic commercial orientation toward ever-changing opportunities for profit. As a result, bathhouses were successful in resisting the disciplinary ambitions of governmental regulation in a roundabout and opportunistic way. The autocratic-paternalistic Russian model of governmentality, armed with a mold for the ideal citizen and a scientifically well-informed understanding of sanitary and hygienic requirements, signally failed to extend the sphere of morally uplifting government influence into the confines of St. Petersburg's bathing culture, either by regulation or by providing municipal alternatives to the commercial bathhouse. And thus, instead of heralding a new age of sanitary bathing, the Bathhouse Ordinance of 1879 contributed to the commercialization of male sex in bathhouses and reinforced the designation of the city's commercial baths as hubs or destinations for queer spatial patterns.

As Foucault has put it, "it became apparent that if one governed too much, one did not govern at all—that one provoked results contrary to those one desired."[131] Far from a successful penetration or appropriation of the city's bathing spaces by progressive regulatory control and spatial ordering, the degree of government influence over these spaces, if anything, declined after 1880, as the increasing commercialization and entrenchment of sex in the bathhouses suggest. St. Petersburg's bathhouse "quasi-commons" survived and flourished. They did this by shifting their resources toward the *nomernaia bania* and the illicit sex that were distinctively urban in their adapted, anonymous forms but at the same time harked back to the village roots of communal bathing as both a necessity and a pastime. These were the rocks on which governmentalization of bathing foundered, and the city administration had no choice but to accept the queer and straight sexual economy that flourished behind closed doors as the lesser of two evils.

Chapter 5

Cruising in the *Pays du Tendre*

In a diary entry dated June 9, 1906, Mikhail Kuzmin describes his impressions while walking home during St. Petersburg's so-called white nights, when the sun sets only briefly and leaves behind an unusual twilight that never quite disappears: "As the three of us were returning home via Gorokhovaia street, [we saw] couples everywhere: on the sidewalk, under the arches, in the cabs; the rose-coloured dawn, the sleeping canals, the bright sky poured out some kind of love."[1] These impressions, along with many others he recorded in his diary around that time, evoke the emotional atmosphere of queer St. Petersburg, a topic that has been neglected in this book so far, as arguably it has been in the study of urban sexuality more generally. Specifically, this passage sheds light on the experiential qualities of cruising or navigating the city as a queer man in the company of other queer men. His spatial practices were not usually solitary, speculative excursions concerned exclusively with sexual gratification; they were infused with friendship, camaraderie, and a collective intimacy.

Kuzmin refers to cruising as an activity involving a "friendly gang" of men walking, chatting, observing, and interacting with others in the city's public and semipublic spaces. Their distinctive traditions of socialization in regular haunts contributed to a visible urban assemblage or milieu that was porous and assertive rather than furtively occult. Many of Kuzmin's diary entries resurrect an atmosphere of romantic adventure and sexualized friendship as opposed to self-consciously transgressional and anonymous sex. Despite his privileges and advantages, which included his aristocratic birth and manifest talent, his experience was hardly esoteric. He was a man in a crowd, meeting regularly to cruise with friends and acquaintances, most of them queer, many of them neither aristocratic nor particularly notable in their accomplishments. Together with Kuzmin, they formed a highly mixed milieu and closely linked their activities and manner of socialization to the physical landscape of the city. Characteristically, Kuzmin locates a vaguely described emotional state—"some kind of love"—not to the couples populating the streets but to the material environment surrounding them.

In this chapter, I focus on the interaction between physical space, patterns of movement, and the vaguer emotional valences of community, desire, love, and friendship that interpenetrated them. By looking at Kuzmin's recollections from the spring of 1906 in particular, a time when he records many instances of cruising, I hope to get a few steps closer to the elusive but not impossible role of the queer milieu as a refuge or sanctuary, a role that is often ignored in historical and geographical work on queer life precisely because these valences are so hard to track down. I acknowledge that Kuzmin's experiences are not capable of indefinite extrapolation—they are neither representative nor esoteric but are reflective of his particular community. Nevertheless, I am not concerned here with a comprehensive mapping of emotions to queer spatial patterns or even an investigation of the boundaries of their extrapolation to other queer men in the city. Instead, I hope to contextualize the queer spatial patterns described thus far by connecting them to one man's experience and bringing them to life there. Kuzmin's diary, which here fulfills the function of an in-depth interview, adds color and depth to what is otherwise a mock miniature of a city populated by wooden figurines or mechanical puppets. Kuzmin's recollections from the spring of 1906 are those of a man whose appetite for social, romantic, and sexual communion is still vast and only mildly differentiating, while his reflection and self-awareness are already those of a mature writer. During that time, his reunions with other regulars of his queer milieu were highly concentrated in one particular space, the Tavricheskii Garden, also known in English as the Tauride Garden, which served as a destination and starting point for his perambulatory adventures. Aside from being a celebrated poet, intellectual, and composer, a prominent figure in Russia's Silver Age, Kuzmin was a flaneur, a dandy, and a *tetka* who met regularly with his friends and acquaintances, with painters and writers but also with hooligans and *tapetkas* in the Tavricheskii Garden for a daytime stroll and humorous chat.[2]

The Tavricheskii Garden is near the city center. At the time of Kuzmin's walks, it boasted glades with fruit trees, picturesque ponds, and winding rivers crossed by neat metal bridges, cropped lawns, several pavilions, an abundance of benches, a restaurant, a café, and, depending on the season, other attractions such as an ice rink. According to Ulla Hakanen, who has written about St. Petersburg and the figures of the Russian Silver Age, the Tavricheskii Garden was an "area that has received surprisingly little attention in literature on St. Petersburg."[3] The Tavricheskii Garden has a fascinating history of its own, but here it is its role in late imperial St. Petersburg's queer milieu that warrants attention. The rambling paths, glades, and embankments of the garden played an important role as regular meeting places for queer men and for some, including Kuzmin, served as a relatively safe social setting—an emotional refuge among the city's public spaces.

I concentrate here on the spring and summer of 1906, during which Kuzmin committed to his diary recollections and anecdotes from his various strolls and encounters with friends in the Tavricheskii Garden, or Tavrida, as he calls it. His early diaries cover the period from 1905 to 1915, but the frequency of his visits to the Tavricheskii Garden peaked during the "season" of 1906, as he terms it.[4] His later entries from the years 1908 to 1915 generally became much briefer, in particular with regard to his meetings with other queer men.[5] For the purposes of the present discussion, therefore, I focus on Kuzmin's recollections from a period when visits to the Tavricheskii Garden occupied much of his attention and prompted him to record detailed descriptions of his movements through the city, his varied experiences of the queer milieu, and his very personal emotional responses. It is likely that even these descriptions are not a complete record of his visits to the garden. Nevertheless, in looking at them as a series and juxtaposing them with what is known about cruising in the historical city from other sources, I hope to reconnect his experience to the city in a way that informs or at least adds vitality to our reading of the spatial patterns discussed in this book.

This chapter starts with a brief description of the garden as a physical space and a hub of queer sociability and spatial practices. The second section connects this description to an emotional or allegorical map of cruising that Kuzmin and Konstantin Somov, a painter and at times Kuzmin's lover, set out to make. The third section explores Kuzmin's experience of flirtation, friendship, love, and confrontation as he participated in cruising patterns that often started in the garden. Finally, the fourth section looks at the interaction between cruising and friendship, tracing modes of queer socialization that suggest a more diffuse and less instrumental sexuality than that often attributed to queer men in the historical city.

Tavrida: A Queer Urban Arcadia

The garden's history began with an amorous and unusual affair. Shortly after having engineered the annexation of Crimea, Grigory Potemkin, who was also known as Prince Potemkin-Tavricheskii, the longtime paramour of Catherine the Great, received permission from the empress to build a palace and garden some two miles up the Neva River from her own palace, the Ermitazh (Hermitage). With the help of the English philosopher and designer of the panopticon, Jeremy Bentham, Potemkin hired William Gould to design a sophisticated landscaped garden in the English style of the time, replete with artificial hills and flowing water brought in through an elaborate system of canals that fed into the Neva. The garden was open by invitation only, and these were mainly sent to members of Catherine the Great's court and the intimates of Potemkin. After Potemkin's death, however, Catherine reappropriated the palace and garden, to which she made various additions, including a pavilion, several bridges, a luxurious villa for Gould, who had gone into her service, and an orangery. Following an interlude as the backyard of a stable and a cavalry regiment under Catherine's successor, the garden was restored and extended by Gould, who had made it his life's work and went on to serve Catherine's grandson, Alexander I. It was not until 1861 that this imagined urban arcadia finally opened to the general public: "On orders of the highest authority from July 24, the Tavricheskii Garden, with the exception of the greenhouse and orchard, is now open to the strolling public."[6]

Its reception was mixed. The garden itself, all agreed, was a work of art. Its location, although it was close to the city center, was problematic. A guidebook from the 1870s complains that the garden was located near residential areas inhabited by relatively poor residents. These included the Peski Borough, which furnished the garden with an unsavory clientele.[7] In 1887, Vladimir Mikhnevich, summarizing newspaper articles from the preceding years, called the garden an "open sore," again blaming the visitors from the neighboring borough for its demographic degradation: "The garden attracts all the wild, bacchanalian, and slothful elements of the local population," he grumbled.[8] Despite a typically vague order in 1888 from the City Duma and the mayor's office requiring strict surveillance and the prevention of "any outrageous or indecent acts whatsoever" in the garden, the complaints continued.[9] Finally, in a set of measures reminiscent of the manner in which the cleanup of the Passazh was attempted, the garden was rezoned and divided into three sections in the first years of the twentieth century. The first section, closest to the Tavricheskii Palace, was closed to the public altogether. The second section was accessible for an entrance fee. Here the city assigned venues for the establishment of commercial hospitality and entertainment, including a restaurant and a seasonal ice-skating rink. Finally, the third section, which encompassed much of the landscaped gardens as well as the ponds, remained open to everyone.[10] Like the reconstruction of the Passazh, the zoning and revitalization of the garden immediately earned it high praise as a uniquely bucolic, seemingly natural landscape in the middle of a teeming metropolis.[11] Queer men were early or perhaps returning enthusiasts and joined the crowds in both the freely accessible and the ticketed sections. Kuzmin was frequently among them. The garden's status as one of the favorite haunts of queer men in the city was hard to miss. In 1908, Vladimir Ruadze, whose investigation of the queer milieu had drawn him there, was one of the first to publicly acknowledge the association of the garden with queer spatial patterns.[12]

The physical landscape of the garden is important in understanding its role as part of the city's queer milieu. It stood apart as an artificial arcadia in miniature set against the background of the imposingly impersonal architecture of the central boroughs. It occupied about 1.5 square kilometers on the border between the Liteinaia and Rozhdestvenskaia Boroughs (see the top right of map 1 in chapter 1).[13] Other landscaped areas in the city, notably the nearby Summer Garden and the Field of Mars, followed classical French or German designs, resembling the Luxembourg Gardens in Paris in their promotion of austere symmetry over playful variation, visibility over privacy, and sand and stone over vegetation and water. Like St. Petersburg itself, these alternative destinations were flat and were visible in their entirety from any point within them or along their perimeter. Thus, they were ideally suited for surveillance. The topography of the Tavricheskii Garden could not have been more different. It had glades, hills, dense bunches of trees that felt like dark forests when one was among them, riverbanks, picturesque foot bridges, sheltered benches, and conversation pavilions. It provided ample opportunity to avoid observation—a familiar theme, of course, in the patterns of queer sociability—but also created a theatrical backdrop productive of surprise and drama for anyone who wished to be seen and noticed.[14] It was a garden made for walking, not standing or sitting, its rivulets and pools set in an undulating landscape that was reminiscent of the English shires or southern Germany. The resulting scenery was especially striking in this flat, planned city surrounded by treeless marshlands and organized around linear streets and waterways used for transport. The garden was versatile in its uses as well. Visitors walking in groups or pairs could present themselves or discreetly avoid observation.[15]

Aside from its landscape, the garden had other attractions. Soon after it reopened in 1892, public toilets and commercial venues such as restaurants, cafés, a summer dance floor, and a winter ice-skating rink appeared, adding modern entertainments to the arcadian atmosphere and creating a contrived and enigmatically modern urban setting for encounters between both strangers and friends.[16] The Tavricheskii Garden was, using the language of Miles Ogborn, "made of spectacles."[17] Functionally, if not aesthetically, like London's Vauxhall Gardens in the late eighteenth century, Tavrida provided a stage on which visitors could enjoy the "pleasures of looking at others."[18] For queer men, the topography offered obvious advantages, including the ability to move freely and quickly between places where observation was possible, indeed unavoidable, and places where lovers or friends could talk without being easily observed.

It would be unwise to generalize from Mikhail Kuzmin's practice and experience of cruising in the Tavricheskii Garden, but his account is that of a member of a community or milieu—a fact corroborated by several other sources, including Ruadze. Kuzmin unambiguously relates his excursions as a routine he shared with a large and diverse group of men. Although his activities and especially his reflections on them cannot be read as representative of all the cruising that took place either there or elsewhere in the city, they certainly do inform our understanding of a prominently visible collective spatial practice. This is doubly unique. For one, we have a source rich in detail and color, introspection and observation. Kuzmin's diary offers one of the very few records of a participant's views of late imperial St. Petersburg's queer milieu, and it is certainly the most detailed, unreserved, and emotionally explicit. For another, Kuzmin's diary complements a record otherwise dominated, as already described, by the prurient and forensic allure of furtive, criminalized sex and clandestine encounters. His recollections of cruising in the Tavricheskii Garden animate some of the routine adventures that were on offer to queer men in the city's public spaces, to add another oxymoron to a collection that already includes the "familiar stranger."

Kuzmin frequented this garden with his "friendly gang," as he called the group of regulars with whom he shared his strolls. Their excursions brought them to the Tavricheskii Garden but did not end there. Frequently the garden was a place to converse, flirt, assemble, make introductions, or meet a stranger before going on to any of a number of nearby destinations frequented by Kuzmin and his friends and acquaintances. These included the Znamenskaia Bathhouse, Morozov's restaurant, Nevsky Prospect, and a number of private rooms or apartments and other nearby public or semipublic locations. These patterns brought Kuzmin into social, romantic, and sexual contact with men from socioeconomic backgrounds entirely different from his own, including the young men he describes as "hooligans," who alternately threatened queer men like Kuzmin and offered themselves for sex, perhaps for a price.[19]

By connecting Kuzmin's experience of cruising in the Tavricheskii Garden to the friendships, patterns of movement, and manners of dress and appearance that marked his association with the queer milieu and provided him with sexual opportunity, one can begin to appreciate that queer cruising, although fraught with perils and pitfalls, was unlike the furtive pursuit of sex. In Kuzmin's case, it provided a social haven and refuge, the focal point of a shared tradition of carefully calibrated deviance in movements, behavior, and appearance that corresponded, of course, to a shared sexual interest. The connections between the queer spatial patterns of late imperial St. Petersburg and Kuzmin's personal, even intimate recollections demonstrate how queer men's participation in a spatial routine characterized their highly varied milieu and meant navigating not only a physical landscape rife with opportunities for sex but also the superimposed and interwoven geographies of affect, violence, and emotion.[20]

The Tavricheskii Garden as an Emotional Refuge

Tavricheskii Garden functioned as an emotional refuge for Kuzmin and his friends and their use of this space for cruising was essential to that function. An emotional refuge has sometimes been described as "a relationship, ritual, or organization (whether informal or formal) that provides safe release from prevailing emotional norms and allows relaxation of emotional effort, with or without an ideological justification, which may shore up or threaten the existing emotional regime."[21] The word "ritual" stands out in this definition, which, oddly, downplays the specific physical setting or stage for this emotional release. In the case of Kuzmin and his friends, a specific place, the Tavricheskii Garden, is so central to the ritual of cruising that the space itself functioned as an emotional refuge. Kuzmin and his companions came there precisely to let down their guard, to obtain "safe release from prevailing emotional norms," to flirt, joke, meet, and interact in a manner that was anything but furtive and reserved.

The term "cruising" itself is illustrative. Etymologically, it is a sailing term describing a pleasurable zigzagging (not functional tacking) on a favorable sea, a motion that does not require intense effort and one that presupposes a degree of safety—the proximity of a safe shore or harbor above all. Following Mark W. Turner and Henning Bech, I deploy this contemporary term in its queer connotation in what I believe is an appropriate anachronism to characterize the strolls of Kuzmin and his associates. The term fills a gap in the Russian language in use at the time.[22] Like the cruising in other cities that Turner described, Kuzmin's strolls in the Tavricheskii Garden engaged him in a collective activity with a dynamic of its own. It was "a process of walking, gazing, and engaging another (or others), and it [was] not necessarily about sexual contact."[23] It is important to underline the fact that here also cruising "isn't only about sex" and that "the dynamics of the gaze may be erotic and stimulating precisely because it does not end in *sex*."[24] Thus, the possibility of subsequent opportunities for sex as a form of potential energy, specifically of illicit or even illegal sex between two men, had to be present for a stroll to qualify as cruising, but it might be only one of several competing valences. For Kuzmin and his friends, this possibility, the hope of making a fortuitous acquaintance that might lead to sex, was a key motive for coming to the garden, but so was the opportunity to converse with like-minded friends. Fortunately for these men, the setting provided them not only with realistic prospects of finding a sexual partner but also with options for socializing and managing their behaviors in such a way as never to remove the cover of deniability, even though Kuzmin and his friends went quite far in displaying their affection for one another and in setting themselves apart from other visitors to the park.

A designation of the garden as a space in which licentious behavior could perhaps be taken a step further than in other locations created a set of opportunities that were at the heart of Kuzmin's experience of the queer milieu. The resulting visible claim of the queer milieu on the Tavricheskii Garden is corroborated most notably by Ruadze's 1908 pamphlet about queer St. Petersburg, but it is also evident in Kuzmin's recollections, which recount his strolls and encounters in the Tavricheskii Garden with queer men who were shopkeepers, tradesmen, hooligans, workers, wealthy merchants, aristocrats, and prominent artists or intellectuals.[25] However, Kuzmin reflections on his interactions and his experience of the park add important emotional and experiential depth to the descriptions of derogatory observers. His diary links the activity of cruising in the Tavricheskii Garden to the concept and reality of an emotional refuge that enabled St. Petersburg's queer milieu to function in this space with greater ease than in other locations across the city.

In applying the concept of an emotional refuge, I draw attention to the possibility of cruising as a sexually charged, but ultimately preeminently social activity in which shared or overlapping sexual inclinations provide an important common ground. This approach is not without precedent, though it has not often been applied to men. Carroll Smith-Rosenberg studies female friendship in nineteenth-century America as a story in which "sexual and emotional impulses," as she calls them, were but one part of "a continuum or spectrum of affect gradations strongly affected by cultural norms and arrangements."[26] Kuzmin's engagement as a queer man with the habitués of Tavricheskii Garden, whether inside or outside the garden, is similarly composed of instances all along this spectrum, an analysis of which helps us understand the role of the Tavricheskii Garden as another hub or haven in the queer urban landscape.

While cruising in Tavricheskii Garden, queer men wore their hearts on their sleeves, so to speak. Kuzmin's descriptions of cruising record not only his and his friends' highly noticeable behavior and appearance on many occasions but also the emotions he felt and believed he shared with his companions. "We were hysterical with laughter," he writes, or "he blushed," or "we missed his incessant complaints." These and other descriptions conjure up a relaxed emotional engagement with the Tavricheskii Garden. For Kuzmin, this was a place of pleasurable irritation, occasional ennui, frequent flirtation and leisurely banter, romantic or sexual potential, and lighthearted social intercourse. It was entirely incongruent with the efficient process of finding a sexual partner in Toronto's Allan Gardens, London's Hyde Park, or New York's Central Park, as described by various historians of these cities' queer milieus.[27]

It has been convincingly argued that, even empirically, "emotions are relational" rather than isolated, internal states, which implies that the emotional role and function of a particular space cannot be understood without attention to the system of relationships being enacted in that space, "producing as much as manifesting what may be felt to belong to one person or another."[28] It is in this sense that Kuzmin's descriptions of interactions with both the members of his "friendly gang" and other presumably queer and male "familiar strangers" and with hooligans, policemen, young ladies, and other visitors to the Tavricheskii Garden must be understood. These interactions are instructive in that they inform a view of the garden in which cruising covered a spectrum ranging from opaquely legible behavior, recognizable only to the initiated, to the flagrant and even flamboyant. Cruising was, for Kuzmin, intertwined in a spatial context that included not only the possibility of friendship, romance and sex but also that of violent beatings by hooligans, observation by police constables, and encounters with casual passersby. He describes a queer world, therefore, but one that is more than a homosocial idyll. His routine and ritual of strolling in the Tavricheskii Garden provided both an emotional refuge and a spatially circumscribed, partial relief from the threat of violence and police interference.

"Voyage du Pays du Tendre au Pays Chaud"

If there is a useful attenuation of the hydraulic portrayal of sexuality—male sexuality in particular, and perhaps iconically, queer male sexuality—it is provided by the notion of *tenderness* and its self-sufficient spatialization in the Tavricheskii Garden. During a stroll on June 15, 1906, as already mentioned in the introduction to this book, Kuzmin and his friend and onetime lover, the painter Konstantin Somov, spoke of creating a map centered on the garden that is the inspiration for the title of this book. On that map, the garden was to figure as the "pays du tendre," the land of tenderness or love—following the then-famous example of Mademoiselle (Madeleine) de Scudéry, a seventeenth-century French writer. Somov was to draft the map and Kuzmin to compose an accompanying poem titled "Voyage du pays du tendre au pays chaud," which meant a trip from tenderness or mere desire to the "hot country," or the land of sexual passion and lust. The French title implies that the map would show a route of travel, perhaps one along which both Kuzmin and Somov regularly traveled. Although the main "land of tenderness" was avowedly the Tavricheskii Garden, the "land of heat" is not explicitly specified. Most plausibly, they included several nearby commercial bathhouses, notably the Znamenskaia or Basseinaia Bathhouse, which we know Kuzmin frequented and which would have added a dimension of characteristically sly humor to their designation, given that these institutions were, indeed, purveyors of heat in the more innocent but by no means exclusive sense.[29]

Kuzmin and Somov's map project suggests the twin aspects of cruising—its emplacement of collective, shared, sentimental affection and embodied passion. In this sense, the two men map the Tavricheskii Garden as an unrepressive, sexualized space in which casual flirtation and friendship were not sublimational conveniences but undetermined pathways animated by the proximity and availability of nearby spaces in which illicit sexual desires could be consummated. This representation reflects their experience as Kuzmin recorded it. In his entry for June 18, 1906, for example, he describes a stroll with his "friendly gang" during which they observed men they fancied, met strangers and acquaintances, and were generally on the lookout for potential sexual partners.[30] In an earlier entry from April 17, 1906, he describes a sexual encounter with a bathhouse attendant in the Basseinaia Bathhouse, a mere five minutes' walk from the Tavricheskii Garden.[31] For Kuzmin and those among his friends and acquaintances who, like him, were not so fortunate as to have a private apartment at their disposal for a sexual tryst, the bathhouse with its separate rooms (or *nomernaia bania*; see chapter 4 on bathhouses) would have offered a nearby alternative. Thus, Kuzmin and Somov's joking resolution to map the route "from a place of tenderness to a place of heat," from love to lust, might have resulted in a visualization of the short walk from Tavricheskii Garden to the Basseinaia or Znamenskaia Bathhouses.[32] Nevertheless, it is clear from Kuzmin's diary that the connection was more conceptual than empirical. In his case, cruising only rarely led to a sexual encounter. On many occasions, communion with his friends was itself the consummation he pursued and this offered a sufficient basis for contented diaristic reflection.[33] The map was allegorical first and foremost, an "inside joke" among the already sufficiently oriented, although, of course, it corresponded to a spatial reality also described in Kuzmin's diary. Perhaps for this reason the map was never drawn. Befitting its conversational and playful provenance, the map's discursive amalgamation of the Tavricheskii Garden with hidden and heated rooms in nearby bathhouses infused the strolls of Kuzmin and Somov with a subversive potential that did not require actual movement along the map's presumed paths to capture the synergies between "tenderness" and "heat."

Underscoring this at once spatial and allegorical configuration, their map is, of course, a reference, whether intentional or not, to Mademoiselle de Scudéry's famous *Carte du Tendre*. That map, replete with its own hydraulic system, including a conspicuous-looking estuary and a landlocked "lake of indifference," first appeared in the novel *Clélie*. Its popularity and acclaim by far eclipsed that of the novel containing it. This prototypical amorous geography would probably have been known to Kuzmin and Somov, who both spoke and read French.[34] It records the stages of romantic propriety and the dangers and temptations awaiting those who stray from the path of mutual affection and esteem. In humorous perversion of the theme, Kuzmin and Somov show a more direct and altogether less allegorical route from social encounter to sexual engagement—and back again. The antipodes of a social round involving, perhaps, some flirtation in the garden and the sexual assignations of the bathhouses stand out. Indeed, the pattern applied regardless of whether the walk was taken alone, with a partner, or in a group, insofar as sex was, as we have seen, on offer in the "land of heat" in any case. Yet theirs too is a spatial abstraction, a recordable pattern of social, sexual, and emotional engagement with urban space, transcribed as an allegorical journey, open to but only occasionally undertaken by some of the queer men who convened in the Tavricheskii Garden. In this sense it echoes de Scudéry's map closely. Thomas McDonough points out that on de Scudéry's map, fictitious landmarks "figured as narratives" that could be passed through in virtually any sequence or inhabited indefinitely. He describes it as a "psychogeographical map . . . each segment of which has a different 'unity of atmosphere.'"[35]

The map discussed by Kuzmin and Somov similarly divided the stations of cruising according to their relational role, although in Kuzmin's own experience this progression was not a strict necessity. The garden as the locus of agreed rendezvous with friends or unexpected, trembling encounters could as readily be a destination as a point of departure toward the baths, where a more passionate, sexual sort of engagement might follow. The patterns, however, could just as easily be reversed. Like the landscape depicted by Mademoiselle de Scudéry, it was, of course, a world of limited privilege that Kuzmin and Somov inhabited. Both were aristocrats and could earn an income from their artistic work, although Kuzmin's income was only about average for men living in St. Petersburg in 1906.[36] From an economic perspective, they represented an urban middle class, by no means the decadent world of the very rich that St. Petersburg was also known for. From their vantage point as accomplished, handsome, sexually active queer men, their map highlights the spatial dynamic of a retrievable and social adventure, the perambulatory activity of cruising in the company of friends and "familiar strangers," infused with the possibility of a much more directed detour to one of the nearby baths. While the proximity of the countries of tenderness and heat was spatial and literal, it also allegorically underpinned a ritual of queer sociability.

That Kuzmin and Somov intended their map to depict physical and more-than-physical movements fits well with William Reddy's emphasis on rituals for creating an emotional refuge. The walk in and from the gardens was capable of facilitating the "safe release" and "relaxation of emotional effort" so characteristic of an emotional refuge.[37] Though it is not known to have been actually painted by Somov, the map he and Kuzmin conceived sheds light on the connections between the spatial, emotional, and sexual sustenance of cruising in the Tavricheskii Garden.

Et in Arcadia Ego: Other "Familiar Strangers"

The "pays du tendre," it must be said, was populated not just by Kuzmin's "friendly gang" but also by constables, hooligans, and other visitors to the garden. The overlap and interactions between Kuzmin's habitual companions and other groups in this diverse social environment characterized the spatial practice of cruising and their particular queer milieu at least as much as the connections between the "pays du tendre" and the "pays chaud." Kuzmin's diary entries from late spring 1906 highlight the role that the Tavricheskii Garden played in his romantic affairs and disappointments, in his friendships and encounters with queer men and other contemporaries.

In the late afternoon of May 28, 1906, Kuzmin joined his friends Stepan and Vasilii, sellers of icons and antiquities in a shop that Kuzmin frequented, for a stroll in the Tavricheskii Garden. His friends, who were already slightly drunk, "teased constables" and made fun of young female passersby.[38] As mentioned in chapter 4, their behavior, which included tripping the young ladies and standing under their umbrellas uninvited, was flagrantly provocative and calculated to attract attention. Evidently, they did not expect this attention to prompt police intervention, even though constables had options available to them (recall the use of petty crimes statutes described in chapter 2).

Beyond their blithe indolence, Kuzmin and his friends self-consciously underlined their frivolity by their choice of dress and appearance. Before setting off to the Tavricheskii Garden, Vasilii wished to put on makeup. Kuzmin expertly counseled him to apply rouge only to parts of the face "where it is unmistakable as rouge and not a blush." Vasilii was not convinced.[39] As for Kuzmin, we know from his diary and the many surviving photographs and portraits of him that he regularly wore makeup and was a punctilious, if eccentric, dresser. In spring 1906, his flirtations with the faith of the Old Believers, whom he had considered joining as a priest, were still relatively recent, and he sometimes wore their stern, double-breasted black overcoat above his signature bright spot of color in the form of a silk tie or yellow shirt. He liked to top it off by pinning a yellow daffodil to his coat, a well-known sign of mutual recognition between queer men, and he often donned a worker's flat cap, which had the effect of softening the clear class distinctions between himself and the hooligans, tradesmen, shop assistants, and workers with whom he associated in the park besides artists and aristocrats.[40] When he was in the Tavricheskii Garden, his dress never exposed him to unwanted attention. This was not the case everywhere, even in the city center. A week later, as he sat waiting in a cab on Nevsky Prospect, a constable asked him pointedly "what sort of uniform" he was wearing, adding that it was not per se "incriminating."[41]

On May 28, as on several other occasions, Kuzmin described his experience of the Tavricheskii Garden as "not very fun," but it still served its purpose as a gathering place in which he could let his guard down, reconnect with friends, make new acquaintances, see young men with whom sex was always on offer for pay, or simply while away the hours before the start of his and his friends' nighttime adventures.[42] When in the garden, they casually exploited the restraint shown by constables, which was by no means the exclusive domain of Kuzmin and his friends. As mentioned in chapter 2, if complaints of anonymous informers and investigative journalists like Ruadze are to be believed, police showed similar restraint toward the hooligans on their own or in interactions with members of other groups.[43] The playfully provocative behavior of Kuzmin's friends on that May 28, 1906, and their flamboyant appearance on this or other occasions should thus be seen in the context of the garden's designation as a "place for some light fun," perhaps a stroll of young lovers, some flirtation, a minor fight or confrontation, and the general mixing of classes and pleasures. Even the revealing continued patronage of the Society for Popular Sobriety suggests that the rezoning had failed to dispel the garden's enduring reputation for license and licentiousness, which constables were unprepared to suppress. Against this background, it is not altogether surprising that during another stroll in the Tavricheskii Garden a month later, Kuzmin proposed holding hands with his lover—a waiter and a regular in his circle—in order to "show everyone our love."[44]

The evening in the Tavricheskii Garden with Stepan and Vasilii proved to be entertaining, but it did not live up to Kuzmin's expectations. His companions, who had raised Kuzmin's hopes of meeting a new potential lover, failed to introduce him to anyone with whom "he might be undisposed to make a closer acquaintance."[45] After the departure of Vasilii, who settled for an old acquaintance, Stepan and Kuzmin departed to the nearby restaurant *Rossiia* affectionately termed Morozov's after the owner, one of Kuzmin's regular haunts. There they were joined by Semen Katkov, a salesman in a shop for undergarments, and Adolf Lange, a young polyglot typesetter of winning appearance whom Katkov had invited on Kuzmin's suggestion. The night ended in disaster. The physical affections exchanged between the men at Kuzmin's table—"caresses," as he calls them—provoked unwanted attention and derogatory remarks from guests at the neighboring table. A minor confrontation ensued, during which Lange hit a woman from the neighboring table. An open brawl was only barely prevented by the establishment's waiters, one of whom had taken a drink with Kuzmin and his friends just before. That waiter escorted the guests at the neighboring table out of the restaurant. It did not end there, however. As Kuzmin learned the next day when he visited Stepan and Vasilii at their shop, soon after he had left, a group of workers, perhaps tipped off and tipped, had attacked the waiters in apparent revenge. In the ensuing fight, Katkov sided with the waiters and was slashed across the forehead with a knife. He lost consciousness and spent the next week recovering in a hospital.

It is clear that even Kuzmin's status as an aristocrat would have done little to protect him had he been there. "If only he had left with me," Kuzmin reflects, "he would not have been caught, but if we had all stayed, we might have seen it all and would have found ourselves in the same danger. I imagine the fight, screams, all the running in different directions in the gray dawn, and the only figure left at the scene—a pale curly-haired boy lying in his blood, whom I had just caressed."[46] A few days later, following another walk in the Tavricheskii Garden and a cab ride across Nevsky, Kuzmin himself was beaten up by eight strangers who had clearly lain in wait for him and his group. Vasilii and Lange had also "been involved in conflicts," which Kuzmin suspects were related to the encounter of the week before in Morozov's restaurant. Kuzmin, in reflecting on this disconcerting series of events, regretfully faults himself for associating with hooligans. For Kuzmin, Katkov's injury and his own involvement in a drawn-out physical confrontation were uncomfortable reminders of the dangers that lay in wait for him when he left the narrow confines of the extensively surveilled but conveniently licentious Tavricheskii Garden and looked elsewhere for amorous adventures with men outside his class.

Kuzmin's experience harks back to the dossier discussed in chapter 1. As an aristocrat, who at thirty-three was no longer quite young, he might easily have qualified as a typical "auntie." He certainly diverted a part of his limited income to provide young men like the would-be icon dealer Pavlik, perhaps the shop clerk Katkov, and the typesetter Lange with contributions toward a more "merry and easy existence" than that which would otherwise have been available to them.[47] Some of the men in this circle, notably Kuzmin's periodic lover Sasha, ticked yet another of the dossier's boxes. Sasha married, although he continued his meetings with Kuzmin. The parallels do not end there, yet they also encompass the sharply contrasting paradigms of Drs. Vladimir Merzheevskii and Veniamin Tarnovskii, who denounced the impecunious youths whom the author of the ministerial dossier was eager to exculpate. Like the bureaucrats and aristocrats Tarnovskii described, who became the victims of blackmail by decidedly unaccomplished ruffians and opportunists, Kuzmin feared the possible consequences of the "caresses" he shared with Katkov and Lange, whom he classed as "hooligans."[48] Not only does he fear that their shared "secret exposes . . . [him] to blackmail," but his entry from June 5 suggests that a poorly dressed middle-aged man who had only just been turned away by a yard keeper had attempted to visit Kuzmin at home and make good on these perceived threats.[49]

Kuzmin's diary, nonetheless, wreaks havoc with the forensic agendas of earlier accounts of the queer milieu by telling a multidimensional story set in the physical spaces that Kuzmin and his friends came to frequent. These stories played out in the real places that according to broadly consistent accounts queer men frequented, but they are also told as they unfold, without hindsight and apparent revision and with the emotional and biographical detail that is usually missing in the otherwise undocumented sexual and romantic relationships of the men who did not get caught. Pavlik, for example, whom Kuzmin met in the Tavricheskii Garden on June 11, 1906, is neither victim nor exploiter in the two men's subsequent relationship. Although Kuzmin occasionally paid Pavlik, who struggled to make ends meet, the latter sharply denied that their relationship depended on these payments and even attempted in an emotional outburst to prevent them.[50] Similarly, Pavlik seemed anything but a reluctant convert to homosexual love and sex. If the diary is to be believed, Kuzmin's support had little influence on Pavlik's sexual proclivities, about which the two men spoke openly. Pavlik confessed an interest in one of Kuzmin's aristocratic friends, but on the same occasion showed an even keener interest in a man of a station similar to his own.[51] Even more important, Pavlik and Kuzmin seemed at times to transcend the transactional and contingent nature of their relationship. Kuzmin dedicated one of his most romantic poems, "Summer Love," to Pavlik, and Pavlik reinforced Kuzmin's impression of their relationship as sincere when he continued seeing Kuzmin during periods when the latter could not pay.[52]

After his adventures of May 28, 1906, and the following week that had started in the Tavricheskii Garden but turned sour elsewhere, and even after his encounter with Pavlik, Kuzmin continued to frequent the garden. There he met Pavlik and other members of his extended gang, which included shop clerks like Stepan and Vasilii as well as luminaries of the artistic world like Sergei Diaghilev and Somov.[53] Their ritual in this space and the role of police, who sustained a minimum degree of safety but did not interfere in any minor instances of licentious or even disorderly behavior, seemed as much a refuge and blessing to Kuzmin as it was odious to other visitors and observers. In 1908, Ruadze describes the Tavricheskii Garden as being dominated by "depraved women, alcoholics who can barely stand up, a huge gang of thieves, hooligans, pimps, and the homosexual world."[54] As though echoing Kuzmin's recollections, Ruadze also points toward a strong degree of overlap between what he calls the "homosexual world" and the demographic of "hooligans," describing a member of the latter group whom he met in the Tavricheskii Garden as "a typical homosexual coquette."[55]

The visits of Kuzmin and his "friendly gang" to the Tavricheskii Garden and their encounters with "familiar strangers" there evince some of the ways participants in the queer milieu navigated the risks and exploited the inherent unruliness of this space to enact strolls that were both collective mutual affirmation and visible performance. Judith Butler describes such performances as decisive in laying claim to and defining an urban space, and this may well have been the case here.[56] For Kuzmin and his "friendly gang," the garden was an environment where queer men *performed* their desires in a recognizable but always deniable spectacle and where their claim of authorship to the regular spatial patterns they carried out enjoyed a considerable degree of resilience.

Cruising as a Sociable Activity

But Kuzmin's queer milieu, as described in his accounts of visits to the Tavricheskii Garden and other locations in the city center, was characterized by a degree of sociability suggestive of a diffuse and community-based sexuality. For him, cruising was an opportunity to reconnect with friends and acquaintances he saw regularly and to extend his social network, to meet men who might merely be like-minded, but who might also become friends, occasional sexual partners, or even longer-term lovers. Going to the garden meant participating in a set of retrievable spatial patterns that integrated him with a loosely knit community of men. These men shared his desire for sex with other men and his willingness, at least during their strolls in this location, to reveal this allegiance. It was anything but a solitary search for a sexual partner in an anonymous and clandestine encounter.

Kuzmin's emphatic hope on some occasions was that a rendezvous with his regulars might lead to an introduction to a potential lover, a man someone in his "friendly gang" was bound to know already. On other occasions, he went there to meet and converse with someone who was already his lover, such as Somov or Pavlik, or simply to socialize and converse with friends—men among whom he could let down his guard. On still other occasions, the Tavricheskii Garden was no more than the departure point for a beeline to Kuzmin's apartment or a nearby bathhouse or perhaps a more extended and potentially more dangerous adventure that took him to other sites in the city center. Kuzmin recorded a total of twenty-nine visits to the Tavricheskii Garden between May 2 and September 10, 1906, the period when his visits seemed to be most frequent. Characteristically, he tends to use the first person plural when he recounts his visits, noting names only of new or irregular companions or of friends he had hoped to meet there but who had failed to come (e.g., "Walter Nouvel and Somov were not there"). In a typical diary entry from March 9, 1907, where he uses a term that I have borrowed throughout this book, Kuzmin writes, "We went for a walk, saw Yusin, Chesnokov, Pavlik, and other familiar strangers."[57] The first person plural refers to Kuzmin and Nouvel, a palace official who was also a musician, and to the company of regulars who had joined them earlier for a game of cards in Nouvel's apartment.

Sometimes Kuzmin recorded their topics of conversation, which revealed a degree of intimacy and a shared jargon that underlay their experience of cruising. They discussed the kinds of men who attracted them. They poked fun at Léon Bakst, a painter and stage designer who "conscientiously and somewhat resignedly inspects youngsters."[58] Kuzmin and his married onetime lover, Sasha, resolved to introduce each other to certain "literate" acquaintances, a designation reserved for men who were eager to have sex with other men. Like enthusiastic but slightly awkward adolescents, they sought each other's advice on how to approach the men they fancied, underscoring the impression of the Tavricheskii Garden and their joint activity of cruising there as not just a sexual but also an emotional and social resource for Kuzmin and his companion. As if to underscore that impression, Kuzmin completed his entry on the previous day with the exclamation: "I am so cheerful and happy, and it is rarely that spring and summer are so bright. I have never had such a friendly gang."[59]

Kuzmin's descriptions of cruising in Tavricheskii Garden as a sociable activity differ from the forensic and journalistic accounts of his day as well as from descriptions of cruising in other contemporary major urban centers.[60] Although fin-de-siècle observers focused on the transactional, often mercenary nature of encounters between men, on what Dan Healey calls "male sexual exchange," Kuzmin's diary indicates that commercial sex was but one aspect of the queer urban milieu territorialized in the Tavricheskii Garden and not necessarily the most prominent one, if his diaristic descriptions are any indication.[61] Kuzmin's use of the Tavricheskii Garden for sociable cruising differs equally starkly from the sordid, solitary, and dangerous search for sex variously described by queer urban historians of Western cities around the same time.[62] Compare cruising around Memorial Square in Toronto, which, during the period from 1890 to 1930, according to Steven Maynard, was an activity explicitly and exclusively aimed at finding a partner for sexual intercourse. Thus, it was carried out "of course, most often at night, under the cover of darkness."[63] This is in marked contrast to Kuzmin's descriptions of languid afternoons and early evening strolls in Tavricheskii Garden, all very much out in the open. Similarly, Matt Cook describes cruising in turn-of-the-century London as a lone prowl in the dark with a specific, entirely sexual objective.[64] Kuzmin's recollections carry the imprint of an entirely different experience: darkness, secrecy, and isolation would all have been quite antithetical to his cruising experience. On no occasion does he record visiting the Tavricheskii Garden at night. Mutual visibility was as important to his practice of cruising as was the sociability of his "friendly gang" and their differentiation by behavior and dress from outsiders. Cruising here seems closer to a socialized and collectivized flanêrie than the furtive and often clumsy escapades that were so much more likely to leave traces in the forensic record of this and other cities. This means that it is paradoxically more obscure but at the same time more valuable to an understanding of the historical geography of the queer milieu.

To Kuzmin, cruising established and reinforced his sense of belonging to a diverse and thematically composed community of queer men, a distinctly urban milieu. His visits to the Tavricheskii Garden established and strengthened social ties among a group of men who shared overlapping illicit sexual desires, but also much more, as it turns out, including an understanding of the city's queer topography, a jargon, manners of dress, favorite haunts, a routine of spatial patterns and modes of socialization—even a sense of humor and, in some cases, aesthetic or sexual tastes and predilections. Membership happened by repetition, advanced in degrees, and was linked to attendance. As Kuzmin and his friends aptly put it in their choice of terms, in the broadest possible sense, queerness for them was a matter of reading the city and its queer milieu, a matter of being "literate," of knowing their way in both geographical and sexual terms from the "pays du tendre" to the "pays chaud." Cruising in the "pays du tendre," the Tavricheskii Garden, was an integrative and constitutive practice for this sociable community.

Kuzmin was certainly an insider who enjoyed the full benefit of the garden as an emotional refuge and social or sexual resource. In his recollections, no spontaneous meetings with complete strangers take place in the Tavricheskii Garden. Rather, when he spoke to a stranger, he either knew him as another habitué or, more likely, was introduced by mutual acquaintances. For Kuzmin and the members of his community, cruising in the Tavricheskii Garden was a perpetual urban excursion into a familiar geography and community rather than a focused pursuit of a narrowly defined goal. In their spatial navigation of the garden, they laid claim to an emotional and social landscape in which their movements and interactions permitted "safe release from prevailing emotional norms," in this case decidedly "without an ideological justification."[65] All the same, it would be going too far to describe cruising as purely a lighthearted affair. Kuzmin often left the garden disappointed, recording that it had been either too busy, too empty, boring, or frequently enough "not very fun." On one occasion he describes the Tavricheskii Garden as being full of "faces that are vapid and ugly to the point of desperation! I understand that one day after such a stroll I might hang myself."[66] When even the garden—which Kuzmin counted on to sustain his sense of community and provide him with sexual and romantic opportunity—failed, he felt with particular acuteness his estrangement in an anonymous and often hostile city. This estrangement centered on what he describes as disappointment in his routine and a sense of alienation from his queer community of "familiar strangers," but it was reinforced by what he experienced as the threat and reality of physical violence that he encountered when he strayed outside the geographical and demographic perimeter he frequented.

For Kuzmin, the spatial practice of cruising in the Tavricheskii Garden was the best option available for the pursuit of community, romance, and sex. His routine in this space provided Kuzmin and his friends with the opportunity to carve out an emotional refuge that they continually reconstituted and extended via new encounters or visits to other nearby locations. As an emotional refuge, it had to be negotiated and integrated with the activities of other—at times overlapping—groups and communities. These included constables, passersby, and a broader milieu of hooligans, whose presence in the garden could be negotiated with a lesser degree of caution than was requisite in other public and semipublic spaces in the city.

Erotically laden and communally queer as it was, cruising in the Tavricheskii Garden was not exclusively focused on sexual gratification. Although Kuzmin does record sexual encounters in his diary, on no occasion does he mention one that took place *in* the Tavricheskii Garden or even in the nearby public toilets. By contrast and proximity, the nearby commercial bathhouses, mentioned in the context of Kuzmin and Somov's literary "map," were already a hybrid space that catered to both sexual and social interactions, offering them like items on a menu. While in the garden, Kuzmin's interactions and relationships were settled within a community, the city's queer milieu, in which sex was prominent but present in this particular space only in a latent capacity. Whether or not encounters and relationships among members of Kuzmin's "friendly gang" or even between them and a larger circle of "familiar strangers" actually culminated in sex on any particular occasion, the possibility was an important feature of their joint strolls and imbued them with a sense of purpose and adventure. So long as this adventure took place in the Tavricheskii Garden, if Kuzmin's recollections are to be believed, his and other men's glances could be direct, as were their conversation and their transparent displays of affection. He and the men he met there regularly did not have to rely on the subterfuge of nocturnal backward glances.

The spatial analogy of a refuge or safe haven helps in deciphering the rituals and relationships supported by Kuzmin's practice of cruising. As a concept that has been explored so successfully by William Reddy, "refuge" applies to a broad range of situations. Here it helps in reading and interpreting Kuzmin's routine of visits to the Tavricheskii Garden. It connects the physical space of the garden to queer sociability, and prompts us as retrospective "readers" to contextualize this refuge, much the way Kuzmin and Somov did in their fanciful contemplation of the map: the journey from the "pays du tendre" to the "pays chaud" and back again.

Just as readily as a stroll in the garden could segue into sex in a location where such an activity was convenient, it could serve as the prequel to a far-flung adventure in the city or a brutal beating in the street. Here, as with less allegorical maps, departing from the known paths could end in discovery or disaster. The Tavricheskii Garden was a familiar and well-marked point of departure, a harbor of sorts from whence Kuzmin and the participants in his milieu embarked on broader spatial patterns that interpenetrated the city. Kuzmin and Somov's "voyage du pays du tendre au pays chaud" is emblematic as the most reliable and reproducible of these patterns. It confirms that specific urban places in the city had well-established and complementary roles in queer socialization and encounters, interlocking with the lives and activities of queer men to form a distinct community and milieu. This and other routes of travel connected the Tavricheskii Garden to a wider landscape of queer sociability. The city was more than a backdrop to this emotional refuge. To Kuzmin, who had come to St. Petersburg as an adult from his native Yaroslavl' and in many ways shared the fate of most migrants by moving in with family members, cruising combined navigation of the city's varied physical spaces with social and sexual exploration.

"The straight lines of Petersburg," Kuzmin wrote, have "their poetry, in the style of some A. Benoit."[67] But the queer milieu was mapped out within and against these arteries and vistas. Much as Kuzmin loved and admired this geometrical city, the Tavricheskii Garden was valuable to him precisely as a space that deviated from the linear architectural rigor of the city's grand design. Kuzmin was not unique in responding to this attraction, although he was perhaps particularly attuned to it, given his literary achievements and preoccupations. According to Matthew Gandy, the tripartite connection between literature, landscape, and male-male sexuality was well established in the pastoral. According to an "eroticized reading of nature and landscape," he writes, "the pastoral genre" has been both an "inspiration for much park design" and a sexually ambivalent "'state of innocence'" with a long-standing literary connection to a "natural state of homoeroticism."[68] This particular pastoral landscape with its undulations, groups of trees, and glades provided a counterpoint in a severe city. To Kuzmin and men like him, it served as a refuge in an otherwise unwelcoming metropolis, accessible to the "literate" through their enactment of the spatial patterns constitutive of the city's queer milieu.

Conclusion

It might be said that this book is not about queer men at all but about the city—more specifically, about efforts by municipal and national authorities to contain, manage, and suppress the queer milieu and about the ways these efforts were frustrated. Such a claim has more than a bit of merit. Among the sources used for this book, the ratio of firsthand testimony by queer men to texts about them by men avowedly eager to suppress the expression of queer desire would be very small. This is a criticism I should be perfectly prepared to accept. For a start, the city is itself a worthwhile subject, all the more so if it can be explored in a new way. But I would also contend that the city—and specifically the efforts of its appointed authorities to compel it to conform to some ideal vision of spatial order—created the mold, later discarded and entirely forgotten, that once surrounded the queerness of St. Petersburg, allowing it to take shape. What I mean is that many factors had a very practical, immediate, and real impact on the lives of queer men. These included precinct-level police protocols, ministerial dossiers, citywide directives, orders for spatial modifications, sanitary regulations, approved designs of urinals, streetlights, tram lines, the landscaping of public gardens, and instruction manuals for police officers. These varied and discreet phenomena, so material but also so mundane, touched these lives more directly than explicitly homophobic laws, since the most draconian were not usually enforced. They also touched them much more frequently than the clinical cases cited in the sexological definition of "the homosexual" and his discursive annunciation. Viewed comprehensively in the ways that I have argued in this book, queer men came into contact with the surfaces created by and described in these documents on a daily basis and whenever they participated in the spatial patterns of queer urban life.

As reflected in efforts to manage its public spaces, the city was always immediate and palpable to queer men, not just as a constraint or even as a set of opportunities. Queer life is not just molded by the city, it is also the result of the friction created by the intersection of different sorts of matter at the meeting point between efforts of spatial ordering and queer lives. We should not forget the violence that is involved in queer history. Foucault wrote of the "infamous man" that his seemingly insignificant and disregarded life left a trace—perhaps preserved in some government archive—only at the point where it painfully intersected with an authority that had the overwhelming power to crush or stifle it. The documentary traces of these lives, later recovered and brought to light, are "snares, weapons, cries, gestures, attitudes, ruses, intrigues for which the words have been the instruments."[1] An intrusive and coercive authority is the condition for the memory of these marginal figures. Archival recovery reenacts, even amplifies, this violence, or at least that is an ever-present danger.

Equally sobering is Foucault's contention that "it is doubtless impossible ever to recapture them in themselves, such as they might have been 'in a free state.'"[2] I do not quite share Foucault's pessimism about the absolute irretrievability of these obscure "infamous lives," about their release from the words written about them and from the pain and power those records embody. The resistance metaphor that has shaped so much of queer history supposes that power and authority were necessarily a threat to queer expression, but this was not always the case. Many actions by municipal authorities were either directly conducive to the emergence of a visible and retrievable queer milieu or else supported an entente, a neutral state not of toleration but of clearly circumscribed noninterference. These actions were nevertheless defining for the queer milieu and queer spatial patterns. Recollect the opportunities created by streetlights, public urinals, trams, family sections in the bathhouse and the redesign of the Tavricheskii Garden. No less important was the restraint (always surprising to those invested in the resistance paradigm) shown by authorities in other contexts. The directive to track down queer men in their own apartments was successfully resisted, not by its potential victims but by constables and precinct supervisors. And consider the decision of the policeman charged with interviewing the young, bereft Johan about the disappearance of his friend, not to call explicitly for an investigation of the queer aspects of this case. Consider also those who determined whether or not to arrest Raikovskii, who had been denounced by a former lover. We do not know and we never will know if the constables in question were motivated by tolerance and forbearance. If they were, they hid it well. More likely, however, they conducted their work routinely, performing a more or less consistent triage across cases such as these. For whatever reason, these spaces or cases did not make the cut. They were crowded out by those for which further action was felt to be warranted, cases that were more manageable, more significant, less embarrassing, less intractable.

This is not to say that constables simply turned a blind eye to queer men. The encounter of Ludwig Zimmel' with the constables policing the easterly stretch of Nevsky Prospect on the night of September 25, 1900, was an outrageously mismatched collision between the individual and the machinery of authority, exactly of the type that Foucault describes so well. But extrapolating indiscriminately from these cases is not only discouraging but also misleading and leaves unexplored much of the experience of queer men in the historical city. By using archival snippets and amalgamating them with all the available sources, it is possible, despite the odds, to move the queer milieu into better focus. We might take the metaphor of sight and lenses further, since it is so important to accounts of power. Here, we have a kind of photographic negative of what cruising, bathing, queer socialization, and the cat-and-mouse game of policing must have been for queer men in their everyday lives. Processing this negative is fraught with difficulty, but it is rewarding. Certainly much more survives than the momentary flash of getting caught, beaten, punished, or expelled, where offenders are startled and shamed in the acts of their apprehension.

I have tried to complement and expand a picture constrained by a prior emphasis on laws, court cases, and medical treatises in the case of late imperial St. Petersburg but have done so in the hope and conviction that this approach will reap benefits in its possible application to other cities as well, especially cities outside of the familiar pale of queer histories focused on a handful of great Western metropolises. In addition to the use of previously unexamined sources, I have allowed myself license to make explicit inferences guided by a transparent reading of ellipses, allusions, and omissions in these and previously known sources and to transfer a number of helpful concepts to this non-Western context in order to decipher the interaction between queer spatial patterns and government action. Finally, I have undertaken to recover the traces of an emotional range of encounters and communion associated with this city's historical queer milieu. In the form of the diaries and fictional works of Mikhail Kuzmin and in the occasional statements of men recorded and plausibly rendered by representatives of the state, these fragments provide a depth that to a small but important degree offsets the lopsidedness of the surviving testimonies. In so doing, I have tried to resurrect the "infamous man" from his ignominy.

These interlocking projects underscore the crucial importance of recognizing and addressing ambiguity as a hallmark of the historical queer milieu. Given this recognition, which strikes me as both traditionally underemphasized and thrillingly useful, the lives of queer men in late imperial St. Petersburg suddenly appear to have a lot in common with the researcher's effort to collate the occasional signs and markers of the queer milieu into a geography of not only sexual opportunity but also social pleasures and emotional sustenance. A similar deciphering and interpreting of highly ambiguous evidence would have been the prerequisite for participation in the city's queer milieu. A participant required not only the map but also the literacy (including the emotional literacy) to read it. Take, for example, Vania, the protagonist of Kuzmin's only novel, *Wings*, an early-twentieth-century fictional account of what one might today describe as a coming-out story set in late imperial St. Petersburg. Although the protagonist's gradual, growing awareness of his desires and how to satisfy them is the main topic of the book, Kuzmin diligently eschews any explicit acknowledgment of what would have been a criminal act. This precaution did not protect him. *Wings* was promptly censored as "pornography," it was forcibly withdrawn from sale, and its author was fined two hundred rubles (the equivalent of at least eight average monthly salaries), with the threat of a jail term if he could not pay.[3] But even if Kuzmin failed to get his work past the censor, who displayed impressive subtlety on this occasion, the author's artistry and artfulness are instructive for the archaeologist of queer life. Unabashedly flirtatious in public in his nonliterary life, Kuzmin here preserved for our reference the nuanced art of detecting and navigating the urban queer milieu.

An illustration of this notion and its connection to ambiguity as an important and unavoidable theme for both the researcher and the participant of the queer milieu comes early in the novel. Vania unexpectedly becomes privy to a seemingly trivial conversation that hints at the homosexual nature of the relationship between two men in his social circle. On the recommendation of a friend, a fellow aristocrat named Stroop, he visits the keeper of an old icon. At this man's house, he hears his host chide another visitor, Stroop's manservant Fyodor, for "indulging himself" with his master.[4] Vania intuitively understands what is meant. At first he hesitates to trust his intuition and for a while is convinced that he is "seeing ghosts." Kuzmin writes, "Vania saw all this as in a dream, feeling as though he were falling into some sort of abyss and that everything was being obscured in a mist."[5] Without ever receiving explicit confirmation, however, it becomes clear in subsequent passages of the novel that Vania was not *seeing ghosts* after all. Fyodor and Stroop were indeed partners in a sexual, if not romantic, relationship. They were participants in the city's queer milieu, which Vania was about to enter.

The fictional Vania's exegetical attitude is implicitly recommended by Kuzmin to his readers and, as is the central assertion of this book, should be deployed with a degree of urgency to the historical scholarship of the queer milieu, which otherwise risks mischaracterizing its object as it grasps for rare certainties. Through Vania, Kuzmin describes a shared engagement, a conversation with "familiar strangers" that left few explicit traces, but was also not a purely introspective and personal preoccupation. What is more, it is an engagement that extends far beyond the fact of sex between men or even an acknowledged desire for it. Hence, its investigation requires moving the focus away from documents that identify criminal and "debauched" acts and the often wretched individuals who were caught committing them. Instead, it shifts into focus the means by which these men—often successfully—navigated their world, the queer milieu, as I have termed it here. This navigation and its retrospective reconstruction require the consideration of a range of people (whether identifying as queer or not) and the places and influences that allowed and constrained, encouraged and enticed queer relationships.

In Kuzmin's *Wings*, Vania's maturation involves a heightened sensitivity to and ultimate engagement with certain patterns that he encounters in the city, a sense of adventure, of something being not quite what it seems to be, of being slightly awkward, but richer and rifer with opportunity than the world he had recognized until then. Characteristically, Kuzmin conveys a sense of the city's queer milieu by engaging his readers' intuition just as his protagonist relies on his. The book's central narrative progress is not a specific change in the protagonist's character or his perseverance in the face of adversity; it is simply a gradual becoming aware of something that was there from the start. His own desires as well as their correspondence to those of a loosely affiliated network of men become increasingly undeniable, having been at first no more than a nuance, legible only to the most attuned among Kuzmin's readers. It works like a film plot in which a sexual relationship between two members of the same sex gradually dawns on the viewer, first becoming plausible and, as the plot progresses, undeniable, with or without the eventual revelation in flagrante delicto. This is precisely the alternative or complement that this book aspires to present to what Matt Houlbrook has called the dominant paradigm in queer histories. It is not the predetermined hunt for correlations between forensic homosexuality and subjective experience and identities. Valuable as this effort has been for many cities, it is fraught with the pitfalls of extrapolation from extremes and the temptations of historical hindsight. Even where these can be successfully navigated, it is bound to succeed better in some settings than in others, and imperial St. Petersburg, like many times and places, does not yield readily to this approach. Instead of starting with a court or medical case or a public scandal, I have proposed to read the city profusely, the way the fictional Vania does. After a while, a surprising term stands out, then crops up again, and a pattern emerges. When explicit records can be correlated to an activity and a response that plausibly reflect a routine, they become not the entry but rather an end point, a confirmation of a hypothesis.

To Vania, unlike the present-day reader of archival materials, this *becoming undeniable* is a personal progression. It describes the arc of identity formation and not merely vision or perception. Although the explicit discourse about queer identities may be more recent than Kuzmin's novel, its noncritical but quite psychological trajectory is very much at the heart of the book's lasting appeal. Following Vania's arrival in and geographical exploration of the city, his allegiance to a milieu populated by men who have sex with men crystallizes tantalizingly slowly. Part of this experience is contingent on his growing adeptness in navigating a queer milieu that accompanied or instantiated his burgeoning self-awareness. Unlike the psychological and cultural dimensions of that narrative, however, his becoming "literate" in navigating the city's queer milieu is accessible to some degree in the historical evidence outside the world of fiction. Much of this evidence is the photographic negative of the queer milieu rather than its direct imprint. Similar to the challenge faced by anyone looking back at the queer milieu through the prism of archival and other accounts, the fictional character Vania discovers quite realistically that some of the most potent, albeit highly ambiguous, clues come from individuals whose relationship with the city's queer milieu is characterized by a duty-bound desire to suppress it. In Vania's case, this was Fyodor's uncle. In our case, it is the constables and planners, the sanitary inspectors and city administrators, the journalists and bureaucrats on whose accounts we largely rely.

The exegetical task for Vania or a present-day reader of the historical city is thus characterized by a motivational shift. What Fyodor's uncle was gently condemning sounded quite enticing to Vania, who decided to look for more rather than recoil. Taken to its extreme, the notion of observing the hunter track the prey has been invoked to describe the activities of queer men in historical settings. In his study of nineteenth-century Paris, for example, Andrew Ross hypothesizes that spatial management inscribed illicit sex in the public sphere in ways that—very much contrary to intention—made it easier to find.[6] Empirically unverifiable even for Paris, a city whose queer milieu is among the best documented, this notion remains provocative and useful for the historiogeographical investigation of *illicit* desire. Moving beyond observation narrowly focused on criminalized sex, this book makes no claim as to whether queer men alive at the fin de siècle found that efforts to manage queer spatial patterns generally enhanced their visibility, but it describes how they adapted, even took advantage of opportunities offered by the routine activities and protracted initiatives of regulators, planners, sanitary commissions, constables, and entrepreneurs to manage queer spatial patterns in a city where courts rarely prosecuted sodomy cases. In these sources, state actors, some of them employed in the lower echelons of administration, recorded their actions and observations vis-à-vis the queer milieu with a range of attitudes from benign indulgence to heightened concern over threats to the state, disease, and moral corruption. Their protocols, reports, correspondence, and directives reflect the movements and encounters, the opportunities and risks facing queer men who, quite frequently, as we have seen, navigated the city and its queer milieu successfully in pursuit of communion and passion, tenderness and heat, without catastrophic consequences.

The analogy between Vania and the historical reader of St. Petersburg's queer milieu is more than skin deep; it cuts right to the heart of the modern city. Vania is compelled to read and recognize an urban milieu that for all its appeal and vitality is associated with breach of law and is subject to formal and informal sanction. He extrapolates from self-consciously elliptical phrases or explicit condemnation to a colorful and enticing set of characteristically urban spaces, patterns, and relations in which his as-yet-undiscovered desires could be realized and this alternative, even illicit, order thus confirmed. The clash of competing orders within cities is as characteristic of their modernization as the initial ordering of space, and the draining of the primordial swamps in the case of St. Petersburg is characteristic of the period of their foundation. The clash between them, which took place in slow motion and resulted in an ever-shifting entente between queer men and the authorities, is evident in particularly sharp relief in late imperial St. Petersburg, where the gradual transition toward increasing homogeneity within a resistance paradigm was not the next step. The search for such an entente allows us to reconceive the historical city and to see it in a way that its governors, administrators, constables, and progressive reformers did not wish it to be seen even by contemporaries. In parallel, this search recasts the municipal archive and other historical sources as an intrinsically misleading landscape in the sense of having been written and set up with the intention of leading those of us who deign to look for something that the city is not expressly designed to offer as far astray as possible. Reading the archives and other historical sources against the grain can therefore be seen as an act of defiance, a reenactment of navigating the queer milieu by contemporaries of St. Petersburg's unique fin de siècle. Its reward, analogous to Vania's voyage of discovery, is the resurrection of a family of ghosts, the ghosts of a milieu and of men whose fate was willfully obscured by participants and observers alike, but was therefore no less—and perhaps much more—characteristic of the clash of orders that defined the city on the eve of the Russian Revolution.

One might be forgiven for confusing or even intentionally conflating the archival figure of the "infamous man" with the "little man," a familiar trope of Russian literature. The "little man" is a tragic observer, even of himself. He can be sufficiently self-aware to recognize the burden of repression, but he remains insufficiently courageous to either incite collective rebellion or opportunistically pursue his deep-seated desires surreptitiously. Usually he does not transgress, but if he does, he masochistically wishes to get caught. The two prototypes are not very far apart, and both are traditionally urban, quintessentially Russian. In fact, Foucault explicitly plays on "infâme" / "infime," infamous and insignificant, detestable and disregardable.[7] Contrary to traditions, however, more than a few men qualifying for membership in either category might have had their revenge long ago and be less in need of retroactive vindication than Foucault and a generation of Russian writers supposed. In the historical city, obscurity did not always mean invisibility, nor did transgression necessarily imply oppression and isolation. A milieu did exist—surely one of several—in which the "infamous man" or the "little man," or whatever epithet one wishes to burden him with, could find a community of like-minded friends. Men who *seem* small and insignificant in historical retrospect, even to the sympathetic historian determined to rescue them from anonymity and authority, could live full and rich lives in the company of "familiar strangers," not merely in a city which officially despised them but within a *milieu* that, however unwittingly, shaped and supported them. Map in hand, they journeyed from the tropics of tenderness to those of heat in the company of friends and associates in a city where strangers were potentially lovers who had not yet met.

Appendix

Key Sources

The archival files on which this book draws are first and foremost from the archives of major municipal institutions (see the full list in the bibliography). They illuminate a great number of otherwise obscure details, such as how certain well-known queer sites were physically laid out, how they were periodically reconfigured, what their intended functions were, and how they actually operated. In these municipal files, we learn about the installation of new public toilets, about changes in the mandatory layout and regulation of commercial bathhouses, the opening hours for public gardens, and the expansion of gas and electric lighting in the city center. These seemingly trivial features of the urban topography proved salient. I also reviewed surviving records of the administrative apparatus reporting to the city's head of police and mayor and the files of the so-called Investigative Department of the police and the borough police stations. These archival files were fundamentally important in trying to reconstruct negotiations over the city's queer spatial patterns. They contained directives, arrest and patrol logs, interrogation protocols, and administrative correspondence for the entire period of investigation.

Finally, I reviewed the records and correspondence of the City Council with other government bodies, such as the Sanitary Commission (TsGIA SPb, fond 210). These further enabled me to clarify the process of decision-making by city officials. In this context, for example, I looked at the correspondence of city administrators with citizens and private companies, which contained petitions and letters from urban residents reacting to demands by the City Council, and in a few cases the responses from City Council officials.

In conducting this research, I juxtaposed archival sources with published newspapers and periodicals. Some of these overlap with Mark Steinberg's sophisticated study of perceptions of the queer milieu as reflected in the city's most widely distributed newspapers.[1] Others were lesser-known regular publications that have not been previously drawn upon by scholars studying St. Petersburg's queer milieu. These include *Vedomosti Sankt-Peterburgskoi Gorodskoi Politsii* and its continuation under the new name *Vestnik Sankt-Peterburgskogo gradonachal'stva i Sankt-Peterburgskoi gorodskoi politsii* (St. Petersburg Police and City Council Information Bulletin), in which various incident reports and executive decisions such as directives and changes to legislation were published. This bulletin also contains detailed information regarding reforms targeting commercial bathhouses, for example. Similarly, St. Petersburg City Duma Information Bulletin (*Izvestiia Sankt-Peterburgskoi gorodskoi dumy*, or *City Bulletin*) contains information about sanctioned physical changes that took place in the city and occasionally offers clues to the rationale behind these changes. Another such publication with an even smaller local distribution, the *Petersburg Flyer* (*Peterburgskii listok*), contains the story of the reconstruction of the Passazh shopping arcade. Recourse to this publication helped establish an explicit link between the Passazh's reconstruction and its role in the queer milieu.

Books published during the period covered by my research, including medico-forensic reports, commentary on legislation, court case compendiums, and published works about the queer milieu by fin-de-siècle contemporaries, were also helpful in contextualizing archival information. Among these published works, I studied the medico-forensic and psychiatric literature already prominently reflected in the subsequent historical discussion of homosexuality. These sources contain medical case histories of individuals who engaged in same-sex relationships as recorded by contemporaries. Although I did not assume that their stories were necessarily representative or entirely accurately told, they did point me to several locations in St. Petersburg, which—based on corroborating evidence from archival sources—turned out to be regular sites of queer encounters. For example, Vladimir Ruadze, a journalist who wrote about St. Petersburg's queer milieu in 1908, describes a spatial link between homosexual prostitution and proximity to military barracks. He and other contemporary commentators also spatially linked heterosexual prostitution—again correlated with the presence of the soldiery—to male homosexual cruising.[2] These links, corroborated by my archival research on the basis of police reports in one area, proved particularly useful in identifying the likely location and extent of other cruising sites. Thus, the proximity of military barracks served as one of several markers that guided my research and was confirmed by archival evidence indicating cruising.

The degree of focus introduced into my research by this contextualization was helpful, but it was always important to remember that the use of published sources necessarily introduced a bias toward cruising that frequently and proximately resulted in sex, as opposed to activities primarily related to queer socialization, because most contemporary published sources refer to cases involving a breach of law. Therefore, primary documents in the form of archival files in various municipal administrative archives always constituted the anchor for any analysis of spatial patterns linked to the queer milieu. These illuminated a broad range of negotiated responses to queer spatial patterns ranging from no action at all to the deployment of building regulations and petty crimes statutes in addressing recognizably queer spatial patterns.

Notes

Abbreviations Used in the Notes

TsGIA SPb	Tsentral'nyi gosudarstvennyi istoricheskii arkhiv Sankt-Peterburga (Central State Historical Archive of St. Petersburg)
RGIA	Rossiiskii gosudarstvennyi istoricheskii arkhiv (Russian State Historical Archive, St. Petersburg)
GARF	Gosudarstvennyi arkhiv Rossiiskoi Federatsii (State Archive of the Russian Federation, Moscow)
TsGAKFD SPb	Tsentral'nyi gosudarstvennyi arkhiv kinofotodocumentov Sankt-Petersburga (Central State Archive of Documentary Films, Photographs, and Sound Recordings of St. Petersburg)
Gorodskaia duma	Sankt-Peterburgskaia gorodskaia obshchaia duma (St. Petersburg City Duma)
Gorodskaia uprava	Sankt-Peterburgskaia gorodskaia uprava (St. Petersburg City Council)
Izvestiia dumy	*Izvestiia Sankt-Peterburgskoi gorodskoi obshchoi dumy* (St. Petersburg City Duma Information Bulletin)
Vedomosti politsii	*Vedomosti Sankt-Peterburgskoi gorodskoi politsii* (St. Petersburg Police and City Council Information Bulletin)
Vestnik gradonachal'stva	*Vestnik Sankt-Peterburgskogo gradonachal'stva i Sankt-Peterburgskoi gorodskoi politsii* (Continuation of *Vedomosti politsii* under a new name)

A Note on Terminology

1. Bleys, *The Geography of Perversion*, 11.
2. Ahmed, *Queer Phenomenology*, 67.
3. Healey, *Homosexual Desire in Revolutionary Russia*, 83–86, 90–92.
4. Halperin, "How to Do the History," 90.

Introduction

1. Steinberg, *Petersburg Fin de Siècle*, 1–2.
2. Note, however, Laura Engelstein's mention of court cases in which homosexual men and a lesbian couple were prosecuted in 1922. These cases indicated "that Soviet

courts tried to repress sexual variation even when homosexuality was not a crime." Whether this suggests a degree of continuity in practices of state repression directed against queer men must be the subject of an entirely separate investigation, given that war and revolution interrupted not only men's lives but also the operation of the state, including the archives on which this investigation largely relies. Picking up the strands of continuity across this divide is a task that can only be contemplated once a relatively stable "before" picture has emerged, which is the project of this book. See Engelstein, "Soviet Policy," 155.

3. TsGIA SPb, fond 1648, opis 1, delo 417 (hereafter, f., d., o.), Kniga sutochnykh dokladov, 7v–8.

4. On the demography of the city, see the study by Christopher Ely, *Underground Petersburg*.

5. RGIA, f. 1683, o. 1, d. 119, Svedeniia o fiziologicheskikh porokakh raznykh lits, 1–13, 2v; see also Rotikov, "Epizod iz zhizni 'golubogo' Peterburga" and Rotikov, *Drugoi Peterburg*. On homosexual topography, see also Healey, *Homosexual Desire in Revolutionary Russia*, 33. The archival file "RGIA, f. 1683, o. 1, d. 119, Svedeniia o fiziologicheskikh porokakh raznykh lits, prozhivaiushchikh v Peterburge, no date" was used by scholars with the wrong reference (Iuri Periutko, Bersen'ev, Markov, who cited "RGIA, f. 1683, o. 1, d. 199"). When I tried to order this file using their reference, I failed to locate it. Thanks to the archivists, I was able to locate the file under the different number (d. 119), so I reference it correctly.

6. TsGIA SPb, f. 1648, o.1, d. 417, Kniga sutochnykh dokladov, 7v–8.

7. This did not happen, however, without a bit more due diligence or hypothesis testing. According to the protocol, the constable interrupted the conversation to check whether Johan's claim that Dmitrii had committed suicide by throwing himself into the river from Nikolaevskii Bridge could be corroborated, an event Johan admitted to having deduced by conjecture rather than having witnessed it. Consequently, the constable placed a telephone call to several police stations. The investigation was surely far from exhaustive but sufficient to discard what at this stage would in any case have been an unlikely hypothesis, namely, that Dmitrii as the initiator of the breakup had subsequently committed suicide. The interviewer diligently recorded that no such incident had been reported and this record provided him with irreproachable grounds to conclude that no missing person investigation was required. The protocol is the only entry in this case file and it is unlikely that any organ pursued the case further. The discretion involved in refraining from formally opening a missing-person investigation and, in all likelihood, ceasing any further activity was coupled with the compromise of leaving the case formally open, not on the grounds of failure to find Dmitrii but on the grounds of "questionable statements" by Johan.

8. The term "familiar strangers" (*znakomye neznakomtsy*) is used in the diary of the fin-de-siècle poet, composer, and flaneur Mikhail Kuzmin. Kuzmin, *Dnevnik, 1905–1907*, 330.

9. I consulted the following censuses available at the National Library of Russia, St. Petersburg: *Sankt-Peterburg po peripisi 10 dekabria 1869 goda*; *Sankt-Peterburg po peripisi 15 dekabria 1881 goda*; *Sankt-Peterburg po peripisi 15 dekabria 1890 goda*; *Sankt-Peterburg po peripisi 15 dekabria 1900 goda*; and *Petrograd po peripisi 15 dekabria 1910 goda*.

10. On the industrialization and urbanization of imperial St. Petersburg, see Bater, *St. Petersburg*; and Bater, "Between Old and New." See also McKean, *St. Petersburg be-*

tween Revolutions; Brower, *Russian City*; Brower, "Urban Revolution"; and Shaw, "St Petersburg and Geographies."

11. Berman, *All That Is Solid*.

12. Among the many works on the connections between autocratic ambition and the reality of the streets, see in particular Steinberg, *Petersburg Fin de Siècle*; McReynolds, *Russia at Play*; Neuberger, *Hooliganism*; Smith and Kelly, "Commercial Culture and Consumerism"; Morrissey, *Suicide*; Ely, *Underground Petersburg*; and Hasegawa, *Crime and Punishment*.

13. Alexander Morrison writes extensively on this topic. See, for example Morrison, *Russian Conquest of Central Asia*.

14. On social inequality in late imperial Russia and St. Petersburg, see Beer, *Renovating Russia*, 62, 68–72. See also Gregory, *Before Command*, 28–36; and Mironov, "Wages and Prices," 52.

15. Ogborn, *Spaces of Modernity*, 132.

16. On the latter point, see, for example, Beachy, *Gay Berlin*, 58.

17. See "A Note on Terminology" in this book regarding the use of the word "queer" in the present discussion.

18. Kuzmin, *Dnevnik, 1905–1907*, 173. On June 15, 1906, Kuzmin wrote, "I remembered how Somov and I were joking that it was necessary to publish a special map of the Tavricheskii Garden, like *du pays du tendre*, and to write a poem [entitled] *voyage du pays du tendre au pays chaud*." I use the translation provided by the editors of Kuzmin's diary, Nikolai Bogomolov and Sergei Shumikhin: *Puteshestvie iz strany nezhnosti v stranu pylkosti*.

19. Notwithstanding Phil Hubbard's insightful critique of a topographical categorization of spaces as public and private, the definitions used throughout this book are simple and based on access (rather than, for example, ownership). Public spaces as referred to here are accessible to all and include the likes of parks, streets, squares, and even enclosed spaces such as shops or exhibition halls, so long as entrance is nonexclusive. Semipublic spaces are spaces that are, in principle, accessible to all on short notice, but entrance to which is commercially regulated with regard to each individual entry or stay. These include pleasure gardens, skating pavilions, restaurants, museums, theaters, music halls, hotels, cabs, streetcars, and bathhouses. Private spaces, for the purposes of this study, are accessible only to certain individuals according to criteria that are determined for more than a few occasions of entry or stay. For example a boardinghouse is a private space, whereas a hotel room or single-family bathing facility is a semipublic space because it is accessible on short notice to anyone or almost anyone for a fee. Private spaces according to this definition include factory dormitories, boardinghouses, apartments, private houses, palaces, government buildings, social clubs, asylums, and military barracks. The categories, as used here, signify a distinction unrelated to ownership or visibility (in the sense of privacy); my definition relates only to terms of access. For a discussion of possible definitions of public, private, and other types of spaces, see, for example, Hubbard, *Cities and Sexualities*, 117–18. See also important works on the categorization of space: Howell, "Public Space and the Public Sphere"; and Dennis, *Cities in Modernity*.

20. Houlbrook, *Queer London*, 9.

21. Another example of a study acknowledging this implication is Ross, *Public City/Public Sex*, 13–14.

22. One of a few signal exceptions is Philip Howell's work on the regulation of prostitution in nineteenth-century Britain and the British Empire, which traces and reconstructs "actually existing" geographies of regulations. Howell argues that "the solution to prostitution is as profoundly spatial as is the problem." The Contagious Diseases Acts of 1864, 1866, and 1869 were spatial fixes based on "the installation of discipline and regulation through enclosure and surveillance" of women. Howell, *Geographies of Regulation*, 2, 10. Regarding imperial St. Petersburg, see Christopher Ely's innovative work on the prerevolutionary underground. He specifically describes the cat-and-mouse game of radical subversion, positioning urban space as the "context in which a radical movement could take shape." Notably, his scope includes an exploration of the seemingly mundane material and tactical aspects of revolutionary struggle. Ely, *Underground Petersburg*, 16–21.

23. International permeability plays an important role in constructing arguments about the evolution of queer identities in the twentieth century. At a time when familiar modern sexual identities evolved in many Western cities in communication with one another via some form of cultural osmosis, significant barriers between the Soviet Union and the West already existed. See Matt Houlbrook, for example, who notes that London "was part of a global network of queer cities. Many men—usually, but not only, the wealthy and privileged—moved easily between London and New York, Vienna, San Francisco, Berlin, Rome, or Paris, to work, to live, or simply for pleasure. These transnational connections underscore this book's organizing theme—that relationship between modern urban life and 'being queer.'" Houlbrook, *Queer London*, 9.

24. See Beer, *Renovating Russia*.

25. For a concise overview of the city's early history, see Bater, *St. Petersburg*, 81, where he writes that "by the late 1840s the city in practice had become an extension of the state government."

26. See, for example, Ely, *Underground Petersburg*; and Hasegawa, *Crime and Punishment*, 27–36.

27. For an overview of St. Petersburg's historiography, see McReynolds, "St. Petersburg," 858.

28. Ely's work on the development of the Russian radical populist movement in the context of urban modernity addresses this Soviet-era stereotype. Ely, *Underground Petersburg*, 12–16. See also Hasegawa, *Crime and Punishment*, 23; and Kelly, *St Petersburg*.

29. Among the many works on autocratic ambition and the reality of the streets, see Steinberg, *Petersburg Fin de Siècle*; McReynolds, *Russia at Play*; Neuberger, *Hooliganism*; Smith and Kelly, "Commercial Culture and Consumerism"; Morrissey, *Suicide*; Ely, *Underground Petersburg*; and Hasegawa, *Crime and Punishment*.

30. See Hasegawa, *Crime and Punishment*, 27–36; and Neuberger, *Hooliganism*, 3–4.

31. McReynolds, "St. Petersburg," 861.

32. In 1914, Magnus Hirschfeld wrote, "Visitors to Russia often told me that they were presented with bathhouse attendants. . . . Aside from bathhouse attendants, cabbies, yard keepers and apprentice boys are particularly inclined to homosexual intercourse." He also notes that sublimated, noncommercial homosexual relationships were widespread "among the Slavs." Hirschfeld, *Die Homosexualität des Mannes*, 590. Also cited in Healey, *Homosexual Desire*, 33n60, and in Healey, "Masculine Purity," 245. Hirschfeld uses the term "mischief," which he attributes to reports he received from Russia.

33. Houlbrook, *Queer London*, 4 (emphasis in original).

34. Houlbrook, *Queer London*, 4, 6. Here, Houlbrook is referring to Jan Lofstrom, among others. See Lofstrom, "Birth of the Queen," 24.

35. Steinberg, *Petersburg Fin de Siècle*, 8.

36. See, for example, Houlbrook, *Queer London*; Cook, *London and the Culture of Homosexuality*; Chauncey, *Gay New York*; Bech, *When Men Meet*; Higgs, *Queer Sites*; Peniston, "Pederasts, Prostitutes, and Pickpockets"; Turner, *Backward Glance*; Ross, *Public City/Public Sex*; Beachy, *Gay Berlin*; Boyd, *Wide Open Town*; and Stewart-Winter, *Queer Clout*.

37. For the archetype of this scholarship, see Castells, *The City and the Grassroots*, 140–43.

38. Karlinsky, "Russian's Gay Literature and Culture," 350.

39. Regarding the theme of sexual liberation, see in particular Engelstein, *Keys to Happiness*.

40. Piriutko published under the pseudonym Konstantin Rotikov. Piriutko explains that his work was prompted by his discovery of one particular archival file in the RGAI about "developments in the capital concerning sex between men." RGIA, f. 1683, o. 1, d. 119, Svedeniia o fiziologicheskikh porokakh. He published works on this topic in 1997 and 2000: Rotikov, "Epizod iz zhizni 'golubogo' Peterburga"; and *The Other St. Petersburg*, which avowedly tells an "alternative history" of nineteenth-century St. Petersburg (Rotikov, *Drugoi Peterburg*). In modern vernacular Russian, the word "goluboi," which denotes the color light blue, has a second meaning denoting something akin to the term "queer." It is mainly used to refer to men. Among publications on the topic by Simon Karlinsky, see in particular "Russia's Gay Literature and Culture," 350. See also Karlinsky, "Death and Resurrection of Mikhail Kuzmin"; Karlinsky, "Gay Life before the Soviets"; and Karlinsky, "Russia's Gay Literature and History."

41. Bersen'ev and A. Markov critically engage with Piriutko's work. They acknowledge its importance but point out the inconsistencies and oversights in Piriutko's research and analysis. According to them, "the scientific value and merit of this undertaking, regrettably, is not significant, as the author approached even the dating of documents inattentively. Any analysis, however robust, of the material is lacking." Bersen'ev and Markov, "Politsiia i gei," 105.

42. Bersen'ev and Markov, "Politsiia i gei."

43. Healey, *Homosexual Desire in Revolutionary Russia*, 7; Healey, "Masculine Purity"; Healey, "Disappearance of the Russian Queen"; Healey, "What Can We Learn?"; Engelstein, "Soviet Policy"; Engelstein, "Combined Underdevelopment."

44. Engelstein, *Keys to Happiness.*

45. The brunt of Engelstein's analysis relates to the progress of bourgeois liberalism in shaping civic discourse about sex and sexual deviance. She detects here many of the same trends as in the West, but also a unique nervousness even among liberal elites about the unfettered pursuit of pleasure, which became idiomatically associated with St Petersburg. Hers is a signal contribution to discussions not of what Russia might have become but what it already was on the eve of World War I. Her approach is broad insofar as it does not prioritize same-sex desire but looks at sexuality comprehensively. Healey, on the other hand, focuses specifically on homosexuality and, as he calls it, "medico-legal conceptions of it," covering a period from the time of publication of the first Russian-language medical works on the topic until the Stalin era (Healey, *Homosexual Desire in Revolutionary Russia*,

15). One of Healey's key contributions lies in challenging views of the 1933–34 Stalinist crackdown on male homosexuals as a sudden reversal. He goes even further. He traces the construction of revolutionary masculinity or heterosexuality back to the medical and ideological sequestration and stigmatization of same-sex love and gender dissent. As to the prerevolutionary era, he discusses the ineffectiveness of sodomy laws, the gradual osmosis of Western medical and legal notions of homosexuality into Russian-language discourse, and the variability of attitudes across national and ethnic boundaries—all important and valid observations on which this book relies. Healey, *Homosexual Desire in Revolutionary Russia.*

46. Houlbrook, *Queer London*, 5.

47. Houlbrook, *Queer London*, 5 (emphasis in the original).

48. Houlbrook, *Queer London*, 273.

49. On the mobility of legislative concepts and medical knowledge, see Healey, *Homosexual Desire in Revolutionary Russia.*

50. Hubbard, *Cities and Sexualities*, 30.

51. Hubbard, *Cities and Sexualities*, 117.

52. On queer visibilities, see the excellent work of Andrew Tucker, *Queer Visibilities.*

53. Here, I refer in particular to the destruction of archives of the City Magistrate Court and the Police Department in February 1917 and October 1917. See more on the official website of TsGIA SPb, https://spbarchives.ru/web/group/information_resources/-/archivestore/guide_page/2-141, accessed July 26, 2018.

Chapter 1. St. Petersburg and Its Familiar Strangers

1. Anichkov Bridge and its popularity among queer men is discussed in historical documents and published materials: RGIA, f. 1683, o. 1, d. 119, Svedeniia o fiziologicheskikh porokakh, 2v; TsGIA SPb, f. 965, o. 1, d. 1614, O pedaraste, 2–2v, 5–5v; Ruadze, *K sudu!* 102–9; *Gazeta-kopeika*, "Nravy nevskogo prospekta," April 2, 1910, 5. Mark Steinberg has also discussed the popularity of Anichkov among the queer men; see Steinberg, *Petersburg Fin de Siècle*, 63, 65.

2. Seliverstov, *Leningrad.*

3. Regarding street crime in late imperial St. Petersburg, see Weissman, "Regular Police in Tsarist Russia"; and Neuberger, *Hooliganism*. For violent crime in imperial Russia, see McReynolds, *Murder Most Russian.*

4. RGIA, f. 1683, o. 1, d. 119, Svedeniia o fiziologicheskikh porokakh, 2, 2v.

5. Bersen'ev and Markov, "Politsiia i gei," 105. As per this hypothesis, one of the most recent files to have been added or updated before the composition of the dossier would have been that of Count Mesherskii, who turned fifty-five, the age indicated for him in the dossier, in 1894, one year after Ostrovskii, a recipient of the dossier, was appointed chairman of the Imperial Governing Council's Legislative Department. The other men mentioned and for whom other historical records are available had aged by more than a year relative to the age indicated in the dossier. Bersen'ev and Markov's dating thus relies on the reasonable assumption that Count Mesherskii's age had been the most recently noted before the time of the dossier's compilation and that corrections for time passed since other individuals' ages had been noted were omitted by bureaucratic oversight.

6. I use the term "assemblage" in reference to assemblage theory, which stresses the heterogeneity and interconnectedness of the elements in a network. For some background, see Deleuze and Parnet, *Dialogues*, 39; Latour, *Reassembling the Social*, 27–43; Price-Robertson, "Realism, Materialism, and the Assemblage"; Marcus and Saka, "Assemblage"; and Legg, "Assemblage / Apparatus." See also the following works by scholars who use assemblage theory to explore specifically the spatiality of elements in an assemblage: Bennett, "Agency of Assemblages"; Li, "Practices of Assemblage"; Anderson and McFarlane, "Assemblage and Geography"; and Gandy, "Cyborg Urbanization." On the application of assemblage theory to social differences, race, and sexuality, see Lim, "Immanent Politics"; and Jaspir Puar, *Terrorist Assemblages*.

7. *Merriam-Webster.com Dictionary*, Merriam-Webster, https://www.merriam-webster.com/dictionary/milieu, accessed July, 12 2020.

8. See chapters 3 and 4 for a discussion of such measures regarding the Passazh and the commercial bathhouses.

9. See more about the term "queer milieu" in Notes on Terminology.

10. RGIA, f. 1683, o. 1, d. 119, Svedeniia o fiziologicheskikh porokakh, 4.

11. RGIA, f. 1683, o. 1, d. 119, Svedeniia o fiziologicheskikh porokakh, 4v.

12. RGIA, f. 1683, o. 1, d. 119, Svedeniia o fiziologicheskikh porokakh, 4.

13. RGIA, f. 1683, o. 1, d. 119, Svedeniia o fiziologicheskikh porokakh, 2.

14. RGIA, f. 1683, o. 1, d. 119, Svedeniia o fiziologicheskikh porokakh, 1.

15. RGIA, f. 1683, o. 1, d. 119, Svedeniia o fiziologicheskikh porokakh, 2.

16. See, for example, Kovalevskii, *Psikhologiia pola*, 209–14, as well as the works of Fredric Zuckerman and of Christopher Ely about surveillance after Aleksandr II's assassination: Zuckerman, *Tsarist Secret Police*; and Ely, *Underground Petersburg*. Finally, see Korobeinikov, "Imagining Post-Imperial Order."

17. RGIA, f. 1683, o. 1, d. 119, Svedeniia o fiziologicheskikh porokakh, 6v.

18. RGIA, f. 1683, o. 1, d. 119, Svedeniia o fiziologicheskikh porokakh, 4.

19. TsGIA SPb, f. 965, o. 1, d. 1933, Prosheniia i zaiavleniia raznykh lits, 13. Regarding the meaning of red handkerchiefs in queer socialization, see the discussion in Healey, *Homosexual Desire in Revolutionary Russia*, 40n90, 281.

20. See Merzheevskii, *Sudebnaia genikologiia*, 252–55. Kovalevskii also notes that the police compiled records of homosexuals in the city; see Kovalevskii, *Psikhologiia pola*, 211. He writes that "in one government department, it is said, only pederasts are employed. In St. Petersburg's police museum I saw an album of Petersburg's pederasts and in it I saw no small number of individuals, who occupy prominent positions, even counts, who, however, had their run-ins with the police as a result of their pederasty." The police undertook two types of surveillance, acknowledged and covert (*glasnoe* and *neglasnoe*). The former was used to monitor and control urban residents convicted of having committed petty crimes, recently released from prison, or returned from exile and the latter aimed to secretly observe any other suspicious individuals. From the surviving archival files, it is clear that one method of surveillance was to gather the testimony of house custodians or yard keepers (*dvornik*), who were legally obliged to "provide ongoing assistance to the police in maintaining order in the city." From this activity, for example, arose a list of urban residents under covert police surveillance in the Admiralteiskoi Borough. See TsGIA SPb, f. 1648, o. 1, d. 40, Kniga o litsakh, sostoiashchikh pod nadzorom politsii, 1898–1906; TsGIA SPb, f. 1648, o. 1, d. 13, Kniga o litsakh, sostoiashchikh pod

nadzorom politsii, 1912–1914. For Kazanskaia Borough, see TsGIA SPb, f. 1648, o. 1, d. 388, Kniga o litsakh, sostoiashchikh pod nadzorom politsii, 1904–1908; and TsGIA SPb, f. 1648, o. 1, d. 393, Kniga o litsakh, sostoiashchikh pod nadzorom politsii, 1908–1912. For Liteinaia Borough, see TsGIA SPb, f. 1648 o. 1, d. 671, Kniga o litsakh pod nadzorom politsii, 1905; TsGIA SPb, f. 1648 o. 1, d. 656, Kniga o litsakh, sostoiashchikh pod nadzorom politsii, 1906; TsGIA SPb, f. 1648 o. 1, d. 673, Kniga o litsakh, sostoiashchikh pod nadzorom politsii, 1909; and TsGIA SPb, f. 1648 o. 1, d. 674, Kniga o litsakh, sostoiashchikh pod nadzorom politsii, 1913. For Spasskaia Borough, TsGia SPb, f. 1648 o. 1, d. 1250, Kniga o litsakh pod nadzorom politsii, 1913. Regarding police surveillance in this earlier period, see, for example, Ely, *Underground Petersburg*. About the role of yard keepers in helping police control the city and maintain order, see *Izvestiia dumy*, "O nadzore za dezhurnymi dvornikami," no. 20 (June 1892); and *Izvestiia dumy*, "O dezhurstve dvornikom," no. 21 (June 1892).

21. Bersen'ev and Markov hypothesize that the dossier was composed by the head of the municipal gendarmerie department. This department was charged with carrying out surveillance of state and political crimes and secret societies. It was formally associated with the military but may well have used police files to carry out its work. On other occasions gendarmes were assigned to assist the police, so connections between these organizations were relatively well developed. Bersen'ev and Markov, "Politsiia i gei," 105.

22. RGIA, f. 1683, o. 1, d. 119, Svedeniia o fiziologicheskikh porokakh, 3.

23. In *Dnevnik, 1905–1907*, 158, Kuzmin recalls the dialogue with his friend Kudriiashev about how to apply makeup fashionably. See more on this subject in chapter 5. Regarding yellow narcissus, see Kuzmin, *Dnevnik, 1905–1907*, 357, 428.

24. RGIA, f. 1683, o. 1, d. 119, Svedeniia o fiziologicheskikh porokakh, 2v.

25. RGIA, f. 1683, o. 1, d. 119, Svedeniia o fiziologicheskikh porokakh, 2.

26. A later journalistic pamphlet informs us that in 1908, a queer man was "beaten in a beastly fashion" by constables, who observed him entering the pissoir on Mikhailovskaia Square twenty times." Ruadze, *K sudu!* 104.

27. RGIA, f. 1683, o. 1, d. 119, Svedeniia o fiziologicheskikh porokakh, 2.

28. RGIA, f. 1683, o. 1, d. 119, Svedeniia o fiziologicheskikh porokakh, 2v–3.

29. RGIA, f. 1683, o. 1, d. 119, Svedeniia o fiziologicheskikh porokakh, 3.

30. RGIA, f. 1683, o. 1, d. 119, Svedeniia o fiziologicheskikh porokakh, 3.

31. TsGIA SPb f. 965, o. 1, d. 1862, Po zhalobe kol. sekr Sarkisova na poruchika Raikovskogo, zarazivshchegosia sifilisom, 1901 (for more about this case, see chapter 2).

32. In September 1883, Fedor Bychkov, then director of a private gymnasium and a state counselor, was sentenced to exile in Siberia for sexually abusing eleven boys aged eleven to thirteen in his gymnasium. Several petitions from prominent citizens on his behalf were unsuccessful. See Bersen'ev and Markov, "Politsiia i gei," 105; and RGIA, f. 1405, o. 83, d. 10544, Po prosheniiu publichnoi biblioteki Afanasiia Bychkova.

33. The view of homosexuality as uniquely urban was by no means unique. In 1908, Kovalevskii wrote that homosexuality is "a typical urban phenomenon." Kovalevskii, *Psikhologiia pola*, 209.

34. RGIA, f. 1683, o. 1, d. 119, Svedeniia o fiziologicheskikh porokakh, 1, 4, 4v.

35. The traditional and simplified conception of the social structure posited the existence of four main estates—nobility, clergy, townspeople, and peasantry. Pogodin writes,

"Every estate has its own role in the state: the clergy pray, the nobles serve in war and peace, the peasants plow and feed the people, and the merchants are the means that provide for each according to his needs"; quoted in Barsukov, *Zhizn' i trudy M. P. Pogodina*, 591. The idea of four estates was, in its slightly more complex form, encoded in Russian law—above all, in the Estate Laws, part of the Legal Code of 1832, which was the first new law code in Russia in nearly two centuries (see *Svod zakonov Rossiiskoi Imperii*, vol. 1, art. 2). By the end of the nineteenth century, individuals no longer neatly corresponded to the demographic reality of the empire. As Alison Smith explains, "although they clearly still existed, at the end of the 19th century these identities had been often understood as obsolescent, if not totally obsolete relics from earlier times. By 1909 the legal practitioner (or scholar) Nikolai Korkunov claimed that 'it is unusual to meet a man who does not himself know to which soslovie he belongs.'" Smith, *For the Common Good*, 1. Scholarly works on the significance of social estates include Freeze, "Soslovie (Estate) Paradigm"; Steinwedel, "Making Social Groups"; and Smith, "Honored Citizens."

36. For a fuller discussion of the complexity of the estate system in cities, see Smith, *For the Common Good*, introduction and chap. 1.

37. *Zakony i postanovleniia*, 24. In 1892, there was a new version of the Gorodovoe Polozhenie. See the section regarding the City Duma: *Gorodovoe polozhenie s zakonadatel'nymi motivami*, 736. Bater writes about this reform in *St. Petersburg*, 194.

38. RGIA, f. 1683, o. 1, d. 119, Svedeniia o fiziologicheskikh porokakh, 1.

39. RGIA, f. 1683, o. 1, d. 119, Svedeniia o fiziologicheskikh porokakh, 3. Regarding the assumption that the highest protector might be a member of the royal family, see Bersen'ev and Markov, "Politsiia i gei," 105.

40. Merzheevskii, *Sudebnaia genikologiia*, 205.

41. Ruadze, *K sudu!* 20.

42. Tchaikovsky, *Dnevniki*, 203.

43. Bersen'ev and Markov, "Politsiia i gei," 106.

44. RGIA, f. 1683, o. 1, d. 119, Svedeniia o fiziologicheskikh porokakh, 4v.

45. About Ostrovskii's career ambition, see Voronov, "Ministerstvo zemledeliia Rossiiskoi Imperii,"188.

46. See also Healey, who mentions a relationship between two workers. Healey, *Homosexual Desire in Revolutionary Russia*, 43.

47. Meslé and Vallin, "Long-Term Trends in Life Expectancy," 6.

48. García, Voss, and Meerkerk, *Selling Sex in the City*. See Hetherington, "Prostitution in Moscow." Other important works on female prostitution in imperial Russia include Bernstein, *Sonia's Daughters*; and Hearne, *Policing Prostitution*. About male prostitution, see Healey, "Masculine Purity."

49. Bater, *St. Petersburg*, 327.

50. As Bater writes, the housing crisis "loomed, arrived, and deepened" in late nineteenth-century St. Petersburg, where "housing conditions for the masses quickly became a scandal." Bater, "Between Old and New," 56. Official surveys regularly reported cases of fifteen or more people per apartment, ten or more to a room, and five or more per bed. See Pazhitnov, "Zhilishchnaia politika," 53. On age and sex percentages, see Kupriianova, *Rabochii Peterburga*, 185–86.

51. On economic and social inequality in the city and living conditions, see Bater, *St. Petersburg*, 328–29, 34–35. On the living conditions in the city more broadly, see

Pazhitnov, "Kvartirnii vopros"; Sviatlovskii, *Zhilishchnyi vopros;* and Viatkin, "Gorodskoe upravlenie."

52. St. Petersburg Census of December 15, 1881 (*Sankt-Peterburg po peripisi 15 dekabria 1881 goda*), 205; see also the discussion in Kupriianova, *Rabochii Peterburga*, 185–86.

53. Simms, "Economic Impact of the Russian Famine," 5; Khaustova, "Pre-Revolution Living Standards"; and Johnson, "Demographics, Inequality and Entitlements."

54. Even by the turn of the twentieth century, men outnumbered women by almost 10 percent, an unprecedented proportion compared to other European capitals at the time. See *Sankt-Peterburg po peripisi 10 dekabria 1869 goda*, part 3, 74–85; *Sankt-Peterburg po peripisi 15 dekabria 1881 goda*, vol. 1: *Naselenie*; and *Petrograd po perepisi 1910 goda*, vol. 1, table 3. For age and gender demographics and family status, see also Bater, *St. Petersburg*, 313, 14–15; Henze, *Disease, Health Care and Government*; and Bater, "Between Old and New."

55. On the issue of female prostitution in imperial Russia, see Bernstein, *Sonia's Daughters*; Hetherington, "Prostitution in Moscow"; Hearne, *Policing Prostitution*; and Hearne, "To Denounce or Defend?"

56. Merzheevskii, *Sudebnaia genikologiia*, 239.

57. RGIA, f. 1683, o. 1, d. 119, Svedeniia o fiziologicheskikh porokakh, 8.

58. Hetherington writes that the "cost for a visit at the highest category of brothels (which employed 110 prostitutes in all) was 5 rubles, while a whole night was 10. In the middle tier of brothels, which employed 304 prostitutes, he [Dubrovskii—the author of a statistical report about prostitution in St. Petersburg] recorded a price of 1–2 rubles per visit and 2–6 rubles for a night, while in the lowest tier, employing 537 prostitutes, a visit was 20–50 kopecks [a ruble was 100 kopecks] and a night was 50 kopecks to 2 rubles" in 1898. Hetherington, "Prostitution in Moscow," 146.

59. Tarnovskii, *Izvrashchenie polovogo chuvstva*, 71.

60. RGIA, f. 1683, o. 1, d. 119, Svedeniia o fiziologicheskikh porokakh, 9v, 10v.

61. RGIA, f. 1683, o. 1, d. 119, Svedeniia o fiziologicheskikh porokakh, 4.

62. Ross, *Public City/Public Sex*, chap. 4, 125–53.

63. RGIA, f. 1683, o. 1, d. 119, Svedeniia o fiziologicheskikh porokakh, 4.

64. On this theme more broadly, see, among others, Lindenmeyr, *Poverty Is Not a Vice*; Rabow-Edling, *Slavophile Thought*; Kolstø, "Power as Burden"; and Bradley, "Subjects into Citizens." On the zemstvo movement more broadly, see Seregny, "Zemstvos, Peasants, and Citizenship"; Gleason and Porter, "Zemstvo and Public Initiative"; and Emmons and Vucinich, *Zemstvo in Russia*. See also Bersen'ev and Markov, "Politsiia i gei," 107.

65. Ostrovskii, *Talents and Admirers*, premiered on the December 20, 1881, in the Malyi Theatre, St. Petersburg.

66. RGIA, f. 1683, o. 1, d. 119, Svedeniia o fiziologicheskikh porokakh, 5.

67. Tarnovskii, *Izvrashchenie polovogo chuvstva*, 72.

68. Tarnovskii, *Izvrashchenie polovogo chuvstva*, 73–74.

69. With regard to the blackmailers, Merzheevskii observes that "the prosecutor's office manages only in exceptional cases to bring them into the dock as the accused"; Merzheevskii, *Sudebnaia genikologiia*, 208.

70. Merzheevskii describes two cases of consensual sodomy involving well-to-do men with impecunious youths. One involves a "universally respected, extraordinarily well-educated and knowledgeable seminary instructor," who stood accused of having

had sex with a "villain of the lowest class." The second case involved a forty-two-year-old aristocrat and a young soldier. In both cases, "both of the accused were convicted " Merzheevskii, *Sudebnaia genikologiia*, 222–23. It is possible that in some of these instances Merzheevskii refers to court cases described in the international literature, to which he refers.

71. Tarnovskii, *Izvrashchenie polovogo chuvstva*, 75–76.

72. Bukhner, *Sudebnaia meditsina*, 5.

73. RGIA, f. 1683, o. 1, d. 119, Svedeniia o fiziologicheskikh porokakh, 4.

74. Dudyrev, "Razrabotka i priniatie ugolovnogo ulozhenie."

75. RGIA, f. 1683, o. 1, d. 119, Svedeniia o fiziologicheskikh porokakh, 4v. Tarnovskii, *Izvrashchenie polovogo chuvstva*, 68–69.

76. Tarnovskii, *Izvrashchenie polovogo chuvstvai*, 69.

77. RGIA, f. 1683, o. 1, d. 119, Svedeniia o fiziologicheskikh porokakh, 1, 1v.

78. Ugolovnoe ulozhenie, visochaishe utverzhdennoe 22 marta 1903 goda (St. Petersburg: Gosudarstvennaia tipografiia, 1903) [Criminal Law of the Russian Empire, 1903], 180–82; see chapter 27, "O nepotrebstve," articles 513–15 where the term "liubostrastnoe deistvie" is introduced.

79. Healey, *Homosexual Desire in Revolutionary Russia*, 98.

80. Although prostitution was legal, a woman or a man who admitted to offering to engage in sex for money in any space accessible to the public could be charged with the administrative offense of "debauchery in public spaces," punishable by article 43 of the Administrative Code, which bestows on the police powers to intervene in cases where constables observe "impudent and seductive behavior in public places." This topic is further explored in chapter 2.

81. Nabokov, *Sbornik statei*, 97.

82. RGIA, f. 1683, o. 1, d. 119, Svedeniia o fiziologicheskikh porokakh, 1, 5.

83. RGIA, f. 1683, o. 1, d. 119, Svedeniia o fiziologicheskikh porokakh, 4v.

84. Bersen'ev and Markov, "Politsiia i gei," 116n8.

85. RGIA, f. 1683, o. 1, d. 119, Svedeniia o fiziologicheskikh porokakh, 4v.

86. RGIA, f. 1683, o. 1, d. 119, Svedeniia o fiziologicheskikh porokakh, 4v, 5.

87. RGIA, f. 1683, o. 1, d. 119, Svedeniia o fiziologicheskikh porokakh, 3v.

88. RGIA, f. 1683, o. 1, d. 119, Svedeniia o fiziologicheskikh porokakh, 6v, 9v.

89. Kovalevskii, *Psikhologiia pola*, 211.

90. Merzheevskii, *Sudebnaia genikologiia*, 207–9.

91. Tarnovskii, *Izvrashchenie polovogo chuvstva*, 62.

92. RGIA, f. 1683, o. 1, d. 119, Svedeniia o fiziologicheskikh porokakh, 12, 3v.

93. RGIA, f. 1683, o. 1, d. 119, Svedeniia o fiziologicheskikh porokakh, 2v, 3.

94. Interestingly, Ross goes further. He argues that attempts by city authorities to "manage" the visibility of the queer milieu backfired, since they only reinforced the rapid standardization of signs for sexual opportunity, rendering the signs of illicit sex central to the city's visual vocabulary. He writes that "the very premise of regulationism . . . necessitated the provision of sexual spaces and signifiers in public space that could never be completely under the control of those who described and built them. Once these spaces and signs are put in place, women who sold sex and men who sought sex with other men were able to rely on them and deploy them to their own ends, muddying their disciplining effects at least for a time." Ross, *Public City/Public Sex*, 14–15.

95. RGIA, f. 1683, o. 1, d. 119, Svedeniia o fiziologicheskikh porokakh, 3.

96. RGIA, f. 1683, o. 1, d. 119, Svedeniia o fiziologicheskikh porokakh, 3.

97. See Healey, *Homosexual Desire in Revolutionary Russia*, 99; and Engelstein, "Soviet Policy," 158.

98. Weissman, "Regular Police in Tsarist Russia"; and Engelstein, "Soviet Policy."

99. See, in particular, Engelstein, "Soviet Policy," 158.

100. Healey writes that the "trail of evidence from the potentialities of 1917 to the first Soviet Russian criminal code of 1922, which decriminalized sodomy, is rather unclear." He cites the view of Karlinsky, who saw the "decriminalization as at best a benign oversight, the result of the elimination of all tsarist law during the Bolshevik revolution." Healey, *Homosexual Desire in Revolutionary Russia*, 115. Regarding the drafting process of the criminal code of 1903 and articles related to homosexuality in particular, see Koneva, "Istoriia razvitiia ugolovnogo zakonodatel'stva."

101. Healey, *Homosexual Desire in Revolutionary Russia*, 95.

102. Ruadze, *K sudu!* 58, 79.

103. Ruadze, *K sudu!* 79.

104. Ruadze, *K sudu!* 92.

Chapter 2. Policing Sex and Desire

1. TsGIA SPb, f. 965, o. 1, d. 1614, O pedaraste.

2. For examples, see police case logs of the two neighboring boroughs: TsGIA SPb f. 1648, o.1, d. 418, Kniga zapisi zaderzhannykh lits; and TsGIA SPb, f. 965, o. 3, d. 72, Ob obkhodakh politseiskimi agentami. Moreover, under the Security Law of 1881 and given St. Petersburg's state of "reinforced security," constables had the right to detain citizens without cause for up to two weeks; see Ponomarev, Dudchenko, and Rasskazov, "Vnesudebnye repressii," 65.

3. TsGIA SPb, f. 956, o. 1, d. 1614, O pedaraste, 2.

4. Kuzmin, *Dnevnik, 1905–1907*, 158.

5. By "constable" I refer to three types of constables that constituted the low-ranking police force in imperial St. Petersburg: *osobii nadziratil'* (the best translation is a special guard), *politseiskii pristav* (police constable), and *gorodovoi* (patrolman); see Vysotskii, *Sankt-Peterburgskaia politsiia*.

6. For discussions of possible changes in attitudes and enforcement patterns in Russia around 1905, see Engelstein, *Keys to Happiness*; Karlinsky, "Russia's Gay Literature and Culture"; and Surh, *1905 in St. Petersburg*.

7. Foucault, "21 February 1973."

8. The discussion is limited to sex and homosexual socialization between men, since sex between women was not criminalized.

9. Chauncey, *Gay New York*; Cocks, *Nameless Offences*; Cook, *London and the Culture of Homosexuality*; Croix, *Chicago Whispers*; Houlbrook, *Queer London*; Maynard, "Through a Hole"; and Peniston, "Pederasts, Prostitutes, and Pickpockets."

10. Weissman, "Regular Police in Tsarist Russia," 68. See also on this topic Hasegawa, *Crime and Punishment*, chap. 1; and McReynolds, *Murder Most Russian*.

11. The statistical significance of these stories is limited. They qualitatively broaden our understanding of queer policing beyond what existing evidence can provide, but

they are not the best of the best among many similar stories reflected in a vast store. Nor are they even a biased sample chosen by me to support my arguments. To the best of my knowledge, they constitute the sum total of evidence of queer policing in the municipal archives, which I believe I have scanned exhaustively. Given that it may never become feasible to load the scales with sufficient evidence to decisively guide the choice between a general tolerance or indifference model of policing and alternative models, the explanatory success of any model proposed needs to be assessed first and foremost in terms of its ability to reconcile the seemingly incongruent stories reflected in an amended but still very limited body of available evidence.

12. Foucault, "21 February 1973."

13. Gromov, *Zakony ugolovnye*, 280.

14. Cook, *London and the Culture of Homosexuality*, 44.

15. Beachy, *Gay Berlin*, xvii, 43–45, 46, 71.

16. Engelstein, "Soviet Policy," 158.

17. Healey, *Homosexual Desire in Revolutionary Russia*, 95. Healey cites Fuks here: "The intimate character of homosexual actions makes these relations virtually undetectable." See also Fuks, *Gomoseksualizm kak prestuplenie*.

18. Healey, *Homosexual Desire in Revolutionary Russia*, 83.

19. Healey, *Homosexual Desire in Revolutionary Russia*, in particular chapters 1 and 3, where he engages with works of Bekhterev, "O polovykh izvrashcheniiakh"; Merzheevskii, *Sudebnaia genikologiia*; Serbskii, *Sudebnaia psikhopatologiia*; Obolonskii, *Izvrashchenie polovogo chuvstva*; Tarnovskii, *Izvrashchenie polovogo chuvstva*; Nabokov, *Elementarnyi uchebnik*; and Fuks, *Gomoseksualizm kak prestuplenie*. See Engelstein, *Keys to Happiness*; and Engelstein, "Soviet Policy."

20. Cook acknowledges the need to look at day-to-day police routines in trying to reconstruct the workings of the historical queer milieu. He does so by analyzing the actions of policemen as described in courtroom evidence from cases explicitly involving a presumed pursuit of or consummation of homosexual sex between men. He further supplements this evidence with newspaper clippings concerning the same court cases. In a revealing aside, however, he acknowledges that "the police had previously used nuisance legislation to prosecute supposed homosexual behaviour." Cook, *London and the Culture of Homosexuality*, 43, see also chap. 2, 42–55.

21. Cook was not alone in recognizing the existence of something outside the scope of his analysis that might be helpfully illuminated in further work. Houlbrook, in his discussion of queer policing in London during the period between 1918 and 1957, draws attention to the deficiency of courtroom evidence, claiming that it does not reflect "the complex and often contradictory ways in which legislation was implemented." Houlbrook, *Queer London*, 20.

22. A separate police institution was formed, the "morals brigade" (*brigade des moeurs*) that initially relied broadly on the analogy between unregistered female prostitutes and men seeking sex with men in order to prosecute the latter under statutes outlawing "public offenses against decency." The scope of such offenses, however, was significantly constrained in 1843 by a regulation "defining the responsibilities of morals brigade." It instructed constables to "abstain from . . . provocation and try above all to catch the person in the act." The result was what Andrew Israel Ross describes as the "tension between knowledge of the person and that of behavior," given that police

"had little legal recourse unless they witnessed an actual act." Although other recourses and methods of policing are not explored in any depth, Ross does note that "this tension frustrated the police, who nevertheless sought to manage the existence of same-sex sexual solicitation." See Ross, *Public City/Public Sex,* 86, 97, 102–3.

23. Ross, *Public City/Public Sex*, 104.

24. See also Petri, "Discipline and Discretionary Power."

25. I reviewed correspondence and archival files of boroughs and precincts (TsGIA SPb, f. 1648), the police investigative department (TsGIA SPb, f. 965), and the police chief's central administrative apparatus (TsGIA SPb, f. 569) for the period from 1883 to 1917. Here, reference is to local city archives as opposed to national archives containing central government files. See the introduction to this book about the destruction of the archive.

26. TsGIA SPb f. 965, o.1, d.1862, Po zhalobe Kol. Sekr Sarkisova, 5v.

27. Healey, *Homosexual Desire in Revolutionary Russia*, 92–94.

28. Some examples of this scholarly tradition include Daly, *Watchful State*; Hasegawa, *Crime and Punishment*; Weissman, "Regular Police in Tsarist Russia"; and Zuckerman, *Tsarist Secret Police.*

29. Healey, *Homosexual Desire in Revolutionary Russia*, 95.

30. Henze, *Disease, Health Care and Government*, 25; and Beer, *Renovating Russia.*

31. See Healey, *Homosexual Desire in Revolutionary Russia*, 82. Healey suspects the existence of another motive for the reluctance of members of the medical professions to stretch their craft for the purpose of incriminating men accused of having homosexual sex: "Russian psychiatric attention, when it was focused on the problem of homosexuality, rejected the full range of stigmatization when applying the discourse to women or members of the lower classes, out of sympathy with their subordination. Psychiatrists themselves suffered from the same subordination in the autocratic state." Healey, *Homosexual Desire in Revolutionary Russia*, 92. The same sympathy with individuals in a subordinate position, however, is notably absent in Merzheevskii's and Tarnovskii's condemnation of young extortionists, where class plays an unmistakable role in exhonorating the victims and incriminating the blackmailers.

32. As Daly summarizes the effect of these reforms, they "restricted arbitrary arrest, established strict criminal procedure, and placed the investigation of all crimes firmly under the supervision of the office or prosecutor." Daly, "On the Significance of Emergency Legislation," 604.

33. In her critique of the Foucauldian disciplinary hypothesis, Engelstein writes that "here, the 'reign of law' had not 'already begun to recede,' as Foucault said of the European nineteenth century, but had not yet arrived." Engelstein, "Combined Underdevelopment," 343.

34. See Daly, "On the Significance of Emergency Legislation," 602, 624. Daly's translation in brackets and italics. See also a broader discussion about the security police in imperial Russia in Daly, *Watchful State.*

35. Daly, "On the Significance of Emergency Legislation," 605.

36. Healey, *Homosexual Desire in Revolutionary Russia*, 94.

37. Piatnitskii, *Polovye izvrashcheniia*, 88; also quoted in Healey, *Homosexual Desire in Revolutionary Russia*, 94, 93.

38. Engelstein, "Soviet Policy," 158.

39. Daly, "On the Significance of Emergency Legislation," 604.

40. Daly, "On the Significance of Emergency Legislation," 617.

41. It is more than likely that this is yet another reason the dossier found its way into one minister's hands. Its proposals were clearly phrased in the partisan language of this negotiation. Its author not only advocates "administrative measures" but also lays the groundwork for classifying "aunties" as politically unreliable. RGIA, f. 1683, o. 1, d. 119, Svedeniia o fiziologicheskikh porokakh. He compares them to the masonry, which had been banned in Russia since 1822, and accuses them of maintaining a secret society that undermined the integrity of state institutions and the military. In 1889, the Council of Ministers required that governors restrict their use of banishment to cases of "political unreliability" but had not yet implemented a requirement that such cases be reviewed by a central committee on exile and banishments. Daly, "On the Significance of Emergency Legislation," 616–17.

42. Daly, "On the Significance of Emergency Legislation," 616.

43. In a case from the 1870s discussed by Tarnovskii, "one of St. Petersburg's highest administrative figures was exposed as [having engaged in] pederasty and was swiftly discharged from service and banished abroad without trial or publicity." Here it is unclear whether emergency legislation was in fact used or whether discharge and banishment had a softer informal character that owed its effectiveness to the existence of the formal procedural options available. Tarnovskii, writing in 1885 in the present tense, writes that other men, bureaucrats in particular, paid blackmailers for fear of a similar fate. Tarnovskii, *Izvrashchenie polovogo chuvstva*, 72. Of note are also the banishments of "depraved foreigners" (*porochnye inostrantsy*) in 1899–1902 (as well as, presumably, other years). See RGIA f. 1284, o. 238, d. 82, Tsirkuliary MVD, 5, 11, 41; RGIA f. 1284, o. 238, d. 8, Tsirkuliary MVD, 24, 103, 118, 150; RGIA f. 1284, o. 238, d. 84, Tsirkuliary MVD, 155, 160, 161, 170, 191, 193, 194, 247; RGIA f. 1284, o. 238, d. 86, Tsirkuliary MVD, 91, 281; RGIA f. 1284, o. 238, d. 88, Tsirkuliary MVD, 135, 267, 302, 326; and RGIA f. 1284, o. 238, d. 89, Tsirkuliary MVD, 112–13. Similarly, the archives of the Office of the Mayor and Chief of Police contain files concerning banishment for "depraved behavior" (*porochnoe povedenie*), unfortunately without specifics. See TsGIA SPb, f. 965, o. 3, d. 147, O vysylke 77 chelovek.

44. For a detailed history of these states of emergency, see Gessen, *Iskliuchitel'noe polozhenie*, 164. On the history of the emergency legislation more broadly, see Makeev and Toldiev, "Chrezvychainoe zakonodatel'stvo"; Zemliakov, "Administrativnaia ssylka"; and Waldron, "States of Emergency."

45. See Daly, "On the Significance of Emergency Legislation," 612.

46. About the regular police in imperial Russia, see Neil Weissman's work, which focuses specifically on the administrative aspects, size, and official scope of police operations in tsarist Russia. He adopts something akin to a binary classification of police work as either kosher law enforcement analogous to contemporary progressive European examples or unkosher arbitrary coercion, which he assumes to be by definition chaotic and oppressive. See Weissman, "Regular Police in Tsarist Russia," 65.

47. Weissman, "Regular Police in Tsarist Russia," 50.

48. TsGIA SPb, f. 965, o. 1, d. 1614, O pedaraste, 2.

49. TsGIA SPb, f. 965, o. 1, d. 1614, O pedaraste, 2v–3.

50. TsGIA SPb, f. 965, o. 1, d. 1614, O pedaraste, 7, 10.

51. Following this second arrest he was banned from residing in the city for two years. TsGIA SPb, f. 965, o. 1, d. 1614, O pedaraste, 5v, 10. Regarding prosecution for civil offenses, see Ministerstvo vnutrennikh del, *Sbornik instruktsii*; Gromov, *Zakony igolovnye*, 667; Kleigel's, *Posobie dlia podgotovki*; and Volkov, *Postateinyi ukazatel'*.

52. TsGIA SPb, f. 1648, o. 1, d. 418, Kniga zapisi zaderzhannykh lits.

53. TsGIA SPb, f. 1648, o. 1, d. 418, Kniga zapisi zaderzhannykh lits, 113, 29.

54. Bernstein, *Sonia's Daughters*; A. Fedorov, "Deiatel'nost' S.-Peterburgskogo vrachebno-politseiskogo komiteta za period 1889–1895 gg."; Bentovin, *Torguiushchie telom*; Koffin'on, *Izvrashchennyi mir*; and Ruadze, *K sudu!*.

55. See TsGIA SPb, f. 965, o. 3, d. 72, Ob obkhodakh politseiskimi agentami; and TsGIA SPb, f. 1648, o. 1, d. 418, Kniga zapisi zaderzhannykh lits. Regarding further cases of arrest under articles 38, 42, and 43 of the so-called Administrative Code, see also the files of the criminal investigation department (a misnomer, if ever there was one)—again, "books of arrests": TsGIA SPb, f. 965, o. 2, d. 140, Alfavitnaia kniga; TsGIA SPb, f. 965, o. 2, d. 141, Alfavitnaia kniga; TsGIA SPb, f. 965, o. 2, d. 156, Kniga zapisi; TsGIA SPb, f. 965, o. 2, d. 184, Alfavitnaia kniga; and TsGIA SPb, f. 965, o. 2, d. 185, Alfavitnaia kniga. These files document the arrests of men and women for "soliciting members of the public," "impudent and seductive behavior in public places," "loitering," and being drunk in public spaces.

56. Kleigel's, *Osnovy politseiskoi sluzhby*, 10. See also Budkov, *Sbornik obiazatelnykh postanovlenii*, 1910; Budkov, *Sbornik obizatelnykh postanovlenii*, 1914; and Obolonskii, *Izvrashchenie polovogo chuvstva*. Regarding the Administrative Code generally, see Gromov, *Zakony ugolovnye*, 685.

57. Kuzmin, *Dnevnik, 1905–1907*, 158.

58. Healey, *Homosexual Desire in Revolutionary Russia*, 105–7.

59. Kuzmin, *Dnevnik, 1905–1907*, 176, 85, 217.

60. TsGIA SPb, f. 965, o. 1, d. 1614, O pedaraste, 2.

61. Bersen'ev and Markov, "Politsiia i gei."

62. See, for example, Ross, *Public City/Public Sex*, 105.

63. The terms "hooligan" and "hooliganism" were in vogue in the early decades of the twentieth century and, imported from the English, acquired their own cultural meaning in St. Petersburg. It was used by the press, by the public, and by constables and government officials. I adopt the usage of the time, of which Joan Neuberger offers a thorough analysis. She writes that although "most hooligans were young, lower-class males, . . . it would be a mistake to view hooliganism purely as class conflict." Hooliganism was a culture of defiance, expressed in public, provocative behavior, and crime. According to her, "hooligans did not defy institutions of power directly but used public and symbolic behavior to challenge existing hierarchies of everyday life." This ingredient of symbolic cultural subversion or defiance was what set hooligans apart, no matter what their behavior, crime, or occupation or lack thereof. See Neuberger, *Hooliganism*, 60, 8, 2; as well as Neuberger, "Stories of the Street," 179.

64. Kuzmin was fined in April 1908, and in July of that year the city's mayor and chief of police issued another secret directive targeting the "eradication of pornography." *Peterburgskii listok*, "Pornografiia" (in section "Magistrate Court"), May 2, 1908. TsGIA SPb, f. 1648, o. 1, d. 180, Sekretnye tsirkuliary. In this file, see the Secret Direc-

tive issued July 31, 1908, no. 9776, "O razvitii protivoestestvennykh organizatsii i iskorenenie pornografii," 99. Both Kuzmin's fine and the issuance of this directive may have been prompted by Ruadze's inflammatory pamphlet, also published that year, in which he specifically mentions Kuzmin's novels, *Wings* and *The Chimes of Love* (Kuranty Liubvi). Ruadze, *K sudu!*, 115.

65. Kuzmin, *Dnevnik, 1905–1907*, 113, 59.

66. Just as in Russia, Beachy notes that in Weimar Germany, where "male prostitution was never specifically criminalized and certain erotic same-sex acts were 'illegal,' the lines dividing prostitution, opportunistic sex, companionship, and love would remain ambiguous and shifting." Beachy, *Gay Berlin*, 188–89. Kuzmin's recollections suggest that a range of exchanges from specific monetary payments, or "tips," for specific sexual acts to sponsorship via gifts or even simply subsidized access to certain venues and modes of consumption added a commercial dimension to some of his sexual encounters. Vis-à-vis hooligans, he specifically recalls restaurant visits during which, presumably, the young men he describes as "hooligans" did not share in the bill, although they were also under no explicit obligation to engage in sex and, at least sometimes, did not. Kuzmin, *Dnevnik, 1905–1907*, 159. Elsewhere, Kuzmin notes: "One needs to explain oneself frankly, otherwise it turns out to be an average between legal marriage and blackmail, to which I do not consent"; Kuzmin, *Dnevnik, 1905–1907*, 243. The distinctions between commercial and noncommercial sex have been explored by historians and cultural geographers, who consistently point out the blurred boundaries between the two, even for heterosexual sex acts and relations. Among others, see Hubbard, *Sex and the City*; Hubbard and Sanders, "Making Space for Sex Work"; Felski, *Gender of Modernity*; and Swanson, *Drunk with the Glitter*.

67. The historian Joan Neuberger explains that hooligans "eluded police control" in the city, as interfering with them could be risky even for armed constables. Neuberger, *Hooliganism*, 26.

68. Gromov, *Zakony ugolovnye*, 685.

69. TsGIA SPb, f. 569, o. 10, d. 104, Tsirkuliary departamenta politsii, 189–90.

70. Responses from three boroughs (Narvskaia, Liteinaia, and Spasskaia), including, fortunately, the replies of constables from almost all precincts in these boroughs, have survived. Unfortunately, responses from the other eleven boroughs appear neither in the archival files of boroughs and precincts nor in those of the police chief's central administrative apparatus or the police investigation department.

71. TsGIA SPb, f. 1648, o. 1, d. 1222, Tsirkuliarnye telegrammy, 48–58.

72. TsGIA SPb, f. 1648, o. 1, d. 1222, Tsirkuliarnye telegrammy, 55.

73. TsGIA SPb, f. 1648, o. 1, d. 855, Tsyrkuliary Peterburgskogo gradonachal'nika, 195–195v.

74. TsGIA SPb, f. 1648, o. 1, d. 651, Sekretnye tsirkuliary, 105, 107v, 108, 108v.

75. TsGIA SPb, f. 1648, o. 1, d. 651, Sekretnye tsirkuliary, 108v.

76. TsGIA SPb, f. 1648, o. 1, d. 651, Sekretnye tsirkuliary, 112.

77. Despite being launched with a similarly vague directive initially, the push to constrain illicit sexual activity in the semipublic spaces of the city's hotels received a more supportive response from constables. Soon after the July directive regarding debauchery in hotel rooms, the city's governor and mayor at the time, Daniil Drachevskii, who was simultaneously also its chief of police, launched a campaign against debauchery

in hotels that lasted beyond his term (1908–1914), and well into the Revolution. Enlisting the help not only of borough police stations but also the city's Medico-Police Committee and regulatory authorities, Drachevskii and his successors tried to stem what they saw as a tide of debauchery in hotels. See in particular, TsGIA SPb, f. 569, o. 17, d. 999, O vzyskanii mer, and TGIA SPb, f. 569, o. 12, d. 118, Delo o soderzhanii gostinits. Both files contained lists of hotels where debauchery was allegedly taking place. Precinct-level constables diligently created these lists for each borough (for example, TsGIA SPb, f. 569, o. 17, d. 999, O vzyskanii mer, 8, 10, 12, 13, 15, 18). In addition to raids, the city administration responded with spatial regulation (see TsGIA SPb, f. 569, o. 17, d. 999, O vzyskanii mer, 1–3). Hotels were barred from playing music, offering billiard tables, and, temporarily, from selling liquor. Petitions from owners to repeal these restrictions led to the withdrawal of the ban on selling alcohol, in part thanks to the involvement of the Excise Duty Collection Office (Upravlenie aktsiznymi sborami), which had an interest in renewing this source of revenues. The campaign was in full swing when it seems to have abruptly stopped or at least its documentary trail broke off well into the Revolution in 1917 (TsGIA SPb, f. 569, o. 17, d. 999, O vzyskanii mer, 1–3 and f. 569, o. 12, d. 118, Delo o soderzhanii gostinits, 1–5).

78. GARF, f. 111, o. 1, d. 2999, Poseshchenie restoranov; see also Ruadze, *K sudu!*, 102.

79. Kuzmin, *Dnevnik, 1905–1907*, 165, 58, 59.

80. Healey, *Homosexual Desire in Revolutionary Russia*, 92–95.

81. See, for example, *Peterburgskii listok*, "Stolichnaia nakip'," February 11, 1900. In addition, one of the most popular boulevard papers, *Gazeta-kopeika*, had a special series dedicated to street life ("Our Street" or "Nasha ulista"), with all its troubles or, as Marc Steinberg calls them, "moral sores of urban life." See, for example, *Gazeta-kopeika*, "Nasha ulitsa," August 11, 1908, 3–4; August 22, 1908, 3; August 24, 1908, 2–3; and Steinberg, *Petersburg Fin de Siècle*, 50. See also the chapter titled "Ulitsa" (Street), in Ruadze, *K sudu!*.

82. Further cases demonstrating the thresholds or boundary conditions for police action include the case of Vasilii Orlikov, a man accused of having compelled his underage nephew to have sex with him (TsGIA SPb, f. 1648, o. 1, d. 566, Kniga zapisi ugolovnykh obvnenii). This case indicates that sex with a male minor or a man in a dependent position, even if not accompanied by assault, was more likely to be persecuted than consensual sex between adult men. A number of the cases mentioned and referenced above as inconsequential arrests for petty crimes indicate that constables responding to street-level disturbances generally acted only when the situation risked attracting public attention or the attention of superiors. Conversely, constables were reluctant to act in cases where the risk of attracting such attention was small, as was evident in the case of Sarkisov and Raikovskii discussed in chapter 1, TsGIA SPb f. 965, o. 1, d. 1862, Po zhalobe Kol. Sekr Sarkisova. Healey also touches on this theme (but he explores other sources) in Healey, *Homosexual Desire in Revolutionary Russia*, 95, 96. See GARF, f. 124, o. 28, d. 686, Delo po prosheniiu K. V. Sizykh; GARF, f. 124, o. 30, d. 1481, Delo po prosheniiu I. Miniaylo; and GARF, f. 124, o. 31, d. 1026, Delo po proshenii V. Pudenko. Notably, the observation in Healey (p. 95) that "police rarely figure as initiators of arrests. Rather, they acted when a denunciation was received or other circumstances drew their attention to a particular 'pederast'" would be neither peculiar to St. Petersburg nor conclusive regarding police activity beyond immediate enforcement of articles 995 and 996 of the criminal code banning male sodomy.

83. Weissman, "Regular Police in Tsarist Russian," 58.

84. Foucault, "The Punitive Society," 32, where he writes that "for an analysis of penality it is important to see that power is not what suppresses civil war, but what conducts and continues it."

85. Chauncey, *Gay New York*; Cocks, *Namelss Offences*, 61–67; and Houlbrook, *Queer London*, 25–31.

86. Ross, *Public City/Public Sex*, 13, 129–36.

87. Lipsky, *Street-Level Bureaucracy*, xiii, xvii.

88. Gilson, "Michael Lipsky, 'Street-Level Bureaucracy,'" 391. Here, Gilson refers to Laws and Haje, "Policy in Practice."

89. On the concept of "pedestrianism," see Blomley, *Rights of Passage*. On the revanchist city, see Smith, *New Urban Frontier*. For an example of analysis combining these two concepts, see Levy, "Revanchism via Pedestrianism."

90. Gilson, "Michael Lipsky, 'Street-Level Bureaucracy,'" 387. Here Gilson refers to Wastell et al., "Children's Services," 317.

91. Recall, for example, that according to Tarnovskii, writing in 1885, high-ranking officials paid blackmailers for fear of exposure. Here it is far from clear that this exposure must necessarily have been to the state. Tarnovskii, *Izvrashchenie polovogo chuvstva*, 72.

92. Foucault, "21 February 1973"; and Engelstein, "Combined Underdevelopment."

93. Foucault, *Discipline and Punish*, 253.

94. Foucault, "'Omnes et Singulatim,'" 319.

95. Foucault, "21 February 1973," 145. The term is also discussed in Markus and Farmer, "Introduction," 2.

96. Bech, *When Men Meet*; Boyd, *Wide Open Town*; Cocks, *Namelss Offences*; Higgs, *Queer Sites*; Houlbrook, *Queer London*; and Maynard, "Through a Hole." Ross is perhaps the exception, in the sense that he treats the containment of queer spatial practices in Paris as an aesthetic matter, one that affects the legibility of sex and that quite possibly provided the signposts along the well-trodden roads to illicit sex in the city. However, his starting point is very different because sodomy was not a crime in eighteenth-century Paris. Ross, *Public City/Public Sex*.

Chapter 3. Queer Streetlife

1. Analyses of scholarly uses of the idea of modernity include Kenny, *Feel of the City*; Giddens, *Consequences of Modernity*; Giddens, *Modernity and Self-Identity*; Harvey, *Condition of Postmodernity*; and Bauman, "Modernity." See also "Historians and the Questions of Modernity," special issue of *American Historical Review* 116, no. 3 (2011).

2. Berman, *All That Is Solid*, 15.

3. On urbanization in late imperial Russia, see Hamm, *City in Late Imperial Russia*; Brower, *Russian City*; and Economakis, *From Peasant to Petersburger*.

4. Kruze and Kuznetsov, "Naselenie Peterburga," 105. See also Bater, *St Petersburg*, 310.

5. On urban conditions during the last decades of imperial reign, see the works of Bater, "Between Old and New," 55–61; and Bater, *St Petersburg*, chap. 6, esp. 342–53. On the crime rate, see Hasegawa, *Crime and Punishment*, 27–36.

6. Steinberg, *Petersburg Fin de Siècle*, 47–69.

7. See, for example, Cook, *London and the Culture of Homosexuality*, 22–29; Chauncey, *Gay New York*, 179–205; and Houlbrook, *Queer London*, 45–48.

8. Turner, *Backward Glances*.

9. Vernon, *Distant Strangers*, xii.

10. Although smartly dressed—even something of a dandy—the flaneur was not necessarily a member of the middle or upper classes. Precisely due to his anonymity in the crowd, his displays of conspicuous consumption, evident in his dress and his lack of an obvious productive occupation, were, arguably, sufficient "street credentials" for individuals of this category. See, for example, Hubbard, *Cities and Sexualities*, 124. Scholarly work also suggests that flaneurism is not a gender-exclusive phenomenon. About the flaneur as a male figure, see, among others, Tester, *Flâneur*; and Lauster, "Walter Benjamin's Myth." About the flaneuse, or the female version of a flaneur, see Dreyer and McDowall, "Imagining the Flâneur as a Woman"; and Tseng, "The Flâneur, the Flaneuse, and the Hostess."

11. Andersson, *Streetlife in Late Victorian London*, 220.

12. Lefebvre, *Production of Space*. For more about "practiced places" in cities in modernity, see Dennis, *Cities in Modernity*, 28.

13. Certeau, *Practice of Everyday Life*.

14. I deploy the term proposed by Peter K. Andersson; see Andersson, *Streetlife in Late Victorian London*.

15. The term "a society of strangers" emerges from Georg Simmel's and Nicholas Vernon's discussions: Simmel, "Metropolis and Mental Life"; and Vernon, *Distant Strangers*, xii. See also the discussion about flaneurs in late imperial St. Petersburg in Steinberg, *Petersburg Fin de Siècle*, 51–52. About streetlife more broadly, see Sennett, *Flesh and Stone*; and Benjamin, *Arcade Project*.

16. The term "familiar strangers" (*znakomye neznakomtsy*), is from the diary of the fin-de-siècle poet, composer, and flaneur Mikhail Kuzmin. Kuzmin, *Dnevnik, 1905–1907*, 330.

17. Simmel, "Metropolis and Mental Life."

18. Dennis, *Cities in Modernity*, 2.

19. Cultural geographers, urban studies scholars, and philosophers have long been concerned with positioning social practices in space. Henry Lefebvre, one of the most important proponents of spatial theory, proposed that space itself is a social construct (based on values and the social production of meanings), in both the physical and built sense and in the sense of spatial practices and perceptions (see Lefebvre, *Production of Space*). Within the body of literature dedicated to special theory, Edward Soja, David Harvey, and Nigel Thrift offer helpful entry points. See Soja, *Postmodern Geographies*; Harvey, *Consciousness*; and Thrift, *Non-Representational Theory*.

20. Certeau, *Practice of Everyday Life*, 123; see also Thompson, "Telling Spatial Stories."

21. Berman, *All That Is Solid*, 232.

22. Bentham, *Panopticon*. On the concept of the panopticon, see Lyon, "Bentham's Panopticon"; and Miller and Miller, "Jeremy Bentham's Panoptic Device."

23. Ogborn, *Spaces of Modernity*, 151, 150.

24. John Lockman (1752), *A Sketch of the Spring-Gardens*, Vaux-Hall, in a Letter to a Noble Lord, p. 13, cited in Ogborn, *Spaces of Modernity*, 151.

25. Browne, *Dark Matters*, 21.

26. Joyce, *Rule of Freedom*; Dennis, *Cities in Modernity*.

27. Here I mean that the city originally developed toward the north (Petrogradsky Island). This is the first phase of construction. The second phase includes the expansion of the city's right riverbank, where the city expanded toward the Fontanka River. During the third phase, commencing in the reign of Nicholas I, the city expanded beyond the Fontanka River. See Darinskii and Startsev, *Istoriia Sankt-Peterburga*; Avseenko, *200 let S.-Petersburgu*; and Enakiev, *Zadachi preobrazovaniia*.

28. See the chapter "Liteinaia Borough," in Eremeev, *Gorod S.- Peterburg*, 619.

29. Eremeev, *Gorod S.-Peterburg*; and see Bater, *St. Petersburg*, 80, 157, 374.

30. Eremeev, *Gorod S.-Peterburg*, 615, 616.

31. Eremeev, *Gorod S.-Peterburg*, 614.

32. On the reactive system of policing, see Weissman, "Regular Police in Tsarist Russia."

33. See the chapter "Liteinaia Borough" in Eremeev, *Gorod S.-Peterburg*, 609–23. See also the archival files about police surveillance around the borough: GARF, f. 111, o. 1, d. 3764, Raion Fontanki dom no. 16; and GARF, f. 111, o. 1, d. 3764, Raion Fontanki dom no. 38.

34. Weissman, "Regular Police in Tsarist Russia," 48.

35. TsGIA, f. 569, o. 10, d. 104, Tsirkuliary departamenta politsii.

36. Andersson, *Streetlife in Late Victorian London*, 16.

37. Eremeev, *Gorod S.-Peterburg*, 609–23. On the building stock, population, and social composition of the borough and the role of Liteinyi Prospect in urban life, see Bater, *St. Petersburg*, 157, 66, 374, 268.

38. Eremeev, *Gorod S.-Peterburg*, 609–23; Rozanov, *Literaturnye ocherki*, 224–26.

39. I studied three contemporary newspapers: a daily official city mayoral newspaper, *Vestnik Sankt-Peterburgskogo gradonachal'stva i Sankt-Peterburgskoi gorodskoi politsii*; a daily popular urban newspaper, *Peterburgskii listok*; and a daily yellow-press newspaper, *Gazeta-Kopeika*), published from 1890 to 1914. Additionally, I studied the *City Duma Information Bulletin* (*Izvestiia dumy*) during the same period.

40. *Sankt-Peterburg po peripisi 10 dekabria 1869 goda*, part 3, 74–85, 74, 85. For estimates on the number of horse-drawn trams and cabs, see also Gorodskaia uprava, *Po voprosy*, 107; and Seliverstov, *Leningrad*.

41. Gautier, *Winter in Russia*, 68.

42. Bater, "Development of Public Transportation," 89.

43. Bater, "Development of Public Transportation."

44. Kuzmin, *Dnevnik, 1905–1907*, 164.

45. Kuzmin, *Dnevnik, 1905–1907*, 338.

46. Kuzmin, *Dnevnik, 1905–1907*, 169.

47. Healey, *Homosexual Desire in Revolutionary Russia*, 23.

48. Kuzmin, *Dnevnik, 1905–1907*, 143.

49. Enakiev, *Zadachi preobrazovaniia*, 30–40; Zanosov and Pyzin, "Gorodskoi transport," 38–46.

50. Bater, "Development of Public Transportation," 89.

51. See, for example, Cherikover, *Peterburg*; and Zanosov and Pyzin, "Gorodskoi transport."

52. *Gazeta-kopeika*, "Kinematograph: v Tramvaie," October 9, 1903; again, Pyzin and Zanosov describe cabs and other means of public transport as places of encounter. See also Steinberg, *Petersburg Fin de Siècle*, 23, on the issue of noise from public transport.

53. Zanosov and Pyzin, "Na ulitsakh," 26.

54. See, for example, the report of the Lighting Supervision Commission organized by the City Council (Komissiia po nadzoru za osveshcheniem), where the members of the commission reported to the City Duma about the unsatisfactory lighting on the city streets and the consequences for urban residents; *Izvestiia dumy*, "Obshchii plan," 997.

55. Schivelbusch, *Disenchanted Night*, 62; and Schlör, *Nights in the Big City*. See also Cresswell, "Night Discourse."

56. Hubbard, *Cities and Sexualities*, 122, 23.

57. Cherikover, *Peterburg*, 36, 37. The report was published on behalf of the Geographic Commission of the Teaching Department of the Society for the Dissemination of Technical Knowledge (Geograficheskaia komissiia uchebnogo otdela obshchestva rasprostraneniia tekhnicheskikh znanii).

58. Nye, "History of Electricity Use," 79–80; see also Schivelbusch, *Disenchanted Night*.

59. Dennis, *Cities in Modernity*, 135. See also Schivelbusch, *Disenchanted Night*, 148, where he refers to the "illuminated window as stage, the street as theater with the passers-by as audience—this is the scene of big-city night life."

60. *Izvestiia dumy*, "Ob elektricheskom osveshchenii," 27–48; *Izvestiia dumy*, "Ob osveshchenii Nevskogo Prospekta ," 855–58.

61. Regarding the development of streetlighting in the early twentieth century, see: *Izvestiia dumy*, "Obshchii plan"; and *Izvestiia dumy*, "Ob usilenii osveshcheniia." See how innovations in electric streetlighting in St. Petersburg were discussed in the foreign press in Fonveille, "Gas and Electricity in Paris."

62. See http://www.lensvet.spb.ru/elektricheskie_fonari, accessed September 12, 2020. Semenovich, *Ulichnoe osveshchenie*, 38.

63. *Izvestiia dumy*, "Ob elektricheskom osveshchenii."

64. Semenovich, *Ulichnoe osveshchenie*, 38.

65. Ruadze, *K sudu!* 55–56, 102–3, where Ruadze talks about Nevsky, Morskaia Street, and Fontanka; RGIA, f. 1683, o. 1, d. 119, Svedeniia o fiziologicheskikh porokakh, 2v; TsGIA SPb, f. 965, o. 1, d. 1614, O pedaraste, 2.

66. For the importance of Nevsky Prospect for socialization and queer socialization, see Steinberg, *Petersburg Fin de Siècle*, 63–66; Ruadze, *K sudu!* 55–56, 102–3; and Healey, *Homosexual Desire in Revolutionary Russia*, 31.

67. Ogborn, *Spaces of Modernity*, 151.

68. N. Popov, *Memoirs*, cited in Karpenko, "Osvesheniie," 75.

69. Healey, "Disappearance of the Russian Queen," 158. The same text appears in Healey, *Homosexual Desire in Revolutionary Russia*, 37. See also Tucker, *Queer Visibilites*.

70. Zanosov and Pyzin, "Magaziny u lavki," 97; Cherikover, *Peterburg*, 5–6.

71. Turner, *Backward Glances*, 52.

72. *Peterburgskii listok*, "Passazh v budushchem"; *Peterburgskii listok*, "Otkrytie passazha."

73. Svetlov, *Peterburgskaia zhizn'*, 51, 105.

74. Cook, *London and the Culture of Homosexuality*, 25.

75. Houlbrook, *Queer London*, 49–52.

76. Peniston, "Pederasts, Prostitutes, and Pickpockets," 172.

77. Ross, *Public City/Public Sex*, chap. 2, 80. Ross's research on the Parisian urinals should be read in the context of Matt Houlbroook's call to examine how public toilets were actually used and policed; see Houlbrook, "Private World," 52.

78. RGIA, f. 1683, o. 1, d. 119, Svedeniia o fiziologicheskikh porokakh. See also Healey, *Homosexual Desire in Revolutionary Russia*, 31.

79. Merts, "Gorodskie retiradniki," 35.

80. Merts, "Gorodskie retiradniki," 36.

81. Merts, "Gorodskie retiradniki," 35.

82. Ross, *Public City/Public Sex*, 65.

83. Ruadze, *K sudu!* 103–4.

84. As Weismann explains, the so-called reactive system of policing required a constable to be placed on each corner; see Weissman, "Regular Police in Tsarist Russia." Also in this area were plainclothes policemen whose primary responsibility was protecting a nearby royal palace. See GARF, f. 111, o. 1, d. 99, Raion Anichkogo mosta, 1914; GARF, f. 111, o. 1, d. 100, Raion Anichkogo mosta, 1915; and GARF, f. 111, o. 1, d. 101, Raion Anichkogo mosta, 1916.

85. For a broader discussion of the role of public toilets in queer encounters in Western cities, see Cook, *London and the Culture of Homosexuality*, 44; Houlbrook, *Queer London*, 49; and Peniston, "Pederasts, Prostitutes, and Pickpockets," 176–77. See also Delph, *Silent Community*; Tewksbury, "Men and Erotic Oases"; and Edelman, "Tearooms and Sympathy."

86. TsGIA SPb, f. 965, o. 1, d. 1614, O pedaraste, 2; see also TsGIA SPb, f. 1683, o. 1, d. 119, Svedeniia o fiziologicheskikh porokakh.

87. Merzheevskii, *Sudebnaia genikologiia*, 254. Merzheevskii describes an incident involving two men who met at the arcade. One of them tried to blackmail the other after having sex with him. See also Healey, *Homosexual Desire in Revolutionary Russia*, 31, as well as the same text in Healey, "Disappearance of the Russian Queen," 157.

88. Tarnovskii, *Izvrashchenie polovogo chuvstva*, 72; see also Koni, *Na zhiznennom puti*, 154–55.

89. RGIA, f. 1683, o. 1, d. 119, Svedeniia o fiziologicheskikh porokakh (the "dossier"); and Tarnovskii, *Izvrashchenie polovogo chuvstva*, 73.

90. Petrov, *Passazh*.

91. Some changes, such as the replacement of the aging glass roof and the installation of electric lights and sockets, were seemingly neutral, although, as discussed, electric lighting also created opportunities for cruising, even as it facilitated surveillance. More important, the gallery was replaced by a second row of shops, and all cafés, restaurants, and rooms by the hour that were directly accessible from the Passazh were closed down. As a journalist of the *Peterburgskii listok* wrote enthusiastically during the reconstruction phase, "precisely in this way the upper gallery shall be removed, which had such an unfortunate reputation in the past. Everything will be different and this should, in the opinion of the builder and manager, Mr. Kozlov, raise the commercial importance of the reopened the Passazh." *Peterburgskii listok*, "Passazh v budushchem."

92. *Peterburgskii listok*, "Razdel 'Mimokhodom'" (emphasis added).
93. Ruadze, *K sudu!* 102–3.
94. S.-Peterburgskoe gorodskoe obshchestvennoe upravlenie, *Putevoditel' po S.-Peterburgu*; Lisovskii, *Arkhitektura Peterburga*.
95. Benjamin, *Arcade Project*.
96. Buck-Morss, *Dialectics of Seeing*; Hanssen, *Walter Benjamin*.
97. RGIA, f. 1683, o. 1, d. 119, Svedeniia o fiziologicheskikh porokakh; Ruadze, *K sudu!* 102–3.
98. Ruadze, *K sudu!*.
99. Andersson, *Streetlife in Late Victorian London*, 7.

Chapter 4. Bathing in the Queer City

1. TsGIA, SPb, f. 569, o. 11, d. 426, Delo o zakrytii ban', 5v. See police resolutions regarding the closure of bathhouses in this file, 13v,34v, 48v, 52v, 63v.
2. TsGIA, SPb, f. 569, o. 11, d. 426, Delo o zakrytii ban', 16v–17.
3. TsGIA, SPb, f. 569, o.11, d. 426, Delo o zakrytii ban', 28, 42–42v; for the reopening of Gustov's baths, see 43.
4. Healey, *Homosexual Desire in Revolutionary Russia*, 33.
5. Healey, *Homosexual Desire in Revolutionary Russia*, 28.
6. Among queer urban historians, whose works were discussed in the introduction, see, for example, Prior and Cusack, "Ritual, Liminality and Transformation"; Holmes, O'Byrne, and Gastaldo, "Setting the Space for Sex"; Hammers, "Making Space?"; and Berube, "History of Gay Bathhouses."
7. Pollock, *Without the Banya*, 103–4 (emphasis added).
8. Pollock, *Without the Banya*, 73–79, 98–119.
9. Gandy, *Fabric of Space*, 13. Regarding my use of the term "common," see Eizenberg, "Actually Existing Commons," 766. To Eizenberg the defining features of an urban common are informal cooperation and a resemblance to a rural "ideal common." Both are in evidence in late imperial St. Petersburg's commercial bathhouses, even though these were, of course, economically motivated operations. Regarding the first, informal cooperation, the purely commercial nature of urban bathing was notably interrupted by the role of mutuality and informal cooperation. In the *prostaia bania*, the cheapest bathhouse sections, attendants were few and far between and visitors had to assist one another in maintaining the proper humidity in the steam room, washing each other, and carrying water from tanks and receptacles (see, e.g., Znamenskii, *O russkikh baniakh*). These are the practices most obviously analogous to the social reproduction involved in the traditional bathing commons, as transplanted to the practices and biopolitics of the metropolis. Here, I follow the spirit if not the letter of arguments in Hardt and Negri, *Commonwealth*. In addition, the role of bathhouse attendants was quintessentially informal, as they worked in highly improvised ways for their lodging and tips. Instead of being employed by bathhouse operators in the modern sense, they were tolerated and expected to support the unique culture of urban bathing by operating at the nexus of monetary and nonmonetary exchange. Their work exemplifies the ways in which the cooperative social reproduction of the "common" or "commons" is supplemented by entrepreneurial activity and by commercial-

ized forms of reward. Finally, regulated prices actually constrained the ability of owners and operators to compete on price alone, leading to attempts to maintain profitability through both commercial improvisation and a reinforcement of informal cooperative and self-regulating activities, both licit and illicit (Siuzor, "Torgovye (narodnye) Bani"). Regarding the second key feature of the urban common, its link to a nonurban ideal common, St. Petersburg's commercial bathhouses bore an obvious connection to rural bathing. Indeed, village bathhouses in Russia provide a surprisingly faithful analogy to the historical English and American village commons so familiar to advocates of common rights and commoning. Like those village commons, the Russian village bathhouses constituted "property with no rights allocation and regulation, and as belonging to everybody and hence to nobody" (Eizenberg, "Actually Existing Commons," 765). Transposed to late imperial St. Petersburg, this amalgamation of village traditions and urban realities established the city's commercial bathhouses as a kind of "quasi-commons"—that is, one in which traditional rural commons practices persisted but were also supplemented and co-opted by commercial imperatives, new urban realities, and government regulation. Building on this linguistic theme, bathhouses were emphatically "common places," a term that Svetlana Boym uses to refer to the organization of space and speech in Russian everyday life, although my borrowing of the phrase sees more vitality and persistence in the idea of the "common" than Boym's history of aestheticized derogation and nostalgia; see Boym, *Common Places*. We can understand St. Petersburg's bathhouses as a mainstream communal social space or "common place" of this stripe, as places where communal practices persisted despite the forces of capitalist modernity.

10. Glassberg, "Design of Reform"; Otter, "Making Liberal Objects"; Osborne and Rose, "Governing Cities"; Renner, "Nation That Bathes Together."

11. Randall, "Cracks in the Granite."

12. With the exception of Ethan Pollock, *Without the Banya*.

13. Dubrovskaia and Dubrovskii, *Russkaia bania i massazh*, 135; Tolstoi, *Slavianskie drevnosti*, 34.

14. A. I. Bogdanov, *Istoricheskoe, geograficheskoe i topograficheskoe opisanie*.

15. I. A. Bogdanov, *Tri veka peterburgskoi bani*.

16. I. A. Bogdanov, *Tri veka peterburgskoi bani*, 27.

17. A. I. Bogdanov, *Istoricheskoe, beograficheskoe i topograficheskoe opisanie*.

18. Polnoe sobranie zakonov Rossiiskoi Imperii, article 71.

19. This regulation is mentioned in the archival file TsGIA SPb, f. 792, o. 1, d. 7705, Po khodataistvu banevladel'tsev, 1, 1v, 2, 2v.

20. TsGIA SPb, f. 210, o. 1, d. 484, Ob ustroistve, 16. See also TsGIA SPb, f. 479, o. 22, d. 1479, O materialakh za 1900.

21. Znamenskii, *O russkikh baniakh*, 3; *Vedomosti politsii*, "Peterburgskie bani"; *Vedomosti politsii*, "Peterburgskie bani: prodolzhenie"; *Illustrirovaniia gazeta*, 22 (June 10, 1871), 324–25.

22. Bailey, "Entertainmentality!" 126.

23. Znamenskii, *O russkikh baniakh*, 34.

24. Eremeev, *Gorod S.-Peterburg*, 507–9, 235–37.

25. *Peterburgskii listok*, "Pisma v redaktsiiu"; Eremeev, *Gorod S.-Peterburg*; P. Siuzor, "Torgovye (narodnye) bani," 136; Znamenskii, *O russkikh baniakh*. Regarding the role

of barbers in bloodletting, see Eremeev, *Gorod S.-Peterburg*, 244–45. See also Pollock, *Without the Banya*, 88.

26. A hundred kopeks make a ruble. Entrance fees were introduced at this level in 1879; see *Vestnik gradonachal'stva*, "Chast' offitsial'naia," no. 172 (July 29, 1879): 1–2. Regarding the ratio of attendants to patrons, see Eremeev, *Gorod S.-Peterburg*, 260–61.

27. Eremeev, *Gorod S.-Peterburg*, 236–37, 507; Znamenskii, *O russkikh baniakh*, 34.

28. Pollock, *Without the Banya*, 103.

29. Eremeev, *Gorod S.-Peterburg*, 236; Pollock, *Without the Banya*, 82.

30. Eizenberg, "Actually Existing Commons," 766.

31. TsGIA, SPb, f. 479, o. 22, d. 1479, O materialakh za 1900, where the number of buckets of water used per year is specified as a basis for taxation.

32. Pollock, *Without the Banya*, 109.

33. Pollock, *Without the Banya*, 104.

34. Rozanov, *Literaturnye ocherki*, 224–26; Eremeev, *Gorod S.-Peterburg*, 235–36. See also Pollock, *Without the Banya*, 104–6.

35. The working day of an attendant could last as long as fifteen hours. The first shift started as early as 4:00 AM and the last one ended well past midnight. Attendants might spend up to thirty sessions in the steam room during a single shift. Eremeev, *Gorod S.-Peterburg*, 262–64, 515–16.

36. Pollock, *Without the Banya*, 85, 91. For a detailed description of the workloads of bathhouse attendants, see Eremeev, *Gorod S.-Peterburg*, 262–64, 515–16.

37. Eremeev, *Gorod S.-Peterburg*, 516–17, 263–64.

38. Znamenskii, *O russkikh baniakh*.

39. Leikin, *Stseny iz kupecheskogo byta*, 113–15, 13.

40. Eremeev, *Gorod S.-Peterburg*, 262–63.

41. Tarnovskii, *Izvrashchenie polovogo chuvstva*, 69. For more about this court case, see Chugin, "Zametka o russkikh baniakh," *Vrach* 35; Chugin, "Zametka o russkikh baniakh," *Vrach* 36; Merzheevskii, *Sudebnaia genikologiia*; Ruadze, *K sudu!*; Fuks, *Gomoseksualizm kak prestuplenie*; and Bentovin, *Torguiushchie telom*. For modern commentary, see Healey, *Homosexual Desire in Revolutionary Russia*, 27–28; and Steinberg, *Petersburg Fin de Siècle*. Regarding the homosexual milieu in Victorian England, see also Potvin, "Vapour and Steam."

42. Znamenskii, *O russkikh baniakh*; and Pollock, *Without the Banya*, 88, 122.

43. Merzheevskii, *Sudebnaia genikologiia*, 207–9. See also Healey, "Masculine Purity."

44. Eremeev, *Gorod S.-Peterburg*, 455.

45. *Nomernye bani* came at all price levels. Cheap ones were very simple with only a tub, a bench, and some hooks on the wall. The most expensive looked like luxurious hotel rooms and had private steam rooms attached. For a detailed description of *nomernye bani*, see Eremeev, *Gorod S.-Peterburg*. The Voronin bathhouse had a *nomernaia bania* with luxurious apartments consisting of several rooms; see Siuzor, *Torgovye (narodnye) bani*.

46. Dennis, *Cities in Modernity*, 1; TsGIA SPb, f. 792, o. 1, d. 7705, Po khodataistvu banevladel'tsev. The law of 1783 forbade mixed-sex bathing in common sections only; see Polnoe sobranie zakonov Rossiiskoi Imperii, article 71. The *nomernaia bania* was separately taxed under the laws of 1835 and 1838, according to which bathhouse owners had to pay an annual tax for each private room they offered. The bathhouse owners

tried to repeal this tax in 1883, but their petition was unsuccessful. See TsGIA SPb, f. 792, o. 1, d. 3682, Po pros'be soderzhatelei, 2v, 3–3v.

47. For heterosexual prostitution, see, among others, Chugin, "Zametka o russkikh baniakh," *Vrach* 36, 587; and Eremeev, *Gorod S.-Peterburg*, 510. For homosexual encounters in the *nomernaia bania*, see Merzheevskii, *Sudebnaia genikologiia*, 207–9. Pollock also mentions an abundance of pornographic accounts of men having sex with women in the *nomernaia bania*. Pollock, *Without the Banya*, 311n59.

48. TsGIA SPb, f. 569, o. 11, d. 426, Delo o zakrytii ban'. This file also contains detailed accounts of sexual encounters of various kinds in *nomernye bani*. For additional explorations on this topic, see Pollock, *Without the Banya*, 85; and Healey, *Homosexual Desire in Revolutionary Russia*, 27.

49. Giliarovskii, *Moskva i moskvichi*, 101.

50. Gol'denberg, *Bani dlia voisk*, 56.

51. Pollock, *Without the Banya*, 79, 101–3.

52. Gol'denberg, *Bani dlia voisk*; Spasskii, "Kratkii ocherk"; Kurlova, "K voprosu o lechenii"; Fialkovskii, "Materialy k voprosu"; Fadeev, " Ucheniiu o russkikh baniakh"; Karvasovskii, *Kratkii ocherk*; Markov, *Voiskovye bani*; Otter, "Cleansing and Clarifying"; Renner, "Nation That Bathes Together"; Crook, "'Schools for the Moral Training of the People.'"

53. Eremeev, *Gorod S.–Peterburg*, 559; *Izvestiia dumy*, "Po voprosu"; TsGIA SPb, f. 515, o. 1, d. 6702, O zaloge imushchestva (this file contains detailed description of several bathhouses in the city provided by the City Credit Society, which organized bathhouse inspections for loan securitization); TsGIA SPb, f. 210, o. 1, d. 319, Ob osmotre domov.

54. TsGIA SPb, f. 515, o. 1, d. 6702, O zaloge imushchestva; TsGIA SPb, f. 210, o. 1, d. 613, Ob organizatsii.

55. *Izvestiia dumy*, Po voprosu.

56. *Izvestiia dumy*, "Vodosnabzhenii v Peterburge."

57. *Izvestiia dumy*, "Vodosnabzhenii v Peterburge"; *Izvestiia dumy*, "O korennom uluchshenii."

58. Renner, "Nation That Bathes Together"; Crook, "'Schools for the Moral Training of the People.'"

59. Otter, "Making Liberalism Durable"; see also Crook, "Power, Privacy and Pleasure"; Sheard, "Profit Is a Dirty Word"; and Joyce, *Rule of Freedom*.

60. Crook, "'Schools for the Moral Training of the People,'" 22.

61. McFarlane, "Governing the Contaminated City," 418.

62. See Shifrin, *Victorian Turkish Baths*.

63. Eremeev, *Gorod S.-Peterburg*, 91. See also Bater, *St. Petersburg*, 342–44; and Karmazinov, *Vodosnabzhenie Sankt-Peterburga*.

64. Pollock, *Without the Banya*, 75.

65. *Peterburgskii listok*, "Mal'tsevskie bani"; *Peterburgskii listok*, "Novye bani"; Siuzor, Torgovye (narodnye) bani. For scholarly works on bathhouse architecture, see Sindalovskii, *Ot doma k domu*; and Isachenko, *Zodchie S.-Peterburga*, 203–508.

66. Rozanov, *Literaturnye ocherki*, 224–26. See a detailed account of Rozanov's view regarding the Russian bathhouse in Pollock, *Without the Banya*, 104–7.

67. Pollock, *Without the Banya*, 104.

68. TsGIA SPb, f. 256, o. 3, d. 357, Ob osvidetel'stvovanii torgovykh ban'. Unfortunately, inspection reports are available only for three city boroughs—Kolomenskaia, Narvskaia, and Spasskaia. These years also saw increasing attention to bathing by medical practitioners. See Gol'denberg, *Bani dlia voisk*; Spasskii, "Kratkii ocherk"; Kurlova, "K voprosu o lechenii"; Fialkovskii, "Materialy k voprosu"; Fadeev, " Ucheniiu o russkikh baniakh"; Karvasovskii, *Kratkii ocherk*; Markov, *Voiskovye bani*; Otter, "Cleansing and Clarifying"; Renner, "Nation That Bathes Together"; Crook, "'Schools for the Moral Training of the People,'" and the discussion in Pollock, *Without the Banya*, chap. 4.

69. *Vedomosti politsii*, "Peterburgskie bani" and "Peterburgskie bani: prodolzhenie."

70. Eremeev, *Gorod S.-Peterburg*, 235–36; *Vedomosti politsii*, "Peterburgskie bani" and "Peterburgskie bani: prodolzhenie." The water supply was a major concern; badly constructed piping led to water shortages and poor water quality. Improper heating resulted in the frequent presence of carbon monoxide in the steam rooms. Bathhouse buildings were, as a rule, poorly maintained and constructed, which led to poor insulation and potentially unsafe conditions across all sections. Drafts, poor ventilation, slippery or grimy floors, and the lack of evacuation routes were among the problems noted.

71. Merzheevskii, *Sudebnaia genikologiia*, 238–41.

72. "Binding Ordinance on the Organization of Public Bathhouses in St. Petersburg," or *Obiazatel'noe postanovlenie ob ustroistve v gorode Sankt-Peterburge obshchestvennykh ban'*; *Vestnik gradonachal'stva*, "Chast' offitsial'naia."

73. It specified, for example, that commercial bathhouses had to have brick walls of a certain minimum thickness to ensure proper insulation, a ceiling height of at least five arshins (3.5 meters) to ensure sufficient air circulation, double-pane windows to protect visitors from the cold, and floors of certain specifications to prevent the buildup of deep-seated grime. Restrictions were also imposed on the ventilation system, the cleanliness and sufficiency of the water supply, and steam-room heating. All this was very much technocratic, from today's perspective, and had little to do with regulating behaviors, including queer spatial patterns. Only one specification among the various construction standards contained in the first part of the ordinance touched directly on behaviors: planning requirements mandated separate entrances to male and female sections to ensure that men and women did not so much as see each other at the bathhouse, let alone bathe together. See *Vestnik gradonachal'stva*, "Chast' offitsial'naia," 1.

74. In what was, presumably, yet another attempt to eliminate spatial patterns that facilitated illicit sex, the ordinance further reinforced gender segregation in bathhouses. It explicitly specified that male attendants were permitted to serve only in the men's sections in bathhouses and female attendants only in the women's sections.

75. See, for example, Eremeev, *Gorod S.-Peterburg*, 517.

76. *Vestnik gradonachal'stva*, "Chast' offitsial'naia."

77. This section of the ordinance also raised entrance fees for the third- and first-class sections by 33 percent and for the second-class section by 25 percent.

78. TsGIA SPb, f. 792, o. 1, d. 3337, Po zaiavleniiui.

79. TsGIA SPb, f. 792, o. 1, d. 3337, Po zaiavleniiu, 4–7. The first inspection took place in August 1882; the second one was six months later. The second round was needed because the majority of the bathhouses were in poor condition, To avoid the closure of 90 percent of the bathhouses, the officials gave the bathhouse operators six-month extensions.

80. TsGIA SPb, f. 792, o. 1, d. 3337, Po zaiavleniiu, 5v.

81. TsGIA SPb, f. 792, o. 1, d. 3337, Po zaiavleniiu, 5v.

82. *Vestnik gradonachal'stva*, "Chast' offitsial'naia," paragraph 32.

83. TsGIA SPb, f. 210, o. 1, d. 613, Ob organizatsii i.

84. TsGIA SPb, f. 792, o. 1, d. 3211, O dopolnenii primechaniem. The City Council and the City Duma took limited measures to tailor the ordinance to the needs of bathhouse operators and owners. Paragraph 10 of the ordinance required changing, washing, and steam rooms of all sections (for both women and men) to be located on the same floor. The City Council realized that this rule could not be easily implemented or would require an utterly unrealistic investment. Prompted by a petition from Mr. Durdin—a bathhouse operator whose bathhouse did not meet the above-mentioned requirement and who complained that to comply, he would need to build a new bathhouse (list 2–2v)—the City Council decided that this particular requirement "does not apply to baths that existed before the ordinance was introduced," list 4.

85. Pollock, *Without the Banya*, 90. Note 63 on that page is a report of the Sanitary Commission and not the Medical Police. Eremeev, *Gorod S.-Peterburg*, 243.

86. TsGIA SPb, f. 792, o. 1, d. 3211, O dopolnenii primechaniem, 2–4. In the 1903 amendment to the ordinance, the exception was introduced into the relevant paragraph itself, whereas until then it had been an "additional note to a comment about paragraph 10." *Vestnik gradonachal'stva*, "Obiazatel'noe postanovlenie."

87. Regarding the new rule introduced in 1887 about the opening hours of the commercial bath houses, see TsGIA SPb, f. 792, o. 1, d. 3337, Po zaiavleniiu, 10. The updated version of the ordinance was introduced in 1903. See the following set of documents related the updated version: (1) the full text can be found in *Vestnik gradonachal'stva*, "Obiazatel'noe postanovlenie"; (2) the archival record from the Archive of the City Duma is TsGIA, SPb, f. 792, o. 1, d. 8532, Ob izmenenii. According to the updated version of the ordinance, the *nomernaia* bathhouse had to be closed by midnight and other sections of the bathhouse could remain open for another half an hour. All sections had to be closed at 2:00 AM and could not reopen until 5:00 AM. In contrast, the 1879 Ordinance did not limit the working hours of the commercial bathhouses. Another four paragraphs of the 1879 Ordinance were revised to address overcrowding; they limited the number of visitors based on the size and parameters of a bathhouse and restricted bathing in bathhouse courts (many bathhouse owners had absorbed courtyards into their operations as an inexpensive measure to expand capacity).

88. TsGIA SPb, f. 210, o. 1, d. 484, Ob ustroistve, 2–3; see also TsGIA SPb, f. 569, o. 11, d. 426, Delo o zakrytii ban', 5. Although this scheme was never realized, its aggressive pursuit by municipal authorities amounts to an inherent admission of the ineffectiveness of the previously attempted reforms. In fact, the sanitary commission's expert report prepared for the City Council in support of funding the first municipal bathhouse specifically described commercial bathhouses as unsanitary places fraught with immoral activity, and characterized bathhouse owners as prepared to optimize income to the detriment of their customers and by breaking the law. Had they been built, such institutions would certainly have closed much of the gap between St. Petersburg and the Western bathhouse movement. As the partially surviving tender documentation makes clear, city officials had decided to create an entirely new type of bathhouse that combined the merits of recent innovations in construction technologies and hygiene. In March 1910, the City

Council chose the Vasilievskii Borough (in the northwest of the city) as the site for the construction of the first public bathhouse. The engineer A. Rozenberg won the tender organized by the City Council with a project cheerfully titled *S legkim parom!* (Enjoy your bath!). The new model bathhouse was to be functional, spacious, and low cost. It was a well-ventilated and well-lit two-story building with separate male and female sections on the first and ground floors, respectively. The size of the building was generously calculated on the basis of the target capacity set out in the tender documentation to provide services to over a thousand bathers at a time, with changing, washing, and steam rooms in the male and female sections. A separate laundry room and gynecologist's cabinet were the only spaces dedicated to auxiliary services. Every other function seems to have been deemed superfluous, including those where enjoyment or leisure was the main draw. For example, the municipal design had no kitchen. Even the habitual dipping pools had been excluded as an unnecessary and unsanitary fixture of the commercial bathing commons. The design for the utilitarian washing facilities, however, met the highest specifications, including state-of-the-art ventilation and heating and a layout specifically designed to optimize the movements of visitors without creating crowds or bottlenecks. Importantly, the planned municipal baths had no *nomernaia bania* where bathers could withdraw for a sexual encounter. Gol'denberg, *Bani dlia voisk*.

89. TsGIA SPb, f. 210, o. 1, d. 484, Ob ustroistve, 16. The City Council allocated over 200,000 rubles to fund the construction of the winning project. This sum would have constituted around 5 percent of the city's ever-growing annual budget for health and sanitation, which is a measure of the importance the city attached to the project, bearing in mind that this municipal bathhouse was supposed to be the first of many. The project, however, as we have already noted, never came to fruition. Financial constraints must have been of the first importance: the start of Russia's costly war effort coincided with an escalation of the estimated project costs by 40 percent, which was reason enough to stop the project. See more in Fedorov, "Finansovoe polozenie Peterburga."

90. Noncompliance created significant additional investment risks, since any newly constructed bathhouse that subsequently fell afoul of the inspectors could by law be forced to remain shut. Furthermore, the cost of compliance for new bathhouses was even higher than for existing ones, since additional requirements applied, including the minimal ceiling height of 3.5 meters. Finally, new bathhouses were now restricted to areas where Neva water was available.

91. In fact, the regular pattern of bathhouse construction did not resume until the first decade of the twentieth century. Up until around 1880, bathhouse construction and migration-driven population increases show roughly parallel linear growth trajectories, starting from the earliest year for which consistent statistical data are available, 1818. After about 1880, despite accelerating population growth, bathhouse construction stopped and did not resume until a significant cushion of pent-up demand had accumulated. A boom-and-bust cycle is not a sufficient explanation for the halt in construction. The rate of construction exceeded population growth only slightly from 1818 to 1881, and it is hardly likely that an unsustainable boom portion of the cycle, which was not supported by sufficient population growth, would have lasted for more than sixty years. At any rate, within a decade after 1881 the population had caught up and the original 1818 proportion of residents to bathhouses was reestablished. Growth, however, did not resume for at least another decade. Thus, the lull in bathhouse con-

struction between 1881 and 1901 corroborates the view that the requirements set out in the ordinance rendered the construction of compliant bathhouses commercially unattractive. It follows—if one puts aside for a moment the relatively minor proportional increase in construction costs resulting from requirements that applied only to new bathhouses—that the owners of existing bathhouses saw their margins temporarily decline roughly by the cost of capital on a risk-adjusted basis.

92. As an example of one of the original distinctions in requirements, only new bathhouses had to achieve a minimal ceiling height of 3.5 meters; see *Vestnik gradonachal'stva*, "Chast' offitsial'naia," 1.

93. TsGIA SPb, f. 792, o. 1, d. 7705, Po khodataistvu banevladel'tsev. See, in particular, the resolution of the City Council from January 25, 1900, recommending to the City Duma an increase in entrance fees to bathhouses (4), as well as the City Duma's decision to reject the proposal (17).

94. See, in particular, TsGIA SPb, f. 792, o. 1, d. 7705, Po khodataistvu banevladel'tsev, 2v; see also Eremeev, *Gorod S.-Peterburg*, 512.

95. TsGIA SPb, f. 792, o. 1, d. 7705, Po khodataistvu banevladel'tsev, 9.

96. As contemplated by the ordinance, the mechanism for closure as a result of noncompliance was that the Sanitary Commission would not renew or rescind a bathhouse's license to operate, whereupon the police would physically close and seal the bathhouse.

97. TsGIA SPb, f. 569, o. 11, d. 426, Delo o zakrytii ban', 25–25v.

98. TsGIA SPb, f. 569, o. 11, d. 426, Delo o zakrytii ban'; see the police resolution from June 6, 1887, in document no. 15075, 12.

99. TsGIA SPb, f. 155, o. 1, d. 186, Ob osmotre domov, 13, 14–14v.

100. TsGIA SPb, f. 569, o. 11, d. 426, Delo o zakrytii ban', 20–20v, 16v–17, 64.

101. TsGIA SPb, f. 569, o. 11, d. 426, Delo o zakrytii ban', 16v–17, 64.

102. TsGIA SPb, f. 569, o. 11, d. 426, Delo o zakrytii ban'. See, for example, letters from Timofei Kriukov (28–28v) and Ivan Petrov (35v), who were both bathhouse operators requesting permission from the Mayor's Office as the highest municipal authority to reopen their *nomernye banii*.

103. See, for example, TsGIA SPb, f. 569, o. 11, d. 426, Delo o zakrytii ban', 18, 25–25v, 29, 37.

104. TsGIA SPb, f. 792, o. 1, d. 3682, Po pros'be soderzhatelei. The City Duma did not immediately ratify the change and it is unclear when or whether it was ratified, although following passage by the City Council it is likely to have been simply a delay, during which it had to be clarified that the old taxes still applied (3v).

105. Ruadze, *K sudu!* 17–19; and *Peterburgskii listok*, "Pisma v redaktsiiu."

106. TsGIA SPb, f. 569, o. 11, d. 426, Delo o zakrytii ban'. See, for example, petitions from Pavel Nikitin (27v) and Adrian Gustov (28v).

107. Healey, *Homosexual Desire in Revolutionary Russia*, 27.

108. Healey, *Homosexual Desire in Revolutionary Russia*, 28.

109. Healey, *Homosexual Desire in Revolutionary Russia*, 35.

110. See, for example, Rozanov, *Literaturnye ocherki*, 224–26; Khrustalev, *Dnevnik velikogo kniazia*; Kuzmin, *Dnevnik, 1905–1907*, 85–86; Bentovin, *Torguiushchie telom*; Pollock, *Without the Banya*, 120–27; and Healey, *Homosexual Desire in Revolutionary Russia*, 33n60.

111. Pollock, *Without the Banya*, 103.

112. Pollock, *Without the Banya*, 112.

113. See Healey, *Homosexual Desire in Revolutionary Russia*, 124. See also an interview with him after the book was published. In the light of newly discovered evidence showing that Kuzmin was censored, the diagnosis of a relaxation in censorship is debatable (see more about this topic in the conclusion of this book).

114. Healey, *Homosexual Desire in Revolutionary Russia*, 33.

115. TsGIA SPb, f. 569, o. 11, d. 426, Delo o zakrytii ban'.

116. TsGIA SPb, f. 569, o. 11, d. 426, Delo o zakrytii ban', 5v.

117. TsGIA SPb, f. 569, o. 11, d. 426, Delo o zakrytii ban'. See, for example, a letter from Adrian Gustov (22–22v).

118. See Ruadze, *K sudu!* 17. Here Ruadze writes about the pimp and bathhouse attendant Gavrila in the Znamenskiaia Bathhouse in the Liteinaia Borough. See also RGIA, f. 1683, o. 1, d. 119, Svedeniia o fiziologicheskikh porokakh, 2.

119. A redoubled emphasis on prostitution and the increased role of the *nomernaia bania* in bathhouse operations were not the only adjustments made to the new legislative and economic environment. Bathhouse owners increased capacity in their common sections by reducing the average time each visitor spent in the bathhouse. They did this both by cranking up the heat in the steam room and, in some cases, imposing caps on the overall time guests could spend in the bathhouse. In many instances, capacity was further increased by appropriating outdoor spaces that could be closed off and used year-round—in the summer for washing and in the winter for cooling off. Still others tried to get around restrictions on serving food and drink in the changing rooms by offering beer and a buffet in the entrance hall instead. See, for example, Siuzor, Torgovye (narodnye) bani; and *Peterburgskii listok*, "Pisma v redaktsiiu."

120. Quoted in Healey, *Homosexual Desire in Revolutionary Russia*, 28. Kuzmin attests to this culture, describing his own experiences of homosexual cruising at commercial bathhouses. In diary entries relating to the period from 1905 to 1907, he records payment for sexual encounters with bathhouse attendants. Two of Kuzmin's longtime lovers were bathhouse attendants and he repeatedly expressed his fondness for the bania and the opportunity for sexual intimacy they provided. See Kuzmin, *Dnevnik, 1905–1907*, November 6, 1905, 66; May 20, 1906, 151; April 6, 1907, 343; and others.

121. Eremeev, *Gorod S.-Peterburg*, 262–63. See also Pollock's discussion of Eremeev's statistics on *banshchiki* in Pollock, *Without the Banya*, 122.

122. Pollock, *Without the Banya*, 122.

123. TsGIA SPb, f. 569, o. 11, d. 426, Delo o zakrytii ban', 70–70v.

124. TsGIA SPb, f. 569, o. 11, d. 426, Delo o zakrytii ban'; see police resolutions regarding the closure of bathhouses on 5v, 13v, 34v, 48v, 52v, and 63v.

125. TsGIA SPb, f. 792, o. 1, d. 7705, Po khodataistvu banevladel'tsev; see the Report of the Sanitary Commission from January 7 and 21, 1900 on 1–4, and 6–9.

126. TsGIA SPb, f. 569, o. 11, d. 426, Delo o zakrytii ban', 22–22v; see also 16v–17, 23, 27v.

127. TsGIA SPb, f. 569, o. 11, d. 426, Delo o zakrytii ban', 7–8, 16, 64.

128. The cost of the visit ranged from 75 kopeks to 10 rubles. The average monthly income of a worker was between 15 rubles and 22 rubles. *Peterburgskii listok*, "Novye bani," 2. On imperial workers' wages, see Bater, *St. Petersburg*, 256.

129. Rozanov, *Literaturnye ocherki*, 224–26.

130. *Vedomosti politsii*, "Peterburgskie bani: prodolzhenie"; Rabinow, *Foucault Reader*, 242, 51.

131. Rabinow, *Foucault Reader*, 242.

Chapter 5. Cruising in the *Pays du Tendre*

1. Kuzmin, *Dnevnik, 1905–1907*, 168.

2. From the French "tapette," also slang for a passive homosexual, which, in turn, derives from the verb "taper," meaning "to touch," "to clap," "to thump," or "to beat." It usually refers to a young man who is not averse to being "tapped," meaning he prefers a passive sexual role.

3. Hakanen, "Panoramas from Above," 200.

4. Diaries of 1921, 1921, 1931, and 1934 are not directly relevant to this discussion.

5. Kuzmin was censored and fined in 1908 for writing pornography. The sentence referred to his novel *Wings*, which contained prose with strong suggestions of sexual relations between men. Kuzmin had to resort to the help of friends to pay the fine and was hard hit by his only novel's withdrawal from sale. He also must have realized that he was now no longer under the radar. It may be no coincidence that his diary, which he frequently read to friends and considered a work of art, changed in 1908. After that year, the unmistakable and often humorous references to sex between men, the names of men in his queer circle, or mention of places in which he frequently met them disappear. It is not unlikely that Kuzmin self-censored his diary to avoid incriminating himself and his friends if readings from his diary were ever overheard by less-than-well-meaning ears or in case of a police raid or investigation. What we do not know, of course, is where this self-censorship ended; whether, for example, he changed his behavior as well.

6. *Severnaia pchela*, Zametki, July 24, 1861.

7. Mikhnevich, *Peterburg ves' na ladoni*, 118–19.

8. Mikhnevich, "Peterburgskie sady."

9. *Izvestiia dumy*, "O poriadke," 815.

10. Aksel'rod, Vesnina, and Demidova, *Sady i parki Leningrada*.

11. Sankt-Peterburgskoe gorodskoe obshchestvennoe upravlenie, *Putevoditel' po S.-Peterburgu*, 225.

12. Ruadze, *K sudu!* 105–7.

13. Punin, *Arkhitektura Peterburga*; Seliverstov, *Leningrad*; Aksel'rod, Vesnina, and Demidova, *Sady i parki Leningrada*.

14. Sankt-Peterburgskoe gorodskoe obshchestvennoe upravlenie, *Putevoditel' po S.-Peterburgu*.

15. Aksel'rod, Vesnina, and Demidova, *Sady i parki Leningrada*; Lisovskii, *Arkhitektura Peterburga*; Keller, *Prazdnichnaia kul'tura Peterburga*.

16. Kerzun, *Kratkii ocherk*; *Khronos*, "O zeleni i gul'iane," March 22, 1909, 3. See also Khmelnitskaia, *Restaurant Life*.

17. Ogborn, *Spaces of Modernity*, 151. Kuzmin mentions the ice rink in *Dnevnik, 1905–1907*, 328.

18. Ogborn, *Spaces of Modernity*, 151. See also other works on pleasure gardens in which the authors talk about "pleasure-seekers" (Bailey's term): Bailey, *Leisure and Class*, 14–15; Connell, "Managing Gardens"; and Gaskell, "Gardens for the Working Class."

19. Regarding being threatened, see Kuzmin, *Dnevnik, 1905–1907*, 168; for possible offers of sex, see 154–55.

20. For more background on this approach, see Reddy, *Navigation of Feeling*; Rosenwein, "Worrying about Emotions"; Rosenwein, "Problems and Methods"; Davidson, Bondi, and Smith, *Emotional Geography*; Pile, "Emotions and Affect"; Plamper, *History of Emotions*; Paterson, *Senses of Touch*; and Gregg and Seigworth, *Affect Theory Reader*. See also works in Slavic studies: Plamper, "Emotional Turn?"; Matich, "Poetics of Disgust"; Kuntsman, "'With a Shade of Disgust'"; Steinberg, "Melancholy and Modernity"; Lapin, *Peterburg*; and Steinberg and Sobol, *Interpreting Emotion*.

21. Reddy, *Navigation of Feeling*, 129.

22. Turner, *Backward Glances*, 60; Bech, *When Men Meet*, 118.

23. Turner, *Backward Glances*, 60.

24. Turner, *Backward Glances*, 61.

25. Ruadze, *K sudu!* 105–7; Kuzmin, *Dnevnik, 1905–1907*, 168, 169.

26. Smith-Rosenberg, "Female World of Love," 28–29.

27. Maynard, "Through a Hole"; Cook, *London and the Culture of Homosexuality*, 13–14, 89; Chauncey, *Gay New York*, 182–85, 91.

28. Bondi, "Making Connections"; Davidson, Bondi, and Smith, *Emotional Geography*; Griffero, *Atmospheres*; Keltner et al., "Emotional Expression."

29. Kuzmin, *Dnevnik, 1905–1907*, 173.

30. Kuzmin, *Dnevnik, 1905–1907*, 176.

31. Kuzmin, *Dnevnik, 1905–1907*, 133.

32. Kuzmin, *Dnevnik, 1905–1907*, 173. In Russian, I use the translation provided by N. Bogomolov and S. Shumikhina: *Puteshestvie iz strany nezhnosti v stranu pylkosti*.

33. Kuzmin, *Dnevnik, 1905–1907*, 139, 58, 73, 76, 79, 83.

34. Malmstad and Bogomolov, *Mikhail Kuzmin*.

35. McDonough, "Situationist Space," 61, 60.

36. Malmstad and Bogomolov, *Mikhail Kuzmin*, 394n8.

37. Reddy, *Navigation of Feeling*, 129.

38. Kuzmin, *Dnevnik, 1905–1907*, 158.

39. Kuzmin, *Dnevnik, 1905–1907*, 158. Vasilii Kudriashev was a clerk in an antique shop.

40. About yellow daffodils, see Kuzmin, *Dnevnik, 1905–1907*, 357, 60.

41. Kuzmin, *Dnevnik, 1905–1907*, 164.

42. Kuzmin, *Dnevnik, 1905–1907*, 158; see also 162.

43. As police looked on, the less savory among the park's visitors were largely left to their own devices and settled scores with one another, but they did more than that. These young men, who were often armed, "chose this garden as their regular meeting place and engage[d] in various kinds of deviant behavior, theft and fighting," according to an anonymous citizen's complaint to the police investigative department in 1900. TsGIA SPb, f. 965, o. 1, d. 1631, Po anonimu o besporiadkakh, 1. The situation was no different in 1909; see *Peterburgskii listok*, "Nadzor za Sadami." See also Neuberger, *Hooliganism*, 26; Kuzmin, *Dnevnik, 1905–1907*, 164–65, notes on June 4 and 5, 1906; and Ruadze, *K sudu!* 105–7.

44. See, for example, notes on June 18 and 29, 1906, Kuzmin, *Dnevnik, 1905–1907*, 176, 85.

45. Kuzmin, *Dnevnik, 1905–1907*, 158.

46. Kuzmin, *Dnevnik, 1905–1907*, 159.

47. RGIA, f. 1683, o. 1, d. 119, Svedeniia o fiziologicheskikh porokakh, 1.

48. Nikolai Bogomolov and Sergei Shumikhin, the editors of Kuzmin's diary, agree. In their annotations they describe Katkov as a "well-known hooligan." Kuzmin, *Dnevnik, 1905–1907*, 158, 578.

49. Kuzmin, *Dnevnik, 1905–1907*, 168.

50. See, for example, a scene where Pavlik professes to love Kuzmin and refuses to take money, which the latter secretly tries to put in his pocket; Kuzmin, *Dnevnik, 1905–1907*, 180.

51. Kuzmin, *Dnevnik, 1905–1907*, 170, 76.

52. Kuzmin, *Dnevnik, 1905–1907*, 210, 243, 319, 323.

53. See, for example, their stroll on June 10, 1906; Kuzmin, *Dnevnik, 1905–1907*, 168.

54. Ruadze, *K sudu!* 105.

55. Ruadze, *K sudu!* 105. See also Kuzmin's entry for February 24, 1906, where he recorded a friendly exchange with a young man he describes as a hooligan. He writes, "I met that same hooligan again: 'Once more, my respects, sir'—and, he added, shouting as he walked away 'each day I meet you here, dear sir—probably you live nearby'"; Kuzmin, *Dnevnik, 1905–1907*, 113.

56. Butler, *Gender Trouble*.

57. Kuzmin, *Dnevnik, 1905–1907*, 330.

58. Kuzmin, *Dnevnik, 1905–1907*, 176.

59. Kuzmin, *Dnevnik, 1905–1907*, 175.

60. Ruadze, *K sudu!* 105–7. See, for example, Houlbrook, *Queer London*, 52–56 and Chauncey, *Gay New York*, 89–90, 182–83.

61. Healey, "Masculine Purity," 235. In Kuzmin's diary, see, for example, the entry on March 11, 1907; Kuzmin, *Dnevnik, 1905–1907*, 331.

62. See, for example, Houlbrook, *Queer London*, 7, 52–56; Chauncey, *Gay New York*, 89–90, 182–83; Bleys, *Geography of Perversion*, 25; Duberman, Vicinus, and Chauncey, *Hidden from History*; and Boyd, *Wide Open Town*, 49–52.

63. Maynard, "Through a Hole," 211.

64. Cook, *London and the Culture of Homosexuality*, 14.

65. Reddy, *Navigation of Feeling*, 129.

66. Kuzmin, *Dnevnik, 1905–1907*, 140.

67. Kuzmin, *Dnevnik, 1905–1907*, 54. Alexandre Benoit, an artist and acquaintance of Kuzmin, had recently achieved fame as a stage designer.

68. Gandy, "Queer Ecology," 738–39.

Conclusion

1. Foucault, "Life of Infamous Men," 79.

2. Foucault, "Life of Infamous Men," 80.

3. On May 2, 1908, a short entry titled Pornografiia (Pornography) appeared in the section "Magistrate Court" of *Peterburgskii listok*, no. 199, 2. According to this source, Kuzmin was prosecuted at the city magistrate court for "publishing a pornographic novel." Due to the fact that the magistrate court and its archives were destroyed in February 1917, the court files regarding Kuzmin's case have been lost. I only recently dis-

covered this note regarding his trial and sentencing in the daily newspaper *Peterburgskii listok*: "The well-known founder of the pornographic literary school, the young writer Kuzmin, [is sentenced] under paragraph 1001 of the criminal code, that is, for dissemination of pornography. His case was heard behind closed doors. The sentence, which was announced in an open-door session [of the court] is a fine of 200 rubles, with the alternative of a jail term of 1 month in case of inability to pay." Kuzmin's biographers, John Malmstad and Nikolay Bogomolov, do not mention this incident, indicating that it had been lost to historians (see Malmstad and Bogomolov, *Mikhail Kuzmin*). Kuzmin's diary entries on the day of sentencing and in the following weeks contain unambiguous references to this event: "They are sounding the alarm with Ivanov because of the appeal, raising to their feet whoever they can. Better if they just obtained 200 rubles and let it go peacefully" (Kuzmin, *Dnevnik, 1908–1915*, 34.) Simon Karlinksy and Dan Healey also do not mention that Kuzmin was fined for the publication of "pornographic material." In a 2016 interview with the Australian Broadcasting Corporation, the interviewer, Annabelle Quince, asked Healey: "So you didn't see a scandal like the Oscar Wilde scandal in Tsarist Russia?" Healey responded: "That's right, there was no major political or cultural moment when Tsarist or imperial Russia actually put homosexuality on the public agenda in that way. The closest thing you come to that is very late in the Tsarist regime. In 1907 a novel is published called *Wings* by a modernist writer, Mikhail Kuzmin, and it's an extraordinary short novel about a young man's coming-out process. And that book is unusual in the European literature of this type, because it actually has a happy ending. And the book caused a fairly big literary scandal at the time, but there was no attempt to censor the book or to bring Mikhail Kuzmin to trial or anything like that. People discussed it in the press of the day, which was relatively uncensored, and it became a succès de scandale, you could say." (http://www.abc.net.au/radionational/programs/rearvision/the-story-of-homosexuality-in-russia/5063950#transcript, accessed March 31, 2019). The date of publication given by Healey is incorrect. The novel was published in November 1906; see Malmstad and Bogomolov, *Mikhail Kuzmin*, 93.

4. For this scene, see the English translation of the book, Kuzmin, *Wings*, 32–36. For the novel in Russian, see Kuzmin, *Kryl'ia*, 43. The first publication was in 1906 in the artistic journal *Libra* (Vesy); its eleventh issue was completely devoted to Kuzmin's publication, "in itself an unprecedented event in the magazine's history." See more about the book's initial publication in Malmstad and Bogomolov, *Mikhail Kuzmin*, 93.

5. Kuzmin, *Wings*, 36.

6. Ross, *Public City/Public Sex*.

7. I refer to a French-language edition of this essay. Foucault, "La vie des hommes infâmes," 28–29.

Appendix

1. Steinberg, *Petersburg Fin de Siècle*, 63–64, 185–87.

2. Ruadze, *K Sudu!*; and Healey, "Masculine Purity."

Bibliography

Primary Sources

Archival Sources Studied

Central State Historical Archive of St. Petersburg (TsGIA SPb)

Fond 14, Imperatorskii Petrogradskii universitet (Petrograd Imperial University)

Fond 155, Sanitarno-epidemiologicheskoe biuro sanitarnoi komissii Petrogradskoi gorodskoi upravy (Sanitary and Epidemiological Bureau of the Sanitary Commission of the Petrograd City Council)

Fond 210, Petrogradskaia gorodskaia sanitarnaia komissiia (Petrograd Sanitary Commission)

Fond 256, Stroitel'noe otdelenie Petrogradskogo gubernskogo upravleniia (Construction Department of the Petrograd City Council)

Fond 479, Petrogradskaia kazennaia palata (Petrograd State Chamber)

Fond 515, Petrogradskoe gorodskoe kreditnoe obshchestvo (Petrograd Credit Society)

Fond 569, Upravlenie Petrogradskogo gradonachal'stva i stolichnoi politsii (Department of the Petrograd Mayor's Administration and the Capital City's Police)

Fond 792, Petrogradskaia gorodskaia duma (Petrograd City Duma)

Fond 965, Petrogradskaia sysknaia politsiia (Petrograd Police Investigative Department)

Fond 1648, Politseiskie uchastki Petrograga (Petrograd Borough Police Stations)

Russian State Historical Archive (RGIA)

Fond 1284, Departament obshchikh del MVD (Department of General Affairs of the Ministry of Internal Affairs)

Fond 1288, Glavnoe upravlenie po delam mestnogo khoziaistva MVD (Main Administration of Municipal Affairs of the Ministry of Internal Affairs)

Fond 1290, Tsentral'nyi statisticheskii komitet MVD (Central Statistical Committee of the Ministry of Internal Affairs)

Fond 1400, Documenty iz unichtozhennykh del senata i ministerstva iustityii (Documents from the destroyed files of the Senate and the Ministry of Justice)

Fond 1405, Ministerstvo iustitsii (Ministry of Justice)

Fond 1406, Redaktsiia zhurnala ministerstva iustitsii (Editorial Office of the Journal of the Ministry of Justice)

Fond 1683, Ostrovskii Mikhail Nikolaevich (1827–1901), Ministr gosudarsktvennykh imushchestv, predsedatel' departamenta zakonov, pochetnyi chlen Akademii nauk, chlen gosudarstvennogo soveta (fond of Mikhail Nikolaevich Ostrovskii)

State Archive of the Russian Federation, Moscow (GARF)

Fond 102, Departament politsii MVD (Department of Police the Ministry of Internal Affairs)

Fond 111, Otdelenie po okhraneniiu obshchestvennoi bezopasnosti i poriadka (Okhrannoe otdelenie) pri Petrogradskom gradonachal'nike (Department for Protecting Public Security and Order, under the Petrograd Mayor)

Fond 124, Ugolovnoe otdelenie pervogo departamenta ministerstva iustitsii (Criminal Division of the First Department of the Ministry of Justice)

Fond 564, Koni Anatolii Fedorovich (Personal Fond of Anatolii Fedorovich Koni)

Archival Sources Cited in the Book

Documents in Russian archives are categorized by their collection (*fond*), section (*opis'*), and file (*delo*), and page number (*list*).

Central State Historical Archive of St. Petersburg (TsGIA SPb)

Fond 155, Sanitarno-epidemiologicheskoe biuro sanitarnoi komissii Petrogradskoi gorodskoi upravy (Sanitary and Epidemiological Bureau of the Sanitary Commission of the Petrograd City Council)

TsGIA SPb, f. 155, o. 1, d. 186, Ob osmotre domov, dvorov, i drugoe, 1910.

Fond 210, Petrogradskaia gorodskaia sanitarnaia komissiia (Petrograd Sanitary Commission)

TsGIA SPb, f. 210, o. 1, d. 319, Ob osmotre domov, dvorov i drugikh mest stolitsi, 1908–1909.

TsGIA SPb, f. 210, o. 1, d. 484, Ob ustroistve gorodskikh narodnykh ban', 1910–1916.

TsGIA SPb, f. 210, o. 1, d. 613, Ob organizatsii i deiatel'nosti gorodskoi sanitarnogo nadzora, 1914.

Fond 256, Stroitel'noe otdelenie Petrogradskogo gubernskogo upravleniia (Construction Department of the Petrograd City Council)

TsGIA SPb, f. 256, o. 3, d. 357, Ob osvidetel'stvovanii torgovykh ban' v Kolomenskoi, Narvskoi, Spasskoi, 1871.

Fond 479, Petrogradskaia kazennaia palata (Petrograd State Chamber)

TsGIA, SPb, f. 479, o. 22, d. 1479, O Materialakh za 1900, 1899–1900.

Fond 515, Petrogradskoe gorodskoe kreditnoe obshchestvo (Petrograd Credit Society)

TsGIA SPb, f. 515, o. 1, d. 6702, O zaloge imushchestva, N. N. Gavrilovoi, N. I. Vul'fson, E. O. Ivanovoi po Suvorovskomu Prospektu, 69, Iaroslavskoi ul. 2, i Iaroslavskoi pl. 2, 1890–1914.

Fond 569, Upravlenie Petrogradskogo gradonachal'stva i stolichnoi politsii (Police Mayoral's central administrative apparatus)

TsGIA SPb, f. 569, o. 10, d. 104, Tsirkuliary departamenta politsii, 1910–1914, 1910, no. 2199, October 21, 1910.

TsGIA, f. 569, o. 10, d. 104, Tsirkuliary departamenta politsii, 1910–1914, Tsyrkuliar ot 3 aprelia 1910 goda, no. 5847.

TsGIA, SPb f. 569, o. 11, d. 426, Delo o zakrytii ban' dopustivshikh besporiadok i razvrat, 1887–1890.

TsGIA SPb, f. 569, o. 12, d. 118, Delo o soderzhanii gostinits prevrashchennykh v pritony razvrata (spiski, otnosheniia, raporta), 26.06.1909–04.10.1919.

TsGIA SPb, f. 569, o.17, d. 999, O vzyskanii mer k nedopushcheniiu razvrata v gostinitsakh, 1908.

Fond 792, Petrogradskaia gorodskaia duma (Petrograd City Duma)

TsGIA SPb, f. 792, o. 1, d. 3211, O dopolnenii primechaniem paragrafa 10 obiazatel'nogo postanovleniia ob ustroistve v S.-Peterburge obshchestvennykh ban', 1881.

TsGIA SPb, f. 792, o. 1, d. 3337, Po zaiavleniiui glasnogo V. I. Likhacheva o neispolnenii upravoi izdannogo v 1879 obiazatel'nogo postanovleniia o baniakh, 1882–1887.

TsGIA SPb, f. 792, o. 1, d. 3682, Po pros'be soderzhatelei nomernykh odnosemeinykh ban' ob otmene trebovaniia s nikh aktsiza v dokhod goroda, 1883.

TsGIA SPb, f. 792, o. 1, d. 7705, Po khodataistvu banevladel'tsev otnositel'no uvelicheniia vkhodnoi platy za pol'zovanie baniami, 1900.

TsGIA, SPb, f. 792, o. 1, d. 8532, Ob izmenenii i dopolnenii obiazatel'nogo postanovleniia ob ustroistve v S.-Peterburge obshchestvennykh ban' i o poriadke proizvodstva bannogo promysla, 1902.

Fond 965, Petrogradskaia sysknaia politsiia (Police Investigative Department)

TsGIA SPb, f. 965, o. 1, d. 1614, O pedaraste Ludvige Adamoviche Zimmel', 1900.

TsGIA SPb, f. 965, o. 1, d. 1631, Po anonimy o besporiadkakh i krazakh, sovershaemykh v Tavricheskom sadu vo vremia gulianii, 1900.

TsGIA SPb, f. 965, o. 1, d. 1862, Po zhalobe kol. Sekr Sarkisova na porutchika Paikovskogo, zarazivshchego Sifilison, 1901.

TsGIA SPb, f. 965, o. 1, d. 1933, Prosheniia i zaiavleniia raznykh lits, 1903.

TsGIA SPb, f. 965, o. 2, d. 140, Alfavitnaia kniga zaderzhannykh lits za 1905 god s bukvy M do S, 1905.

TsGIA SPb, f. 965, o. 2, d. 141, Alfavitnaia kniga zaderzhannykh lits za 1905 god s bukvy T do Ia, 1905.

TsGIA SPb, f. 965, o. 2, d. 156, Kniga zapisi zaderzhannykh lits za 1906 god, 1906.

TsGIA SPb, f. 965, o. 2, d. 184, Alfavitnaia kniga zaderzhannykh lits za 1907 god s bukvy A do Zh, 1907.

TsGIA SPb, f. 965, o. 2, d. 185, Alfavitnaia kniga zaderzhannykh lits za 1907 god s bukvy M do S, 1907.

TsGIA SPb, f. 965, o. 3, d. 72, Ob obkhodakh politseiskimi agentami tsentral'nikh ulits Peterburga, vokzalov, sadov i drugikh mest poseshcheniia publikoi v nochnoe vremia s tsel'iu zaderzhaniia podozritel'nykh lits i narushitelei blagochiniia, 1904.

TsGIA SPb, f. 965, o. 3, d. 147, O vysylke 77 chelovek za porochnoe povedenie cherez soveshchatel'noe prisutstvie, 27.05.1914–12.06.1914.

Fond 1648, Politseiskie uchastki perodraga (Borough Police Stations)

TsGIA SPb, f. 1648, o. 1, d. 13, Kniga o litsakh, sostoiashchikh pod nadzorom politsii, 1912–1914.

TsGIA SPb, f. 1648, o. 1, d. 40, Kniga o litsakh, sostoiashchikh pod nadzorom politsii, 1898–1906.

TsGIA SPb, f. 1648, o. 1, d. 180, Sekretnye tsirkuliary Peterburgskogo gradonachal'nika, rasporiazheniia okhrannogo otdeleniia o rozyske i vysylke lits, o podchenenii lits neglasnomu nadzoru politsii, 1908.

TsGIA SPb, f. 1648, o. 1, d. 388, Kniga o litsakh, sostoiashchikh pod nadzorom politsii, 1904–1908.

TsGIA SPb, f. 1648, o. 1, d. 393, Kniga o litsakh, sostoiashchikh pod nadzorom politsii, 1908–1912.

TsGIA SPb, f. 1648, o. 1, d. 417, Kniga sutochnykh dokladov pristava uchastka o proishestviiakh, 1910–1911.

TsGIA SPb, f. 1648, o. 1, d. 418, Kniga zapisi zaderzhannykh lits, 1910.

TsGIA SPb, f. 1648, o. 1, d. 566, Kniga zapisi ugolovnykh obvnenii, 1866–1915, Protokol po zaiavleniiu kr. Smolenskoi gub. Elizavety Vasil'evny Orlikovoi (Fontanka 28) o snoshenii ee muzha, Vasiliia Nikifirova Orlikova s ego plemianikom Pavlom Alekseevichem Kurochkinym, prozhivaiushchim u nego, 1913, register number 68, September 3, 1913.

TsGIA SPb, f. 1648, o. 1, d. 651, Sekretnye tsirkuliary departamenta politsii i Peterburgskogo gradonachal'nika, 1906–1910.

TsGIA SPb, f. 1648, o. 1, d. 656, Kniga o litsakh, sostoiashchikh pod nadzorom politsii, 1906.

TsGIA SPb, f. 1648, o. 1, d. 671, Kniga o litsakh pod nadzorom politsii, 1905.

TsGIA SPb, f. 1648, o. 1, d. 673, Kniga o litsakh, sostoiashchikh pod nadzorom politsii, 1909.

TsGIA SPb, f. 1648, o. 1, d. 674, Kniga o litsakh, sostoiashchikh pod nadzorom politsii, 1913.

TsGIA SPb, f. 1648, o. 1, d. 855, Tsyrkuliary Peterburgskogo gradonachal'nika, rasporiazheniia i perepiska s Okhrannym otdeleniem o litsakh, sostoiashchikh pod nadzorom politsii, 1910.

TsGIA SPb, f. 1648, o. 1, d. 1222, Tsirkuliarnye telegrammy i perepiska s okhrannym otdeleniem ob usilenii nadzora za nastroeniem rabochikh fabrik i zavodov, za litsami sostoiashchimi pod nadzorom politsii, 1910.

TsGIA SPb, f. 1648, o. 1, d. 1250, Kniga o litsakh pod nadzorom politsii, 1913.

Russian State Historical Archive (RGIA)

Fond 1284, Departament obshchikh del ministerstva vnutrennikh del (Department of General Affairs of the Ministry of Internal Affairs)

RGIA, f. 1284, o. 238, d. 8, Tsirkuliary MVD za vtoruiu polovinu 1900 goda, 1900.

RGIA, f. 1284, o. 238, d. 82, Tsirkuliary MVD za pervuiu polovinu 1900 goda, 1900.

RGIA, f. 1284, o. 238, d. 84, Tsirkuliary MVD za pervuiu polovinu 1901 goda, 1901.

RGIA, f. 1284, o. 238, d. 86, Tsirkuliary MVD za vtoruiu polovinu 1901 goda, 1901.

RGIA, f. 1284, o. 238, d. 88, Tsirkuliary MVD za pervuiu polovinu 1902 goda, 1902.

RGIA, f. 1284, o. 238, d. 89, Tsirkuliary MVD za vtoruiu polovinu 1902 goda, 1902.

Fond 1405, Ministerstvo iustitsii (Ministry of Justice)

RGIA, f. 1405, o. 83, d. 10544, Po prosheniiu publichnoi biblioteki Afanasiia Bychkova, 1883–1884.

Fond 1683, Ostrovskii Mikhail Nikolaevich (1827–1901), Ministr gosudarsktvennykh imushchestv, predsedatel' departamenta zakonov, pochetnyi chlen Akademii nauk, chlen gosudarstvennogo soveta (fond of Mikhail Nikolaevich Ostrovskii)

RGIA, f. 1683, o. 1, d. 119, Svedeniia o fiziologicheskikh porokakh raznykh lits, prozhivaiushchikh v Peterburge, no date.

State Archive of the Russian Federation, Moscow (GARF)

Fond 111, Otdelenie po okhraneniiu obshchestvennoi bezopasnosti i poriadka (Okhrannoe otdelenie) pri Petrogradskom gradonachal'nike (Department for Protecting Public Security and Order, under the Petrograd Mayor)

GARF, f. 111, o. 1, d. 99, Raion Anichkogo mosta, 1914 Fontanki dom no. 16, 1914.

GARF, f. 111, o. 1, d. 100, Raion Anichkogo mosta, 1915.

GARF, f. 111, o. 1, d. 101, Raion Anichkogo mosta, 1916.

GARF, f. 111, o. 1. d. 2999, Poseshchenie restoranov, 1911.

GARF, f. 111, o. 1, d. 3764, Raion Fontanki dom no. 16, 1914; f. 111, o. 1, d. 3764 Raion Fontanki dom no. 38, 1913.

Fond 124, Ugolovnoe otdelenie pervogo departamenta ministerstva iustitsii (Criminal Division of the First Department of the Ministry of Justice)

GARF, f. 124, o. 28, d. 686, Delo po prosheniiu K. V. Sizykh o pomilovanii ee syna A. Sizukh, osuzhdennogo Irkutskim okruzhmym sudom 11 marta 1910 goda po st. 995 i 996 Ulozh. O nakaz., 1910.

GARF, f. 124, o. 30, d. 1481, Delo po prosheniiu I. Miniaylo, osuzhdennogo Ekaterinodarskim okruzhnym sudom po st. 995, 2 p. 31 ulozh. o nak. o pomilovanii, 1912.

GARF, f. 124, o. 31, d. 1026, Delo po proshenii V. Pudenko, osuzhdennogo Rostovskim-na-Donu okruzhnym sudom po st. 152, 995, 996, i 1642 v 1910–1913, ob otbytii sroka nakazaniia v gorode Rostov-na-Donu, 1913.

Published Primary Sources (including Criminal Codes, Urban Laws, Periodicals, and Books)

Criminal Codes, Urban Laws and Censuses

Gorodovoe polozhenie s zakonadatel'nymi motivami, raz'iasneniiami i dopolnitel'nymi uzakoneniiami, sostavitel', S. G. Shcheglovitov. St. Petersburg: Tip. Stasiulevicha, 1892.

Petrograd po peripisi 15 dekabria 1910 goda. Petrograd: Izdanie gorodskoi upravy po statisticheskomu otdeleniiu, 1883–1914.

Polnoe sobranie zakonov Rossiiskoi Imperii, ustav Blabochiniia, vol. 27, xx 468, no. 15379 (8 aprelia 1782), paragraf 71.

Sankt-Peterburg po peripisi 10 dekabria 1869 goda. St. Petersburg: Izdanie tsentral'nogo statisticheskogo komiteta, ministerstva vnutrennikh del, 1872, 1875. 3 vols.

Sankt-Peterburg po peripisi 10 dekabria 1869 goda. St. Petersburg: Gorodskaia uprava po statisticheskomu otdeleniiu, 1875.

Sankt-Peterburg po peripisi 15 dekabria 1881 goda. St. Petersburg: Sankt-Peterburgskaia gorodskaia uprava po statisticheskomu otdeleniiu, 1883–1884.

Sankt-Peterburg po peripisi 15 dekabria 1890 goda. St. Petersburg: Gorodskaia uprava po statisticheskomu otdeleniiu, 1892.

Sankt-Peterburg po peripisi 15 dekabria 1900 goda. St. Petersburg: Gorodskaia uprava po statisticheskomu otdeleniiu, 1903–1905.
Svod zakonov Rossiiskoi Imperii, 9. St. Petersburg, 1832, vol. 1.
Ugolovnoe ulozhenie, visochaishe utverzhdennoe 22 marta 1903 goda. St. Petersburg: Gosudarstvennaia tipografiia, 1903.
Zakony i postanovleniia: vysochaishee utverzhdennoe 16-go (28-go) iiunia 1870 goda, gorodskoe polozhenie. 3rd ed. St. Petersburg: Ministerstvo vnutrennikh del, 1870.

Periodicals Studied

Arkhiv psikhiatrii, nevrologii i sudebnoi psikhopatologii
Arkhiv sudebnoi meditsiny i obshchestvennoi gigieny (later *Vestnik obshchestvennoi gigieny, sudebnoi i prakticheskoi meditsiny*)
Gazeta-kopeika
Illustrirovaniia gazeta
Izvestiia Moskovskoi gorodskoi dumy
Izvestiia Sankt-Peterburgskoi gorodskoi obshchoi dumy
Obozrenie psikhiatrii
Peterburgskii listok
Vedomosti Sankt-Peterburgskoi gorodskoi politsii (later *Vestnik Sankt-Peterburgskogo gradonachal'stva i Sankt-Peterburgskoi gorodskoi politsii* and *Vedomosti stnik Sankt-Peterburgskogo gradonachal'stva*)
Vrach
Zodchii: Arkhitekturnyi i khudozhestvennyi zhurnal

Books and Cited Periodicals

Avseenko, Vasilii. *200 let S.-Peterburgu: istoricheskii ocherk*. St. Petersburg: S.-Peterburgskaia gorodskaia duma, 1903.
Barsukov, Nikolai. *Zhizn' i trudy M. P. Pogodina*. St. Petersburg: Izd. Mamontova, 1902.
Bekhterev, Vladimir. "O polovykh izvrashcheniiakh, kak patologicheskikh sochetatel'nykh refleksakh." *Obozrenie psikhiatrii* 7–9 (1915): 1–26.
Benjamin, Walter. *The Arcade Project*. Edited by Howard Eiland and Kevin McLaughlin. Cambridge, MA: Harvard University Press, 2002.
Bentham, Jeremy. *Panopticon; or, the Inspection House: Containing the Idea of a New Principle of Construction Applicable to Any Sort of Establishment, in Which Perfons of Any Defcription Are to Be Kept under Inspection*. Dublin, 1791.
Bentovin, Boris. *Torguiushchie telom: ocherki sovremennoi prostitutsii*. Moscow: Krumbiugel', 1907.
Bogdanov, Andrei Ivanovich. *Istoricheskoe, geograficheskoe i topograficheskoe opisanie Sankt-Peterburga ot nachala zavedeniia ego, s 1703 po 1751 god*. St. Petersburg, 1779.
Budkov, Mikhail Mikhailovich. *Sbornik obiazatelnykh postanovlenii dlia goroda S.-Peterburga i prigorodnykh politseiskikh uchastkov: s prilozeniem pravil i raz'iasnenii*. St. Petersburg: Tipografiia Peterburgskogo gradonachal'stva, 1910.
Budkov, Mikhail Mikhailovich. *Sbornik obizatelnykh postanovlenii dlia petrograda i prigorodnykh politseiskikh uchastkov*. Petrograd, 1914.
Bukhner, Ernst. *Sudebnaia meditsina dlia vrachei i iuristov*. St. Petersburg: Meditsinskii departament, 1870.

Cherikover, Semen. *Peterburg*. Moscow: Tipografiia T-va I. D. Sytina, 1909.
Chugin, V. I. "Zametka o russkikh baniakh v saniternom otnoshenii." *Vrach* 35 (1880): 577–78.
Chugin, V. I. "Zametka o russkikh baniakh v saniternom otnoshenii." *Vrach* 36 (1880): 585–86.
Enakiev, Fedor. *Zadachi preobrazovaniia Sankt-Peterburga*. St. Petersburg: T-vo R. Golike i A. Vil'borg, 1912.
Eremeev, Ivan. *Gorod S.-Peterburg s tochki zreniia meditsinskoi politsii: sostavleno po rasporiazheniiu gospodina S.-Peterburgskogo gradonachal'nika general-maiora N. V. Kleigel'sa*. St. Petersburg: Tip. M. D. Lombovskogo, 1897.
Fadeev, A. K. "Ucheniiu o russkikh baniakh." Doctoral diss., University of St. Petersburg, 1890.
Fedorov, A. "Deiatel'nost' S.-Peterburgskogo vrachebno-politseiskogo komiteta za period 1889–1895 gg." *Vestnik obshchestvennoi gigieny, sudebnoi i prakticheskoi meditsiny* 11 (1896): 178–94.
Fedorov, M. "Finansovoe polozhenie Peterburga." *Gorodskoe delo* 1 (1909): 13–17.
Fialkovskii, S. Iu. "Materialy k voprosu o vliianii bani na zdorovyi i bol'noi glaz cheloveka." *Vrach* 9 (1881): 137–40.
Fonveille, W. "Gas and Electricity in Paris." *Nature* 21, no. 534 (1880): 283.
Fuks, Iosif Borisovich. *Gomoseksualizm kak prestuplenie: iuridicheskii i ugolovno-politicheskii ocherk*. St. Petersburg: Tip. t-va Obshchestvennaia pol'za, 1914.
Gautier, Theophile. *A Winter in Russia*. New York: Henry Holt, 1874.
Gazeta-kopeika. "Kinematograph: v tramvaie," October 9, 1903.
Gazeta-kopeika. "Nasha ulitsa," August 11, 1908.
Gazeta-kopeika. "Nasha ulitsa," August 22, 1908.
Gazeta-kopeika. "Nasha ulitsa," August 24, 1908.
Gazeta-kopeika. "O zeleni i gul'iane," March 22, 1909.
Gazeta-kopeika. "Nravy Nevskogo prospekta," April 2, 1910.
Gessen, Vladimir. *Iskliuchitel'noe polozhenie*. St. Petersburg: Iurid. kn. skl. Pravo, 1908.
Giliarovskii, Vladimir Alekseevich. *Moskva i moskvichi: vospominaniia*. Moscow: Vserossiiskii Soiuz Poetov, 1926.
Gol'denberg, Nikodim. *Bani dlia voisk i dlia marodnykh mass*. St. Petersburg: Tipografiia E. Evdokimova, 1898.
Gorodskaia Khronika. "Retiradniki," no. 9–10, 1897.
Gorodskaia uprava. *Po voprosy o dal'neishem eksplotatsii Konno-Zheleznykh Dorog 1-ogo tovarishchestva, po okonchanii 31 avgusta 1898 goda sroka kontsesii*. St. Petersburg: ISPGD, 1989.
Gromov, Nikolai Andreevich, ed. *Zakony ugolovnye: ulozhenie o nakazaniiakh ugolovnykh i ispravitel'nykh, ustav o nakazaniiakh, nalagaemykh mirovymi sud'iami*. St. Petersburg: Izdatel'stvo Ministerstva vnutrennikh del, 1909.
Hirschfeld, Magnus. *Die Homosexualität des Mannes und des Weibes*. Berlin: Loius Marcus, 1914. https://doi.org/10.1515/9783110867800.
Izvestiia S.-Peterburgskoi gorodskoi dumy. "Ob elektricheskom osveshchenii chasti Nevskogo prospekta ot Anichkogo mosta do Znamenskoi ploshchadi i po Bol'shoi morskoi ulitse," no. 1 (November 1886): 27–48.
Izvestiia S.-Peterburgskoi gorodskoi dumy. "Ob osveshchenii Nevskogo prospekta i Bol'shoi morskoi ulitsy," no. 44 (November 1886): 838–58.

Izvestiia S.-Peterburgskoi gorodskoi dumy. "Obshchii plan usilenia osveshcheniia gorodskikh ulits," no. 18 (May 1907): 997–1019.

Izvestiia S.-Peterburgskoi gorodskoi dumy. "Ob usilenii osveshcheniia," no. 23 (May 1912): 2153–58.

Izvestiia S.-Peterburgskoi gorodskoi dumy. "O dezhurstve dvornikov," no. 21 (June 1892): 759–60.

Izvestiia S.-Peterburgskoi gorodskoi dumy. "O korennom uluchshenii vodosnabzheniia S.- Peterburga," no. 17 (April 1911): 577–630.

Izvestiia S.-Peterburgskoi gorodskoi dumy. "O nadzore za dezhurnymi dvornikami," no. 20 (June 1892): 670.

Izvestiia S.-Peterburgskoi gorodskoi dumy. "O poriadke i blagochinii v obchshestvennykh sadakh," no. 19 (May 1888): 815–16.

Izvestiia S.-Peterburgskoi gorodskoi dumy. "Po voprosu o prinuditel'nom ozdorovlenii goroda S.-Petersburga," no. 173 (March 1909): 1443–49.

Izvestiia S.-Peterburgskoi gorodskoi dumy. "Vodosnabzhenii v Peterburge," no. 26 (June 1914): 2993–3000.

Karvasovskii, I. A. *Kratkii ocherk istorii ban' i znachenie ikh v gigienicheskom i terapevticheskom otnosheniiakh*. Kiev: V. Izopol'skii, 1884.

Kerzun, A. P. *Kratkii ocherk deiatel'nosti S.-Peterburgskogo gorodskogo popechitel'stva o narodnoi trezvosti 1898–1912*. St. Petersburg, 1913.

Khronos, "O zeleni i gul'iane," March 22, 1909.

Kleigel's, Nikolai Vasil'evich. *Osnovy politseiskoi sluzhby*. St. Petersburg: Tipografiia SPb. gradonachal'nika, 1905.

Kleigel's, Nikolai Vasil'evich. *Posobie dlia podgotovki na dolzhnosti klassnye i okolotochnykh nadzeratelei S.-Peterburgskoi stolichnoi politsii*. St. Petersburg: Tip. Sankt-Petersburgskogo gradonachal'stva, 1900.

Koffin'on, A. *Izvrashchennyi mir: o polovom voprose*. Moscow: Tipo-Litografiia Torgovogo doma E. Konovalova i Ko, 1908.

Koni, Anatolii Fedorovich. *Na zhiznennom puti: iz zapisok sudebnogo deiatelia; zhiteiskie vstrechi*. 2 vols. Vol. 1. St. Petersburg: Tipografiia T-va Trud, 1912.

Kovalevskii, Pavel Ivanovich. *Psikhologiia pola: polovoe bessilie i drugie izvrashcheniia i ikh lechenie*. St. Petersburg: Tip. M. I. Akinfieva, 1909.

Kupriianova, L. *Rabochii Peterburga*. St. Petersburg, 1914.

Kurlova, M. G. "K voprosu o lechenii ozhireniia goriachimi vannami i russkoi parovoi banei." *Vrach* 42 (1884): 715–16.

Kuzmin, Mikhail. *Dnevnik, 1905–1907*. Edited by Nikolai Bogomolov and Sergei Shumikhin. St. Petersburg: Izdatel'stvo Ivana Limbakha, 2000.

Kuzmin, Mikhail. *Dnevnik, 1908–1915*. Edited by Nikolai Bogomolov and Sergei Shumikhina. St. Petersburg: Izdatel'stvo Ivana Limbakha, 2009.

Kuzmin, Mikhail. *Kryl'ia*. St. Petersburg: Skorpion, 1907.

Leikin, Nikolai. *Stseny iz kupecheskogo byta*. St. Petersburg: Tipografiia S. V. Zvonareva, 1871.

Markov, K. V. *Voiskovye bani i prachechnye*. St. Petersburg: Tip. i Lit. V. A. Tikhanova, 1900.

Merts, Ivan. (1872) "Gorodskie retiradniki v S.- Peterburge." *Zodchii: Arkhitekturnyi i khudozhestvennyi zhurnal* 7 (1880): 34–36.

Merzheevskii, Vladimir Osipovich. *Sudebnaia genikologiia dlia vrachei i iuristov.* St. Petersburg: Izdanie B. G. Ianpol'skogo, 1878.
Mikhnevich, Vladimir. *Peterburg ves' na ladoni.* St. Petersburg: Izdanie Knigotorgovtsa K. N. Plotnikova, 1874.
Mikhnevich, Vladimir. "Peterburgskie sady i ikh etnografiia." In *Iazvy Peterburg: sbornik gazetnogo fol'klora kontsa XIX–nachala XX veka*, edited by Lev Lurye. 1887; repr., Leningrad: Leningradskoe otdelenie sovetskogo fonda kul'tury, 1990.
Ministerstvo vnutrennikh del. *Sbornik instruktsii, zakonopolozhenii i rasporiazhenii dlia nizhnikh chinov politsii i politseiskikh uriadnikov.* St. Petersburg: Tipografiia ministerstva vnutrennikh del, 1908.
Nabokov, Vladimir Dmitrievich. *Elementarnyi uchebnik osobennoi chasti russkogo ugolovnogo prava.* 2 vols. Vol. 1. St. Petersburg: Senatskaia tipografiia, 1903.
Nabokov, Vladimir Dmitrievich. *Sbornik statei po ugolovnomu pravu.* St. Petersburg: Tipografiia Tovarishchestva "Obshchestvennaia pol'za," 1904.
Obolonskii, Nikolai Aleksandrovich. *Izvrashchenie polovogo chuvstva.* Kiev: Tipographiia Imperatorskogo Universiteta, 1898.
Ostrovskii, Aleksandr Nikolaevich. *Talents and Admirers.* Premiered on December 20, 1881, Malyi Theatre, St. Petersburg.
Pazhitnov, K. "Kvartirnii vopros v Moskve i v Peterburge." *Gorodskoe delo* 7 (1910): 1413–19.
Pazhitnov, K. "Zhilishchnaia politika gorodskoi dumy goroda petrodrada." *Izvestiia Moskovskoi gorodskoi dumy* 10 (1914).
Peterburgskii listok. "Mal'tsevskie bani," August 19, 1876.
Peterburgskii listok. "Nadzor za Sadami," May 15, 1900.
Peterburgskii listok. "Novye bani," December 21, 1880.
Peterburgskii listok. "Otkrytie Passazha," November 12, 1900.
Peterburgskii listok. "Passazh v budushchem," April 2, 1900.
Peterburgskii listok. "Pisma v redaktsiiu," February 2, 1900.
Peterburgskii listok. "Pornografiia" (in section "Magistrate Court"), May 2, 1908.
Peterburgskii listok. "Razdel 'Mimokhodom,'" October 1, 1901.
Peterburgskii listok. "Stolichnaia nakip'," February 11, 1900.
Piatnitskii, Boris Ivanovich. *Polovye izvrashcheniia i ugolovnoe pravo.* Mogilev: Tipografiia I. B. Klaza, 1910.
Rozanov, Vasilii. *Literaturnye ocherki.* St. Petersburg, 1902.
Ruadze, Vladimir. *K sudu! gomoseksual'nyi Peterburg.* St. Petersburg: Kommercheskaia tipografiia Vilenchik, 1908.
Sankt-Peterburgskoe gorodskoe obshchestvennoe upravlenie. *Putevoditel' po S.-Peterburgu: obrazovatel'nye ekskursii.* St. Petersburg: Novoe vremia, 1903.
Semenovich, G.L. *Ulichnoe osveshchenie goroda Sankt-Peterburga: ocherk razvitiia osveshcheniia stolitsi so vremeni ee osnovaniia po 1912 g.* Petrograd: Gorodskaia tipografiia, 1914.
Serbskii, Vladimir Petrovich. *Sudebnaia psikhopatologiia: lektsii, chitannye v Imperatorskom moskovskom universitete. Vypusk vtoroi: Klinicheskaia psikhiatriia.* Moscow: Izd. M. i S. Sabashnikovykh, 1900.
Severnaia pchela, "Zametki," July 24, 1861.

Simmel, Georg. "The Metropolis and Mental Life." In *Georg Simmel on Individuality and Social Forms*, edited by Donald N. Levine, 324–39. Chicago: University of Chicago Press, 1971.

Siuzor, P. Iu. "Torgovye (narodnye) bani Voronina." *Zodchii: Arkhitekturnyi i khudozhestvennyi zhurnal* 1–8 (1872): 134–38.

Spasskii, I. T. "Kratkii ocherk vrachebnykh otnoshenii ban'." *Drug zdravlia* 1 (1895): 24–27.

Svetlov, Sergei. *Peterbugskaia zhizn' v kontse XIX stoletiia*. St. Petersburg, 1892.

Sviatlovskii, Vladimir. *Zhilishchnyi vopros s ekonomicheskoi tochki zreniia*. St. Petersburg: Tipografiia Ministerstva putei soobshcheniia, 1902.

Tarnovskii, Veniamin. *Izvrashchenie polovogo chuvstva: sudebno-psikhiatricheskii ocherk*. St. Petersburg: Tipografiia Stasiulevicha, 1885.

Tchaikovsky, Petr I. *Dnevniki, 1873–1891*. St. Petersburg: Severnyi olen', 1993.

Vedomosti Sankt-Peterburgskoi gorodskoi politsii. "Peterburgskie bani," no. 118 (May 27, 1871): 1–2.

Vedomosti Sankt-Peterburgskoi gorodskoi politsii. "Peterburgskie bani: prodolzhenie," no. 119 (May 28, 1871): 1–2.

Vedomosti Sankt-Peterburgskogo gradonachal'stva. "Obiazatel'noe postanovlenie ob ustroistve v gorode Sankt-Peterburge obshchestvennykh ban'," no. 132 (June 20, 1903): 1–2.

Vestnik Sankt-Peterburgskogo gradonachal'stva i Sankt-Peterburgskoi gorodskoi politsii. "Chast' offitsial'naia: usloviia ustroistva obshchestvennykh ban'," no. 172 (July 29, 1879): 1–2.

Viatkin, M. P. "Gorodskoe upravlenie i gorodskoe khoziaistvo Peterburga." In *Ocherki istorii Leningrada*, edited by M. P. Viatkin, 887–913. Moscow-Leningrad: Institut istoriii SSSR (Akademiia nauk SSSR), 1956.

Volkov, Vasilii Vasil'evich. *Postateinyi ukazatel' podsudnosti ugolovnykh del, predusmotrennykh ulozheniem o nakazaniiakh, ugolovnym ulozheniem i ustavom o nakazaniikh, dlia obshchikh, mirovykh i volostykh sudakh po zakonu o preobrazovanii mestonogo suda*. St. Petersburg: Tip. inzh. G. A. Bernshteina, 1914.

Vysotskii, Ivan Petrovich. *Sankt-Petersburgskaia politsiia i gradonachal'stvo 1703–1903*. St. Petersburg: T-vo R. Golike i A. Vil'borg 1903.

Zanosov, Dmitrii, and Vladimir Pyzin. "Gorodskoi transport: izvoshchiki, konka, tramvai." In Zanosov and Pyzin, *Iz zhizni Peterburga*, 38–46.

Zanosov, Dmitrii, and Vladimir Pyzin. "Magaziny u lavki, restorany i traktiry." In Zanosov and Pyzin, *Iz zhizni Peterburga*, 96–104.

Zanosov, Dmitrii, and Vladimir Pyzin. "Na ulitsakh i ploshchadiakh stolitsy." In Zanosov and Pyzin, *Iz zhizni Peterburga*, 22–37.

Zanosov, Dmitrii, and Vladimir Pyzin, eds. *Iz zhizni Peterburga 1890–1910-ykh godov: zapiski ochevidtsev*. Leningrad: Lenizdat, 1991.

Znamenskii, V. N. *O russkikh baniakh v gigienicheskom otnoshenii*. St. Petersburg: Tipografiia I. Markova i Ko, 1861.

Secondary Sources

Ahmed, Sara. *Queer Phenomenology: Orientations, Objects, Others*. London: Duke University Press, 2006.

Aksel'rod, V. I., N. Vesnina, and D. A. Demidova. *Sady i parki Leningrada*. Leningrad: Lenizdat, 1981.

Anderson, Ben, and Colin McFarlane. "Assemblage and Geography." *Area* 43, no. 2 (2011): 124–27.

Andersson, Peter. *Streetlife in Late Victorian London: The Constable and the Crowd*. New York: Palgrave Macmillan, 2013.

Bailey, Peter. "Entertainmentality! Liberalizing Modern Pleasure in the Victorian Leisure Industry." In *The Peculiarities of Liberal Modernity in Imperial Britain*, edited by S. Gunn and J. Vernon, 119–33. Berkeley: University of California Press, 2011.

Bailey, Peter. *Leisure and Class in Victorian England: Rational Recreation and the Contest for Control, 1830–1885*. London: Routledge, 2014.

Bater, James H. "Between Old and New: St. Petersburg in the Late Imperial Era." In Hamm, *City in Late Imperial Russia*, 43–78.

Bater, James H. "The Development of Public Transportation in St. Petersburg. 1860–1914." *Journal of Transport History* 2, no. 2 (1973): 86–93.

Bater, James H. *St Petersburg: Industrialization and Change*. London: McGill-Queen's University Press, 1976.

Bauman, Zygmunt. "Modernity." In *The Oxford Companion to Politics of the World*, edited by Joel Krieger. Oxford: Oxford University Press, 1993.

Beachy, Robert. *Gay Berlin: Birthplace of a Modern Identity*. New York: Vintage Books, 2014.

Bech, Henning. *When Men Meet: Homosexuality and Modernity*. Chicago: University of Chicago Press, 1997.

Beer, Daniel. *Renovating Russia: The Human Sciences and the Fate of Liberal Modernity 1880–1930*. Ithaca, NY: Cornell University Press, 2008.

Bell, David, and Jon Binnie. "Authenticating Queer Space: Citizenship, Urbanism and Governance." *Urban Studies* 41, no. 9 (2004): 1807–20.

Bell, David, and Jon Binnie. *The Sexual Citizen: Queer Politics and Beyond*. Cambridge: Polity, 2000.

Bell, David, and Gill Valentine. *Mapping Desire: Geographies of Sexualities*. London: Routledge, 1995.

Bennett, Jane. "The Agency of Assemblages and the North American Blackout." *Public Culture* 17 (2005): 445–46.

Berman, Marshall. *All That Is Solid Melts into Air: The Experience of Modernity*. London: Verso, 1983.

Bernstein, Laurie. *Sonia's Daughters: Prostitutes and Their Regulation in Imperial Russia*. Los Angeles: University of California Press, 1995.

Bersen'ev, Vladimir, and A. Markov. "The Police and Gays: An Episode from the Era of Aleksandr III." *Risk: Al'manakh* 3 (1998): 105–16.

Berube, Allan. "The History of Gay Bathhouses." *Journal of Homosexuality* 44, no. 3 (2003): 33–53.

Bleys, Rudi. *The Geography of Perversion: Male-to-Male Sexual Behavior Outside the West and the Ethnographic Imagination, 1750–1918*. London: Cassell, 1996.

Blomley, Nicholas. *Rights of Passage: Sidewalks and the Regulation of Public Flow*. New York: Routledge, 2010.

Bogdanov, Igor Alekseevich. *Tri veka Peterburgskoi bani*. St. Petersburg: Iskusstvo S.-Peterburg, 2000.

Bondi, Liz. "Making Connections and Thinking through Emotions: Between Geography and Psychotherapy." *Transactions of the Institute of British Geographers* 30, no. 4 (2005): 433–88.

Boyd, Nan Alamilla. *Wide Open Town: A History of Queer San Francisco to 1965*. Los Angeles: University of California Press, 2003.

Boym, Svetlana. *Common Places: Mythologies of Everyday Life in Russia*. Cambridge, MA: Harvard University Press, 2009.

Bradley, Joseph. "Subjects into Citizens: Societies, Civil Society, and Autocracy in Tsarist Russia." *American Historical Review* 107, no. 4 (2002): 1094–123.

Brower, Daniel. *The Russian City between Tradition and Modernity, 1850–1900*. Berkeley: University of California Press, 1990.

Brower, Daniel. "Urban Revolution in the Late Russian Empire." In Hamm, *City in Late Imperial Russia*, edited by Michael F. Hamm, 319–55. Bloomington: Indiana University Press, 1986.

Browne, Simone. *Dark Matters: On the Surveillance of Blackness*. Durham, NC: Duke University Press, 2015.

Buck-Morss, Susan. *The Dialectics of Seeing: Walter Benjamin and the Arcades Project*. Cambridge, MA: MIT Press, 1991.

Butler, Judith. *Gender Trouble: Feminism and the Subversion of Identity*. London: Routledge, 1990.

Castells, Manuel. *The City and the Grassroots: A Cross-Cultural Theory of Urban Social Movements*. London: Edward Arnold, 1983.

Certeau, Michel de. *The Practice of Everyday Life*. Berkeley: University of California Press, 1984.

Chauncey, George. *Gay New York: Gender, Urban Culture, and the Making of the Gay Male World, 1890–1940*. New York: Basic Books, 1994.

Cocks, Harry. *Namelss Offences: Homosexual Desire in the 19th Century*. London: I. B. Tauris, 2003.

Connell, Joanne. "Managing Gardens for Visitors in Great Britain: A Story of Continuity and Change." *Tourism Management* 26, no. 2 (2005): 185–201.

Cook, Matt. *London and the Culture of Homosexuality, 1885–1914*. Cambridge: Cambridge University Press, 2003.

Cresswell, T. "Night Discourse: Producing/Consuming Meaning on the Street." In *Images of the Street*, edited by Nicholas Fyfe, 268–79. London: Routledge, 1998.

Crook, Tom. "Power, Privacy and Pleasure: Liberalism and the Modern Cubicle." *Cultural Studies* 21, no. 4–5 (2007): 549–69.

Crook, Tom. "'Schools for the Moral Training of the People': Public Baths, Liberalism and the Promotion of Cleanliness in Victorian Britain." *European Review of History: Revue Europeenne d'histoire* 13, no. 1 (2006): 21–47.

Daly, Jonathan W. "On the Significance of Emergency Legislation in Late Imperial Russia." *Slavic Review* 54, no. 3 (1995): 602–29.

Daly, Jonathan W. *The Watchful State: Security Police and Opposition in Russia 1906–1917*. DeKalb: Northern Illinois University Press, 2004.

Darinskii, Anatolii, and Vitalii Startsev. *Istoriia Sankt-Peterburga*. St. Petersburg: Glagol, 2007.

Davidson, Joyce, Liz Bondi, and Mick Smith, eds. *Emotional Geography*. Farnham: Ashgate, 2005.

de la Croix, St. Sukie. *Chicago Whispers: A History of LGBT Chicago before Stonewall.* Madison: University of Wisconsin Press, 2012.

Deleuze, Gilles, and Claire Parnet. *Dialogues.* New York: Columbia University Press, 1977.

Delph, Edward William. *The Silent Community: Public Homosexual Encounters.* London: Sage, 1987.

Dennis, Richard. *Cities in Modernity. Representation and Production of Metropolitan Space, 1840–1930.* Cambridge: Cambridge University Press, 2008.

Dreyer, Elfriede, and Estelle McDowall. "Imagining the *Flâneur* as a Woman." *Communication* 38, no. 1 (2012): 30–44.

Duberman, Martin, Martha Vicinus, and George Chauncey. *Hidden from History: Reclaiming the Gay and Lesbian Past.* London: Penguin Books, 1989.

Dubrovskaia, A., and V. Dubrovskii. *Russkaia bania i massazh.* Moscow: Vlados-Press, 2008.

Dudyrev, Fedor. "Razrabotka i priniatie ugolovnogo ulozhenie 1903 goda." *Aktual'nye problemy ekonomiki i prava* 4 (2009): 193–98.

Economakis, Evel. *From Peasant to Petersburger.* London: Macmillan, 1998.

Edelman, Lee. "Tearooms and Sympathy, or, the Epistemology of the Water Closet." In *Homographesis: Essays in Gay Literary and Cultural Theory*, edited by Lee Edelman, 148–72. London: Routledge, 1994.

Eizenberg, Efrat. "Actually Existing Commons: Three Moments of Space of Community Gardens in New York City." *Antipode* 44, no. 3 (2012): 764–82.

Ely, Christopher. *Underground Petersburg: Radical Populism, Urban Space, and the Tactics of Subversion in Reform-Era Russia.* DeKalb: Northern Illinois University Press, 2016.

Emmons, Terence, and Wayne S. Vucinich, eds. *The Zemstvo in Russia: An Experiment in Local Self-Government.* Cambridge: Cambridge University Press, 1982.

Engelstein, Laura. "Combined Underdevelopment: Discipline and the Law in Imperial and Soviet Russia." *American Historical Review* 98, no. 2 (1993): 338–53.

Engelstein, Laura. *The Keys to Happiness: Sex and the Search for Modernity in Fin-de-Siècle Russia.* Ithaca, NY: Cornell University Press, 1992.

Engelstein, Laura. "Soviet Policy toward Male Homosexuality." *Journal of Homosexuality* 29, no. 2–3 (1995): 155–78.

Felski, Rita. *The Gender of Modernity.* Cambridge, MA: Harvard University Press, 1995.

Foucault, Michel. *Discipline and Punish: The Birth of the Prison.* London: Penguin Social Sciences, 1991.

Foucault, Michel. "The Life of Infamous Men." In *Power, Truth, Strategy*, edited by Meaghan Morris and Paul Patton, 76–91. Sydney: Feal, 1979.

Foucault, Michel. "'Omnes et Singulatim': Toward a Critique of Political Reason." In Michel Foucault, *Power: Essential Works of Foucault 1954–1984*, edited by James D. Faubion, 298–325. London: Penguin Books, 2002.

Foucault, Michel. "The Punitive Society: Lectures at the Collège de France 1972–1973." Edited by Bernard E. Harcourt. Houndmills: Palgrave Macmillan, 2015.

Foucault, Michel. "21 February 1973." In *The Punitive Society: Lectures at the Collège De France 1972–1973, Translated by Graham Burchell*, edited by Arnold I. Davidson, 139–54. Houndmills, Basingstoke: Palgrave Macmillan, 2015.

Foucault, Michel. "La vie des hommes infâmes." *Cahiers du chemin* 29 (January 1977): 12–29.

Freeze, Gregory L. "The Soslovie (Estate) Paradigm and Russian Social History." *American Historical Review* 91, no. 1 (1986): 11–36.

Gandy, Matthew. "Cyborg Urbanization: Complexity and Monstrosity in the Contemporary City." *International Journal of Urban and Regional Research* 29, no. 1 (2005): 26–49.

Gandy, Matthew. *The Fabric of Space: Water, Modernity, and the Urban Imagination.* Cambridge, MA: MIT Press, 2014.

Gandy, Matthew. "Queer Ecology: Nature, Sexuality, and Heterotopic Alliances." *Environment and Planning D: Society and Space* 30, no. 4 (2012): 727–47.

García, Magaly Rodríguez, Lex Heerma van Voss, and Elise van Nederveen Meerkerk, eds. *Selling Sex in the City: A Global History of Prostitution, 1600s–2000s.* London: Brill, 2017.

Gaskell, Martin. "Gardens for the Working Class: Victorian Practical Pleasure." *Victorian Studies* 23, no. 4 (1980): 479–501.

Giddens, Anthony. *The Consequences of Modernity.* Stanford, CA: Stanford University Press, 1990.

Giddens, Anthony. *Modernity and Self-Identity: Self and Society in Late Modern Age.* Cambridge: Polity Press 1991.

Gilson, Lucy. "Michael Lipsky, 'Street Level Bureaucracy: Dilemmas of the Individual in Public Service.'" In *the Oxford Handbook of Classics of Public Policy and Aministration*, edited by Stella Balla, Martin Lodge, and Edward Page, 383–404. Oxford: Oxford University Press, 2015.

Glassberg, David. "The Design of Reform: The Public Bath Movement in America." *American Studies* 20, no. 2 (1979): 5–21.

Gleason, William, and Thomas Porter. "The Zemstvo and Public Initiative in Late Imperial Russia." *Russian History* 21, no. 1–4 (1994): 419–37.

Gregg, Melissa, and Gregory Seigworth, eds. *The Affect Theory Reader.* Durham, NC: Duke University Press, 2010.

Gregory, Paul R. *Before Command: An Economic History of Russia from Emancipation to the First Five-Year Plan.* Princeton, NJ: Princeton University Press, 1994.

Griffero, Tonino. *Atmospheres: Aesthetics of Emotional Spaces.* Farnham: Ashgate, 2014.

Hakanen, Ulla. "Panoramas from Above and Street from Below: The Petersburg of Viacheslav Ivanov and Mikhail Kuzmin." In *Petersburg/Petersburg: Novel and City, 1900–1921*, edited by Olga Matich, 208–11. Madison: University of Wisconsin Press, 2010.

Halperin, David M. "How to Do the History of Male Homosexaulity." *GLQ: A Journal of Lesbian and Gay Studies* 6, no. 1 (2000): 87–123.

Hamm, Michael F., ed. *The City in Late Imperial Russia.* Bloomington: Indiana University Press, 1986.

Hammers, Corie J. "Making Space for an Agentic Sexuality? The Examination of a Lesbian/Queer Bathhouse." *Sexualities* 11, no. 5 (2008): 547–72.

Hanssen, Beatrice. *Walter Benjamin and the Arcades Project.* New York: Continuum International, 2006.

Hardt, Michael, and Antonio Negri. *Commonwealth.* Cambridge, MA: Harvard University Press, 2009.

Harvey, David. *The Condition of Postmodernity: An Enquiry into the Origins of Cultural Change.* Oxford: Basil Blackwell, 1989.

Harvey, David. *Consciousness and the Urban Experience: Studies in the History and Theory of Capitalist Urbanization.* Baltimore: Johns Hopkins University Press, 1985.

Hasegawa, Tsuyoshi. *Crime and Punishment in the Russian Revolution: Mob Justice and Police in Petrograd.* Cambridge, MA: Belknap Press of Harvard University Press, 2017.

Healey, Dan. "The Disappearance of the Russian Queen, or How the Soviet Closet Was Born." In *Russian Masculinities in History and Culture*, edited by Barbara Evans Clements, Rebecca Friedman, and Dan Healey, 152–71. New York: Palgrave Macmillan, 2002.

Healey, Dan. *Homosexual Desire in Revolutionary Russia: The Regulation of Sexual and Gender Dissent.* Chicago: University of Chicago Press, 2001.

Healey, Dan. "Masculine Purity and 'Gentlemen's Mischief': Sexual Exchange and Prostitution between Russian Men, 1861–1941." *Slavic Review* 60, no. 2 (2010): 233–65.

Healey, Dan. "What Can We Learn from the History of Homosexuality in Russia?" *History Compass* 1, no. 1 (2005): 1–6.

Hearne, Siobhan. *Policing Prostitution: Regulating the Lower Classes in Late Imperial Russia.* Oxford: Oxford University Press, 2021.

Hearne, Siobhan. "To Denounce or Defend? Public Participation in the Policing of Prostitution in Late Imperial Russia." *Kritika: Explorations in Russian and Eurasian History* 19, no. 4 (2018): 717–44.

Henze, Charlotte E. *Disease, Health Care and Government in Late Imperial Russia: Life and Death on the Volga, 1823–1914.* London: Routledge, 2010.

Hetherington, Philippa. "Prostitution in Moscow and St. Petersburg, Russia." In *Selling Sex in the City: A Global History of Prostitution, 1600s–2000s*, edited by Magaly Rodríguez García, Lex Heerma van Voss, and Elise van Nederveen Meerkerk, 138–70. London: Brill, 2017.

Higgs, David. *Queer Sites: Gay Urban Histories since 1600.* London: Routledge, 1999.

Holmes, Dave, Patrick O'Byrne, and Denise Gastaldo. "Setting the Space for Sex: Architecture, Desire and Health Issues in Gay Bathhouses." *International Journal of Nursing Studies* 44, no. 2 (2007): 273–84.

Houlbrook, Matt. "The Private World of Public Urinals: London, 1918–57." *London Journal* 25, no. 1 (2000): 52–70.

Houlbrook, Matt. *Queer London: Perils and Pleasures in the Sexual Metropolis, 1918–1957.* Chicago: University of Chicago Press, 2005.

Howell, Philip. *Geographies of Regulation: Policing Prostitution in Nineteenth-Century Britain and the Empire.* Cambridge: Cambridge University Press, 2009.

Howell, Philip. "Public Space and the Public Sphere: Political Theory and the Historical Geography of Modernity." *Environment and Planning D: Society and Space* 11, no. 3 (1993): 303–22.

Hubbard, Phil. *Cities and Sexualities.* London: Routledge, 2012.

Hubbard, Phil. *Sex and the City: Geographies of Prostitution in the Urban West.* Aldershot: Ashgate, 1999.

Hubbard, Phil, and Teela Sanders. "Making Space for Sex Work: Female Street Prostitution and the Production of Urban Space." *International Journal of Urban and Regional Research* 27, no. 1 (2003): 75–89. https://doi.org/10.1111/1468-2427.00432.

Isachenko, Valerii. *Zodchie S.-Peterburga: XIX–nachalo XX veka*. St. Petersburg: Tsentropoligraf, 2010.

Johnson, Eric M. "Demographics, Inequality and Entitlements in the Russian Famine of 1891." *Slavonic and East European Review* 93, no. 1 (2015): 96–119.

Joyce, Patrick. *The Rule of Freedom: Liberalism and the Modern City*. London: Verso, 2003.

Karlinsky, Simon. "Death and Resurrection of Mikhail Kuzmin." *Slavic Review* 38, no. 1 (1979): 92–96.

Karlinsky, Simon. "Gay Life before the Soviets: Revisionism Revised." *Advocate* 339, no. 1 (1982): 31–34.

Karlinsky, Simon. "Russia's Gay Literature and Culture: The Impact of the October Revolution." In *Hidden from History: Reclaiming the Gay and Lesbian Past*, edited by Martin Duderman, Martha Vicinus, and George Chauncey, 347–64. London: Penguin Books, 1989.

Karlinsky, Simon. "Russia's Gay Literature and History." *Gay Sunshine* 29/30 (1979): 1–7.

Karmazinov, Feliks, ed. *Vodosnabzhenie Sankt-Peterburga*. St. Petersburg: Novyi zhurnal, 2003

Karpenko, I.A. "Osvesheniie." In *Tri veka Sankt-Peterburga: Entsiklopediia 19 vek*, edited by A. V. Tereshchiuk, 773–76. St. Petersburg: Fililogicheskii fakul'tet SPbGU, 2005.

Kashin, Konstantin, and Ethan Pollock. "Public Health and Bathing in Late Imperial Russia: A Statistical Approach." *Russian Review* 72, no. 1 (2013): 66–93.

Keller, Elena. *Prazdnichnaia kul'tura Peterburga: ocherki istorii*. St. Petersburg: Mikhailov, 2001.

Kelly, Catriona. *St Petersburg: Shadows of the Past*. New Haven, CT: Yale University Press, 2014.

Keltner, Dacher, Disa Sauter, Jessica Tracy, and Alan Cowen. "Emotional Expression: Advances in Basic Emotion Theory." *Journal of Nonverbal Behavior* 43, no. 2 (2019): 133–60. https://doi.org/10.1007/s10919-019-00293-3.

Kenny, Nicolas. *The Feel of the City: Experiences of Urban Transformation*. Toronto: University of Toronto Press, 2014.

Khaustova, Ekaterina. "Pre-Revolution Living Standards: Russia 1888–1917." Paper presented at the Annual Conference of the Economic History Society, 2013.

Khmelnitskaia, Irina. *Restaurant Life of St. Petersburg and Moscow in Late Imperial Russia*. St. Petersburg: Evropeiskii universitet, 2008.

Khrustalev, V. M., ed. *Dnevnik velikogo kniazia Konstantina Konstantinovicha (K. R.)*. Moscow: PROZAiK, 2013.

Kochakov, B. *Ocherki istorii Leningrada, period imperializma i Burzhuazno-demokraticheskikh Revoliutsii*, vol. 3. Moscow-Leningrad: Nauka, 1956.

Kochakov, B. *Ocherki istorii Leningrada, period kapitalizma, vtoraia polovina XIX veka*, vol. 2. Moscow-Leningrad: Nauka, 1957.

Kolstø, Pål. "Power as Burden: The Slavophile Concept of the State and Lev Tolstoy." *Russian Review* 64, no. 4 (2005): 559–74.

Koneva, Marina. "Istoriia razvitiia ugolovnogo zakonodatel'stva za deistviia gomoseksual'nogo kharaktera." *Ugolovnoe pravo* 2 (2003): 42–44.

Korobeinikov, Aleksandr. "Imagining Post-Imperial Order: Nationalism, Regionalism, Autonomism, and State Socialism in Northeast Russia, 1905–1922." Ph.D. diss., Central European University, 2019.

Kruze, E., and D. Kuznetsov. "Naselenie Peterburga." In *Ocherki istorii Leningrada*, edited by Mikhail Viatkin. Moscow: Institut Istorii Akademii nauk SSSR, 1956.

Kuntsman, Adi. "'With a Shade of Disgust': Affective Politics of Sexuality and Class in Memoirs of the Stalinist Gulag." *Slavic Review* 68, no. 2 (2009): 308–28.

Kuzmin, Mikhail. *Wings*. London: Modern Voices, 2007.

Lapin, Vladimir. *Peterburg: zapakhi i zvuki*. St. Petersburg: Evropeiskii dom, 2007.

Latour, Bruno. *Reassembling the Social: An Introduction to Actor-Network-Theory*. Oxford: Oxford University Press, 2005.

Lauster, Martina. "Walter Benjamin's Myth of the Flâneur." *Modern Language Review* 102, no. 1 (2007): 139–56.

Laws, David, and Maarten Haje. "Policy in Practice." In *The Oxford Handbook of Public Policy*, edited by Robert E. Goodin, Michael Moran, and Martin Rein, 409–24. Oxford: Oxford University Press, 2008.

Lefebvre, Henry. *The Production of Space*. Oxford: Blackwell, 1991.

Legg, Stephen. "Assemblage / Apparatus: Using Deleuze and Foucault." *Area* 43, no. 2 (2011): 128–33.

Levy, Joshua. "Revanchism via Pedestrianism: Street-Level Bureaucracy in the Production of Uneven Policing Landscapes." *Antipode*, December 15, 2020. https://doi.org/https://doi.org/10.1111/anti.12702.

Li, Tania M. "Practices of Assemblage and Community Forest Management." *Economy and Society* 36, no. 2 (2007): 263–93.

Lim, Jason. "Immanent Politics: Thinking Race and Ethnicity through Affect and Machinism." *Environment and Planning A* 42, no. 10 (2010): 2393–409.

Lindenmeyr, Adele. *Poverty Is Not a Vice: Charity, Society, and the State in Imperial Russia*. Princeton, NJ: Princeton University Press, 1996.

Lipsky, Michael. *Street-Level Bureaucracy. Dilemmas of the Individual in Public Services*. New York: Russell Sage Foundation, 2010.

Lisovskii, Vladimir. *Arkhitektura Peterburga*. St. Petersburg: Slaviia, 2004.

Lofstrom, Jan. "The Birth of the Queen/the Modern Homosexual: Historical Explanation Revisited." *Sociological Review* 45, no. 10 (1997): 24–41.

Lyon, David. "Bentham's Panopticon: From Moral Architecture to Electronic Surveillance." *Queen's Quarterly* 98, no. 3 (1991): 596–616.

Makeev, Vasilii, and Alaudin Toldiev. "Chrezvychainoe zakonodatel'stvo v sisteme gosudarstvennoi okhrany Rossiiskoi Imperii (vtoraia polovina XIX–nachalo XX veka)." *Filosofiia prava* 5, no. 66 (2014): 34–38.

Maliepaard, Emiel. "Bisexuals in Space and Geography: More-Than-Queer?" *Fennia—International Journal of Geography* 193, no. 1 (2015): 148–59.

Malmstad, John E., and Nikolay Bogomolov. *Mikhail Kuzmin: A Life in Art*. Cambridge, MA: Harvard University Press, 1999.

Marcus, George, and Erkan Saka. "Assemblage." *Theory, Culture and Society* 23, no. 2–3 (2006): 101–9.

Markus, Dubber, and Lindsay Farmer. "Introduction: Regarding Criminal Law Historically." In *Modern Histories of Crime and Punishment*, edited by Dubber Markus and Lindsay Farmer, 1–13. Stanford, CA: Stanford University Press, 2007.

Matich, Olga. "Poetics of Disgust: To Eat and Die in Andrei Belyi's 'Petersburg.'" *Slavic Review* 68, no. 2 (2009): 284–307.

Maynard, Steven. "Through a Hole in the Lavatory Wall: Homosexual Subcultures, Police Surveillance, and the Dialectics of Discovery, Toronto, 1890–1930." *Journal of the History of Sexuality* 5, no. 2 (1994): 207–42.

McDonough, Thomas F. "Situationist Space." *October* 67 (Winter 1994): 58–77.

McFarlane, Colin. "Governing the Contaminated City: Infrastructure and Sanitation in Colonial and Post-Colonial Bombay." *International Journal of Urban and Regional Research* 32, no. 2 (2008): 415–35.

McKean, Robert B. *St. Petersburg between Revolutions: Workers and Revolutionaries, June 1907–February 1917.* New Haven, CT: Yale University Press, 1900.

McReynolds, Louise. *Murder Most Russian: True Crime and Punishment in Late Imperial Russia.* Ithaca, NY: Cornell University Press, 2012.

McReynolds, Louise. *Russia at Play: Leisure Activities at the End of the Tsarist Era.* Ithaca, NY: Cornell University Press, 1991.

McReynolds, Louise. "St. Petersburg: The National Destiny in the Cityscape." *Journal of Urban History* 33, no. 5 (2007): 857–63.

Meslé, France, and Jacques Vallin. "Long-Term Trends in Life Expectancy and the Consequences of Major Historical Disasters." In *Mortality and Causes of Death in 20th-Century Ukraine*, edited by France Meslé and Jacques Vallin. London: Springer Science and Business Media, 2012.

Miller, Jacques-Alain, and Richard Miller. "Jeremy Bentham's Panoptic Device." *October* 41 (1987): 3–29.

Mironov, Boris. "Wages and Prices in Imperial Russia, 1703–1913." *Russian Review* 69, no. 1 (2010): 47–72.

Morrison, Alexander. *The Russian Conquest of Central Asia: A Study in Imperial Expansion, 1814–1914.* Cambridge: Cambridge University Press, 2020.

Morrissey, Susan K. *Suicide and the Body Politic in Imperial Russia.* Cambridge: Cambridge University Press, 2007.

Neuberger, Joan. *Hooliganism: Crime, Culture, and Power in St. Petersburg, 1900–1914.* Los Angeles: University of California Press, 1993.

Neuberger, Joan. "Stories of the Street: Hooliganism in the St. Petersburg Popular Press." *Slavic Review* 48, no. 2 (1989): 177–94.

Nye, David E. "History of Electricity Use." In *Concise Encyclopedia of the History of Energy*, edited by Cutler J. Cleveland, 76–89. San Diego: Elsevier, 2009.

Ogborn, Miles. *Spaces of Modernity: London's Geographies, 1680–1780.* New York: Guilford Press, 1998.

Osborne, Thomas, and Nikolas Rose. "Governing Cities: Notes on the Spatialisation of Virtue." *Environment and Planning D: Society and Space* 17, no. 6 (1999): 737–60.

Oswin, Natalie. "Critical Geographies and the Use of Sexuality: Deconstructing Queer Space." *Progress in Human Geography* 32, no. 1 (2008): 89–103. https://doi.org/10.1177/0309132507085213.

Otter, Chris. "Making Liberal Objects: British Techno-Social Relations 1800–1900." *Cultural Studies* 21, no. 4–5 (2007): 570–90.

Otter, Chris. "Making Liberalism Durable: Vision and Civility in the Late Victorian City." *Social History* 27, no. 1 (2002): 1–15.

Otter, Christopher. "Cleansing and Clarifying: Technology and Perception in Nineteenth-Century London." *Journal of British Studies* 43, no. 1 (2004): 40–64.

Paterson, Mark. *The Senses of Touch: Haptics, Affects and Technologies.* London: Bloomsbury, 2013.

Peniston, William A. "Pederasts, Prostitutes, and Pickpockets in Paris of the 1870s." *Journal of Homosexuality* 41, no. 3–4 (2001): 169–87.

Petri, Olga. "Discipline and Discretionary Power in Policing Homosexuality in Late Imperial St. Petersburg." *Journal of Homosexuality* 66, no. 7 (2019): 937–69. https://doi.org/10.1080/00918369.2018.1485302.

Petrov, Genadii. *Passazh: Sankt-Peterburg, 1848–1998; istoricheskii ocherk.* St. Petersburg: Artdeko, 1998.

Pile, Steve. "Emotions and Affect in Recent Human Geography." *Transactions of the Institute of British Geographers* 35, no. 1 (2010): 5–20.

Plamper, Jan. "Emotional Turn? Feelings in Russian History and Culture. Introduction." *Slavic Review* 68, no. 2 (2009): 229–37.

Plamper, Jan. *The History of Emotions: An Introduction.* Oxford: Oxford University Press, 2015.

Pollock, Ethan. *Without the Banya We Would Perish: A History of the Russian Bathhouse.* Oxford: Oxford University Press, 2019.

Ponomarev, Evgenii, Iuliia Dudchenko, and Viacheslav Rasskazov. "Vnesudebnye repressii kak mera bor'by po okhrane gosudarstvennogo stroia v Rossii vo vtoroi polovine XIX–nachale XX veka." *Filosofiia prava* 5, no. 55 (2014): 62–67.

Potvin, John. "Vapour and Steam: The Victorian Turkish Bath, Homosocial Health, and Male Bodies on Display." *Journal of Design History* 18, no. 4 (2005): 319–33.

Price-Robertson, Rhys. "Realism, Materialism, and the Assemblage: Thinking Psychologically with Manuel Delanda." *Theory and Psychology* 26, no. 1 (2015): 58–76.

Prior, Jason, and Carole Cusack. "Ritual, Liminality and Transformation: Secular Spirituality in Sydney's Gay Bathhouses." *Australian Geographer* 39, no. 3 (2008): 271–81.

Puar, Jaspir. *Terrorist Assemblages: Homonationalism in Queer Times.* Durham, NC: Duke University Press, 2017.

Punin, A. L. *Arkhitektura Peterburga serediny i vtoroi poloviny XIX veka.* 2 vols. Vol. 1. St. Petersburg: Kriga, 2009.

Rabinow, Paul, ed. *The Foucalt Reader: An Introduction to Foucault's Thought.* New York: Pantheon Books, 1984.

Rabow-Edling, Susanna. *Slavophile Thought and the Politics of Cultural Nationalism.* Albany: State University of New York Press, 2012.

Randall, Dills. "Cracks in the Granite: Paternal Care, the Imperial Façade, and the Limits of Authority in the 1824 St. Petersburg Flood." *Journal of Urban History* 40, no. 3 (2014): 479–96.

Reddy, William M. *The Navigation of Feeling: A Framework for the Histories of Emotions.* Cambridge: Cambridge University Press, 2001.

Renner, Andrea. "A Nation That Bathes Together: New York City's Progressive Era Public Baths." *Journal of the Society of Architectural Historians* 67, no. 4 (2008): 504–31.

Rosenwein, Barbara H. "Problems and Methods in the History of Emotions." *Passions in Context: Journal of the History and Philosophy of the Emotions* 1, no. 1 (2010): 1–32.

Rosenwein, Barbara H. "Worrying about Emotions in History." *American Historical Review* 107, no. 3 (June 2002): 821–45.

Ross, Andrew Israel. *Public City/Public Sex: Homosexuality, Prostitution, and Urban Culture in Nineteenth-Century Paris.* Philadelphia: Temple University Press, 2019.

Rotikov, Konstantin. "Epizod iz zhizni 'golubogo' Peterburga." *Nevskii arkhiv: Istoriko-kraevedcheskii sbornik* 3 (1997): 449–66.

Rotikov, Konstantin. *Drugoi Peterburg.* St. Petersburg: Kul'torologiia, 2000.

Schivelbusch, Wolfgang. *Disenchanted Night: The Industrialization of Light in the Nineteenth Century.* Berkeley: University of California Press, 1995.

Schlör, Joachim. *Nights in the Big City: Paris, Berlin, London 1840–1930.* London: Reaktion Books, 1998.

Seliverstov, Iurii, ed. *Leningrad: istoriko-geograficheskii atlas.* Moscow: Glavnoe upravlenie geogezii, 1989.

Sennett, Richard. *Flesh and Stone: The Body and the City in Western Civilization.* New York: W. W. Norton, 1996.

Seregny, Scott J. "Zemstvos, Peasants, and Citizenship: The Russian Adult Education Movement and World War I." *Slavic Review* 59, no. 2 (2000): 290–315.

Shaw, Denis. "St Petersburg and Geographies of Modernity in Eighteenth-Century Russia." In *St Petersburg, 1703–1825*, edited by Anthony Cross, 6–29. London: Palgrave Macmillan, 2003.

Sheard, Sally. "Profit Is a Dirty Word: The Development of Public Baths and Wash-Houses in Britain 1847–1915." *Social History of Medicine* 13, no. 1 (2000): 63–86.

Shifrin, Malcolm. *Victorian Turkish Baths.* Liverpool: Liverpool University Press, 2015. Also available at http://www.victorianturkishbath.org/thebook.htm.

Simms, James Y. "The Economic Impact of the Russian Famine of 1891–92." *Slavonic and East European Review* 60, no. 1 (1982): 63–74.

Sindalovskii, Naum Aleksandrovich. *Ot doma k domu . . . Ot legendy k legende: Putevoditel'.* St. Petersburg: Norint, 2008.

Smith, Alison Karen. *For the Common Good and Their Own Well-Being: Social Estates in Imperial Russia.* Oxford: Oxford University Press, 2014.

Smith, Alison Karen. "Honored Citizens and the Creation of a Middle Class in Imperial Russia." *Slavic Review* 76, no. 2 (2017): 327–49.

Smith, Neil. *The New Urban Frontier: Gentrification and the Revanchist City.* New York: Routledge, 1996.

Smith, Steve, and Catriona Kelly. "Commercial Culture and Consumerism." In *Construction Russia Culture in the Age of Revolution 1881–1940*, edited by Catriona Kelly and David Shepherd, 106–55. Oxford: Oxford University Press, 2005.

Smith-Rosenberg, Carroll. "The Female World of Love and Ritual: Relations between Women in Nineteenth-Century America." *Signs* 1, no. 1 (1975): 1–29.

Soja, Edward. *Postmodern Geographies: The Reassertion of Space in Critical Social Theory.* London: Verso, 1989.

Steinberg, Mark D. "Melancholy and Modernity: Emotions and Social Life in Russia between Revolutions." *Journal of Social History* 41, no. 4 (2008): 813–41.

Steinberg, Mark D. *Petersburg Fin de Siècle.* New Haven, CT: Yale University Press, 2011.

Steinberg, Mark D., and Vladimir Sobol, eds. *Interpreting Emotion in Russia and Eastern Europe*. DeKalb: Northern Illinois University Press, 2011.

Steinwedel, Charles. "Making Social Groups, One Person at a Time: The Identification of Individuals by Estate, Religious, Confession, and Ethnicity in Late Imperial Russia." In *Documenting Individual Identity: The Development of State Practices in the Modern World*, edited by Jane Caplan and John Torpey, 67–82. Princeton, NJ: Princeton University Press 2001.

Stewart-Winter, Timothy. *Queer Clout: Chicago and the Rise of Gay Politics*. Philadelphia: University of Pennsylvania Press, 2016.

Surh, Gerald D. *1905 in St. Petersburg: Labor, Society, and Revolution*. Stanford, CA: Stanford University Press, 1989.

Swanson, Gillian. *Drunk with the Glitter: Space, Consumption and Sexual Instability in Modern Urban Culture*. London: Routledge, 2007.

Tester, Keith, ed. *The Flâneur*. London: Routledge, 1994.

Tewksbury, Richard. "Men and Erotic Oases." *Sociology Compass* 4, no. 12 (2010): 1011–19.

Thompson, Victoria E. "Telling Spatial Stories: Urban Space and Bourgeois Identity in Early 19th Century Paris." *Journal of Modern History* 75, no. 3 (2003): 523–56.

Thrift, Nigel. *Non-Representational Theory*. London: Routledge, 2008.

Tolstoi, N. *Slavianskie drevnosti: etnolingvisticheskii slovar'*. 5 vols. Vol. 1. Moscow Nauka, 1995.

Tseng, Ching-Fang. "The Flaneur, the Flaneuse, and the Hostess: Virginia Woolf's (Un) Domesticating Flanerie in Mrs. Dalloway." *Concentric: Literary and Cultural Studies* 32, no. 1 (2006): 219–58.

Tucker, Andrew. *Queer Visibilites: Space, Indentity and Interaction in Cape Town*. Oxford: Wiley-Blackwell, 2009.

Turner, Mark. *Backward Glances: Cruising Queer Streets in New York and London*. London: Reaktion Books, 2003.

Vernon, Nicholas James. *Distant Strangers: How Britain Became Modern*. Berkeley: University of California Press, 2014.

Voronov, Ivan. "Ministerstvo zemledeliia Rossiiskoi imperii: XIX–nachalo XX vv." PhD diss., St. Petersburg State University, 2016. https://disser.spbu.ru/disser2/disser/Voronov_Diss.pdf.

Waldron, Peter. "States of Emergency: Autocracy and Extraordinary Legislation, 1881–1917." *Revolutionary Russia* 8, no. 1 (1995): 1–25.

Wastell, David, Karen Broadhurst, S. White, and S. Peckover. "Children's Services in the Iron Cage of Performance Management: Street-Level Bureaucracy and the Spectre of Švejkism." *International Journal of Social Welfare* 19, no. 3 (2010): 310–20.

Weissman, Neil. "Regular Police in Tsarist Russia, 1900–1914." *Russian Review* 44, no. 1 (1985): 45–68.

Zemliakov, Aleksandr. "Administrativnaia ssylka v Rossiiskoi imperii kontsa XIX–nachala XX vv." *Omskii nauchnyi vestnik* 2, no. 23 (2003): 17–20.

Zuckerman, Fredric S. *The Tsarist Secret Police and Russian Society, 1880–1917*. New York: New York University Press, 1996.

INDEX

Page numbers in *italics* indicate illustrations.

CPSIA information can be obtained
at www.ICGtesting.com
Printed in the USA
LVHW101623090622
720900LV00002B/78